Lives of Dust and Water

Lives of Dust and Water

An Anthropology of Change and Resistance
in Northwestern Mexico

María Luz Cruz-Torres

The University of Arizona Press

Tucson

The University of Arizona Press
© 2004 The Arizona Board of Regents
All rights reserved

First paperback printing 2008
ISBN 978–0-8165-2747-2 (pbk. : alk. paper)

Library of Congress Cataloging-in-Publication Data
Cruz-Torres, María Luz
Lives of dust and water : an anthropology of change and resistance in
northwestern Mexico / María Luz Cruz-Torres.
p. cm.
Includes bibliographical references and index.
ISBN 0-8165-2388-6 (cloth : alk. paper)
1. Rural poor—Mexico—Sinaloa (State)—Social conditions. 2. Rural poor—
Mexico—Sinaloa (State)—Economic conditions. 3. Rural development—
Mexico—Sinaloa (State). 4. Social change—Mexico—Sinaloa (State).
5. Sinaloa (Mexico : State)—Social conditions. 6. Sinaloa (Mexico : State)—
Economic conditions. 7. Sinaloa (Mexico : State)—
Rural conditions. I. Title.
F1219.I.S56C78 2004
305.8'9707232—dc22
2004008526

Manufactured in the United States of America on
acid-free, archival-quality paper.

13 12 11 10 09 08   7 6 5 4 3 2

All photographs in this book are by the author.

Le dedico este libro con mucho amor y cariño a

(I dedicate this book with much love and affection to)

mi hija preciosa (my beautiful daughter) Nayely

y a mis padres (and to my parents)

María L. Torres-Velázquez and Jesús Cruz-Burgos

Nosotros tenemos unas vidas de polvo y agua. Durante la sequía el sol lo convierte todo en polvo. Ya ves el calor tan grande que hace y el polvo que se levanta de la tierra cuando uno camina. El polvo se nos mete en los ojos y nos ciega y también en la garganta y nos hace toser. También cubre nuestras casas, nuestras plantas y nuestros animalitos. El polvo es como una maldición que alguien nos debió echar cuando luchamos por este cerro para hacer nuestro ranchito. La sequía en este ranchito hace que nuestras vidas sean tristes porque el polvo nos agobia. Pero en las aguas es cuando de veras volvemos a renacer. Renace el quelite y renace la esperanza de que tengamos mejor siembra y de que haya más camarón en los esteros. Llegan las aguas y llega la vida.

[Our lives are dust and water. During the dry season, the sun turns everything into dust. You know how hot the sun gets, and how when you walk it stirs up the dust on the ground. The dust gets in our eyes and blinds us, and it gets in our throats and makes us cough. It covers our houses, our plants, and our animals. The dust is like a curse that someone must have cast on us when we fought to have this hill as our own little village. The drought in this little village makes our lives miserable because the dust overwhelms us. But with the arrival of the rainy season, we are truly reborn. The quelite is reborn and hope is reborn that we will have a better harvest and that the shrimp will abound in the estuaries. The rain comes, and with it, life.]

—Don Chico Flores, El Cerro, 1989 (my translation)

Contents

Illustrations

Maps

Figures

Tables

Photographs

Acknowledgments

This book would not have been possible without the great help and advice of so many people. My deepest respect and appreciation go to the people whose lives are portrayed in this book. I thank them immensely for welcoming me into their communities and their homes and for sharing themselves with me. I hope they find this work as honest and respectful as it is meant to be. I would especially like to thank those in El Cerro, the Flores-Rodriguez family, particularly Maguey, María Félix, and Cornelio. Thanks also to my compadres Carmen and Jorge, don Cruz Zambrano, Toño, don Pilar, doña Concha, don Manuel, Elisa, and Rosa. My sincere thanks go to those in Celaya, doña Angelita and don Poncho, doña Ramona, doña Carolina and don Ismael, Irma, Magui, Rosa, Santos, Olga, Sylvia, Manuel, Paloma, Wendy, Miros, and Adela.

I am also very grateful to the people from the towns of Rosario and Escuinapa for their support, good humor, and friendship. Special thanks go to the Páez-Miramontes family, Rafael Simental, Jorge Simental, Conchita Grave, Jorge Macías, José Luis, Marissa, Aurelio, and Carlos Hubbard. Millions of thanks go to my colleagues in Mazatlán, Francisco Flores Verdugo, Ramón Enrique Morán, Gildardo Izaguirre Fiero, and Lourdes Patricia Lyle for their assistance and collaboration during various stages of the research. For inspiration and advice I thank Sarah Meltzof, David Grifith, Susan Stonich, Linda Stearns, Thomas Patterson, Juan Vicente Palerm, and Manuel Valdez Pizzini.

I would also like to acknowledge the following organizations and institutions for providing funds at various stages of this research: Wenner Gren Foundation for Anthropological Research, the University of California

Academic Senate, the University of California Regents, The Ernesto Galarza Applied Research Center, the University of California Institute for Mexico and the United States (UC-MEXUS), and the Center for U.S.–Mexican Studies at the University of California, San Diego.

This book has benefited from the insightful comments and suggestions of people who were kind enough to take time from their busy schedules to read portions of the manuscript. My colleagues Michael Kearney, Paul Gelles, Gene Anderson, Karl Taube, and Leo Chávez deserve special thanks. Robert Patch and Augustine Kposowa also provided helpful suggestions.

The work of three lively, smart, and dedicated research assistants was crucial in the analysis of data, transcription of interviews, and the compilation of the bibliography. They are Griselda Rodríguez, Gina Núñez, and Aidé Acosta.

I am also indebted to the University of Arizona Press, especially Dr. Christine Szuter for her great enthusiasm and support, and to Dr. Allyson Carter and the anonymous reviewers whose comments were invaluable. Special thanks to Patricia Rosas, Barbara H. Firoozye, Robin Whittington, and Melanie Mallon for editorial assistance and translation. Thanks also to Linda Bobitt and Jacalyn García-López for designing the maps and figures in this book.

Two very important women in my life deserve special recognition: Dr. Alida Ortiz, a marine biologist, and Dr. Bonnie J. McCay, an anthropologist. They are the best mentors in the world. They both instilled in me perseverance, a passion for learning, and a yen for the unusual.

My heartfelt thanks go to my parents, my sisters, and the rest of my extended family for nurturing and encouraging me over the years, across the distance. Two extra special people have lived through the many lives of this book. One is my daughter Nayely, who gave me a "hug supreme" every time I completed a chapter. The other is my companion, colleague, and friend Carlos Vélez-Ibáñez, who has traveled with me to southern Sinaloa, met and listened to the families in the communities, and whose presence was instrumental for my getting a perspective on the world of rural men. His insightful comments and suggestions on the many drafts of this book have been of tremendous help.

Abbreviations

CAADES	Confederación de Asociaciones Agrícolas del Estado de Sinaloa (Federation of Sinaloan Growers Associations)
CNC	Confederación Nacional Campesina (National Campesino Confederation)
CONASUPO	Comisión Nacional de Subsistencias Populares (National Commission of Popular Subsistence)
COPLAMAR	Coordinación General del Plan Nacional de Zonas Deprimidas y Grupos Marginados (General Coordination of the National Plan for Depressed Zones and Marginal Groups)
DIF	Desarrollo Integral de la Familia (Family Development Programs)
IMSS	Instituto Mexicano del Seguro Social (Mexican Social Security Institute)
IMSSS	Instituto Mexicano del Seguro Social–Solidaridad (Solidarity Program of the Mexican Social Security Institute)
INEGI	Instituto Nacional de Estadística, Geografía, e Informática (National Institute of Statistics, Geography, and Computing)
NAFTA	North American Free Trade Agreement (Tratado de Libre Comercio)
PROCEDE	Programa de Certificación de Derechos Ejidales y Titulación de Solares Urbanos (Program for the Certification of Ejido Land Rights and the Titling of Urban House Plots)
PROFEPA	Procuraduría Federal para la Defensa del Medio Ambiente (Office of the Attorney for Environmental Defense)
PROGRESA	Programa de Educación, Salud, y Alimentación (Program for Education, Health, and Nutrition)

PRONASOL	Programa Nacional de Solidaridad (National Solidarity Program)
RCA	Asociación Rotativa de Crédito (Rotating Credit Association)
SEMARNAP	Secretaría del Medio Ambiente, Recursos Naturales, y Pesca (Secretariat for the Environment, Natural Resources, and Fisheries)
UAS	Universidad Autónoma de Sinaloa (Autonomous University of Sinaloa)
UC-MEXUS	The University of California Institute for Mexico and the United States (El Instituto de la Universidad de California para Estudios sobre México y los Estados Unidos)
UGOCM	Unión General de Obreros y Campesinos de México (Mexican General Union of Workers and Peasants)

Lives of Dust and Water

Introduction

A Journey of Many Paths

> There is unrest and discontent in the countryside. In many places, this unrest has now become exasperation; in other places, the discontent is often translated into acts of desperate violence. This is natural: industrialization and development have been paid for, in great part, by our rural population.
> —Octavio Paz, *The Labyrinth of Solitude*

In August 2000, during one of my field visits to El Cerro, I learned details about the murder of El Profe, the owner of one of the largest and most profitable shrimp farms in southern Sinaloa. At my *compadres'* home, under the shade of a *palapa* (palm hut) they had recently built to shelter them from the sun that continued to accost them despite the rain, I listened attentively to the version of the story that circulated in the community. The burning midday sun peeked out from among the large white clouds that floated in the indigo blue sky, which framed the contours of the newly verdant hills. It was one of those tranquil days when people were at home or under the palapas, chatting pleasantly, and the only other sounds were *norteño* music coming from neighboring houses and dogs barking when a chicken or pig passed them warily. The layer of dust that clothed the town in gray during the dry season had been washed away by the summer rains, which had arrived, as they do each year, like an omen of renewed life and spirits for the community's residents. The fuchsia pink of the bougainvilleas and the bright red of the *tabachín* flowers made the village seem happy and colorful again, features it had been robbed of during the dry season.

On that peaceful day, while life seemed to continue with the normality characteristic of all rainy seasons when I had visited southern Sinaloa, my compadres and my friends sat in a circle and told me the story of the murder of a man about whom I had heard much, but whom I had never met. They told me the story baldly and with much passion and enthusiasm. It was as if they were recounting the plot of an action film, in which the protagonist, because of the circumstances life threw in his path, succumbs without realizing it to the ill fortune destiny holds in store for him. While they talked, the music of the *narco-corridos* from neighboring houses served as background to give the story an air of mystery and suspense. The words of one song told how a man named Perales was shot to death in June 1973; apparently based on a true story, it filled in the conversational lapses. I felt that the story my compadres were recounting now would one day, in a similar way, become a *corrido* played in cantinas or during parties in the *ranchos,* the region's rural communities.

According to their story, "El Profe," as the people of Agua Verde and El Cerro called the shrimp farm owner, had indeed been a professor at the Universidad Autónoma de Sinaloa (UAS), in Mazatlán, before turning to the shrimp aquaculture business. No one knew for certain how he had come to be interested in aquaculture or why he decided to build two shrimp farms and a laboratory to produce the larvae. Those who knew him at UAS remember him as having serious political convictions and a strong sense of justice and humanity. In his youth in the 1970s, he had been a *guerrillero,* as had other young men and women who rose up against the Mexican government. Both in Agua Verde and El Cerro, El Profe was beloved by the people. He became the godfather of several children, lent money to people and never asked for its return, and, most important, he hired men and women from El Cerro to work in his shrimp farms and laboratory.

According to rumors, which are now part of the region's oral traditions, El Profe's murder occurred suddenly, without forewarning. It surprised everyone who knew him, but more significant than the murder itself was the way it happened. One night, leaving his house in a suburb of Mazatlán, he and his wife were ambushed by men who surrounded the car and shot them so many times that their flesh was ripped to pieces. The news spread rapidly throughout the region, and the attack was attributed to connections that El Profe supposedly had with drug traffickers. Although the drug traffickers' reasons for killing him and his wife were never clarified, rumors circulated that the murders were revenge for an unpaid debt owed to a leader of one of the cartels.

The murders caused shock and confusion, but even more so when people heard that while the murders took place, armed men had vandalized the shrimp laboratory while searching for something they never found. The workers were so terrified that they quit their jobs. A few months after the murders, armed men also killed both of El Profe's sons in Culiacán, and two of his compadres were shot to death in the town of Rosario.

When the tale ended, I felt a chill run through my body from the top of my head to the tips of my toes. For the first time in the nearly thirteen years that I had been doing fieldwork in southern Sinaloa, I was afraid. This was not the first time that I had heard a story like this. Indeed, similar stories abound throughout the region. They appear daily in the local newspapers; they have been immortalized in narco-corridos; and the people recount them as part of the region's oral traditions. However, this was the first time that one of these stories affected me deeply, to the point of making me consider the dangers that I might have faced had I asked the wrong questions. Only a month before the murders, while I was studying the effects of neoliberal policies and changes in the Ley General de Pesca (General Fisheries Law) on shrimp farming, I had toured the facilities at El Profe's laboratory and farms. The biologists who worked there gave me the tour, and so I never met El Profe personally. Now, seated under the palapa, I was struck for the first time by the reality that Sinaloans, including the residents of the communities this book tries to represent, confront daily.

Sinaloa is typecast within and beyond Mexico as "the cradle of drug traffic." This reputation began years ago, when the first Chinese immigrants arriving in Mazatlán cultivated and smoked opium (Wald 2001). Marijuana cultivation in Sinaloa's mountain regions, while providing a livelihood for a major segment of the rural population living there, has fortified that reputation. Sinaloans control the cocaine traffic across the border, and the heads of most Mexican drug cartels are from the state (Wald 2001). Drug traffic is so important to the Sinaloan economy that all Sinaloans know the names of the former and current heads of the Sinaloan cartel. Intimately tied to drug trafficking is the wave of violence and bloodshed, which has grown enormously and now reaches even the most remote corners of the state. Nevertheless, despite violence and kidnappings, popular culture, as expressed in oral tradition and in the narco-corridos, glorifies drug trafficking and converts the traffickers into immortal heroes, or Mexican Robin Hoods.

Clearly, drug trafficking and the narco-corridos are two of Sinaloa's most striking features, and indeed, drugs and narco-corridos are two of the state's most important commodities: The former are a major sector of the economy, and the latter enrich regional culture while the profits from their sale, both nationally and in the United States, also contribute to the economy. However, behind this image of drugs and violence, which has such a strong hold on the state, there is another Sinaloa that few people know: It is much older and kinder and continues to retain its own space and identity in the midst of chaos and disruption. This is rural Sinaloa, or, as Octavio Paz would call it, *el otro México* (the other Mexico). It has its own history of land wars, social conflicts, and personal, family, and community struggles for survival. And although drug trafficking is part and parcel of the transnational economy of the present, as are agriculture and fishing, this book is about that other Sinaloa.

This work is the culmination of thirteen years of anthropological research on the political ecology of human survival in one of the most important ecological regions of Mexico. It seeks to explain how rural localities emerge and are influenced by regional, national, and global economies. Almost paradoxically, the region's human localities studied and reported on in this volume are as much the creations of the state as they are the creations of local labor, energy, sacrifice, and individual daily struggle. The supra-local development process is the base from which the state derives its legitimacy, power, and symbolic and mythic continuance. Once established, the local communities emerge as additional sources of human labor to be used for the benefit of local, national, and global political and economic interests. In a very particular sense, these localities are the wellspring of labor used in complex regional, national, and transnational processes of production and distribution. However, the populations discussed here have access to only the barest of the necessities required for their survival.

Nevertheless, these people cannot be reduced to simple labor commodities or to unwilling victims of the state and the global economy. Surrounded by limited resources, poverty, illness, sudden death, and daily oppression, the women, men, and children depicted in this work are innovative, inventive, and possessed of an unbreakable will. Theirs is a hard lot, yet their struggle is not without successes, hopes made realities, and laughter. Part of this book is devoted not only to how these populations manage to survive or adapt in the midst of horrendous circumstances, but also to how they transcend those impediments with dignity, a certain élan, and devotion to their families, friends, and community.

Themes and Goals of This Book

This is an anthropological study of two rural communities and the northwestern region of Mexico in which they are located. Northwestern Mexico is undergoing deep ecological, economic, and political transformations. Most of these changes are related to the growing demand in national and global markets for fishing- and agriculture-based commodities. That demand is directly linked to state and regional economic development policies supporting the use of natural resources for commercial export. The resulting environmental pressures have contributed to the degradation of coastal and marine ecosystems.

Despite all these changes, northwestern Mexico continues to be a region little studied by anthropologists (for exceptions, see Sheridan 1988; Yetman 1998; McGoodwin 1979, 1980, 1982; and Lara Flores 1998). Those who study Mexican *campesinos* (people of the countryside) still tend to concentrate on the central and southern areas of the country, perhaps because, to their way of seeing it, these regions have a well-established agrarian tradition. The northwest is usually considered a region of haciendas, mines, and Jesuit missions. Nevertheless, several years ago, Ralph Beals recognized the importance of northwestern Mexico as an area of study for anthropologists when he mentioned "the long-neglected potential for anthropological studies in northwestern Mexico" (1987, 95). During the 1930s and 1940s, there was fairly strong interest in doing anthropological research in that region, but most of those studies focused on deciphering various aspects of the way of life, including rites and customs, of its indigenous populations: the Seris, Yaquis, Mayos, Coras, and Huicholes (Beals 1987).

In the specific case of Sinaloa, the few ethnographies that exist have tended to concentrate on the agricultural areas of the state's central and northern regions. In his essay on the trajectory of anthropological research in Sinaloa, Andrés Latapí Escalante accurately points out that "anthropological studies have been few in proportion to the richness of the zone" (1988, 139).

This book fills that vacuum in the anthropological literature on northwestern Mexico, particularly in the field of cultural anthropology. The book's main goal is to explain how contemporary rural Mexican communities survive in the midst of the economic and ecological changes affecting the entire nation. The focus is the residents of two rural communities, tenacious and enterprising people who managed to build, practically from scratch, two culturally and socially rich communities. Among the subjects I discuss are the historical processes that directly and indirectly influenced the formation and development of these communities. Within that history, the significance that natural resources have for the inhabitants' survival is as visible as an oasis in the desert. I also discuss the history of the struggles, triumphs, and defeats of certain individuals who challenge the government, themselves, and nature as they struggle to make a place for themselves within a changing rural environment. Social and economic inequality, contradictions, paradoxes, and conflicts continue to distinguish this region.

As I will detail, daily life for the rural population of Sinaloa is plagued by heated, ongoing struggles that seem endless. Most are fought and resisted within the households. It is within the households where, year after year, worry and uncertainty are experienced: Will the rainy season arrive in time to plant the crops and to fill the lagoons so that the shrimp grow abundantly? Will there be enough money to cover the basic household necessities, enough for food, education, and health care?

The struggles also emerge at the community level. These are expressed in such things as, for example, a group of women organizing to collect signatures to take to the municipal president, demanding that he close the cantina where their husbands are spending the small sums they earn. The struggles also emerge when the community's residents blockade the entrance to a road leading to the lagoons and marshes to prevent people of other communities from coming there to fish for shrimp. Another reflection of these struggles is visible when members of a community, seeking land on which to build homes, invade the adjacent lands belonging to a commercial farmer. The Sinaloans who live in rural areas of the state live on a reef of symbiotic relations with the government, each other, and the environment that surrounds them, and from which they are unable to disentangle themselves. Nevertheless, what they can do is resist, protest, bargain, or change these relations.

Analytical Challenges

One of the challenges that we face as academics studying in rural settings is how to analyze contemporary Mexican rural communities. The debate around two theoretical orientations, *campesinista* (peasantization school) and *decampesinista* (proletarianization school), so popular in the 1970s, did not provide a complete picture that would allow us to decipher with exactness how rural communities adapt to new processes that affect them. For example, Michael Kearney (1996, 2) noted that "any genuinely anthropological approach to rural communities must theoretically situate them within global contexts and must attend to the history of the nation-state and its position within global society." Thus, any definition of community must go beyond geographic borders, which circumscribe a group of people within a given physical space, in order to include the relations and interactions among its inhabitants and members of other communities, both within and outside of Mexico. That definition of community must also provide for an understanding of the articulation between the local and the global within a regional context, which has certain historical, political, economic, and ecological characteristics particular to it.

The rural communities of southern Sinaloa formed not only as a result of local forces but also because of ones at the regional, state, and national levels. These communities are not entirely isolated, nor do they exist in a vacuum. For many years, through the production of agricultural and marine export commodities, both have been incorporated within a global process of capital and markets, and in a similar manner drug trafficking now serves similar functions. These global forces with local forces influence how the people in these communities live. Thus, instead of trying to distinguish the local processes from the regional, national, and global ones, my intention is to show how they interacted to establish these communities, and how they continue to shape how these communities survive today.

Another challenge that we face as academics is how to define people who live in rural communities. In the specific case of the two communities discussed here, the use of the term "campesino" is problematic. First, when one asks the residents how they themselves define that term, the most common answer is, "We are campesinos because we live in the countryside and not necessarily because we live off the land." This statement is revealing when one examines in depth how the people in these communities survive through a combination of different productive and economic activities. Most of the inhabitants are involved in a productive cycle in which farming represents only one phase. The residents of the communities are farmers, day laborers, fishermen, shrimp farmers, heavy equipment operators, domestic employees, vendors, peddlers, and so forth. Second, the location of the two communities on the coast complicates the question of whether their inhabitants can be classified solely as campesinos, because many identify themselves as fishermen. Indeed, many were fishermen before they became farmers.

To date, few anthropological studies have dealt clearly or effectively with the topic of the dynamic and complex relationships between Mexican rural communities and natural resources, especially fishing resources (see Quezada Dominguez 1995; Alcalá Moya 1999). Few efforts have been made to understand, in their totality, the full range of productive activities in which coastal rural communities engage. Among these, the work of Yván Bretón and Delfín Quezada in the Yucatan peninsula notes the importance of the articulation of agriculture and fishing for the economy in these communities and how, little by little, the agricultural labor force is being displaced and moved into the exploitation of fishing resources (Quezada and Bretón 1987).

This book will contribute to the development of a more precise understanding of how rural coastal communities in Mexico emerged and continue developing. I discuss these communities' role in the social, economic, and political development of two major assets for northwestern Mexico—land and fishing resources. I also discuss how the conflicts over the exploitation of fishing resources arose, and how those conflicts are played out at the local level. The relationship between the inhabitants of the rural coastal communities of southern Sinaloa and the natural resources they depend on for survival is one of the major themes of this book, but to contextualize and analyze this relationship, I rely on a political ecology approach as my theoretical framework.

Using the political ecology approach, I examine the history and importance of natural resources for the sustenance of southern Sinaloa's rural coastal population. My analysis builds on the insights of the scholars reviewed below by attempting to determine the relationship among the dominant ideology guiding natural resource exploitation, environmental degradation, and economic impoverishment in rural northwestern Mexico. The research discussed in this book considers the household as the basic unit of analysis in order to gain a true understanding of the dynamic relationship between human populations and their environment at the local level. As Sheridan (1988) points out, the household is the basic unit of production, consumption, and resource control in Mexican peasant communities. This study expands Sheridan's argument by treating the household as a social space where people are in a continuous and active process of making choices, generating opportunities, and reorganizing existing resources to meet the household members' basic needs (Feldman 1992, 10).

The analysis builds on the work of scholars who have analyzed relationships between local and global economic and political forces in order to uncover the causes and impact of environmental change. Following Sheridan (1988), this book uses a political ecology approach to determine how the use and allocation of natural resources in southern Sinaloa are shaped by differential relationships of power within and outside rural communities. The influential work of Eric Wolf was an important precursor to the use of a political ecological perspective in anthropological research (Sheridan 1988; Stonich 1993; Gezon 1999). Scholars have followed in Wolf's steps as they analyzed interconnections between the environment and the economic, political, and historical processes experienced by human societies in a variety of geographic settings.[1] For example, some have used political ecology to analyze the social, historical, political, and economic causes of deforestation, and its effects on local populations (Schmink and Wood 1987 and Painter 1995). Similarly, but with a twist, Dodds (1998) analyzed the relationship among wage labor, subsistence agriculture, and deforestation in order to correlate household participation in the lobster-export industry with a reduction of human pressures on local forests.

Other studies have focused on the effect of national economic development policies on natural resources and the implications of this for local populations. For example, Painter (1995) has examined the impact of Bolivia's export-based economy on rural lands and its effect on the peasant population. Stonich (1993) studied how the export of agricultural commodities, such as melons, and fishing commodities, such as shrimp, has accelerated the degradation of coastal Honduras.

Studies in political ecology have also recognized the importance of local social and economic differences for determining which sectors of society will have access to a specific natural resource. Sheridan (1988) analyzed economic and social differences among peasants, private ranchers, and the absentee elite in the municipio of Cucurpe, Sonora, and how these differences influenced these groups' ability to gain or maintain control over land.

Recently, scholars have also recognized the need to incorporate gender within political ecology studies to address the differential effect of environmental degradation and poverty on women and men. These scholars "treat gender as a critical variable in shaping resource access and control, interacting with class, caste, race, culture and ethnicity to shape processes of ecological change, the struggle of men and women to sustain ecologically viable livelihoods, and the prospects of any community for 'sustainable development'" (Rocheleau, Thomas-Slayter, and Wangari 1996, 4). For example, Dianne Rocheleau, Barbara Thomas-Slayter, and Esther Wangari (1996) addressed the interrelationship between gender and ecological, cultural, political, and social factors in order to uncover relations of production within households in Kenya. They also showed how women's access to natural resources, such as water, land, and trees, influences the gender relations of production and women's involvement in collective efforts to protect the environment.

Research in political ecology has also addressed the relationship between environmental destruction and poverty and the responses developed by local communities to deal with these threats (Sheridan 1988; Stonich 1995; Painter 1995). Painter and Durham (1995) conclude that economic impoverishment, resulting from scarcity of land or displacement from forest habitats, prompted the members of affected households to either increase production or migrate. Stonich (1993) points out that peasants' responses to economic impoverishment in southern Honduras included the diversification of the household economy, increased participation of women in the labor force, and the transformation and intensification of agricultural systems. As this book will show, rural households in southern Sinaloa have developed similar responses.

But Why in Sinaloa? The Beginning of a Much-Traveled Journey

"Why in Sinaloa?" is one of the questions that I repeatedly have had to answer when someone asks me where I did my anthropological research.

Others have asked, "What could be of interest in Sinaloa, where there isn't even a strong presence of indigenous peoples?" For many, including academics in Mexico and beyond, Sinaloa is nothing more than a "nest of drug traffickers," where violence is the daily bread for the state's inhabitants. Still others view the state's central and northern regions as meccas for economic development, which is fueled by the commercial agriculture predominant in the large valleys. And for others, Sinaloa equates to the tourist golden coast of Mazatlán. Many people do not know that Sinaloa, and in particular the southern region—which is the focus of this book— has a long trajectory of economic, ecological, and social change that is the base of a partly written history waiting to be further developed.

It was not the drug trafficking nor the commercial agriculture nor the tourism that initially aroused my interested in doing fieldwork in Sinaloa. Rather, I had been interested in studying the production phase of another of the commodities that the state produces: shrimp. At the end of the 1980s, the northwestern region of Mexico, and in particular Sinaloa, was being converted into a laboratory for experimentation with shrimp aquaculture. The "pink gold," as shrimp is called in Mexico, has always been one of the country's most important commodities, but its wild stocks began to decline during the 1970s. Given the favorable results of aquacultural production and profits realized in countries such as Ecuador, the Mexican government chose to follow the same path to expand shrimp production levels. At that time, the Fisheries Law awarded the right to fish for and cultivate shrimp only to those rural populations organized in fishing cooperatives. The possibility of studying the social and environmental impact of shrimp cultivation in the communities where the projects were being developed motivated me to do my doctoral dissertation fieldwork in Sinaloa. Thus, one January morning when the snowflakes still covered the branches and stems of leafless trees at Rutgers University in New Jersey, I left for Mexico, setting out on what would become a long trajectory of fieldwork in Sinaloa.

One of the biggest difficulties that I encountered on my arrival in Mexico was convincing academics and government officials that shrimp cultivation could be a topic studied from the perspective of cultural anthropology. Many still held the notion that the focus of anthropology should be indigenous groups and that topics such as the environment or rural development were the purview of economists or ecologists. This initial reaction was to be expected given the long tradition of indigenous studies within

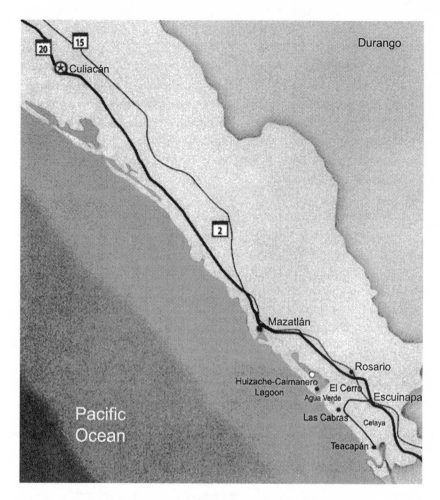

Map 1
The study area

Mexican anthropology. Many people in Mexico tried to persuade me to concentrate my work on one of the country's many native peoples. At the insistence of several biologists who were working for what was, at that time, the Secretaría de Pesca (Fisheries Department), I went to Sonora. There other biologists insisted that I should not leave Mexico without having first visited an indigenous community. They accompanied me as I traveled through the desert of Sonora, arriving finally at the coast of the Sea of Cortez, across from Isla Tiburón, where the Seri Indians live. This was my first visit to an indigenous community, and it made me reflect deeply on the role that anthropology plays and the perceptions in Mexico about this academic field of study. The experience also reinforced my desire to do fieldwork in non-Indian communities and in a region, such as northwestern Mexico, where few ethnographic studies have been done.

The two communities where I chose to do my fieldwork—El Cerro and Celaya in southern Sinaloa—were similar in that both were experiencing the development of commercial shrimp farming, motivated by outside forces (see map 1). In each community, the men who were interested in participating had organized into cooperatives. Yet, social and economic conflicts were already appearing, primarily because of disagreements among the cooperative members, the biologists, and the owners of the companies building the shrimp farms.

Despite those similarities, one thing immediately caught my attention, and it appeared to be one of the greatest differences between the two communities given their geographic proximity: Visible at a glance were topographic and ecological contrasts. El Cerro was built on a hillside amid scrubland and more hills, and Celaya was built on a plain surrounded by lagoons. This, in turn, determined the types of crops that could be planted on the lands. In El Cerro, the most frequently grown crops are corn and beans; in Celaya, coconut and mango. Another difference is related to the system of landholding. El Cerro is an *ejido* (a community of common landholders); whereas in Celaya, land is held privately.

Another important difference I perceived at that time was related to the political structure of each community. In El Cerro, it seemed that the political structure was closely linked to the ejidal system, whereas in Celaya, it seemed to be more closely linked to the cooperative and to the elementary school. Some facets related to the founding of the communities also were in contrast: One was established on vacant land whereas the other was built on land expropriated from a hacienda.

Living in the two communities during this first stage of my fieldwork gave me the opportunity to reflect on how rural Mexican communities are conceptualized in the literature. For example, a common argument in the anthropological literature is that these communities are, for the most part, very conservative, traditional, and resistant to change. It was quite clear that neither of the communities I studied fit that image. Nevertheless, government bureaucrats and the local elite still used those ideas to blame the inhabitants of rural communities for the failure or ineffectiveness of development projects that had been implemented. In these two rural communities, however, which are similar to others in the region, residents were experimenting with a relatively new and considerably risky enterprise of shrimp cultivation.

During that time, I could also see that the communities were not internally homogeneous, even though, at first glance, they seemed so. In terms of their participation in economic and productive activities, tremendous heterogeneity was visible among the residents. I could establish that most were involved in a cyclical web in which aquaculture was merely one among many activities. This heterogeneity was also reflected in the types of houses and furnishings in those houses, and residents themselves perceived that class and identity differences existed within the communities.

When I finished this phase of my fieldwork, I was concerned that the Mexican rural communities generally were much more complex than earlier anthropological studies had indicated. To understand these communities more accurately, I saw the need for a broader and longer-term study. I went back to Rutgers University, convinced that someday I would return to Sinaloa to do that more profound work. When I finished my dissertation, I stored it in a box that I carried with me throughout various moves I made following graduation. Two years passed before I opened the box and reread my dissertation. When I did, it aroused in me the desire to return to Sinaloa and undertake a deeper and more complete investigation. My principal goal was to produce a study that would encompass the complexity and the processes of change that rural Mexican communities were experiencing at that time.

My Return Journey to Southern Sinaloa

When I returned to southern Sinaloa in the summer of 1993, Mexico was experiencing an acute transformation, politically and economically. The results had, and continue to have, a great impact on the rural areas. In particular, two significant events—the reform of Article 27 of the Mexican Constitution and the passage of the Nueva Ley de Reforma Agraria (New Agrarian Reform Law)—represented abrupt about-faces in the historical and legal trajectory of the landholding and ejido system. These events, in turn, strongly influenced the political, ecological, and economic changes occurring in Sinaloa, especially those related to the accelerating development of commercial agriculture and shrimp cultivation.

This second visit was very important because it gave me the opportunity to strengthen my bonds of friendship and trust with the residents of El Cerro and Celaya. As an anthropologist, I felt trepidation about how the people would react upon seeing me arrive again in their community. It had been three years since I had conducted fieldwork, and I was not sure if they would remember me. To my surprise, they received me joyously, with many hugs. Many seemed surprised that I remembered them and that I had returned. Others said that they knew I would be back because, when I had been there the first time, I ate snapper and sucked out its eye: In the region, a saying goes that those who eat the eye of a snapper will always return to the place where they ate the fish.

During my first season, people did not know what to make of my presence. It was obvious that I did not fit within the stereotype that they held of Americans—white skin, blue eyes, blonde hair. In vain, I explained that I was studying at a U.S. university, where I had lived for the last four years. It was also in vain that I told them I was Puerto Rican: None of them had ever heard of Puerto Rico! Finally, they created various identities for me. Most believed that I was a biologist, from some other part of Sinaloa or another state in Mexico, who had come to do social service in the region. Others believed that I was a crazy girl, who had run away from home, and that I was fleeing my parents. Others still thought that I was an ambassador from a South American country, who had been sent to Mexico to learn aquaculture techniques. Regardless of what I told them about my family and my country, they looked at me as if I were lying. They could not believe that a young woman from another country would come to visit places they viewed as such poor and remote communities. Many ended up with the idea that Puerto Rico was a town located on Sinaloa's northern coast.

Partly because of that reaction during my initial fieldwork, I was very surprised by the reception I got on my return in the summer of 1993. This welcome was due largely to people finally understanding that a country called Puerto Rico really existed. The week before I arrived, the popular Mexican television show *Siempre en Domingo* (*Always on Sunday*) had aired a segment that had been filmed in San Juan and showed many pictures of Puerto Rico. Through that program and the magic of videotape, the rural people in southern Sinaloa encountered Puerto Rico for the first time. One of the first people I saw in El Cerro, Lucía, told me that she now understood that I was not Mexican but Puerto Rican because she had seen pictures of the island on television, particularly of El Viejo San Juan (Old

San Juan) and the tourist zone. Lucía also told me that she was struck by the strong resemblance, in her eyes, between Mazatlán and San Juan, because both were ports. From that day on, the roles were reversed: The communities' residents, whom I supposedly had come to study, became the anthropologists, and I, bombarded and cross-examined with all kinds of questions, was converted into the subject of study. This was my first real taste of globalization at the local level.

Girls who saw me walking in the street called to me to ask if I knew Chayanne or Ricky Martin, two Puerto Rican celebrities. They asked me if I knew what had become of the members of the Puerto Rican band Menudo. Women invited me to eat in their homes, and they took the opportunity to ask about life for Puerto Rican women. Some asked if Puerto Rican women also suffered and if their husbands drank and beat them; others wanted to know if the women had washing machines and televisions in their homes. They also asked me if we ate tortillas, beans, and *nopales,* and if we raised chickens and pigs. For their part, the men, chatting at midday under the palapa, would see me and invite me to sit with them, and then they would begin to interrogate me. They wanted to know what kinds of crops are grown in Puerto Rico, and specifically how and when they are planted. They also asked if the people fished, and what species were most commonly caught. Others were interested in knowing if the peso was the official currency in the country, and whether or not the island was autonomous. They also asked me how far Puerto Rico was from Sinaloa, and if they could get there by train or boat.

All these questions, and people's curiosity to learn more about me and my country of origin, made me reflect on the role that anthropologists play and our relationships to the people about whom we write. Other anthropologists have also addressed this in their writings (see, for example, Alonso 1995; Behar 1993; McClusky 2001). Cynthia Hewitt de Alcántara (1984), discussing the history of social anthropology and rural sociology, referred to the distance that often exists between practitioners of these disciplines and their subjects of study. According to her, "Those who studied primitive, or peasant or rural society were, then, by definition outsiders; they came to their subject matter imbued with the culture of an urban, and quite frequently a metropolitan, society. At the same time, they were the intellectual product of particular educational experiences, shaped within specific socioeconomic contexts, during concrete historical periods. They could not entirely escape the determination of relevant enquiry exercised by the social dynamics of their own time and place, nor would the product of their thought have found echo had they done so" (1984, 1).

This situation does not seem to have changed much in recent years if we take into account that most anthropological studies on Mexico have been done by people who come from a very different class and cultural reality than that lived by the people whom they study. In my case, however, I am not a complete outsider to the reality lived by the residents of El Cerro and Celaya. I was born and raised in a rural community similar to theirs. My grandparents were campesinos, men and women of the Puerto Rican countryside, for whom the land was a symbol of pride and identity and agriculture, the base of their daily sustenance. The rural community where I grew up shared many characteristics with southern Sinaloa's rural communities. Both are characterized by the importance of family networks and by the strength of their social networks. In both, households represent the primary social and economic unit. Additionally, in both places, events and anecdotes form part of the rural setting's ambience and oral traditions. Thus, my roots in a rural context have given me a perspective that is much closer to the reality of rural Mexico.

During that summer of 1993, my interest was focused on gaining a more exact idea about what it meant to be a rural community in northwestern Mexico given the drastic economic and political changes occurring. Some of the questions I posed were aimed at investigating how a household made use of scarce resources in order to guarantee the survival of its members. One of my goals was to learn how the people exploited the kinship and *compadrazgo* (co-godparenthood) networks within and beyond the community to benefit the household. During my stay, I learned that, in reality, the differences between the two communities were not so great when examined in a regional context. Both had a common history centered on the struggle for land, and in both, the residents were already connected to a global economy through their participation in shrimp fishing and commercial agriculture. The agrarian struggles, particularly, were a theme that always came up in my conversations with the people, especially when they told me stories of how the communities were established. These struggles remain engraved in the memories of the inhabitants and now form part of the oral tradition of each community. The struggle for access to fishing resources, particularly shrimp, is an experience that the two communities also share and that forms part of the region's oral tradition.

Throughout the years, I have continued my fieldwork in southern

Sinaloa, and I have seen how, over the last nine years, my bonds of friendship and trust with the people have solidified even more. The communities' residents have watched my transformation, as I grew from a young student into a professional woman and a wife and mother. The trust and friendship reached its maximum expression when I was invited to be the godmother of one of the children born in El Cerro. Living in southern California has helped me to develop that friendship. Many people have family members in that region of the United States, and they have given me telephone numbers so that I could call these relatives. They also send messages with me, and they have given my telephone number to their relatives so that they can reach me. Thus, a transnational reciprocity has developed, through which the people from these communities call me at home to ask me to bring them something on my next visit. When their relatives and friends who have been on a visit to southern Sinaloa return to Southern California, they, in turn, bring greetings and gifts to me. For me, their locality and my locality intersect in bonds that are transnational, and I, like them, move within these localities with ease and with little thought.

A Note on Methodology: Ethnography and Process

The idea of writing this book emerged partly from my experience and personal interest. My intention is to understand how other people, who live in a similar social and cultural context to the one in which I grew up, struggle and defend themselves against the adversities they must confront daily. In this sense, I share with Ana Alonso (1995, 9) the fact that "my interest in Anthropology is not motivated by 'imperialist nostalgia' (Rosaldo 1989, 69) but instead by a curiosity about the emancipatory visions of marginal people and the possibilities and limitations they articulate."

As is true of all anthropological ethnographies, mine is also the product of specific times and historical moments. During the 1990s, as my research unfolded, Mexican society underwent important changes, as did my research questions. Many of these changes profoundly affected the country and had huge implications for rural areas and ultimately the kinds of questions I was to ask.

Three of these changes relate to the replacement of the model of import-substitution industrialization with a neoliberal development model, implemented during the presidency of Carlos Salinas de Gortari. One of the most significant changes was the reform of Article 27 of the Mexican Constitution, which amended the laws regulating the ejido sector and radically altered the distribution of land and the privatization of the ejido. Another change was the implementation of the North American Free Trade Agreement (NAFTA) in 1994, which contributed directly to the acceleration of commercial agricultural development. This rapid agricultural development, in turn, has resulted in increased poverty and marginalization for the rural population (Otero 1996). The quality of life for the rural population deteriorated further following the devaluation of the peso at the end of December 1994, an event that forced the Mexican government to implement severe austerity measures that significantly reduced social programs and assistance to smallholders.

Two other events also affected how I would conduct the research. First, the Zapatista Rebellion in Chiapas during January 1994 demonstrated the enormous capacity of the Mexican campesino population to organize and fight for its rights and causes. On many occasions during my research, informants commented on historical wrongs and on the uprisings that developed in response in and around the communities of El Cerro and Celaya. This led me to ask very different historical questions from the ones that I had anticipated asking. Second, the approval of Proposition 187 in California, on November 9, 1994, was widely discussed and criticized in southern Sinaloa. Many people in the rural communities asked me why the gringos did not want them to come to live in California when all that Mexicans were seeking was simply to earn an honest living. From their point of view, this further closed down opportunities to alter their conditions; from my point of view, it called for an examination of the transnational character of local interests.

For the next nine years, specifically between 1993 and 2002, these changes forced me to adopt a much broader series of questions that expanded my research horizons to include regional ecology, agriculture, political economy, and national and global relations of production and consumption. The broadening of my research horizons in turn encouraged me to expand the methodologies I would employ. These heightened and broadened interests led me to search out the dusty corners of municipal archives to gather municipal and regional histories, to visit fishing cooperatives in mangrove swamps to inquire about the salinity of the estuaries, and to gather crop estimates from local farmers. But these were basically analytical necessities. The human dimensions of my research could be captured only by extended and systematic participant observation of the local communities. I conducted hundreds of open-ended and structured interviews, organized numerous focus groups, and developed community and household survey instruments to ensure unbiased and representative data to test the insights gleaned from other sources of information (see the appendix). I collected extensive life and oral histories to capture the dynamic process of community formation. I created informant-ranking exercises to examine socioeconomic stratification, and I daily participated in informal conversations and rituals that took place within the webs of *confianza* (mutual trust) among women.

All the people portrayed in this book are real, although a few are no longer living. I have used pseudonyms to protect their identities. In some cases, people told me what names they wanted me to use instead of their real ones; in other cases, they left it up to me to decide. This book truly has been an extended qualitative and quantitative journey, spanning more than a decade, through which both my work and I have evolved, as have the people of El Cerro and Celaya.

Organization of This Book

This book is divided into three parts. Part I analyzes the historical, social, cultural, economic, and ecological factors that have shaped the definition and development of the southern Sinaloa region. In chapter 1, I discuss the economic, cultural, and environmental history of southern Sinaloa to set the stage for the various modes of production that emerged from the pre-Columbian through the colonial, national, and current transnational periods. Chapter 2 presents an overview of the ecology, geography, and political and social organization of southern Sinaloa to provide context for the research, and analyzes and formulates the relationship among globalization, natural resources, and environmental change.

Part II analyzes the role of the state and of regional and local processes in the settlement and formation of southern Sinaloa's rural communities. Chapters 3 and 5 present the history of the settlement of the two communities, El Cerro and Celaya, and their major ecological characteristics. Chapters 4 and 6 analyze how these communities are internally structured and organized, socially, politically, and economically, and how they have changed over time.

Part III focuses on how rural households in these communities struggle to survive in the midst of environmental degradation and economic impoverishment. Chapter 7 investigates the various gendered responses generated by households to assure the well-being and provisioning of their members. It specifically focuses on the participation of household members in the subsistence, formal, and informal sectors of the local, regional, and global economies. Chapter 8 discusses the various socially and culturally based mechanisms women use to combat economic uncertainty and isolation. I demonstrate that women are not mere passive victims of globalization and that instead they use all resources available to them to guarantee the survival of their families. The conclusion integrates the themes of resistance, economic and environmental change, and the impact of globalization and national policies on rural Mexican communities. Finally, the afterword addresses some of the current changes taking place within the communities of El Cerro and Celaya.

Part I

The Regional Context

History, Development, and Human Processes

The Flores-López family.

Introduction to Part I

What is a region? Regions are often classified according to their perceived common geographic, cultural, economic, and ecological characteristics. As Bryan Roberts (1992, 228) has noted, "There are many possible ways of defining a region: by physical or administrative boundaries, by the distribution of cultural practices, or by a particular concentration of economic activities." Commenting on Mexico, Eric Van Young has observed, "If one reads very far in the very recent literature on Mexican regional history, politics or culture, one rather quickly discovers an interesting fact: regions are like love—they are difficult to describe, but we know them when we see them" (1992, 3). Diana Liverman and Altha J. Cravey (1992, 39) have pointed out that Mexican regions "are very dynamic, serving a range of intellectual, cultural, and political purposes."

Within anthropology, regions are considered important units of analysis, especially for the understanding of the linkages between local communities and the broader society in which they are embedded. Eric Wolf (1982) paid special attention to the manner in which regions developed in association with the production of specific commodities. Regional specialization, according to him, was not limited to the production of raw materials or food but also produced the labor force that sustained agriculture and industry.

Sinaloa covers an area of 58,090 square kilometers, making it Mexico's seventeenth largest state (Heredia Trasviña 1990). The state of Sinaloa and the states of Nayarit, Sonora, Baja California Norte, and Baja California Sur constitute the northwestern region of Mexico (see map 2). Sinaloa borders the states of Sonora and Chihuahua to the north, Durango to the

Map 2
Northwestern Mexico

east, and Nayarit to the south. The Sea of Cortez and the Pacific Ocean mark its northwestern and southwestern boundaries, respectively.

Sinaloa is divided into three regions: north, center, and south. Ecological characteristics partly determine this, because both the center and north have a more desertlike climate than the tropical south. Locally, people talk about cultural and social differences that they think exist among the three regions. The two communities on which this book focuses are located in Rosario and Escuinapa, the two southernmost Sinaloan *municipios* (similar to U.S. counties).

This section's two chapters sketch the history of natural resource use in Sinaloa from the pre-Hispanic period to the present day. The section focuses on the southern region, *el sur de Sinaloa* (southern Sinaloa), which has a long history of natural resource use that has been marred by struggles and conflicts that developed first along ethnic and later class lines. Another salient feature of the region's history of natural resource use is the production of specific commodities during different historical periods destined for regional, national, and global markets. This section pays special attention to how conflicts developed around the attempts to gain control of natural resources for their exploitation. It also discusses the major ecological and geographic characteristics of the region and the factors that have contributed to its environmental degradation.

1

El Sur de Sinaloa

A Historical Portrait of a Land and a People

> Life in northwestern Mexico has been a logical consequence of the
> unique conditions that determined its colonial evolution: the struggle
> to control the environment; the struggle to counteract geographic
> isolation; the struggle to possess fertile land and the water to irrigate
> it; the clash of cultures, racial struggles, and caste antagonisms.
> —Miguel de Medízabal, *La Evolución del Noroeste de México*
> (my translation)

Sinaloa is known today as "the land between the sierra and the sea," but
the Cahítas (inhabitants of the region in pre-Hispanic times) called it "the
place of the *pitahaya*." For the Spanish conquistadors who arrived in
Mexico, this region was part of the northwestern frontier of New Spain.
Both the conquistadors and the Jesuit missionaries, who attempted to colonize, pacify, and settle in Sinaloa, described it and the rest of the northwest as inhospitable and barbarous. Today, for many, Sinaloa is a land of
extraordinary contrasts, where the past and the present merge with the
geography to create a complex and unique cultural and social mosaic.

My first encounter with the contrasts of Sinaloa came when I began my
doctoral dissertation fieldwork, which I carried out in the southern part of
the state. I first observed the magnitude of these contrasts in Mazatlán, a
thoroughly urban area, which encompasses three different ecological, social, and economic zones in one space. On one side is the *zona dorada* (the
golden zone), as it is locally known, famous for its mixture of hotels, folk
art markets, boutiques, discotheques, and restaurants. This is the Mazatlán
that stands for progress and disorder. It is a sophisticated city, controlled

largely by foreign investment and the local elites. Most Mazatlecos are integrated into this zone only to the degree that they provide manual labor to the service industries catering to the tourist trade. Yet another Mazatlán, known as El Viejo Mazatlán (Old Mazatlán) or el centro (downtown), is set apart by its colonial architecture. It was here that the first attempts at urban development occurred, and here, in recent years, that urbanization has accelerated. Viejo Mazatlán's church, plaza, market, narrow streets, colonial buildings, and municipal palace are silent witnesses to a Spanish legacy that began with the arrival of Nuño Beltrán de Guzmán in 1529. This is a dynamic Mazatlán motivated by commerce. The third zone, on the outskirts of the city, consists of *colonias populares*, or poor working-class neighborhoods. It is the semi-urban, poor side of Mazatlán, whose inhabitants struggle to live a hand-to-mouth existence. It is also the Mazatlán that reflects the growing migration from rural areas to the city of those seeking work.

Mazatlán is not the only part of southern Sinaloa where contrasts abound. When one gets away from the city, leaving behind the U.S. and Canadian tourists, the traffic congestion, and the comings and goings of the Mazatlecos, one enters a space where contrast is woven with a thread that bastes the outline of a historical legacy that has refused to become merely a memory on a schoolbook page. Going south, one finds a rural landscape marked by the contours of the hills, the greenery of the *cardones* (cacti) and other vegetation, dead in the dry season but turning exuberantly green when the first rains caress the soil. This countryside is notable for dirt roads that begin with green-lettered metal signs bearing the names of the communities to which they lead. The communities, most of them ejidos, are the legacy of the Mexican Revolution, class struggle, and agrarian reform, and many Sinaloans reside there. In these places, small-scale agriculture is still the base of subsistence, and close economic and social relationships are the fundamental fibers of a community.

Alongside the ejidos are fields of deep-green grass, where horses, cows, and burros graze tranquilly. In these fields, irrigated by pumps, flower spectacular crops of mangoes, chilies, papayas, and plums, mostly destined for regional, national, and global markets. These lands belong mostly to private business owners and represent the polar opposite of the revolutionary ideal, agrarian reform, and class struggle. Until 1992, it was precisely in these two systems of land tenure, the corporate and the private, where one of Sinaloa's greatest contrasts lay.

When traveling through the region and going into its rural areas, one becomes aware that, at one time, an indigenous people gave life to this rural countryside. In the rural communities, stories abound about traces of ceremonial centers built on hilltops or about rock figurines shaped like people, which, upon being spotted, vanish by hiding and camouflaging themselves in the vegetation. Archaeological sites, shell mounds, and buried artifacts in many of these rural communities add veracity to these stories and breathe new life into the pre-Hispanic past that is so enduring in the region's history. Even though the native population was almost entirely exterminated during the Spanish conquest, its ceramics, petroglyphs, game of hulama, and fishing *tapos* (weirs) today are a source of Sinaloan pride. Sadly, these cultural manifestations represent yet another contrast between the idealization of an indigenous past and the reality of the population's brutal extermination by abuse, disease, marginalization, cultural repression, and ecological imperialism.

The origin of all these contrasts is embedded in the region's history, and one comes to understand why and how present-day Sinaloa became a political and population center by studying this history. To read the history of Sinaloa is to enter a labyrinth blotched with the scars of violence, struggle, conflict, loss, failure, and triumph.

Two themes dominate in this history: the importance of natural resources in maintaining human settlements in the region, and the class struggle that has been waged precisely to monopolize and control those resources. Throughout Sinaloa's history, these two themes have come and gone in waves of blood and violence that have splattered against even the most hidden corners of the events forging this region. The fight for natural resources in southern Sinaloa is not recent in origin but instead has its roots in the Spanish conquest and colonization. To understand these two characteristics, it will be necessary to place them in the context of the region's history.

This chapter focuses on the southern region of the state to present the most important historical aspects that contributed to forging present-day Sinaloan society. It briefly sketches a description of the first inhabitants of the area and their relationship to the environment and natural resources; the impact of the Spanish conquest and colonization upon the native population and the natural resources; the creation of a class structure and its impact on the region's economy and society; the struggles for and conflicts over access to and control of natural resources; and the role of the state in supporting or limiting access by certain sectors of the population to these resources. The chapter concludes with a review of the conditions that have shaped the ideology that today governs the use and exploitation of natural resources, and the relationship of this ideology to the class system that predominates in the region.

The Indigenous Landscape of Preconquest Southern Sinaloa

Several centuries before the European invasion of northwestern Mexico, the region's native population lived in widely dispersed and varied types of *pueblos*. These were located across the region's ecological zones, which can be distinguished by their climate, flora, fauna, and altitude. The subsistence patterns of these *naciones* were intimately related to the availability of natural resources in the different zones.

Archaeological studies have revealed the principal characteristics of the naciones that lived in northwestern Mexico. Using linguistic traits and level of cultural and agricultural development as a reference point, preconquest northwestern Mexico was divided into three areas: Mesoamérica, Oasisamérica, and Aridamérica. However, only the area known as Mesoamérica is relevant because present-day southern Sinaloa is in the northwest corner of this greater region.

The Mesoamerican cultural area lies within the region that is present-day central and southern Sinaloa. Archaeological work has revealed that southern Sinaloa was densely populated when the conquistadors arrived and that this density was possible thanks to the indigenous groups' establishment of some very sophisticated organizational and productive strategies (Reff 1991). These studies also show that the indigenous groups had one of the most highly developed technologically complex cultures in northwestern New Spain.

The Totorame were the largest indigenous group inhabiting what is today southern Sinaloa. Their population was spread over twenty-two pueblos that constituted the geographic region that became the province of Chametla, which includes the present-day municipios of Escuinapa, Rosario, Concordia, Mazatlán, and San Ignacio (Verdugo Quintero 1997). Even though we cannot know the exact number of Totorames, Ortega Noriega (1993) believes that approximately 410,000 lived in Chametla, making it the most densely populated subregion in northwestern New Spain. The Totorame were a sedentary people, with most of their settlements of dispersed villages made of adobe located along Sinaloa's coastal plain. Totorame society was stratified, and tribute was paid to a cacique leader who had available a well-equipped and well-organized army to protect its region.

The Totorame economy was based on a form of intensive rain-fed and riverine agriculture that was more advanced than that of native peoples in neighboring cultural areas. The Totorames grew corn, beans, squash, cotton, and tobacco for subsistence and for trade. Textile and ceramic manufacture also formed an important part of their internal production and commercial trade exchanges. As well, they exploited coastal resources, such as mining salt from the ocean. When the ocean salt water evaporated in the estuaries during the dry season, salt was mined naturally, but at other times, the Totorames created salt flats by constructing ditches into which seawater would enter at high tide and then evaporate in the sun. Salt preserved food, but more important, it was used in commercial exchanges with other indigenous groups living in the mountains.

The Totorames also fished in the estuaries, lagoons, and rivers, where they took advantage of the high tides to place tapos across the inlets of these bodies of water, a technique used to this day. At low tide, fish, shrimp, and other organisms were trapped, making them easy to catch. The Totorames also used barbasco leaves to poison the water where the fish swam. Once dead or at least paralyzed, the fish floated on the surface where the fishermen could collect them with ease. Finally, Totorames supplemented their marine and agricultural diet by collecting wild fruits and plants and by raising ducks, turkeys, curassows, and dogs, and keeping beehives to produce wax and honey (Reff 1991).

The other group that inhabited southern Sinaloa was the Xiximes, a highland agricultural and gathering nación that lived in the Sierra Madre. Although they cultivated a variety of crops, such as corn, beans, and squash, they lacked the more advanced agricultural system practiced by the Totorames. The Spanish chroniclers categorized the Xiximes as a "fierce and cannibalistic people," who came down to raid Totorame settlements along the coastal plain (Valdés Aguilar 1998).

How these groups interacted with their environment is not known except by hypothetical implication in relation to their productive complexity. Although precise information exists for other Mexican indigenous groups, such as the Maya, it is almost nonexistent for the peoples who lived in southern Sinaloa due to their annihilation during the European conquest. In any case, whatever may have been the general relationship between the southern Sinaloan indigenous groups and their environment, the latter was altered drastically by the Spanish conquest and colonization of the region.

The European Invasion of Southern Sinaloa

Driven by legends of the Land of the Amazons and the Seven Cities of Cíbol, both of which were alleged to abound with great riches, the Spanish military and ecological conquest of northwestern New Spain began with Nuño de Guzmán's brutal entry into southern Sinaloa in 1529. After having nearly wiped out the indigenous populations living in what are today the states of Michoacán and Jalisco, Guzmán and his men arrived in the province of Aztatlán, located in present-day Nayarit. There they again committed innumerable atrocities against the native people, but the harshness of the *tierra caliente* (lowlands), including storms, floods, and illnesses, finished off a large part of Guzmán's forces as well as the few indigenous survivors (Ortega Noriega 1999).

The arrival of Nuño de Guzmán in the northwest seriously changed the native countryside, leaving in its wake blood, destruction, and violence. Sauer and Brand summarized the impact that this first Spanish penetration had on the region: "By a single entrada, in 1530–1531, Nuño de Guzmán ruined the native scene. Behind he left a trail of smoking ruins and shambles. Survivors were driven out in gangs and sold as slaves; in a few years, the lowlands of Sinaloa and Nayarit became almost a wilderness" (1932, 7). The Indians symbolized this conquest as *"una vibora que cae de las nubes sobre la tierra"* ("a snake that falls to earth from the sky") (De Mendizábal 1930, 18). In only two years, the Spanish invasion of northwestern Mexico achieved what internal fighting among the many indigenous naciones had never achieved: their destruction.

Thus, after the Spaniards had invaded and established groundwork for colonization, the coastal plains of southern Sinaloa were essentially depopulated. At different times, indigenous groups migrated from the mountains to settle on the coast and occupy what was left of the Totorames' communities. Eventually, other Spanish conquistadors followed in the steps of Nuño de Guzmán and invaded the region. These later expeditions, such as that of Francisco de Ibarra, had the same goal as Guzmán's: the exploitation of natural resources and the utilization of Indian labor. In contrast, however, later invasions sought to found Spanish settlements and to Christianize the Indians.

Colonialism, Society, and the Environment

Guillermo Bonfil Batalla (1987) has noted accurately that the Spanish colonization of Mexico was a venture of exploitation whose main target was the Indian. In the specific case of southern Sinaloa, two important factors affected colonization: the different strategies used by the Spaniards to control the region and its indigenous population, and the environmental and social implications and consequences of Spanish colonization.

In southern Sinaloa, as in the rest of Mexico and more generally throughout Latin America, the Spanish colonial regime achieved domination of indigenous society and the environment by methods that arose as much in response to local reality as for external reasons. In southern Sinaloa, local conditions were shaped by the high level of cultural development reached by the Totorames compared to other indigenous groups in northwestern Mexico. The well-defined social and economic organization of the Totorames facilitated the imposition of Spanish institutions.

Those Indians who survived the abuse of the Spanish were subjugated through the imposition of institutions whose central objective was the creation of a new social, political, and economic regime based on a new class structure. In northwestern New Spain, slavery, the *encomienda* system, and *repartimiento* were the first three institutions the Spaniards imposed.[1] Hand in hand with the encomiendas came the *cabildos* (town councils), judicial institutions that controlled the social, political, economic, and ecclesiastic activities of the village.[2] From the outset, the encomenderos dominated the cabildos. They exercised jurisdiction over the distribution of building lots, orchards, farms, and livestock, which made it possible for them to solidify their own power (Himmerich y Valencia 1991).

These first attempts to settle southern Sinaloa were not entirely successful, but European colonization took a new turn with the arrival of Francisco de Ibarra. Under his encouragement, a new group of Spaniards suffering from gold fever settled in the region. Ibarra's reconquest of the northwest had several consequences, including further distribution of encomiendas, the founding of settlements, and the discovery of rich veins of mineral ore, which led to the creation of a new institution, the *reales de minas* (mining centers). While encomienda, repartimiento, and slavery were the key institutions of the conquest, the three most important colonial institutions in northwestern New Spain were *presidios*, reales de minas, and missions.[3] In the southern provinces, however, only the reales de minas and, to some extent the missions, had a significant impact, for reasons to be discussed later.

Along with the founding of towns, the discovery of rich mines led to the creation of reales de minas, whose significance was rooted as much in their productive structure as in their social organization. In economic terms, they were private property; the Spaniards who had been granted mines by the Spanish crown were the owners of the means of production. However, Spanish law awarded subsoil rights and mineral resources to the Spanish king, so mine owners were obliged to pay a tax, consisting of one-fifth of all ore produced (Ortega Noriega 1999).

The founding of the reales de minas created a new system of regional commerce based on the delivery of goods and services necessary for the functioning of the mines. Work animals, food eaten by the laborers, and equipment and materials used in mining were among the items imported from other regions. These were paid for with ore, primarily silver. The historian of Sinaloa Rafael Valdés Aguilar has aptly described this system, which was based on the flow of merchandise into and out of the reales de minas: "the *reales de minas* were the nucleus of commercial circuits of the localities and the marrow of the labor market; they were also the point of confluence of commercial routes to other regions, to which arrived the imports and from which the ore flowed to Mexico City" (1998, 140).

The establishment of the reales de minas in northwestern New Spain was also closely linked to the new class structure that had begun to appear with the establishment of the first Spanish villages in the region and that was predicated on the ethnic and racial differences between the indigenous peoples and the Spaniards. The new system served to support and protect the so-called *pureza de sangre* (bloodline purity) of the Spaniards. Racial difference was used to create a *régimen de castas* (caste system), which had at the top the *gente de razón*—Spaniards and Creoles, who were people of Spanish descent born in Mexico. The gente de razón controlled the mines, salt flats, fisheries, land, livestock, and mule trains (Ortega Noriega 1999). They had political and economic control and social prestige. Only the peninsular Spaniards, however, controlled the production of ore and the commercial system that revolved around it.

The reales de minas were populated primarily by Indians, black slaves, and mestizos. By means of the repartimiento system, the Spaniards kept the Indians subjugated, forcing them to work as *tapisques* (drafted workers) in the mines. The blacks, Indians, and mestizos were given the most arduous and dangerous jobs in the extraction and processing of the precious metals.

The establishment of the reales de minas had two important consequences for the southern provinces. One was the role the region came to play as a place to receive Spanish emigrants and Indians from other regions. The flow of immigrants to the reales de minas was linked to the availability of mining jobs. Poor Spaniards, Indians, and mestizos came to get jobs as day laborers. They supplemented their livelihoods by fishing, extracting salt, selling dried fish, cattle ranching, and making handicrafts.

Environmental degradation was the other important consequence of mining. With the boom following the discovery of new lodes, the demand for natural resources used in processing silver increased. In the northwest, two principal techniques were employed: smelting and amalgamation. Smelting separated high-content silver from other minerals such as lead. To melt the silver required ovens, which burned charcoal made from the trees in the area. This resulted in deforestation of large tracts of land, a necessary evil to sustain the functioning of the mines. Amalgamation was the technique used to process low-grade silver. It required a constant supply of three primary materials: salt, mercury, and water. Known as the patio process, this technique had been invented in Mexico during the 1550s (Andrews 1983). It involved crushing and sifting the mineral ore and then transferring it to cauldrons, where it was boiled with salt and water (Valdés Aguilar 1998). When mercury was added to the mixture, the silver separated from the other minerals. The air and water became contaminated with mercury, and gases from the silver processing harmed the health of the laborers, who were also dying from silicosis, tuberculosis, and bronchitis (Valdés Aguilar 1998).

The huge quantities of salt required by this process were sent from the coastal marshes of the Pacific Ocean to the mines in the sierra. For example, salt from Chametla was sold to neighboring reales de minas and even shipped by mule train as far as Durango. The mayor of the province directly managed the salt marshes of Chametla, and the Xiximes Indians were forced to mine the salt. The Consejo de Indias and the Consejo de Hacienda de Castilla were responsible for supplying the mines with mercury that was produced in Almadén in southern Spain (Valdés Aguilar 1998).

The reales de minas played an important role as an economic institution that helped cement the military conquest while simultaneously serving as an agent for the expansion of Spanish ecological and economic imperialism in northwestern New Spain. The reales de minas established an active economic relationship with the mission settlements.[4] Such was the case for the Real de Minas del Rosario, where the Spanish colonizers had commercial links with the Jesuit missionaries of Elota and Culiacán (Ibarra Escobar, Aguilar Alvarado, and Valdés Aguilar 1997). The creation of a system of economic exchange between the two institutions led, in turn, to interdependency. The missionaries demanded silver in return for food, mules, horses, and Indian laborers, which they supplied to the mines. The Indians in the mission settlements were obliged to work in the mines as tapisques, under a system of forced labor (Ortega Noriega 1993). The silver that the missions received was spent primarily to solidify Catholicism by constructing more churches and missions. What money was left over went to endow the work of the Society of Jesus in the rest of New Spain. The relationship between the reales de minas and the Jesuit missions continued in the northwest until 1776, the year of the Jesuit expulsion as a result of the Bourbon reforms.

Besides the impact on the mission system, the Bourbon reforms led to other significant changes that affected the indigenous population. One was the reorganization of the landholding system, and with it, the transformation of communal lands into private property. All usable land was susceptible to distribution. This radically transformed the structure of the systems of production in the indigenous communities, which served to weaken the traditional structures of communal organization.

According to Ortega Noriega, the privatization of land and other means of production "was the means by which—through sale, fraud, or dispossession—the lands passed to non-Indian owners" (1993, 103). The regularization of land tenure occurred rapidly in those areas settled by the gente de razón. The reforms also promoted the conversion of empty land into private property, and water and other natural resources that had been part of the indigenous communities were also privatized. The Bourbon reforms resulted in "the destruction of the communities and the assimilation of the Indians into a third social group," that comprising mulattos and mestizos (Ortega Noriega 1999, 153).

By the beginning of the eighteenth century, in the northwest as in the rest of New Spain, social and economic inequality had become ever more marked. The class system that had been born with the founding of the first Spanish settlements was now completely institutionalized. The *peninsulares* (Spaniards) remained at the top of the social pyramid and controlled the social, political, religious, and economic life of the region. The *castas* (mixed races), made up of the Creoles, mestizos, and mulattos, constituted the second tier of the social hierarchy. Although the castas were the most numerous, they were considered socially and culturally inferior to the peninsulares but superior to the Indians. The sobriquet gente de razón continued to be used, emphasizing and justifying the social and ethnic differences between the castas and the Indians. The Creoles constituted the largest segment of the casta class, and they were influential in the political and economic systems of the region because many were rich miners and hacienda owners. The remainder of the casta class, mestizos and mulattos, worked for Creoles and peninsulares in the mining industry, on haciendas, and in agriculture. For example, in southern Sinaloa between 1790 and 1810, most of the workforce in the mines was mulatto (Ramírez Mesa 1993). Indians were on the bottom rung of the social ladder and continued to be forced to labor for Spanish business interests. Many worked as servants, peons, day laborers, and manual laborers in the mines and on the haciendas belonging to the Spaniards (Grande 1998).

During the final stages of the colonial period, a class of regional elite had begun to form in northwestern Mexico. It mostly consisted of rich and educated Creoles from distinguished and influential families. Known as *Los Notables*, they lived in the region's urban centers and exercised control over mining, agriculture, ranching, and commerce. Some exercised great political power locally through their domination of the town and provincial councils. In southern Sinaloa, Los Notables, as Voss explains, "were living on borrowed time in the wake of independence; and were orphaned to a republican, externally oriented future for which they were little prepared, but which temptingly held great promise" (1982, 34).

As colonization continued, the class struggle intensified, especially between the peninsulares and the Creoles, over access to the means of production and to the centers of the political system. It was interrupted, however, by the clamor for an end to Spanish colonialism. The War of Independence exploded, and its effects—although minimal in the northwest—were sufficient to awaken a class consciousness among the exploited groups of the region. These groups would later become the principal protagonists in the history of their own struggle. In Sinaloa, the first declaration in favor of independence was affirmed at the Real de Minas del Rosario (Grande 1998).

Post-Independence, the Porfiriato, and the Emergence of Regionalized Economies

After the storm provoked by the War of Independence, a sense of false calm temporarily pervaded northwestern Mexico. According to Voss, the first decade following independence was "a time of definition, a time for designing the nature and direction of the new nation" (1982, 62). A series of changes occurred that altered the political and economic structures of the region.

One important change was the ending of restrictions on commerce and the opening of several ports to transoceanic shipping, which helped to insert southern Sinaloa into the international economy, and led to the expansion of Mazatlán and Guaymas. Mazatlán became the major port of northwestern Mexico, and between 1824 and 1830, foreign merchants, who would later transform the Sinaloan elite, settled there.

These new foreign merchants all represented the most important American, English, Spanish, German, and French trading companies of the period (Ortega Noriega 1999). Some of these traders married into the regional social elite. Others never actually joined the Sinaloan elite but exercised significant political and economic influence in the region nevertheless.

Another significant change was the increase in agriculture and ranching in the state as both ceased to be "occupations appropriate for Indians," becoming instead activities "worthy" of *hacendados*, wealthy landowners. Agriculture expanded with the shift to land as private property and the stimulus from foreign investment. As collective tenure declined, ever more land ended up in the hands of los notables and other wealthy landowners, who promoted industrial agriculture based on single-crop farming. Indians, mulattos, and mestizos, who were now paid wages, provided agricultural labor.

These changes took place after independence, but they continued to favor the local elite and the hacendados. The mestizos, Indians, and mulattos, many of whom had become campesinos, did not benefit at all, socially, politically, or economically. To the contrary, those groups became even more exploited.

The campesino class of southern Sinaloa continued growing. Between 1867 and 1877, the period known as the Restoration Republic, campesinos from Nayarit and other states settled around the Río Baluarte in Rosario. They supported themselves largely by cultivating corn and beans, raising livestock, and working in mining.

During the Porfiriato (1877–1909), or Cañedismo, the economic and political situation of the campesinos deteriorated. The governor of Sinaloa, Francisco Cañedo, faithfully followed the political and economic ideology mandated by Porfirio Díaz. As a result, Sinaloa saw the start of changes whose repercussions still echo in the collective memory of its inhabitants. During this period, Sinaloa and northwestern Mexico in general were integrated into the national economy and society, at last ending the isolation that had characterized the region since the time of the Spanish conquest. United States economic imperialism in northwestern Mexico also reached its greatest expression, and there arose in Sinaloa a new capitalist ideology that legitimated the interests of the property-owning classes. During the Porfiriato, profound changes took place in the pillars of the Sinaloan economy: mining, agriculture, textiles, and commerce, all of which were modernizing and becoming more dependent on foreign capital. These changes laid the groundwork for the model of economic development to be followed in the three regions that make up modern-day Sinaloa: the south, highly dependent on mining and commerce; and the center and north, dominated by industrial agriculture.

Foreign interests influenced many changes during the Porfiriato. The presence of foreigners was on the increase because of laws promoting and favoring foreign capital investment in the different sectors of the state's economy. For example, the Ley Sobre Deslinde y Colonización de los Terrenos Baldíos (The Law for Boundary Demarcation and Occupation of Unclaimed Lands), promulgated in 1883, especially favored foreign business. This law authorized private companies to participate in the surveying of land boundaries in exchange for receiving one-third of that surveyed land. In this way, landholding continued the same pattern of privatization imposed by the Bourbon reforms. Of the ten companies involved in land surveys between 1877 and 1910, eight were of U.S. origin (Ortega Noriega 1999). With the blessing of this law, haciendas proliferated in Sinaloa, many owned by the companies that had surveyed their boundaries.[5] Because of capital investment by these companies and others belonging to U.S. interests, agriculture during the Porfiriato followed a pattern of industrial, capitalist development that continues today, especially in the central and northern parts of the state.

Porfirian legislation permitted foreign investors to exploit mines in Mexico's northern border and Pacific coastal states, and it also awarded investors subsoil rights and rights to the products produced from it (Ortega Noriega 1999). Consequently, the mining sector also thrived as a result of these laws. As with agriculture, many of these laws favored foreign capital investment, but this meant that foreign companies controlled the mines almost exclusively.[6] Not only did foreigners own the best mines, but many also held high-ranking positions on the board of Sinaloan mining companies owned by Mexicans. In addition, they controlled mining by monopolizing material required to run the mines, such as dynamite (Carrillo Rojas 1991).[7]

During the Porfiriato, textiles and commercial trade also flourished in the southern and central parts of the state. The development of regional commerce was closely tied to the state's agricultural and mining production, the output of which was exported worldwide as well as nationally.

Foreign businesses controlled most of the imports and exports that passed through the port of Mazatlán. Spaniards and Germans who owned five important trading companies located there exercised a monopolistic control over the regional market (Román Alarcón 1991). During thirty-two of the Porfiriato's thirty-five years, Sinaloan governor Francisco Cañedo ruled with an iron hand, keeping the repressive Porfirian policies in place. Although it is true that during the dictatorship, Sinaloa entered into a new stage of industrial and commercial expansion driven by foreign capital, it is also true that such expansion created further class divisions and underpaid labor sectors and was regionally uneven. As Ortega Noriega explains: "Modernization in Sinaloa occurred along the coast where it was possible to build roads and mechanize agriculture. The highlands remained at the margin of development, except where there was foreign investment in mining" (1999, 264).

As a direct consequence of this uneven development, there arose several unequal and contrasting Sinaloas at the beginning of the twentieth century. One is the technologically complex Sinaloa of the valleys and the coastal region and the other is the economically isolated Sinaloa of the mountains (Ortega Noriega 1999). As well, two contrasting regional economies coexist: the Sinaloa of commerce and mining in the southern part of the state and the industrial, commercial agricultural Sinaloa of the central and northern regions. As a result of the predominance of Spanish culture and the region's relationship with the United States, two additional contrasting Sinaloas live side by side: one deeply rooted in colonial tradition, and the other economically dependent on the United States.

Under the Porfirian dictatorship, social and economic differences were widened to such a degree that tension and unrest soon reverberated throughout the state. As a result of the growing discontent among the working class and the campesinos, several *caudillos* (revolution leaders) in Sinaloa came forward to dedicate themselves to overthrowing the Porfirian regime. In southern Sinaloa, Heraclio Bernal, known as the Rayo de Sinaloa, played an important role as the mouthpiece for the state's dispossessed. Bernal, a miner of humble origins, challenged the Porfirian regime with a manifesto that brought to light its outrages against the marginalized classes.

During the final decade of the Porfiriato, Sinaloa was predominantly a rural region, with most of the inhabitants making a living in agriculture. According to the general census of 1900, 484,633 persons were agricultural workers, of whom 70 percent were *peones,* or day laborers (Ortega Noriega 1999). The remaining were ranchers or farmers, but the peones, along with fishermen, miners, and workers, made up the largest segment of exploited classes. According to Héctor Olea, Cañedismo's legacy to the Sinaloan people meant the complete subjugation of Sinaloa to foreign monopolies, hacendados, and a state-sponsored dictatorship; the unmitigated exploitation of miners, peones, and railroad workers; and the wholesale suppression of civil and human rights—all accentuated by extreme class divisions (1964, 10).

Such conditions unleashed a series of popular movements, which culminated on November 20, 1910, with the launching of the Mexican Revolution. The revolt began with the expulsion of Porfirio Díaz from the presidency and the termination of the general's dictatorship, and it concluded in different forms in 1940 at the end of the presidential administration of General Lázaro Cárdenas.

In Sinaloa, the revolution brought about abrupt changes that deeply transformed the state's economy and society but retained privileges for the few as well. For the Sinaloans, according to Ortega Noriega, "This was not only a period of violent, profound, and regenerative change but also of notable continuities, some intentional and others not—being instead imposed by the inertia of the times" (1999, 20). During this revolutionary time, natural resources were an important part of state politics. Both the land and the fishing resources were the focus of various policies, whose essential objective was the legal allocation of these resources to an already emerging social sector.

During the presidency of Francisco I. Madero (1911–1913), the first plans for agrarian reform began to be hammered out. Madero emphasized the importance of fishing resources as an essential food source for Mexico's population. The political constitution he developed reaffirmed the "inalienable rights" of the Mexican government to fishing grounds, as well as to territorial waters of the high seas and the waters of lakes and lagoons (Hernández Fujigaki 1988). Nevertheless, Madero, like Porfirio Díaz, ignored promises made to restitute land to Mexico's indigenous communities: Thus, little was accomplished during his tenure.

With the ascension to power of Venustiano Carranza in 1916, Article 27 of the Mexican Constitution of 1917 was approved, mandating that land be distributed to campesinos. In its original form, the article returned to the Mexican state the ownership of the land, water, subsoil, and mineral rights throughout the country's territory, and it laid the legal groundwork for agrarian reform.

In 1920, when General Alvaro Obregón became president, the first agrarian distributions took place; at the same time the power exercised by local caudillos following the revolution was put in check (Ortega Noriega 1999). On May 31, 1923, the Obregón administration established the Dirección de Pesquerías (Department of Fisheries). On December 20 of that same year, Obregón declared the Reglamento de la Pesca Marítima y Pluvial (Regulations for Ocean and River Fishing), which established a hierarchical order in which fishing resources could be exploited, as well as dictating who would be the principal beneficiaries of those resources. According to this decree, the principal beneficiaries were to be Mexico's coastal populations (Hernández Fujigaki 1988). Supplying regional, national, and international markets with fish was of secondary importance in the list of priorities relating to the use and exploitation of fishing resources.

During the presidency of Plutarco Elías Calles (1924–1928), the first fishing licenses were issued, an official fishing season was declared, and restrictions were placed on the use of certain types of fishing gear. By 1930, when Emilio Portes Gil was Mexico's president, promotion of cooperative organizations began, along with deep-sea fishing for shrimp in the waters of the northern Pacific. During the administration of Abelardo Rodríguez, cooperative organizations received full support with the drafting of the Fisheries Law, which was passed on August 31, 1932. This law was a pillar upon which Mexico's fishing cooperative movement was built. It also formally marked the rise of the term "social sector" and the organization into cooperative societies of members of that sector. This law gave high priority to and supported fishermen "whose objective is the improvement of their social and economic situation" so that they might organize themselves in *cooperativas de producción pesqueras* (fishing cooperatives) (Hernández Fujigaki 1988, 3).

In general, during the two decades following the revolution, the economy of Sinaloa, like that of the rest of Mexico, continued to develop largely along the lines set by the Porfirian regime. In the southern part of the state, industry and commerce continued to constitute the primary sectors of the economy, while in the central and northern parts, intensive commercial agriculture was the engine for the state's economic development. Nevertheless, it was not until the administration of Lázaro Cárdenas that the deepest and most significant changes were made, changes that would radically alter Mexico's economy and society. Before Cárdenas, "the promises about agricultural reform had been only timid attempts and false starts" (Padilla 1993, 13).

It was during the Cárdenas administration that agrarian reform in rural Mexico truly came about. In Sinaloa, it took the form of the expropriation of foreign-owned *latifundia* and haciendas to create ejidos and develop private smallholdings (*pequeñas propiedades*). A power struggle among groups openly defending their own interests, namely campesinos, workers, landowners, and the government, marked the agrarian reform in Sinaloa. In addition to its direct consequences, agrarian reform was also a precursor for the formation of the many popular social movements that are still active in Sinaloa.

Cardenismo, Agrarianism, and the Struggle for Land

In 1924, a group of campesinos ambushed and murdered the son of Miguel León, one of the foremen who managed lands belonging to a family named Montero. Weeks later, in the plaza of Mazatlán, one of the accused, Juan Medrano, was calmly waiting to tell the authorities his version of the events when, suddenly, he also was murdered. These homicides apparently had their roots in events of 1918, when Medrano and his brothers had organized a Comité Agrario (Agrarian Committee) in the town of Escamillas, near Mazatlán. The group's goal was to apply formally for a portion of the property owned by Angela Montero, the widow of the head of the Montero family. The land covered large areas in different rural settlements, but most of it lay fallow and was not under cultivation. The campesinos renewed their application in 1921, during the presidency of Alvaro Obregón, and the Comisión Nacional Agraria (National Agrarian Commission) awarded them a land grant. General Angel Flores, governor of Sinaloa and a very close friend of Montero's widow, opposed the grant, and so it was never made. Recognizing that the Montero foremen were repeatedly and consistently harassing them, the campesinos decided to take matters into their own hands and kill the men. Six months after the death of Juan Medrano in 1924, Alvaro Obregón personally awarded the campesinos legal title to the lands. Thus, the town of Escamillas became the first ejido in Sinaloa, and Juan Medrano became the first *agrarista* (activist in the agrarian reform movement) to be murdered in the name of the revolution.[8]

This event marked the start of the most recent phase in the long struggle over land in southern Sinaloa. Like those before, it has been bloody and violent, and certain sectors of the population have defended their self-interests *a capa y espada* (by cloak and dagger). The conflicts heightened as the ideology of the Lázaro Cárdenas administration questioned the agrarian structure and class system prevalent in the region. Agrarian reform in the Cárdenas period was based on several specific objectives and the assumption that these objectives could be achieved with a uniform nationwide process. However, the responses of the various social classes, and even of the government in some states of Mexico, were far from homogeneous. In Sinaloa, agrarian reform and the land struggles had their own distinctive characteristics, shaped by such things as topography, agrarian structure, the class system, and the prevalent ideology about land use existing in Sinaloa's many different regions, all of which affected how the agrarian struggles unfolded, the kind of reception accorded Cárdenas's agrarian reform program, and the reaction of municipal governments throughout Sinaloa.

The principal objectives of the Cárdenas administration's Program for Agrarian Reform were outlined in his Presidential Plan.[9] One key goal was to convert one million peones into independent farmers in order to promote Mexico's agricultural development. Based on the ideology advocated in Article 27 of the 1917 Constitution, Cárdenas made the ejido the focal point of his plan.[10]

The Ley de Dotación de Tierras y Aguas (Land and Water Grants Law), written in 1917 as part of Article 27, launched a massive campaign for distributing and restituting land to create ejidos, farming and ranching settlements, and agrarian communities. The endowment and restitution of lands were linked to the expropriation of large haciendas, a step designed to eliminate *terratenientes* (landholders), and favored a new system of landholding based on three forms of tenure: communal property, smallholdings, and the ejido.

In Sinaloa, agrarian reform during the Cárdenas administration was based on granting land to petitioners who had none. In contrast to other Mexican states where the primary objective of agrarian reform was the restitution of lands taken from indigenous communities during the Porfiriato, in Sinaloa few Indian settlements had survived Spanish colonization. Consequently, until 1935 agrarian redistribution proceeded slowly in the state, and it did not succeed in affecting the structure of landholding or the class system. The breakdown of the agrarian structure did not begin until 1936–1937. In a massive distribution during those years, Cárdenas turned the best lands in Sinaloa over to peones from the haciendas, transforming them into collective ejidos (Grammont 1990).[11] Along with land distribution, the class structure was also transformed, as thousands of peones became campesinos.

With the transformation of the agrarian and class structures, the social and political struggle in the region increased. Confrontations between the terrateniente oligarchy and the farmers were not long in coming. With so few farming settlements in the state, peones from the haciendas made up the majority of the agrarian sector. The thousands of landless farmers who had migrated from other states with the hope of having their own plot of land also became agraristas. The Cárdenas administration's policies appeared in southern Sinaloa at the same time that the supporters of land reform were gaining political power. In the eyes of the terratenientes, the agraristas had become an imminent threat to the landholding status quo.

In southern Sinaloa, several prominent families held most of the political and economic power of the region. Known as the Group of 33, these families, based in Mazatlán, had acquired their power during the Porfiriato through large capital investments in commerce, mining, and fishing (Padilla 1993). In contrast to the central and northern regions, southern Sinaloa had no large valleys that could support vast landholdings, and thus the southern terratenientes had never owned the immense tracts of land that were characteristic of the oligarchy in the central and northern parts of the state (Padilla 1993).

The struggles intensified in 1937 when the agraristas invaded property held by terratenientes and asked the government to turn it over to them. In the struggle to defend their interests, the agraristas were supported by campesino organizations such as the Liga de Comunidades Agrarias (League of Agrarian Communities) and the Confederación Nacional Campesina (National Campesino Confederation, or CNC), both of which had been created by the government as part of the agrarian reform plan. The agraristas were also supported by a militia composed of armed peasants under the command of the federal army.

The terratenientes continued to oppose the distribution of their lands, and to combat the agraristas, they formed the paramilitary group Los del Monte. This group was composed of young men, most of whom were peones or owners of small plots in the agrarian communities. Over many years, they had maintained a close and paternalistic relationship with the terratenientes. Los del Monte became the principal armed group that the oligarchy used against the agrarian movement in southern Sinaloa. Their most common tactic was to murder the leaders of agrarian committees to spread terror among the leaders of the ejido.[12]

The violence increased in 1938 when Los del Monte murdered eleven agraristas in cold blood in the town of El Quemado, in the municipio of Mazatlán. This massacre made it possible for the government to take direct action. General Federico Montes Alanis, head of the military zone in Sinaloa, brought in a group of detectives to find those responsible for the murders. Following an investigation, the detectives themselves murdered Tomás Hernández, the leader of Los del Monte, in the marketplace in Mazatlán. In turn, Los del Monte murdered more agraristas. In 1938 alone, the agrarian revolts in Sinaloa left in its wake 216 dead (Padilla 1993).

In the struggle for land in southern Sinaloa, the agraristas, despite the support they received from the government and campesino organizations, were always disadvantaged. The victims of the conflicts were mostly the campesino leaders and other leaders sympathetic to Cárdenas. It is true that the government gave the campesinos legitimacy to exert a certain level of power in their struggle for land. Nevertheless, it is also true that this power was always linked to a form of state paternalism that denied the campesino social movement any genuine autonomy. Thus, "in southern Sinaloa, the same thing happened to the campesinos that had happened elsewhere in the country: by accepting the assistance offered them by the government, in the end they were subjected to its own decisions and robbed of their capacity for self-management" (Padilla 1993, 81).

Following the Cárdenas administration, agrarian reform in Mexico, and particularly in Sinaloa, took a new turn. The number of grants and beneficiaries declined considerably, and the development of commercial, export-oriented agriculture became the top priority for new state policies. With the end of the Cárdenas project, lands that had been private small-holdings before the Cárdenas administration began to be returned to the original owners, and agrarian laws were created, aimed at protecting lands belonging to terratenientes (Padilla 1993, 83).

In southern Sinaloa, the campesino communities continued to claim land in the name of agrarianism and the revolution well into the 1970s and continue to do so to this day. In their demands, they use the same language that the campesinos who had preceded them had used during the agrarian movement of the Cárdenas period. Slogans such as *"La tierra es de quien la siembra"* ("The land belongs to he who tills it"), *"Sembrar la tierra es hacer patria"* ("To cultivate land is to build a nation"), and *"Tierra, Justicia, y Libertad"* ("Land, Justice, and Liberty") were frequently included as slogans at the end of petitions asking for land redistribution or in written complaints made to the municipal presidents (or mayors) or the campesino organizations, as the following case study illustrates.

The Fight for Land

The following case, recounting the history of an agrarian struggle and the formation of an ejido in southern Sinaloa, illustrates how the campesinos in their struggle to win land employed certain discourses and state-level institutions to invoke an *identidad campesina* (peasant identity), which had been legitimized during the Cárdenas administration.

In 1947, a group of campesinos that sought to win a land grant went before Culiacán's Departamento de Asuntos Agrarios y Colonización (Department of Agrarian and Colonization Issues), asking to be allowed to create a new farming settlement located in a place called Abrevadero el Bosque in the municipio of Escuinapa. The new settlement would be called Isla del Bosque. The petition was not approved because the lands were already granted for a period of twenty-five years to the Compañía Industrial Agrícola y Ganadera (Agricultural and Ranching Industrial Company). Five years later, in 1952, sixty-nine campesinos from Escuinapa petitioned the CNC for a grant of the same land. Their objective was to form a *colonia agrícola y ganadera* (agricultural and ranching settlement), to be named José María Morelos y Pavón. The efforts of this group were also fruitless.

In 1957, the Unión General de Obreros y Campesinos de México (Mexican General Union of Workers and Peasants, or UGOCM) organized a statewide meeting in Los Mochis, Sinaloa, on behalf of the petitioners of the *nuevos centros de población agrícola* (new rural settlements). One of the meeting's principal proposals was to pressure the government to proceed with the distribution of land. The first article of convocation declared, "If the federal government does not begin distributing land during 1957, the petitioning campesinos will take matters into their own hands" (Rubio Ruelas and Hirata Galindo 1985, 68). The meeting also addressed the campesinos' concerns over the new direction that agricultural development in Sinaloa was taking and the fear that private property would completely supplant the ejido system. Perhaps it was because of this new euphoria that appeared around the struggle for land that hundreds of groups of Sinaloan campesinos reignited the revolutionary ideal of demanding land that had at one time been denied to them.

The petition of both groups, Isla del Bosque and José María Morelos y Pavón, were fused into one and approved eight years later by the Department of Agrarian and Colonization Issues. A presidential decree was passed on May 21, 1960, and published on July 4, 1960, in the *Diario Oficial de la Federación* (*Official Journal of the Republic*). The new settlement was named Isla del Bosque.

On August 23, 1960, the Department of Agrarian and Colonization Issues sent the campesinos a communiqué ordering all beneficiaries of the presidential order of May 21 to attend an election in Colonia Morelos, municipio of Escuinapa, which would be held to select the representatives to the new community's ejido commission and its Consejo de Vigilancia (Surveillance Committee). This event would mark the transfer of the awarded land. As a parting shot, the campesinos were told in a paternalistic tone that attendance was mandatory—no excuses or pretexts for failure to attend would be accepted.

Three days before the ceremony celebrating the transfer of the lands, on August 26, 1960, engineer Manuel Cázares Flores, head of the Engineers Brigade for the States of Sinaloa and Sonora, appeared before the CNC for the legal execution of the presidential order transferring the land to the campesinos. At that moment, he learned that the Casa Toledo, owner of the Compañía Industrial Agrícola y Ganadera, had appealed the implementation of the presidential order. This company owned the most fertile land in the Isla del Palmito el Verde, municipio of Escuinapa, including the important Hacienda Las Cabras, which still exists. Natividad Toledo was the owner of Las Cabras and father of Antonio Toledo Corro, who would become the governor of Sinaloa (1981–1988) and the new owner of the hacienda. Former peones of Las Cabras founded Celaya, one of the communities on which this ethnography focuses.

The ceremony for the transfer of the lands never took place, but on August 31, 1960, the newspaper *El Sol,* published in Culiacán, reported that certain members of the UGOCM, who had tried to take possession of the ejido's lands, had accompanied Cazares Flores during his visit to the CNC. On November 4, the ejidatarios of Isla del Bosque sent a letter to the secretary general of the League of Agrarian Communities in Culiacán to defend their position as steeped in revolutionary discourse and agrarian ideology. The campesinos also sought protection through the designation by the Mexican state of *campesinos auténticos* (genuine campesinos) to identify their group. This identity, in the eyes of the government, differentiated them from other individuals who wished to gain access to the same land, but who were not necessarily campesinos or residents of the locality that was petitioning for the land.

At this point, Toledo, manager of the Compañía Industrial Agrícola y Ganadera, authorized five hundred hectares of company land to be set apart "to satisfy the farming needs of the applicants."[13] A month later, in December 1960, the lands were turned over to the *comisariado ejidal* (ejido's officers) of Isla del Bosque.

From that time on, a series of political and social conflicts were unleashed within the ejido as the groups attempted to gain control of the land. Two primary factors caused the conflict. First, the two factions, José

María Morelos y Pavón and Isla del Bosque, had never succeeded in fusing themselves into one community. Second, the land had been awarded to the two groups by means of the same presidential order. The conflict worsened when no campesino representatives for the José María Morelos y Pavón group were selected or recognized as members of the comisariado ejidal. Some strife also appeared because people from other states tried to join the ejido. These campesinos "no auténticos" replaced *jefes de familia* (male household heads) who had lived many years in the locality. The Municipal Agrarian Committee of Escuinapa often expounded vigorously concerning who constituted "authentic" ejidatarios, migrants from other states, and class interests not originating from the communities.[14] Thus demographic pressures from outside Sinaloa increased migration to the area, exacerbating conflicts over access to land; claims to originality as "authentic" campesinos as a response created the cultural basis for divisions between groups, and the roles of the state at times serving different groups and class interests created volatile conditions.

The conflicts between both groups escalated to such a degree that three representatives from campesinos in the José María Morelos y Pavón group appeared in the offices of the presidencia municipal in Escuinapa. They brought with them a petition that was signed with the catch phrase *"Sembrar la tierra es hacer patria."* It asked that the presidente municipal (mayor) intervene in the conflicts.[15]

Due to the violence generated by the conflicts over control of the ejido, the campesinos of the Isla del Bosque faction asked the Department of Agrarian and Colonization Issues to appoint an engineer to survey the boundaries of the lands and grant the corresponding area to each group. On March 28, 1961, the secretary general of the National Executive Committee sent a memorandum to the head of the Department of Agrarian and Colonization Issues asking that the presidential resolution be implemented in its entirety.[16]

After numerous legal confrontations, physical violence, and political maneuvers, in 1962, the head of the Department of Agrarian and Colonization Issues went to Isla del Bosque to verify the territorial division of the ejido's two factions. In making the division, the size and quality of lands and proportionality in regard to number of ejidatarios were taken into account. Finally, on September 8, 1962, in a meeting held in the community, the parceling and distribution of the ejidal plots of land to individual campesinos was done. The land was divided into 489 parcels, measuring between six and eighteen hectares, and distributed to 486 ejidatarios.[17]

It seems that when the division was made, the conflicts between the factions stopped once and for all. During the meeting, Mateo Camacho Ontiveros, secretary general of the Regional Agrarian Committee 15, expressed his satisfaction at seeing that the ejidatarios had arrived at an agreement to end the conflict. According to the record, Camacho Ontiveros, "after giving the ejidatarios some useful advice, expressed his joy upon seeing that the membership of the ejido has arrived at an agreement benefiting everyone equally and ending the problems that the factions have suffered. His greatest wish was that, having been finally reconciled, they would go forward down the same road, under the same banner, and with the same revolutionary ideal, for the betterment of their ejido."[18]

During the 1970s, the struggle for land and the social movements in Sinaloa continued. Nevertheless, the available literature indicates that these efforts were concentrated in the central and northern parts of the state. Two important factors account for this. First, these regions have large irrigation districts and the greatest concentration of large landholdings in the state; however, only 9 percent of this land has been converted into ejidos (Rubio Ruelas and Hirata Galindo 1985). Second, export-oriented commercial agriculture has developed in this region. In fact, the globalization of Sinaloan agriculture has converted these areas into poles of capital accumulation, which attract, and largely depend on, cheap labor (Cisneros 1988). Whether as *jornaleros* (day laborers) or *asalariados agrícolas* (agricultural wageworkers), this labor is provided mostly by migratory flows from the states of Veracruz, Guerrero, Oaxaca, Michoacán, Jalisco, Zacatecas, and Durango. These laborers work seasonally in the cultivation of cotton, garden produce, and sugarcane (Cisneros 1988).

During the 1980s, as a result of the Mexican economic crisis, the government developed new policies guaranteeing commercial farmers and ranchers greater security in regard to land tenure (Shadle 1994). With these new policies, both agrarian reform and agrarianism became things of the past. Nevertheless, the age of agrarianism and land struggles is still latent in the collective memory of the Sinaloan people. Proof of this can be heard in the corridos that tell the story of the *héroes agraristas* (heroes of the agrarian struggle); these songs have become part of the popular culture of rural Sinaloa.[19] The ideology spread by the agrarianism movement is still alive, and it appears in the actions of the rural population when, for example, they invade lands belonging to agribusiness because the ejido land is no longer sufficient to satisfy the demands of a growing population.

During the 1990s, agrarian reform in Mexico took a drastically new direction. Using the argument that the failure of the ejidal system is due to a series of problems, including corruption, lack of credit, and demographic growth, the administration of Carlos Salinas de Gortari amended Article 27 of the 1917 Constitution (Shadle 1994). An important part of this revision was the elimination of the mandate that had established agrarian reform. With the revision of Article 27, land distribution ended, the ejidal system was privatized, and new policies were implemented to encourage the development of industrial agriculture, and with it came even greater impoverishment, migration, and familial stress.

Cooperativism, Globalization, and the Struggle for Shrimp

In summer 1996, Marines from the Mexican Navy, under contract to the fishing cooperatives in the municipio of Rosario, arrested two young men for fishing illegally during the closed season. The Marines asked the men their names, to which they answered, "I'm Antonio Aguilar," and "I'm Porfirio Díaz." The Marines thought that the youths were kidding, so one of them answered back, "So now, you're giving yourselves the names of a famous singer and a president, you sons of bitches. I'm going to hit you with my belt until you tell the truth." The Marines proceeded to confiscate the men's *atarrayas* (fishing nets) and beat them up.

Although salted with the humor that characterizes Sinaloa, this anecdote illustrates the struggle over shrimp fishing that has developed in southern Sinaloa since the 1930s. There are thousands of stories similar to this one that reveal the social and political struggle among sectors of the population in southern Sinaloa that are struggling to gain access to shrimp. These anecdotes also tell of the human rights abuses and physical violence that victimize those who have less power in the hierarchy that controls the use and exploitation of the region's fishing resources. How and why did these conflicts originate? Who are the social actors? What have been the consequences?

In 1928, Mexican President Plutarco Elías Calles issued a new decree creating specific fishing areas (*zonas de pesca*) within the lagoons and estuaries of southern Sinaloa. The zones were to be allocated only when fishing cooperatives in localities specified in the decree had been organized, and only those rural working men whose primary occupation was fishing were eligible to join. Once having been formed, a cooperative could solicit a defined "zone of capture" from the local fishing authority.

This coincided with the increase in demand for shrimp in national and global markets. In Mexico, the government built processing and packing plants for shrimp export along the Pacific and Gulf coasts. In 1932, another decree established that full-time fishermen could organize cooperatives with the goal of improving their social and economic situation. However, for those who were unable or unwilling to join, subsistence fishing remained legal. This situation created a "class" of part-time or subsistence fishermen, known as *pescadores libres*.

From then on, fishing cooperatives in Mexico became a tool for rural development programs. Indeed, in 1938, President Lázaro Cárdenas enacted the Ley General de Sociedades Cooperativas (General Law on Cooperative Associations), which again emphasized and encouraged the organization of rural working people into fishing cooperatives. This, according to President Cárdenas, would integrate the social sector of the fishing industry (Hernández Fujigaki 1988). In 1940, Cárdenas added a new decree to the Ley General de Sociedades Cooperativas that restricted the commercial exploitation of shrimp exclusively to fishing cooperatives. The law, however, continued to allow the rural coastal population to catch shrimp for subsistence purposes, but any excess had to be sold to fishing cooperatives at whatever price they established.

Throughout Mexico all fishing cooperatives were required to turn their shrimp catch over to packing plants at a price established by the government. In general, the fishing cooperatives organized in southern Sinaloa operated with relative success for a number of years, due primarily to the abundance of shrimp resources, a static demographic growth, and the small number of fishing cooperatives at that time.

Gradually, conflicts over the access to shrimp emerged as a result of three main factors: (1) coastal population growth; (2) increased economic value of shrimp in global markets; and (3) the organization of ejidatarios into fishing cooperatives. These factors increased the pressure on the shrimp resources and led to a war among the rural groups that were disputing the right to fish commercially for shrimp. The struggle to gain legal access to the shrimp at the same time gave rise to a new ideology about its exploitation. This ideology, intimately linked to state policies, was based on a social hierarchy, which was headed by the fishing cooperatives whose formation had been supported by the government.

Population growth in coastal southern Sinaloa was directly related to the formation of ejidos in the aftermath of the agrarian reform policies of the 1950s. As noted above, people from other states migrated to Sinaloa searching for a piece of land to farm. However, in many cases, the land they received was of poor quality, so ejido members needed to turn to other economic activities to guarantee the survival of their families. This need, which existed for both ejidatarios and campesinos in general, coincided with a growing demand for shrimp in global markets. In those ejidos that were located near coastal ecosystems, such as lagoons and estuaries where shrimp were abundant, the members naturally turned to fishing to supplement their incomes. They soon realized that fishing was more profitable than farming because it required less physical effort and less capital investment. Thus, ejidatarios became pescadores libres.

For many years, these pescadores libres sold their catch to the fishing cooperatives, while waiting to be accepted as members. However, the fishing cooperatives were reluctant to admit them because the members believed that they were the only ones with the historical rights and patrimony to harvest shrimp. Although the existing fishing cooperatives attempted to control the commercial exploitation of shrimp, in 1968, ejidatarios began a protracted struggle to organize their own fishing cooperatives, giving rise to one of the most intense conflicts in the history of coastal southern Sinaloa.

The conflicts between ejidatarios and cooperatives deepened in 1972 when a new decree was added to the Ley Federal para el Fomento de la Pesca (Federal Law for Fisheries Development). This decree made it legal for ejidatarios to fish for shrimp commercially, as long as they did so in lagoons and estuaries located near the ejido. It also allowed ejidatarios to organize their own fishing cooperatives, known as *cooperativas de producción pesqueras ejidales* (Lobato 1989).

The fishing cooperatives, on the other hand, tried every means to stop the ejidatarios. In pressuring the government to cancel the registration of the cooperativas de producción pesqueras ejidales, and in their general struggle to continue to monopolize the commercial exploitation of shrimp, members of the traditional cooperatives constructed a series of arguments to present before the state. One claim was that the new cooperatives invaded fishing grounds that the state itself had granted exclusively to the traditional cooperatives, even in those cases where the fishing grounds were located on or near an ejido. The traditional cooperatives also pointed out that they had made considerable capital investments in tapos and opening new canals to facilitate the migration of shrimp larvae to the lagoons and estuaries. Additionally, the members of the fishing cooperatives believed that they alone had the historical right to catch shrimp. This inalienable right, legalized by the government, resulted from social struggles they had fought.

In stressing their rights, the members of the traditional fishing cooperatives also employed some of the discourse that had been developed by campesinos in their struggle for access to land. The concept of *autenticidad* (authenticity), used by campesinos, became a critical issue for members of fishing cooperatives. Autenticidad, in this case, was used to distinguish ejidatarios and fishermen, farming and fishing, and land and water. Fishing cooperatives claimed they were *pescadores auténticos*, while ejidatarios were first and foremost farmers, having only recently turned to fishing. For the members of the traditional cooperatives, fishing was the only available occupation, whereas ejidatarios both fished and farmed. Cooperative members also complained that ejidatarios did not know how to fish because their medium was not water but land. In their dialogue with the state, the fishing cooperatives used the issue of the long-term conservation of coastal resources. They argued that the organization of more fishing cooperatives in southern Sinaloa would lead to the overexploitation and depletion of the shrimp and to disastrous competition.

Conflicts intensified when the cooperativas ejidales gained legal access to some of the best shrimping grounds, which had belonged to the fishing cooperatives but were located on ejidal land. The cooperativas ejidales were not passive in these quarrels, and the rivalry led to physical confrontations and violence. A fisherman from the region recalled the conflicts between a fishing cooperative, Lázaro Cárdenas, and a cooperativa ejidal, Los Pachines: "The members of the Lázaro Cárdenas cooperative and Los Pachines beat each other up with rocks and sticks. They filled bags with stones, and they carried clubs in their hands."

The new cooperativas ejidales developed strategies to defend their government-mandated right to exploit shrimp commercially. One consisted of blocking the local roads on their lands to prevent fishermen from reaching the fishing grounds or transporting ice or shrimp back and forth (Lobato 1989).

The state was the mediator in all these conflicts, but often its role was ambiguous, contradictory, and accommodating. On the one hand, it encouraged and supported the organization of ejidatarios into fishing cooperatives. On the other hand, it provided the traditional cooperatives with military personnel to guard their fishing grounds, something that exacerbated, and even appeared to condone, the continuation of violence.

During 1977 and 1978, state intervention in these conflicts resulted in the elaboration of a series of agreements between the traditional and ejidal cooperatives. Some of the most pressing items included in these agreements were the joint exploitation of fishing zones; the merging of the two types of cooperatives (traditional and ejidales); the allocation of offshore fishing permits to certain cooperatives; the permission for cooperativas ejidales to use equipment, such as pickups, owned by the fishing cooperatives; allocation of specific shrimp grounds; and the assignment of more inspectors from the Fisheries Department to regulate fishing.[20]

These agreements finally ended the conflicts between the two types of cooperatives, now known as *cooperativas tradicionales* and *cooperativas ejidales*. By 1983, both were able to fish commercially for shrimp without violence. Today this conflict is only a part of a regional collective memory, and both ejidatarios and fishermen can talk about it with a sense of humor.

Although the conflicts between traditional and ejidal cooperatives have for the most part been resolved, the struggle over shrimp fishing itself has continued. State policies for the development and management of shrimp, most of which have continued to favor the commercial export—oriented sector, are partly to blame. To the degree that the value of shrimp increased in the global marketplace, its importance as a generator of foreign exchange also increased in Mexico. Shrimp became one of the nation's top ten, non-oil export commodities (Miller 1990), and due to its economic importance, shrimp came to be known in Mexico as *oro rosa* (pink gold).

The struggle over shrimp fishing in Sinaloa is far from resolved. Russ McGoodwin described the overall situation in the shrimp industry of southern Sinaloa. Although based on anthropological fieldwork conducted during the early 1980s, his explanation of some of the conflicts in the industry are still valid for and applicable to southern Sinaloa: "In south Sinaloa, by permitting contradictory rights to shrimp in hopes of solving two problems, one basically political, the other economic, the onus of a contradictory managerial policy was placed square in the lap of the rural population. The result has been widespread conflict over rights to shrimp which pits neighbor against neighbor, fishermen against campesinos, a people against its government, and the entire rural-inshore population against the offshore sector of the shrimp industry" (1987, 228).

Conclusion

The history of southern Sinaloa has been characterized as a constant class struggle for access to and control of natural resources. The emergence of a class structure related to the exertion of power over productive resources began with the Spanish conquest. The appearance of this new class structure was intimately linked to the power that the upper classes exerted over the use and exploitation of the abundant natural resources of the region. Over time, and as the class structure solidified, it was obvious that the social and economic advantages of one class came at the cost of social, economic, and political marginalization of the other classes. Ultimately, the social stratification led to struggles fought by the marginalized social classes over control of natural resources. In southern Sinaloa, these class struggles assumed various forms and levels of intensity. The struggle for land was one of the bloodiest and longest in the region. In its wake, a new class structure appeared that comprised campesinos, *minifundistas* (small-land owners), and terratenientes. These groups were intimately linked to the rise of a new agrarian structure composed of ejidos, smallholdings, and latifundia.

In Mexico, the state has always played an important role in delineating the relationship among the various social classes and the natural resources. During the colonial period, government policies were aimed at supporting mining and the use of land and water by Spaniards, and limiting the access of Indians, mestizos, and mulattos to those resources. During the Porfiriato, the regional elite, mostly comprising Creoles and foreigners, benefited from government policies on natural resource use and exploitation. As a result of the 1917 Revolution, the government took on a paternalistic role in guaranteeing the traditionally marginalized classes access to the use and exploitation of productive resources. In the case of the struggle for land, both Article 27 of the 1917 Constitution and the agrarian reforms had as a central axis a legal basis that guaranteed access to a plot of land for campesinos, workers, and peones. In many cases the quality and quantity of distributed land was not uniform, reflecting the influence that the dominant social classes of the region continued to exert, even after the revolution.

Other examples of the government's paternalistic policies were fishing laws that supported the formation of cooperatives and restrictions on the exploitation of commercially valuable fishing species that favored the rural working sector. These policies were designed to protect the state's own interests in those resources with a high commercial value that contributed to the generation of foreign exchange, which the government for the most part collected.

For many years, the Mexican state played a double role in the elaboration of its policies on the use and exploitation of land and shrimp. On one hand, it took on a paternalistic role, disguised as protection for the marginalized classes, and on the other, it was entrepreneurial, supporting the social classes that controlled power and the necessary capital for the supposed economic development of the country. Nevertheless, and despite state protectionism, the marginalized social classes continued to become ever more marginalized.

This double role of the state was radically transformed during the 1990s, as a result of neoliberal policies. Specifically, from 1989 to 1994 the Mexican government underwent changes directed toward the development and implementation of a new economic model, based on market and trade liberalization and private investment. The neoliberal economic model changed the relationship between rural people and the coastal and marine resources they traditionally used (DeWalt 1998). One significant feature of the new economic model was the amendment of Article 27 of the 1917 Mexican Constitution, which allowed for the privatization of the ejido sector. Another was the amendment of the Ley General de Pesca (General Fisheries Law), legalizing both national and foreign private investment in the shrimp industry. These changes have important implications for the understanding of the current state of the relationship among rural communities in two municipios of southern Sinaloa—Rosario and Escuinapa— and natural resources and the state. The changes are especially important because the struggle over natural resources in the rural communities of these municipios continues today and is growing worse as a result of globalization, neoliberal policies, and increased economic impoverishment.

2

Rosario and Escuinapa

The Globalization of Two Coastal Municipios

This is no longer Wonderland where reality triumphed over the fairy tale, and the trophies of the conquest, the deposits of gold, and the mountains of silver humiliated the imagination. Nevertheless, the region still works as the servant girl. It continues to exist at the service of foreign needs, as the source and reserve of petroleum and iron, copper and meat, fruits and coffee—the raw materials and the foods that are destined for the rich countries that gain so much more consuming those things than Latin America gains producing them.
　　—Eduardo Galeano, *The Open Veins of Latin America*

In October of 1993, the residents of Ejido Agua Verde, on the coast of the municipio of Rosario, had decided that the rainy season was over and no more rain would fall that year. It was then that a huge and unexpected storm hit. No one thought it was even going to sprinkle. The sky was blue, and the large and white clouds showed no sign of ominous gathering. Nevertheless, around mid-afternoon, some men from the Civil Defense Department of the municipal headquarters appeared, sounding the bullhorn and announcing that a terrible storm was about to arrive. People thought it was a mistake, like so many other times when the weather report turned out wrong, so everyone went on about his or her daily routine. Some were snoozing under the shade of the palapas, some were eating, some were working in their fields—the *milpas* (cultivated fields) or *chilares* (chili fields)—while others did housework, gossiped, or watched a *telenovela* (soap opera). With the first drops of rain, the people still didn't believe that a storm was coming. That is why, when the downburst broke, it was already too late to go to El Cerro to wait it out while the waters subsided, something they were accustomed to doing every year during every *temporal* (heavy rain). That day, it rained so much that a huge quantity of water filled the dam on which Agua Verde relied. Someone decided to open the floodgates to let it empty a little. Instead, however, the water from the dam dispersed forcefully through every street in the town, leveling whatever it found in its path. The houses flooded; the beds and other furniture were soaked; clothes, shoes, toys, and chairs went floating, with the drowned animals, washed away in the torrent of water, seeking its refuge in the sea. Many people climbed up on rooftops, taking their animals and the few belongings that they had rescued with them. Most people lost all their material goods, as well as their crops and the food they had stored. Hunger was unleashed.

The torrent of rain dragged along with it a cow, which, it seemed, had just drowned. Several men dragged the carcass from the rushing water, and they agreed to share its meat with the inhabitants of the ejido. Nothing from that cow went to waste. Its bones were cooked in a soup, its intestines were made into a *menudo*, and its head was raffled off.

The day after the flood, the presidente municipal arrived in Agua Verde. He went around asking everyone whether, by chance, anybody had seen one of his cows that had strayed away, exactly at the time of the storm. Someone finally told him that a dead cow had come floating past in the stream of rushing water, and they had eaten it. After some further investigation, the mayor found one of those who had eaten a piece of the cow and asked him, "What part did you get?" and the man answered, "the flank." The mayor also asked him whether he had seen a brand on the cow, and if so, would he please describe it. From the description the man gave him of the branding-iron mark on the flank of the cow, the mayor deduced that the cow that had been eaten was the one that had strayed from his herd. So he decided to keep investigating to find out which residents had eaten his cow. He spent a long time asking around until finally he found the responsible parties. Then he ordered them to appear before him, one by one, and he sent them to have their heads shaved as punishment. From then on, those whose heads were shorn were identified in Agua Verde and nearby communities as "those who dined on the presidente municipal's cow." And the people in Agua Verde, to tease them, nicknamed them *"los come vacas,"* or "the cow-eaters." This story, known as the "Story of the Storm of the Cow," has become a part of the oral tradition and one of the stories that the inhabitants of El Cerro tell with great humor, while resting out of the sun under a palapa or seated on a balcony of a house, watching the rainfall.

The Uruguayan writer Eduardo Galeano, in his widely read and controversial work *The Open Veins of Latin America*, indicates that in Mexico, "the pasture that the cows eat has more protein than the diet of the campesinos who care for them, and the meat of these cows is destined for the mouths of those privileged people within the country and, even more, in the international market" (1999, 461). Although the epilogue was written in 1978, this observation still holds for many parts of Mexico that have developed economically based on export commodities. It is certainly the case for the state of Sinaloa, in which cattle raising, shrimp fishing, and the cultivation of fruits and vegetables produce commodities that the state uses to satisfy the demand of domestic and global markets. This is also specifically the case for the two southernmost municipios in the state, Escuinapa and Rosario, which have followed this norm that continues to set a pattern for economic development in Sinaloa.

This chapter examines the emergence of a pattern of regional differentiation and its relationship to the production of commodities and social-class formation in the municipios of Rosario and Escuinapa. I argue that to understand how rural communities like El Cerro and Celaya have been historically, socially, and economically structured, it is imperative to understand the place of such communities within broader regional, ecological, economic, and social processes. This chapter is organized in five sections. The first presents an overview of the most important ecological and environmental characteristics of Sinaloa. The second analyzes the links among commodity production, globalization, the emergence of a *regionalismo*, or regional identity, and an ideology of natural resource use and exploitation within Sinaloa. The third section presents the major social, economic, and political features of the two municipios and the types of human settlements they comprise. The fourth section discusses the emergence and the role of export commodities in the economy of the two municipios. The last section links the relationship between export-commodity production and environmental change in southern Sinaloa.

The Ecology and Environment of Southern Sinaloa

The first impression that one forms of southern Sinaloa depends on the time of year that one visits or lives there. There are only two seasons: wet and dry. During the dry season, the vegetation seems dead, and its gray color gives a lugubrious aspect to the landscape. Because the dry season is longer than the rainy season, the grayish color of the vegetation characterizes the Sinaloan landscape throughout most of the year. During the rainy season, which lasts from the end of June until September, the vegetation becomes exuberant, the grass begins to grow at the sides of the highways, and the livestock grows fat.

Because the Tropic of Cancer crosses the state through northern Mazatlán, weather varies from extremely warm and wet during the summer in the coastal area to cold in the mountains year round. This variation divides the state into three main climatological zones: warm, humid, and tropical wet—based on altitude and latitude. According to Schmidt (1976), mostly warm weather characterizes the dry lowlands of the northwest; a humid, moderate weather characterizes the highlands of the Sierra Madre; and, in the southern coastal plain, the climate alternates between wet and dry.

Temperature and Rainfall

The temperature in these three climatic regions varies according to the season of the year. For example, in the coastal plain, July is the warmest month, whereas the highlands reach their highest temperatures during June. The annual mean temperature at Mazatlán, during the 1986–1997 period, was 24.9 Celsius (Instituto Nacional de Estadística, Geografía, e Informática [INEGI] 1999). During that same period the monthly mean temperature oscillated between 19.5 and 29.0 Celsius (INEGI 1999).

Rainfall is a significantly limiting factor in Sinaloa. The annual amount of rainfall affects both fishing and agriculture industries, which are dependent on rain. The state's experiences with variation in precipitation range from severe floods, caused by tropical storms and hurricanes, to droughts. The northern region of the state suffered droughts during the twelve years between 1990 and 2002. The state has also been the victim of hurricanes and storms during the last decade, some of which formed as the result of El Niño. Floods during the rainy season are very common in both urban and rural areas of the coastal southern region. The beginning of the rainy season, *las aguas,* at the end of June is usually marked by a thunderstorm followed by a temporal. Most of the annual precipitation takes place during the early months of the rainy season, from late June through August.

According to the most recent INEGI data for the southern Sinaloa region, the annual mean precipitation at Mazatlán during the 1986–1997 period was 822 millimeters. During the same period, the lowest annual precipitation was 370.5 millimeters and the highest was 1072.8 millimeters (INEGI 1999). Monthly mean precipitation for Mazatlán during this period ranged from 0.1 millimeters to 247.4 millimeters (INEGI 1999). The driest month during this period was May and the wettest was August.

Natural Resources

Sinaloa has a varied natural resource base, which not only is crucial for the livelihood of the rural population but also plays a key role in this state's economy. Among the most important resources are water, land, plants and animals, and the coastal ecosystems.

Water. Because of the state's economic dependency on export agriculture, water is one of the most valuable natural resources of Sinaloa. The hydraulic resources of Sinaloa comprise principally the rivers, dams, and reservoirs in the state. The eleven major rivers of the state provide water not only for agriculture but for other uses as well. The two largest, the Río Fuerte and the Río Culiacán, are located in the north and central regions, respectively. The three most important rivers in southern Sinaloa are Río Presido, near Mazatlán; Río Baluarte, in Rosario; and Río Cañas, in Escuinapa. Most Sinaloan rivers have their origins in the Sierra Madre and flow into the Pacific Ocean.

Sinaloa's water resources are managed and stored in dams, artificial lakes, and reservoirs throughout the state. There are eleven *presas* (dams) currently operating, most located in the irrigation districts of the central and northern regions of the state. Most of these dams store water from the rivers and were built under the Plan Hidraúlico del Noroeste (Northern Hydraulic Plan), a government program developed to transport water from the south and store it in the central and northern regions (Ceceña Cervantes, Burgueño Lomeli, and Millán Echeagaray 1973). They generate electrical power and support the irrigation infrastructure of the state's agriculture industry.

Sinaloans are acutely aware of the importance of water as a natural resource, and of the conflict over its multiple uses for domestic consumption, agricultural irrigation, and tourism. In September 2000, academics and government officials organized a local conference in Mazatlán to discuss the most pressing issues surrounding the water resources of this municipio. The conference, "La Problemática del Agua en Mazatlán: Cobertura y Tratamiento" ("The Problem of Water in Mazatlán: Coverage and Treatment"), focused on the economic, social, ecological, technological, and financial dimensions of water, and it covered such topics as the multiple uses of competing demands for water, reservoirs, sewage treatment, and the creation of sustainable water-management programs (Universidad Autónoma de Sinaloa and Consejo Ecológico de Mazatlán 2000).

Land. In Sinaloa, land has always been at the core of many agrarian struggles and social conflicts, which have centered on the state's social and economic classes in their struggle to gain access to, and control over, land. The nature of the social conflicts is related to the land-tenure systems existing in the state.

Two major types of land-tenure systems predominate in Sinaloa: *latifundio* and *minifundio.* The former consists of a small number of landowners, mostly agricultural entrepreneurs, who own and control large extensions of land. The latter is represented by ejidatarios and *pequeños propietarios* (small-land holders), who are numerous, but who own only small extensions of land. Both systems of land tenure represent distinct forms of agricultural development. Minifundios represent the traditional agricultural activity in Sinaloa, which is based on family labor. The latifundio is usually associated with capitalist, export agriculture, mostly predominant in the coastal valleys of the central and northern regions.

According to the 1991 census, 59.6 percent of the land was in the hands of ejidos, whereas 33.5 percent was privately owned (INEGI 1991). Ejidos own larger extensions of land in Culiacán, Guasave, Ahome, and El Fuerte, Sinaloa's central and northern municipios, whereas the private sector owns the largest extensions of land in the municipios of Mazatlán, Rosario, Culiacán, El Fuerte, and Ahome. The great majority of the private land is located within the irrigation districts of the Great Valleys of the municipios of Guasave, Ahome, Culiacán, Navolato, and Sinaloa. These five municipios concentrate 77.1 percent of the irrigated land in the state (INEGI 1991).

Land suitable for agriculture in Sinaloa is categorized as *de riego* (irrigated) or *de temporal* (rain-fed). The great majority of the irrigated land is located in the irrigation districts of the central and northern valleys of the state. State policies have favored the development of irrigation projects in regions such as the Culiacán and El Fuerte valleys, where industrial agriculture dominates the economy.

Rain-fed land, on the other hand, is located mostly in the highlands and the southern regions of Sinaloa, where farmers practice mostly seasonal subsistence agriculture and small-scale, commercial, rain-fed agriculture. Most of the rural communities in southern Sinaloa, including El Cerro and Celaya, practice seasonal rain-fed subsistence agriculture.

Plants and Animals. Over time, activities such as farming, woodcutting, and overgrazing have damaged Sinaloa's natural vegetation, but its flora remains diverse (Schmidt 1976). Depending on the region, cacti or tropical trees, such as the tabachín, dominate the landscape. The vegetation differs according to the state's two main ecological zones; however, thorn forest of two types, Selva *Baja caducifolia* and Selva *Mediana caducifolia,* make up most of the state's vegetation. Differences within each type of thorn forest depend on climatological factors, such as temperature and precipitation, which limit the distribution, growth, and height of the vegetation. The Selva *Baja* is an entirely deciduous and short-thorn forest, whereas the Selva *Mediana* is a thorn forest of medium height and is almost completely deciduous. Sinaloa also has oak and pine forests, oak forests, small-leaved desert shrubs, and semideciduous forests.

Sinaloa's terrestrial fauna is also diverse. The characteristics of the various ecological zones influence this diversity. Based on these characteristics, Schmidt (1976) classifies the fauna of Sinaloa in three major groups: animals having specific habitats throughout the state, such as pumas, skunks, coyotes, and river otters; animals inhabiting the foothills and the highlands of the Sierra Madre, such as wolves, black bears, squirrels, and wild turkeys; and animals inhabiting the southern zone of the coastal lowlands, such as jaguars, armadillos, ocelots, cottontails, and crested guans.

Coastal Ecosystems. Traveling along the coast of Sinaloa, the intense, high waves and the deep-blue color of the waters of the Pacific Ocean strike one immediately. One is also struck by the ecological and geomorphological diversity of this coast. In certain places, enormous rock formations seem to serve as natural walls protecting the coast from the strong wave action. In other areas, steep cliffs make the shoreline almost inaccessible. In still other places, the coastline is a series of gentle curves, tracing in outline the wave motion on the sandy beach.

One of the salient features of coastal Sinaloa is the presence of a variety of ecosystems, such as lagoons, estuaries, mangrove forests, salt marshes, and bays. These ecosystems contain a great diversity of flora and fauna and have been crucial to sustaining the human populations that have been settled in the region ever since pre-Columbian times. For example, the presence of shell middens (*conchales*) of *Tivela* and oysters in some of the mangrove-estuarine complexes of southern Sinaloa is witness to the importance that these ecosystems had for the indigenous population (Flores Verdugo et al. 1997).

The Huizache-Caimanero Lagoon Complex is one of the most valuable coastal ecosystems in southern Sinaloa. It is located in the municipio of Rosario near El Cerro. The Huizache-Caimanero is representative of the region's coastal ecosystems, and, as such, it illustrates the complexity, importance, and diversity of these. It shares the characteristics of many other coastal ecosystems in southern Sinaloa: It supports similar flora and fauna; mangrove forests surround it; the rural population uses it as a common-property resource; fishing is the major economic activity practiced in it; its hydrological cycle is strongly influenced by the wet and dry seasons; and it is an important potential site for the construction of shrimp farms.

Because it is one of the most productive fishing grounds in the area, several research studies undertaken at different times have focused on the Huizache-Caimanero Lagoon Complex. This research has been crucial to understanding the ecological, physical, and biological processes taking place in southern Sinaloa's coastal ecosystems. Previous chemical and ecological studies conducted in the Huizache-Caimanero lagoon system focused on the hydrological and productive characteristics, as well as on the flora and fauna found in it.[1] These studies have provided information significant to the understanding of factors influencing the various ecological processes within the lagoon complex. For example, salinity is a principal environmental variable influencing the complex's hydrological cycle. Fluctuations in salinity levels are directly related to levels of precipitation.

Throughout the rainy season, at the end of June, salinity levels decrease as the direct result of fresh water entering the system. During the dry season, when there is no rainfall, salinity levels increase sharply. Changes in salinity have important implications for the understanding of the biological and ecological characteristics of the fauna and flora living in or near the lagoon complex.

Fringes of mangrove forests surround the lagoon complex. As in most of southern Sinaloa's coastal ecosystems, the four most important species of mangrove found in the Huizache-Caimanero are *Rhizophora mangle* (mangle rojo), which grows in the inundated zone; *Avicennia nítida* (mangle negro), which grows right behind *Rhizophora*; and *Laguncularia racemosa* (mangle blanco) and *Conacarpus erectus* (botoncillo), growing farthest from the waterline. The detritus formed from the litter of mangrove leaves and other plants serves as an important source of energy for the life inhabiting the lagoon complex.

The source of the lagoon's productivity lies in its role as a nursery and habitat for aquatic organisms, some of which reside permanently in the ecosystems, while others migrate to it only as juveniles or as adults. In general terms, the aquatic fauna includes species of mollusk, amphipods, gastropods, decapods, fish, and crustaceans. They are distributed along the various ecological zones the lagoons comprise, and along the three main ecosystems associated with the lagoon complex: salt marshes, estuaries, and mangrove forests. Forty different species of fish have been identified in the Huizache-Caimanero Lagoon Complex (Romero Peña 1998). Besides fish, various species of crabs and shrimp also inhabit the ecosystem. Among those having a significant economic value are the two shrimp species that form the bulk of the fishing activity in southern Sinaloa: *Penaeus vannamei* (white shrimp) and *Penaeus stylirostris* (blue shrimp). The Huizache-Caimanero Lagoon Complex is also a habitat for seasonal migratory birds, and forty different species of bird have been identified (Romero Peña 1998).

Coastal ecosystems, such as the Huizache-Caimanero Lagoon Complex, are undergoing rapid environmental transformation due to a series of factors that will be discussed next. The environmental transformation of coastal ecosystems has had very serious repercussions for the healthy functioning of the ecosystem per se, but also for the rural population who must depend on these ecosystems.

Globalization, Development, and Natural Resources

Occasionally during my fieldwork in El Cerro, I would stop to greet Consuelo in front of her house. After saying hello, her husband, Miguel, an ejidatario and fisherman, would ask me if I had finished writing the book and if I had picked the name I was going to give it. I would answer that I had not yet decided. Then I would ask if he had one in mind. He suggested, *El Sur de Sinaloa: Los Olvidados de Diós* (*Southern Sinaloa: The Land God Forgot*) because, he said, the government was always making them promises it never kept, so that the southern part is poorer and less developed than the central and northern regions of the state.

Miguel is not the only person in El Cerro or the other rural communities of southern Sinaloa who think that way. The general impression held locally of the state, both in rural and urban areas, is that there are two regions: The center and north are developed and prosperous, while the south has been left behind, sunk in backwardness and underdevelopment. Many years before, Macedo López had already expressed the sentiments of Miguel. He wrote, "The south is the child that is ignored or remembered only as certain interests find it convenient" (1978, 20).

Nevertheless, people in other parts of Mexico and in the United States tend to view Sinaloa as an entirely homogenous state, whose agricultural production is the sole basis for its prosperity and affluent economic development. This image of Sinaloa is reaffirmed through the state's extensive exportation of agricultural commodities, for the most part destined for global markets. In other words, the globalization of agriculture in Sinaloa means, for example, that the population of the state of California has become one the principal consumers of Sinaloan produce, primarily fruits and vegetables that are sold in southern California supermarkets. Bell peppers and cucumbers, grown and packed by Sinaloan companies—such as Exportalizas Mexicanas, S. A. de C. V., in Culiacán; Big Products, S. A. de C. V., in Navolato; and Agrícola Cuadras in Ahome—are sold in the Ralph's supermarket chain in Riverside, California.

Sinaloa provides an appropriate case study for the examination of the relationship among economic development, globalization, and the environment from a political ecological perspective. The state has traditionally relied on the exploitation of its natural resources for the generation of profits in domestic and global markets and is currently undergoing radical socio-economic and environmental changes in response to increased demand for agricultural and fishing commodities. That demand is directly linked to state and regional economic development policies.

In a case study of southern Sinaloa, a focus on development and globalization can reveal the links between local (a specific place) and global economic and political forces, and how these influence and shape the natural environment. Both concepts—development and globalization—have been at the core of past and recent anthropological studies (Roseberry 1989; Kearney 1995; Escobar 1995; Edelman 1999). Often "development" has been couched in notions of "progress," "modernization," and "sustainability." However, regardless of the many definitions, interpretations, and applications attributed to the concept of development, it is not my intention at this point to engage in an interpretive analysis of the term. Rather, my usage of "development" in this chapter, and in this book in general, stems from its relevance as an analytical framework within which to conceptualize the economic, social, and environmental changes taking place in the southern Sinaloa region.

Globalization, on the other hand, has been defined as a series of "social, economic, cultural, and demographic processes taking place within and transcending nations" (Kearney 1995, 548). Implicit in this definition is the idea that globalization, as a process, connects localities with the world, and that events occurring on one side influence and shape those events occurring on the other side. I tend to agree, however, with Sassen (1998) that in order to analyze how economic globalization is operationalized, implemented, and maintained, a focus on "place" becomes necessary. The relationship between a place and the global economy has important implications for the understanding of the concrete effects and consequences of this relationship.

In the specific case of Sinaloa, the reliance upon the production of agriculture-based commodities has meant that agricultural development is the indicator used to measure the degree of modernization in each region of the state. The view holds that the more complex the technology and the more capital invested and generated, the more "modern" the region. Both the center and the north are considered to be the most modern regions of the state.

In classifying the residents of Sinaloa, bureaucrats also use the level of agricultural development as an indicator. The center and north are associated with people who have an "entrepreneurial point of view" and a "modern vision," while the south is associated with "backward" and "conflictive" inhabitants. In other cases, people will attribute the failure or success of state-promoted development projects (such as, for example, the cultivation of shrimp) to the traits they assume characterize the inhabitants of the center and north in contrast to those of the south.

One cannot deny that Sinaloan agriculture has contributed to the state's economic well-being. Nevertheless, this well-being has benefited only fifty-six families—the *clase dorada,* or golden class—and the few companies that control the state's agricultural production (Valdés Aguilar 1998). For the majority of the population, however, Sinaloan agriculture industry has had very serious consequences. Among these are the exploitation and marginalization of the manual labor pool, agrarian struggles led by workers from the fields, and the impact of pesticides and fertilizers on people's health and on coastal ecosystems.[2]

The industrialization of Sinaloan agriculture brought with it two other significant consequences (Lara Flores 1998). One of them is an increase during the 1990s in the number of women and children who work in the industry. The other is an increase in the number of migrants, most of them indigenous people and campesinos from the states of Oaxaca, Guerrero, and Michoacán, who come to work primarily during the harvest.

As we shall see later in this chapter, commercial agriculture in Rosario and Escuinapa reflects the same pattern of production of export commodities encouraged in the center and north of Sinaloa. However, in these two southern municipios, the production of agriculture-based commodities is a much more recent phenomenon. Long before Rosario and Escuinapa entered the commercial export–agriculture boom, precious metals and shrimp were the commodities traditionally identified with these two locales. Indeed, the influence of fishing and mining in these municipalities has been so great that it persists even today, despite the decline of mining since the 1940s and the ever-increasing scarcity of shrimp. This influence is so strong that even the history and the legends surrounding the founding of the municipios are tied to the production of gold, silver, and shrimp. The immense significance that mining and fishing have had on the municipios is also seen in the names with which the inhabitants of both areas refer to each other: the "*Chupapiedras*" and the "*Hediondos*" (the "Rock Suckers" and the "Stinkers").

Rosario: From a Real de Minas to a Tourist Attraction

Mining is no longer Rosario's economic pillar, as it was in the seventeenth century, but its legacy still persists in every corner of the municipio. This heritage is apparent in the colonial architecture, in the predominant class system, in the oral and written histories, and in the many poems, stories, legends, and accounts that talk about the town's experiences during the age of mining.[3] One first notices the heritage of the colonial mining period upon entering the town and passing through its arches, on which are inscribed the name and date of its founding, "Ciudad Asilo del Rosario 1655," and on seeing to the left the imposing Catholic church with its gold-leaf altar.

I had my encounter with the mining legacy when I went—somewhat by accident—to live in Rosario for the first time, while carrying out fieldwork for my doctoral thesis. I arrived during the dry season, when dust covered the streets, trees, and houses, and the children played in the streets under a burning midday January sun. My arrival coincided with the arrival of the "Húngaros," as the people of Rosario call the Gypsies. It was during my stay in the town and through the opportunity I had to meet many of the residents that I was able to gain a better understanding of what the mining era had meant to southern Sinaloa in general, and to this community in particular.

During the time that I lived in Rosario, I couldn't get over the strong features of its colonial architecture: the houses, attached one to the other, forming a single large building on each side of the street, marked by wide doors and interior patios; the winding cobblestone streets without any signs to indicate the name or the direction the traffic should go; and the impressive Catholic church, product of the colonial legacy and of Rosario's history as a mining town.

The people I met told me the history of Rosario. They explained, with great nostalgia, that it had been, at one time, a real de minas. They spoke like people who are remembering something long gone, something no more than a memory, but, at the same time, they were extremely proud of what this history means for present-day Rosario. It is precisely this history as a real de minas that has given the people of Rosario (*los Rosarenses*) the nickname of the "Chupapiedras," because, it is said, whenever they spot a sparkling rock on the ground, they pop it in their mouths to see if it is gold or silver.

The modern municipio of Rosario is a geographic space full of contradictions, where the past and the present fuse. It is a municipio characterized by a diverse and dynamic population. Although it declined as a result of the downturn in the mining industry, it grew during the 1950s and 1960s with the establishment of ejidos and the region's commercial development of fishing and agriculture. According to the 2000 national census, the municipio had a population of 47,911 inhabitants (INEGI 2000). Present-day Rosario comprises 196 communities, of which 193 are rural and 3 are urban (Maradiaga Ceceña and Ancona Quiroz 1996). The town of Rosario, which is the county (or municipio) seat, continues to be the largest urban center, and the focal point for the political, social, and economic life of the municipio. Today, it is also a tourist attraction, a colonial city, which national and international tourists come to visit to see the church, travel the cobblestone streets, and contemplate the old Spanish cemetery or the lakes that have formed where the mines used to be.

Escuinapa: The Place of the Water Dog

Escuinapa, whose name in Nahuatl means "The Place of the Water Dog," has always been identified as a fishing town. The various archaeological zones that have been discovered, the shell middens, and the technique of fishing with tapos are witness to the municipio's past and its pre-Hispanic legacy. It shares a common history with Rosario. The history goes back to when Escuinapa was a town in the province of Chametla, where today the municipio of Rosario is located. During many years, even after independence from Spain, Escuinapa continued to be a settlement that was tied politically and economically to the municipio of Rosario. It was not until 1915 that Escuinapa was established as a municipio in its own right. Despite sharing a common history and being so close to each other, the two municipios are quite different. This is reflected in the social and economic influence that shrimp farming has had for Escuinapa. As an economic complement to mining, a small group of residents caught shrimp in the coastal region of the province of Chametla. With each downturn in the mining industry, fishing became a more important economic activity in settlements, such as Escuinapa, that were located along the coast. Just as the productivity of the mines of Rosario was nationally recognized, the productivity of the marshes and lakes that surround Escuinapa was also known throughout Mexico.

Called the "Hediondos" by their neighbors in Rosario, life for the *Escuinapenses* revolves around their relationship to the lagoons, estuaries, and the ocean that form the coast of the municipio and to the fishing resources that these ecosystems offer them. In contrast to Rosario, the municipal seat of Escuinapa is located very close to the lagoons and estuaries, so that even the city people recognize and appreciate the important role these fishing resources and the salt beds play in the municipio's social and economic life. One only has to taste the cuisine, examine the social events, or read about Escuinapa to notice the influential presence that coastal ecosystems and fishing have on the life of the municipio.[4]

Today, Escuinapa is still distinguished for its fishing activities, but it is also an agricultural and ranching area. It is a municipio that is undergoing rapid economic development, but this development has occurred primarily in the town just as is the case with Rosario. In political terms, Escuinapa is organized in five *sindicaturas* (mayor population centers) and 122 communities (Maradiaga Ceceña and Ancona Quiroz 1996). In contrast to Rosario, the municipio is primarily urban; 75.4 percent of its population is concentrated in the four localities that represent the urban sector of the municipio (INEGI 1995). Another significant characteristic is that approximately 13.4 percent of its total population comes from other states, such as Nayarit and Michoacán, which places it among the top five Sinaloan municipios as measured by the size of the immigrant population (Maradiaga Ceceña and Ancona Quiroz 1996).

As is true in Rosario, Escuinapa has been incorporated into the region's tourist industry, which is concentrated in Mazatlán. Tourists, both U.S. and Mexican, are taken on tour buses from Mazatlán to Escuinapa to take excursions in skiffs through the mangrove forests of Teacapán, a fishing settlement, or to see the beaches, lagoons, and estuaries that surround the municipio. Several real-estate development projects aimed at tourists have also appeared on the coast, such as the Isla Paraíso, tourist condominiums inhabited primarily by Americans.

Pueblos, Colonias, and Ranchos: Settlement Patterns and Class Structure

The organization of Mexican municipios is still based on the pattern imposed by the Spaniards during the colonial period. This pattern is characterized by a nucleus of power that is concentrated in the pueblo (town or city) and by a peripheral area composed of numerous communities called ranchos, most of which are rural. Rural migration has tended to concentrate largely on the outskirts of towns, in marginal lands that are usually uninhabited or uncultivated. The communities that have formed as a result of rural migration are known as colonias populares. The populations of Rosario and Escuinapa are distributed in these three types of communities.

The Pueblos

The town of Rosario, as is true with other Mexican settlements, was designed in the image and likeness of Spanish towns. The Spanish heritage is seen in its large Spanish-style municipal palace, its central plaza, its church, and its market. It also exhibits many modern stylistic traits, which are represented by the banks, the pharmacies, doctors' offices, stationery stores, grocery stores, restaurants, clothing stores, shoe stores, photography studios, schools, and hospitals. Also modern in style are the government offices, such as the Secretaría del Medio Ambiente, Recursos Naturales, y Pesca (Secretariat for the Environment, Natural Resources, and Fisheries, or SEMARNAP), the headquarters of the Partido Revolucionario Institucional (PRI), the offices of agrarian reform, and the cultural center, which houses a library and offers dance classes and cultural events. There are two bus stations, one taking people from the town to the rural communities and the other offering service to Mazatlán. There is even a bottling plant for purified water. Rosario also has its share of cantinas, ice cream parlors, pizzerias, a Lion's Club, various hotels, *tortillerías* (tortilla bakeries), bakeries, hardware stores, beauty parlors, funeral parlors, and postal and telegraph offices.

Although the pueblo of Rosario strives to be a modern town, it retains two traits from the era when it was a real de minas: Catholicism and the social class structure. Rosario continues to be a Catholic town in which the church bell marks the quiet rhythm of the cycle of time for its inhabitants. It is a town in which Catholicism and daily life appear to go hand in hand. Around 5 a.m., one hears the first bells, announcing the first mass and the beginning of a new day. The Rosarenses awaken and prepare to perform their daily routine. Throughout the day, the church celebrates other masses so that those who could not attend in the early morning can do so at an hour that is more convenient for them. One also begins to hear the human traffic in the narrow and dusty streets as it goes toward the market, the bakery, the schools, the little plaza, or to the bus stop to catch a ride to one of the rural villages, or to Mazatlán or Escuinapa. Then, around 2 or 3 p.m., people begin to return from work, and students come home to eat and rest. The doors of the houses close to the world as do commercial establishments. The town sinks into a profound lethargy while the sun and the heat add to the impression that one truly finds oneself in the bowels of a mine. Women, in front of their homes, sprinkle water from buckets to keep down the dust so that it won't get inside their houses.

By 7 p.m., everything is completely dark and only a few lights illuminate the streets. People in their houses watch telenovelas or pray the rosary. Because there are no movie theaters or other entertainment spots for young people in the town, the youth meet in the little plaza to chat or they attend the 7 p.m. mass. For most young people, mass, in addition to being a religious rite, is also a social event. Before mass begins, the people greet each other and talk over what has happened during the day, and sweethearts greet each other and converse for a while before the mass starts.

While I lived in Rosario, every afternoon a group of young people with whom I had made friends invited me to accompany them to 7 p.m. mass. It was during my trips to church that I was first acquainted with the Húngaros. They had installed themselves and their trailer next to the church, precisely so that they could get the attention of the parishioners as they came to and went from mass. The Gypsies had tied up their animals around the trailer: turkeys, chickens, and goats. The townsfolk, passing near the Gypsies, averted their gaze, walking quickly to avoid the possibility of having a spell cast on them. The Gypsies didn't care that the people wouldn't greet them and ignored them when they would call out to invite them to come for a palm reading, something the Rosarenses considered a sacrilegious and irreverent act in the eyes of God. Their presence fascinated and charmed me, and I would start to walk over to them when one of my friends would brusquely take my arm and say, "Don't go over there, because they'll take you, and that'll be the last we'll hear of you!" During the two weeks that the Gypsies stayed in the town, I could never go near them—not because I was afraid, but because I didn't want to reinforce the rumor that had begun to go around town that I couldn't possibly be Catholic because I came from a country near Cuba and Haiti, which many of the "cultivated" residents of Rosario associated with voodoo and Santería. During the day, nevertheless, I watched the Gypsy women walk freely through the streets of the town, showing off their brilliantly colored and frilly skirts and their long loose hair.

Besides the Catholicism inherited from the first Spaniards who exploited the early mines in the town, the formation of various social classes that today make up the town also comes from the social stratification that arose around the mining industry. The descendants of some of the families that controlled the mines reside in the town, and they are, basically, still those who control the cultural, political, and economic life of the municipio. There are also *familias de abolengo* (the hereditary elite) who control most of the land and own the banks and the town's businesses. Despite Rosario's small size, this class system makes the town a closed community to which it is difficult to gain access if one is an outsider. People know each other, and, based on one's last name, they know each other's social positions.

The other town, Escuinapa de Hidalgo, is the county seat of the municipio of Escuinapa. When entering the town, one rapidly perceives that it is thoroughly modern, with an abundance of stores, hotels, and restaurants. In contrast to what has occurred in Rosario, the processes of economic development have unfolded rapidly here.

The first things that can be seen are the fruit-packing plants and the fields of mango and papaya that lie on each side of the international highway that runs through town. On the outskirts, women selling fresh shrimp or dried, salted shrimp, and mango sellers greet the visitor. Once inside town, it does not take long to notice the dynamism of the Escuinapenses, reflected in an active commerce, and the traffic of people walking or on bicycle, going here and there, stopping to greet one another or chat. Commerce in Escuinapa de Hidalgo is represented by its banks, hotels, pharmacies, clothing stores, shoe stores, groceries, photography studios, hardware stores, toy stores, candy stores, restaurants, jewelry stores, craft shops, furniture stores, video stores, and dozens of food stands belonging to street vendors. Escuinapa also has some chain stores, well known throughout Sinaloa and Mexico, such as la Tienda Ley and the furniture store Coppel, which have displaced many of the smaller businesses belonging to the Escuinapenses. The various medical offices, schools, hospitals, government offices, cultural center, discotheques, movie theaters, and offices of Alcoholics Anonymous complete the town's infrastructure. The mango- and shrimp-packing plants and orchards of coconut, mango, and chili testify to the agricultural and fishing bonanza the town has experienced. The two local bus stations take people from the town to the ranchos, to Rosario and to Mazatlán. There is also a national bus line station, Estrella Blanca, that takes Escuinapenses to other parts of Mexico.

Another peculiar characteristic of the town of Escuinapa is its municipal market. This, in contrast to the one in Rosario, is a concrete building with colonial archways built near the plaza. In this market, known as El Mercado Hidalgo, one can see firsthand the economic dynamics of the Escuinapenses. Starting at 5 a.m., when the church bells first ring, the vendors start out for the market to open their stalls. At home, those who awaken early get dressed to go to market. The families that have domestic help give them money to run errands at the market, a ritual known as *el mandado*. Within the market, the smell of hot bread mixes with that of freshly slaughtered chickens and the aroma of fresh oranges. The people, crowding together in front of different stands, comment on the heat or the price of the product that they are buying, and they also take advantage of the time to talk about the news of the day. At the stands, vendors using loudspeakers announce their wares: oranges, vegetables, pork, homemade cheese, bread, and other items. The market's great assortment of stalls ranges from small food stands, where people go to eat breakfast or have a fruit smoothie, to stalls selling clothes and shoes, electronics, candy, toys, flowers, and gifts for birthdays, baptisms, and weddings, and even to large butcher shops and dairy stores.

At the seafood stands, one can see the *changueras* (women shrimp traders) seated with their buckets, selling shrimp. People come up to ask them whether the shrimp are from an estuary or a farm. The changueras hawk the shrimp to everyone who passes: "Fresh estuary shrimp, just thirty pesos a kilo!" In the flower stands, both the buyers and sellers are, for the most part, women. Women from both the town and the ranchos come to buy flowers to take to the Virgin in the church or to a sick friend.

The social and professional elite of the municipio live in Escuinapa de Hidalgo. Nevertheless, in contrast to Rosario, very few are from the familias de abolengo. Here the top of the class structure comprises a professional elite, mostly doctors, and a few families that control agriculture and commerce. In Escuinapa everyone knows who the successful businesspeople and wealthy professionals are. Some of them have even been kidnapped, and others have suffered attempts.

The Escuinapenses who live in town also recognize the importance of rain for agriculture and fishing. Watching for the arrival of the first rains in Escuinapa is something of a pastime. During the dry season, in the late afternoons as the sun sets, the people take chairs and other furniture outside, and they sit on the street in front of their homes waiting for the rain. All talk focuses on rain because, according to them, when there is no rain, the fishing is also no good. People are always looking up at the sky in search of signs that it will soon rain. When the first drops fall, the children go out into the streets to play, and the adults watch the rain from behind the windows of their houses or wherever they may be at the moment. For many years, when the rains were late in coming, or if it didn't rain at all, it was the custom to organize religious processions through the town's streets, with the people carrying the statue of St. Francis of Assisi, the patron saint of Escuinapa, to ask him to send the rain. These processions stopped being held when the arm of the statue was broken during a procession, and the town's priest got so angry that ever since he has refused to lend the statue for processions.

The first impression that a person forms of Escuinapa de Hidalgo depends on the time of year in which one arrives there. If visiting in May, one runs the risk of finding an empty town, because during this time the well-known Fiestas de las Playas are celebrated, and most of the people go to live and celebrate at the beach for several days. If one visits in December, one finds a town full of life and joy, with fiestas held in honor of the names of the streets, or a Catholic town, whose residents walk in procession to the Capilla del Gallo (Rooster Chapel) to celebrate the Día de la Virgen de Guadalupe (December 12, the day the Catholic calendar dedicates to the Virgin of Guadalupe). If one visits during the day, one runs into the hustle and bustle of the residents and the dynamism of the town's commerce. If one visits at night, the band music and corrido songs come spilling out of the cantinas and night spots and spread to all corners of the town, and the dozens of strolling food vendors who decorate the streets give a sense of continuity and hope to the life of the town.

The Colonias Populares

The colonias populares represent part of the urban zone, even though they are located on the outskirts of town. Here marginality and urban poverty is visible. In most cases, the people themselves build their own houses on lots where they are squatters. In Rosario and Escuinapa, these neighborhoods comprise people who have migrated from the rural communities to the towns looking for greater economic opportunities and social well-being.

People in the neighborhoods earn their living as street vendors, field hands, or by selling food, clothes, or basic goods from their houses. Many of these neighborhoods lack drinking water, sewer and rain-drainage systems, paving, telephone services, health clinics, and schools. Some also face grave environmental problems such as contamination from garbage dumps or sewage.

The Ranchos

Most of the settlements in the municipios are ranchos, of the type that El Cerro and Celaya represent very well. Approximately 59 percent of the population lives in these rural communities (Maradiaga Ceceña and Ancona Quiroz 1996). The ranchos are connected politically with the *ayuntamiento municipal,* or city hall, through the formation of community committees and through the election of political representatives. However, the structural relationship between the city and the countryside continues to be one of subordination and dependence on the part of the latter. The subordination is related to the existing class structure in which the control over productive resources is concentrated in the hands of the professional elite and the familias de abolengo.

The people of the towns of Escuinapa and Rosario refer to the people of the countryside as "the people from the ranchos," or the campesinos. Implicit in these classifications is the idea that the ranchos are homogenous human settlements in which life opportunities are approximately the same for all residents. Also implicit in the classification, however, is an acknowledgment of the difference in social class, because the term "people from the ranchos" has a pejorative meaning. For example, when I lived in Rosario, many people I knew could not understand why I was studying a rancho, because I should, supposedly, be much more interested in the town, a colonial locale with "much culture." Others scolded me for wasting time going to the ranchos, when I should be spending more time going to church and to the cultural events that the Casa de la Cultura sponsored. In reality, the people of the towns know very little about the ranchos. They are unaware of the history of the founding of these communities, the economic and productive activities of the residents, how the communities are organized politically and socially, and what life is like for the people who live there.

For most of the people in towns, the ranchos "are all the same" and when "you've seen one, you've seen them all." In part, this characteristic of homogeneity, which the urban elite attributes to ranchos, is based on the perception of a social class and the marked geographic and political divisions that exist between the town—the "center"—and the ranches—the "periphery." The belief that all the rural inhabitants are ignorant and poor is still deeply rooted among many professionals and elite townspeople. In reality, however, each rural locality in the municipios has its own history, individual economic and social structures, and specific human struggles for survival. Townspeople, however, recognize the economic contribution of rural settlements to the economy and business of the towns. They understand very well that many of their businesses depend on the people from the ranchos who come to town to shop, and that the bulk of the human labor, which sustains the production of export commodities, comes from these rural communities.

Export Commodities of Rosario and Escuinapa

When going into the rural areas of the municipios, one of the most notable features of the countryside is the extensive fields of chili and mango. The green of the leaves of the chili plants and the mango trees jumps out from the ash color that characterizes the region's vegetation during the dry season. This greenery is possible thanks to fields that are irrigated by pumping stations, drawing water from a nearby canal. Nearer the coast, the fields of coconut palms bordering the rural communities give the impression that one has landed on a tropical island, and this illusion, for a brief instant, makes one forget the heat, the sun, and the gray landscape. Along the coast and during the nighttime, around the lagoons and estuaries, one perceives the presence of thousands of fishermen with lanterns, who, from their *pangas* (small wooden boats), extract the pink gold to sell in the local or global markets.

The production of agricultural and fishing-based commodities is an important part of the economy of Escuinapa and Rosario. Today, in addition to shrimp, the production of nontraditional agricultural commodities, especially fruit, constitutes one of the principal economic sources in Rosario and Escuinapa. The production of these commodities does not occur by accident or chance but is something that has been carefully planned by various administrations holding power in the state government and by the powerful social classes. The elite, with government support, has taken advantage of the global demand for these commodities to promote their production. For example, the governor of Sinaloa from 1963 to 1968, Leopoldo Sánchez Celis, is credited with the development of mango-export agriculture because he founded the first large nurseries and launched on a major scale the production of fruits (Confederación de Asociaciones Agrícolas del Estado de Sinaloa [CAADES] 1987). Another Sinaloan governor, Antonio Toledo Corro (1981–1986), a native of Escuinapa, developed and implemented a program of coconut cultivation in the southern part of the state while he held the state post of secretary for agrarian reform. The program's primary goal was to produce copra for use in beauty products based on coconut oil.

The development of fruit horticulture, especially the cultivation of mango in the municipio of Escuinapa, is also attributed to the professional elite who reside in the town. This is true to such an extent that in Escuinapa the cultivation of mango for export is know as the hobby of the doctors, because they were the ones who started the cultivation of this fruit in the municipio (CAADES 1987).

In the municipio of Rosario, after the collapse of the mining industry, many people who were left without work began to plant crops on the banks of the Río Baluarte, and they built the first irrigation dams also along that river. The promotion of agriculture in this municipio is attributed to Francisco del Rincón and Guillermo Elizondo, who introduced the use of tractors and gave financial assistance to the growers (CAADES 1987).

The cultivation of fruit for export took off in these municipios when the growers organized. The Asociación de Agricultores del Río Baluarte (Río Baluarte Growers Association) formed on January 10, 1950, and included growers in Mazatlán, Concordia, Rosario, and Escuinapa. In 1985, the growers in Escuinapa formed their own association, called Asociación de Agricultores del Río Las Cañas (Rio Las Cañas Growers Association). Both organizations belonged to the Confederación de Asociaciones Agrícolas del Estado de Sinaloa (Federation of Sinaloan Growers Associations, or CAADES).

Fruit horticulture production is important not only because of the great volume of fruit produced but also because of its industrial processing. Escuinapa grows slightly more than one-fourth of the state's entire fruit crop, and the processing of mango, plums, and lemons is industrialized (Maradiaga Ceceña and Ancona Quiroz 1996). Next to Escuinapa, Rosario is the municipio with the greatest area planted in fruit orchards in the state. Its economically most important orchard products are mango, avocado, Spanish plum (red mombin), lemons, and coconuts. Besides fruit, chili and sorghum (broomcorn) are two other commodities grown in the municipios.

Both chili and mango are also grown in the valleys of the municipios, and the produce, although sold locally, is mostly destined for U.S. markets. Both smallholders, representing primarily wealthy families and the professional elite, as well as ejidatarios grow these crops. The technology used consists of pump-irrigation systems, fertilizers, and pesticides, which come mostly from Culiacán and are purchased in the *agroquímicas,* stores that specialize in agricultural products, from seeds to pesticides. Agronomists, who are up-to-date on agricultural developments in the central and northern regions of the state, own many of these stores. These individuals often travel to Culiacán and other municipios in the state to familiarize themselves with the techniques and products used in agricultural activities, which they then bring back to Escuinapa and Rosario to disseminate among the agricultural growers.

Coconut is grown in the areas near the lagoons and coast of the municipios. Most campesinos who live in the communities near the plantations take part in the planting and harvesting of the coconut crop, and both fresh and dry coconuts are sold. The unripe coconut is sold au natural, for its water, in local restaurants, the central and northern parts of the state, and other states of Mexico such as Sonora. Merchants buy the dry coconut, sold as copra, directly from the plantation, and they then resell it to cosmetic or soap factories in Guadalajara.

The increasing demand for these commodities in regional and global markets is transforming the environment in these two municipios through its impact on natural resources. To understand the nature of environmental change in southern Sinaloa, one must ask two basic questions: (1) How is the production of agricultural and fishing-based commodities contributing to environmental degradation in this region? and (2) How is environmental degradation affecting southern Sinaloa's rural population? The first question is answered next; the second will be addressed in subsequent chapters.

The Declining Natural Resource Base of Southern Sinaloa

One of the challenges that I faced when I began research for this book was the lack of studies addressing the nature and causes of environmental change in southern Sinaloa. However, as I began to write this book, I also started to make contacts with Mexican scholars and researchers working at universities and other government institutions in the southern Sinaloa region. Their research has been instrumental for my analysis of the relationship between commodity production and environmental degradation in southern Sinaloa. It has also been crucial for the elaboration of a broader picture portraying the various social, economic, and ecological processes linked to environmental change in this region. Moreover, their research demonstrates that there is a growing concern among Mexican academics, and, in particular, scientists, to elucidate the causes and impact of environmental degradation and to contribute to finding a viable solution. From these studies, one can easily deduce that the agriculture, fishing, and shrimp aquaculture industries are among the primary causes of environmental change in southern Sinaloa.

The development of a commercial agriculture industry in Sinaloa is contributing to environmental degradation in two ways. First, it is increasing soil erosion and desertification, which already affect up to 80 percent of the land in Mexico (Carabias, Provencio, and Toledo 1994). In southern Sinaloa, agroindustrial deforestation of natural areas is partly to blame for erosion and desertification, but subsistence farming and the raising of cattle and other domestic animals have also done their share of damage (Perales Rivas and Fregoso Tirado 1994; Reyes Jiménez and Loaíza Meza 1996).

In a desperate effort to increase crop production, subsistence farmers continue to cultivate infertile and marginal land, sometimes without allowing sufficient fallow periods between crops. The lack of fertile land has prompted many campesinos to expand their subsistence farming to areas bordering the lagoons and estuarine ecosystems. This expansion of the agricultural frontier has resulted in the loss of natural vegetation, thus modifying the landscape and altering the biochemical cycles of the lagoons and estuaries (Ruiz-Luna and Berlanga-Robles 1999).

The second contributing factor to environmental degradation, frequently discussed in the literature, is the effect of fertilizers, pesticides, and other agrochemicals on the soil and water (Wright 1990; Carabias,

Provencio, and Toledo 1994; Galindo Reyes et al. 1997; Galindo Reyes 2000; Páez-Osuna, Guerrero-Galván, and Ruiz-Fernández 1998; Berlanga-Robles 1999; Ruiz-Luna and Berlanga-Robles 1999). Pesticides not only have a detrimental effect on the health of agricultural wageworkers, but they harm the region's coastal ecosystems as well. Pesticides and fertilizers, carried by the rains and agricultural runoff, end up in the estuaries and lagoons of southern Sinaloa, threatening the survival of aquatic animals and mangrove forests (Galindo Reyes et al. 1997; Galindo Reyes 2000; Páez-Osuna, Guerrero-Galván, and Ruiz-Fernández 1998).

During my fieldwork in the region, fishermen claimed that agricultural runoff was killing the shrimp and fish. Biological and chemical studies of lagoon and estuarine systems in southern Sinaloa show that water quality is deteriorating as a result of agricultural effluent, which, in turn, is decreasing shrimp production within these ecosystems (Galindo Reyes et al. 1997; Galindo Reyes 2000; Páez-Osuna, Guerrero-Galván, and Ruiz-Fernández 1998; Romero Beltrán and González Gallardo 2000).

Sinaloa has been historically considered one of Mexico's primary shrimp-producing states. However, since 1987, overall shrimp production has declined due to a combination of factors such as climate change, water pollution, destruction of natural habitats, increasing population, and overfishing (Plan Nacional de Desarrollo 1995; SEMARNAP 1997; Berlanga-Robles 1999; Galindo Reyes 2000). People in rural communities whose livelihood depends on shrimp fishing are beginning to accept that this natural resource is close to depletion.

The mayor of the municipio of Escuinapa summarized the decline in shrimp production and its economic and social consequences. In a public speech, which addressed the people of Escuinapa, he clearly echoes some of the concerns Mexican scholars and government officials have expressed.

Our people, with their deep and profound vocation for fishing, have found catching shrimp to be a chief support for their economic betterment. Now, however, we have been observing with tremendous concern the decrease in the amount of shrimp harvested during the past three seasons. This has consequently affected hundreds of families that depend on the labor of these hard-working fishermen. During 1988, production was approximately 700 tons of shrimp. However, during the 1990 and 1991 seasons, production did not exceed 200 tons. In this decline experienced in recent seasons, a variety of factors have combined to create this sorry panorama. These include the eutrophication of the lagoon and estuary systems, where the fishing cooperatives of our municipio traditionally work; the growing social pressure that independent fishermen exert on fishing grounds by capturing this resource throughout most of the year, without respecting fishing seasons established by the authorities in the Fisheries Department; and the gradual pollution that is affecting the ecology of the estuaries. (Simental Beaven 1990, 34; my translation)

In an attempt to relieve some of the pressure on shrimp and other commercially valuable fishing resources, the Mexican government launched a massive campaign during the 1980s to promote a shrimp aquaculture program. Initially, this program was conceived as a rural development strategy directed towards the diversification of economic activities and the generation of income in rural areas. Shrimp farms in coastal Sinaloa have proliferated: The number of commercial shrimp farms grew from 1 in 1984 to 167 by 1998 (SEMARNAP 1998). In the municipio of Escuinapa, the number of shrimp farms grew from 8 in 1989 to 41 by 1997, and in Rosario, the number of shrimp farms grew from 2 in 1989 to 13 by 1997 (SEMARNAP 1998).

This rapid growth is creating a new set of environmental problems for the lagoon and estuarine ecosystems (Instituto Nacional de la Pesca 1998). Among the most pressing is the negative effect of shrimp farm construction on water quality, mangrove forests, and the wild stocks of shrimp (Flores-Verdugo et al. 1992; Ramírez-Zavala, Ruiz-Luna, and Berlanga-Robles 1997; Páez-Osuna, Guerrero-Galván, and Ruiz-Fernández 1998; Berlanga-Robles 1999; Ruiz-Luna and Berlanga-Robles 1999; Cruz-Torres 2001).

Another significant negative effect of the shrimp aquaculture industry is water pollution. Discharge from shrimp ponds is one of the more recent and direct sources of pollution in Sinaloa's coastal waters (Galindo-Reyes et al. 1997; Páez-Osuna, Guerrero-Galván, and Ruiz-Fernández 1998; Berlanga-Robles 1999). The wastewater contains large amounts of organic material, fertilizers, chemicals, and antibiotics, which cause eutrophication in the lagoons and estuaries.

The shrimp aquaculture industry has also harmed the mangrove forest ecosystems (Flores-Verdugo et al. 1997). The effect of shrimp aquaculture on mangrove forests is still a controversial topic in Mexico, and not many scientific studies have addressed the issue. However, the building of shrimp ponds often requires partial clearing of the surrounding mangrove forests (Flores-Verdugo et al. 1992; Ramírez-Zavala, Ruiz-Luna, and Berlanga-Robles 1997). According to Flores-Verdugo and co-authors (1997, 43), "shrimp farming is a recent activity which is transforming the local mangrove landscape, mainly on the seasonal floodplains."

The negative effects of shrimp aquaculture on the wild stocks of shrimp constitute another environmental problem (Berlanga-Robles 1999). Over-harvesting of wild postlarvae significantly depletes the natural shrimp stocks of Sinaloa. In coastal northwestern Mexico generally, the shrimp industry relies on two sources of supply for postlarvae: hatcheries and wild stock. Although nine hatcheries currently operate in Sinaloa, the industry prefers wild postlarvae because they seem healthier and more resistant to viral diseases and are cheaper than hatchery-raised postlarvae. The dependence of the industry on wild postlarvae has even prompted the emergence of a black market. In addition to depleting the natural stock of commercially sold shrimp, the harvesting of wild postlarvae also captures and destroys the fry of many fish and shrimp species.

Environmental problems associated with the shrimp aquaculture industry are affecting the livelihood and the quality of life of rural coastal people. During the rainy season, southern Sinaloa's coastal lagoons are habitats for a variety of fishing resources that the rural coastal population exploits as common property. When these lagoons dry up at the end of the rainy season, the individual residents and some cooperatives have traditionally mined them for salt, for both home consumption and sale. Today, to guarantee a permanent water supply, the shrimp farms have built canals to connect the lagoons with estuaries or the ocean, leading to permanent flooding. By granting concessions—mostly to private investors—to build shrimp farms in these coastal lagoons, the Mexican government has converted a highly diverse coastal ecosystem into a monocrop system. By transforming common-property lagoons into a privately owned resource, the government has exacerbated southern Sinaloa's social conflicts over the use of fishing resources.

Conclusion

Today, the two most important natural resources in southern Sinaloa, particularly in the municipios of Rosario and Escuinapa, are the land and the coastal ecosystems. There is no doubt that economic, social, and ecological factors have contributed to the transformation of both. Currently, one can attribute the environmental degradation of these natural resources in part to economic development policies that seek to maximize the use of those natural resources for the production of commodities to generate profits.

James O'Connor (1998) has discussed the importance of recognizing the dynamic relationship between economic development and natural resource degradation. Writing about the interconnections of economic and environmental crises, he remarked that "there is a global economy that is undergoing a process of 'accumulation through crisis' that is impoverishing tens of millions of people, destroying communities, degrading hundreds of thousands of bioregions, and exacerbating a global ecological crisis" (O'Connor 1998, 267). For him, economic crisis and environmental crisis are mutually interrelated. Case studies, such as the one presented here, that focus on the connection between economic development and regional patterns of natural resource access and distribution can shed light on the various layers and ramifications of environmental degradation.

There are several factors contributing to the degradation of natural resources in southern Sinaloa: population growth, development policies, environmental phenomena such as El Niño, class inequalities, and globalization. The last factor, globalization, is intimately linked to the increasing demand in global markets for agricultural and fishing-based commodities, such as shrimp, mangoes, chilies, and broomcorn. There is no doubt that closely related to the increasing demand for these commodities in global markets, there is also an increasing demand for local labor to produce them. However, as we will see in following chapters, the jobs created by either commercial agriculture or fishing are not sufficient to economically provision rural households in coastal southern Sinaloa.

Environmental degradation, in turn, is jeopardizing the livelihoods of the people who are most dependent on these resources: the rural population. Rural communities, such as Celaya and El Cerro, must face the contradiction of relying ever more heavily on a natural resource base that is diminishing day by day. As I will show in further chapters, in rural communities, such as those presented in this book, impoverished households must increasingly rely on coastal habitats and on their agricultural lands as a source of food. Consequently, this also contributes to exacerbating the environmental degradation of natural resources. Most rural households face a predicament: The daily struggle to survive requires that they engage in practices that accelerate the deterioration of the resources on which they most depend.

Part II

Localities

Their Emergence and Transition within National

and Global Processes

A group of Celayan women and children going to the beach.

Introduction to Part II

Political ecology is concerned with how regional, national, and global processes shape and influence events taking place at the local level. Anthropologists have long studied local-level communities to analyze and understand how they function, and communities have been considered appropriate sites to study the interconnections among environmental, political, and economic processes emerging regionally, nationally, and even globally.

When defining community, Jeffrey Cohen (1999) warns us not to overemphasize the importance of geography so as to neglect the importance that social practice has to the meaning of a community. He defines a community as "a context of actions and result of actions but not as a thing" (Barth 1992, 31; Eriksen 1991, cited in Cohen 1999, 14). This definition allows for the understanding of the linkages between a community and external processes, such as globalization, and of the relations that people develop within and outside the community in order to construct a sense of self-identity and place.

The chapters in this section provide an account of the formation, structure, and function of rural communities in southern Sinaloa. In examining the definition and formation of these communities, the focus is on the influence of local history, as part of a collective memory, and of regional, national, and global processes. Two of these processes, migration and the struggle for land, are central to the understanding of how these communities emerged and developed over time.

Celaya and El Cerro, the two communities portrayed in these chapters, are in some ways representative of the types of rural coastal communities found in southern Sinaloa. The two communities, locally known as ranchos, share a common history rooted in the struggle for land among the rural population, while having unique social, economic, and political structures, and a history of specific local conflicts.

One of the major differences between the communities lies in the land-tenure system. El Cerro is an ejido, a creation of Mexico's agrarian reform process following the 1910 Mexican Revolution. Until the mid-1990s, when new agrarian legislation was enacted, ejidatarios in El Cerro held the land communally. Celaya was also the product of early agrarian reform efforts in Mexico, but each household has traditionally held its land privately.

In the mid-1990s, the reform of Article 27 of the Mexican Constitution radically altered land-tenure patterns in southern Sinaloa, and it has had significant repercussions for these communities, especially El Cerro. This section examines the nature of these changes and discusses how the people of El Cerro and Celaya lived before and after the land reform of the 1990s.

3

Gypsies, Peones, and Ejidatarios

A Political Ecology of El Cerro

> Our life is hard, but in other places, it is worse. Like over there in
> Africa, where they don't have enough food to eat. You see it on TV,
> and you see them suffering, and it makes you sad. But what can we
> do? We're nothing more than a bunch of poor campesinos.
> —Trinidad, 1993

When the people of El Cerro saw the Gypsies for the last time, during the
summer of 1997, the rainy season was about to begin. It was the Gypsies'
custom to stop in the community for a few days during their yearly excur-
sion through southern Sinaloa. Each year, the residents anticipated their
arrival, which they connected with the start of rains. They were in the
habit of watching the sky during the month of June, searching for a black
cloud, a bolt of lightning, or some other sign that it was about to rain. As
soon as they got that signal, people would begin saying, "Now it's going to
rain, and the Húngaros will be here soon." No one ever knew for certain
which day or hour the Gypsies would arrive, because they always appeared
unannounced. In 1997, they turned up on a Saturday around midday in
the middle of heat and sunlight that was so strong it seemed to be stran-
gling the *ranchito* (small village), raising a cloud of dust along the way.
The Gypsies entered El Cerro in their large white trailer, on the community's only passable street. At their appearance, people got up from
hammocks and cots where they were taking a siesta, and others stopped
whatever they were doing to go greet them. The children ran behind the
trailer in great excitement, and they held on to it, while shouting in chorus, *"Los Húngaros llegaron!"* ("The Húngaros are here!"). As they did

each year, the Gypsies pitched their camp at the side of the school because that was the only level place anywhere in the ranchito.

The people whose houses were near the school gathered to watch carefully as the Gypsies stepped out of the trailer. Three tall women, with light skin and long brown hair, wearing long skirts, got down first, followed by two men with long hair and beards. They quickly set up a tent at one side of the trailer and placed chairs around. Then they began talking among themselves. A little while later, the women got up and went to hunt the few chickens that were running around clucking, frightened by the crowd. The children joined the Gypsies to help them trap the chickens. When they caught a bird, the Gypsies would grasp it by the neck, giving it a couple of good twists to kill it. Afterwards, in their broken Spanish, they asked the group that had gathered around how much money they owed the owners of the chickens they had killed. After paying for them, on a bonfire improvised in the middle of the street, the Gypsies cooked the birds in a soup with potatoes and carrots. One asked one of the women from El Cerro for the loan of a white sheet, with which she would improvise a movie screen. In this way, the Gypsies set up their Traveling Cinema, the only movie theater El Cerro has ever had. The Gypsies announced through a loud speaker that that evening they would be showing an action picture, one about drug traffickers.

The children ran to their houses to ask their parents for permission and the five pesos that it cost to get in to see the show. The price of admission included a plate of chicken soup and a glass of Coca Cola. Around 6 p.m., the men and children began to arrive, and the Traveling Cinema filled up. On Sunday night, the Gypsies showed another picture, but this time it was a love story. On Monday morning, very early, before the sun rose, the Gypsies were gone. They left in their trailer, without any goodbyes, leaving in their wake an immense wave of dust, and accompanied by dogs that ran barking behind the trailer. Since that time, they have not returned, and the community, tired of waiting for them, began building a church on the same spot where the Gypsies had always set up the traveling theater.

In contrast to the nomadic existence of the Gypsies, the people of El Cerro have desperately attempted to establish a deep-rooted locality in the hardscrabble soil of the community. In this chapter I detail the process of how El Cerro emerged from nothing, and how as it developed, so did I as an anthropologist. I came to understand the social, economic, political, and ecological trials, conflicts, struggles, and personal tragedies that encompass the daily lives of a very brave people.

The first impression that I had of El Cerro was that it was a small settlement, a lost and lonely ranchito in the midst of dry, lifeless hills. Its landscape contrasted greatly with the rest of the rural landscape, where plantings of chili, mango, and corn, with their brilliant green leaves, jumped out like emeralds from the midst of the gray color of the rest of the vegetation. At first glance, El Cerro seems to be an inhospitable place, one that would be hard to visit unless one had some specific reason for doing so. Its location, relative isolation, lack of amenities, and poverty combine to give one the impression that this ranchito is nothing more than a sack of miseries.

When I went there for the first time to do fieldwork, the idea of a closed campesino community was the first thing that came to mind. Nevertheless, on getting to know the community, and living with its people, I soon realized that the first impression that I so hastily formed was only a passing mirage. I learned that El Cerro, like other rural communities of southern Sinaloa, is a dynamic place where people are always coming and going, for one reason or another. Outsiders like the Gypsies arrive to break the routine and monotony for the residents, bringing them a diversion. Others arrive to work during the fishing season or in the harvesting of mangoes. Others leave to work in chili or broomcorn harvests in nearby communities. Some arrive to sell vegetables or used clothes, while others go in search of firewood or to get water that they haul back to town. Some come from Tijuana or California to visit, and others leave for Tijuana or California to work.

I first visited El Cerro during the dry season, *tiempo triste* ("the sad time"), as the people call that part of the year. I arrived during January, when the hills that surround the ranchito had already lost their vegetation and the only thing that struck one was the landscape's ash color. Sent from the Ministry of Fisheries in Mexico City, I had arrived at the regional fisheries office in Mazatlán to find out how to contact some of the shrimp farms operating in the region. The biologists who worked in the office told me that one of largest and most productive shrimp farms was in an ejido in the municipio of Rosario. The director of the aquaculture section asked two biologists to take me to see the farm and to introduce me to its board of directors. Before leaving, I told them my intention to live in the community in order to carry out my fieldwork. The biologists tried to persuade me to live in Mazatlán and travel daily to Rosario. They were worried that something might happen to me.

In a white pickup truck with my luggage in the back, I arrived in El Cerro around midday as the sun, with a soul of fire, burned everything with its potent rays. The heat was so strong that it was almost hard to breath. The streets and houses of El Cerro were covered with dust. In front of the houses, some women with buckets in their hands splashed water to settle the dust. Half-naked children, burned by the sun, with faces, heads, legs, and backs covered with dust, played in the middle of the street. When they saw our pickup truck arrive, they greeted us with laughter. The burros and the pigs, also covered with dust, tried vainly to evade the thin dogs that harassed them. We passed through the ranchito, on the only passable road, and the vehicle kicked up a wave of dust behind us. When we arrived at the shrimp farm, all the members of the cooperative were harvesting shrimp from the ponds.

Returning from the farm, we stopped in front of the house of Lupe, to see if she would let me live in her home for a while. It had become the custom that all the women students who came to do social service in El Cerro lived in her house. The biologists assumed that the process of doing fieldwork for my doctoral dissertation was very similar to social service that Mexican university students are required to perform. She greeted us, and asked us to come in. The biologists told Lupe that I had come to do my social service in El Cerro. She looked at me and said, "Well, here we're all one big family. At night, we all sleep on the floor in a big heap. If you want to stay here for a few days, stay, but I don't think you're going to be very comfortable." Because Lupe was not exactly excited at the idea of my staying in her house, the biologists promised that they would help me find another place to live. That was how I came to live in the town of Rosario, in the home of a marine biologist who was their friend.

El Cerro is only twenty minutes by car from Rosario. Each day early in the morning, I caught the bus to El Cerro. The driver, Pancho, a man from Agua Verde, greeted me every day and asked about my social service work. Pancho had thought that I was a native of Sinaloa, and the day he asked me what town I was from, I told him that I was not Mexican but Puerto Rican. He thought Puerto Rico was a Central American country, and he said, "Be very careful when you walk around alone. Always bring your papers with you. The other day, they caught two Central Americans—I

The main street of El Cerro.

think they were Guatemalans—and they sent them back to their home-land." From that day on, to avoid running the risk of my deportation to Central America, as he feared might happen, Pancho never mentioned that I was not Mexican.

When I formally began my fieldwork in January of 1989, I spent time visiting the shrimp farm and talking with the biologists in charge of managing it as well as with the members of the cooperative. During my return from one of these trips, I met the person and his family who would become my best informants. Leoncio, the president of the aquaculture cooperative, insisted that I meet Chico, the man who was one of the principal founders of El Cerro. That day, when I went to the shrimp farm, he gave me a ride to meet Chico.

On the left side of the unpaved road that leads to the marshes where the shrimp farm is located are the ejidatarios' plots, planted with corn, beans, and chilies. Leoncio parked alongside one of the fields. Bent over among the chili plants, picking the biggest chilies, was Chico. He greeted us and gave us both chilies. After Leoncio explained who I was and what I was doing, Chico invited us to come to his house right then, and we gave him a lift in the truck.

From that day on, Chico, his wife, Trinidad, and his children became my adoptive family. It was through them that I would learn what it meant to live within the context of rural Mexico and what an ejido really is. It was in his house where I first ate corn tortillas with refried beans, drank *agua de Jamaica,* and tasted *chiles rellenos* and *nopales.* It was also in his house where each afternoon, after making my rounds through the ranchito, I would sit to chat with the couple and their children, while drinking lemonade under the tamarind tree that was planted in the patio behind his house.

After I began my fieldwork in El Cerro, it did not take long to notice that Chico was not an ordinary man, as I initially believed. With time, I came to understand that he was actually somewhat of a celebrity—like a character from a Gabriel García Márquez story, and very similar in fact to José Arcadio Buendía of Macondo. Chico kept history books, old and dusty, which only he, out of his entire family, could understand, and which he proudly showed to everyone who visited his house. He wore a tight belt and sunglasses with palm trees drawn on the lenses. He was a very thin man, small, with a deliberate manner of speaking. He thought before he spoke. He was always curious to understand and eager to explain the events that surrounded him. He looked like a living mannequin who had survived the bitterness of life. He told me about his trips to the "border," to Mexicali, where he had lived with his two sons from his first marriage. He talked about it as if it were a strange region, beyond the limits of the imagination. During the years that he was president of the ejido, he concerned himself with seeing to it that each family had land to cultivate. Even when he was no longer president, his successors consulted him frequently, whenever they had to make an important decision or had to fill out forms to apply for loans.

Trini was also a good informant. She had a magnificent memory; she knew all the details about the founding of the community and about each of the families that reside there. She gave birth to twenty children, of whom she raised eleven to adulthood, the others having died. She did all her own housework and helped Chico farm his parcels of land. The more I got to know Trini, the more impressed I became with the attention she gave to each detail as she described the community to me. Her knowledge of fishing and agricultural practices in El Cerro and the political organization of the ejido has been tremendously useful to me.

As my time in the community passed, the impressions that I formed about it and each one of its inhabitants changed. At times, I thought it was a ranchito where nothing much happened. I thought it was much too tranquil and normal to provide an interesting anthropological study. It also seemed to me to be a homogeneous community, because the poverty in which most of its inhabitants lived was so obvious at a glance that other details of the community could pass unnoticed. There were many times when I sensed that under that calm and that passive and mild silence there must be hidden some secret, some detail that would betray the true reality in which the people lived.

The opportunity to learn more about the family life of each of the households presented itself one day while I was walking down the main street. A group of women was gathered under a tree, embroidering and knitting, and they called me over, inviting me to chat with them. By this time, the people had assumed that I was a marine biologist who was doing her social service duty at the shrimp farm in the community. One of the women asked me if that was true. "Well," I said, "I am a biologist, but I am studying anthropology." The women did not understand what I was trying to say with this business of studying anthropology, and they continued referring to me as "the biologist who came to do her social service in El Cerro." Another woman asked me if I was "taking the census for the rancho." She proceeded to tell me that I should conduct one, because all the students who had come to do their social service had made it the practice to take the census, and it had been several years since the ejido had had its last census, and they did not know how many inhabitants the town now had.

This was how I started my fieldwork in the community, not by doing participant observation, nor by establishing rapport as I had planned in my thesis proposal, but by administering a questionnaire. Nevertheless, administering that questionnaire at the start of my stay in El Cerro was the best thing I could have done. It gave me the opportunity to visit and interview the people in each of the homes in the community, to see their houses, to gain entrée, and to know them personally. Completing each questionnaire took no longer than half an hour. However, when people finished filling it out, they would continue to talk with me for two or three more hours. They talked about the problems in the community, conflict over lands, fishing, their relatives, and their lives.

By the time I finished administering the questionnaire in all the homes, my impression of El Cerro had changed. That thick calm that covered the surface of the lives of the people was, in reality, like an onion. When I had taken off the top layer of skin and thought I had it all figured out, another layer appeared, one even more complicated, and which I had to decipher. Chico, Trini, and their family helped me largely to understand each layer that I peeled off that onion.

The last day of my fieldwork in the community, I went to their house to say goodbye and thank them for all the help they had given me. As soon as Chico saw me, the first words out of his mouth were, "Girl, I almost died!" A few days earlier, the truck in which he had been traveling with other members of the aquaculture cooperative flipped over, and now he was in terrible pain. Two years later, when I returned to El Cerro to carry out most of the fieldwork on which this book is based, he had, indeed, died. The first to tell me the news of his death was Rosa, a neighbor who, as soon as she saw me pass in front of her house, remembered and greeted me. Later that day, when I visited Trini, she told me the details of Chico's death. "Since that accident, Chico was never the same," adding "Chico died here in the house, in my arms. He died tranquilly, no scolding everything and being against everyone, as he had been during his life. He never wanted to go to see the doctors for fear that they would open him up and take his organs for the medical students to study." His death certificate, which Trini showed me, listed the cause as generalized pulmonary tuberculosis. The death certificate said that he died on February 20, 1991. He was seventy-five years of age.

To honor the work that Chico accomplished in founding El Cerro, the community decided to name the building where the ejidatarios meet after him. Nine months after Chico's death, on November 7, 1991, the president of Mexico, Carlos Salinas de Gortari, announced his intention to reform the country's agrarian legal framework by the promulgation of a new text amending Article 27 of the Mexican Constitution (Cornelius and Myhre 1998). In some ways, Chico's life encompassed the beginning and the end of an important historical stage in Sinaloa, the agrarista era. Chico died one year before the neoliberal policies of the Salinas administration radically altered the agrarista ideals for which he had fought. He died without seeing how the neoliberal policies would affect the community that he had worked so hard to help create and preserve.

A principal thesis of this book is that natural resources in southern Sinaloa are the principal base on which a rural population supports itself. Another argument is that the use and exploitation of these resources have engendered a series of social conflicts over a long period. In previous chapters, I discussed how these conflicts have played out at regional and municipal levels, and in the following section I will show how these also occur at the local level. The family of Chico and Trini illustrate this point. Since El Cerro formed as a community, down to the death of Chico, events were unleashed that are related to, on one hand, agrarian struggles and, on the other, local conflicts within the community and the family. These events are interwoven with the history of the founding of El Cerro as a community.

Of Love and Land: An Ethnohistory of El Cerro

Trini and Chico were married for forty-five years. They met when she was barely a teenager, only fourteen years of age. When she saw him for the first time in a ranchito in Nayarit, Chico was twenty-eight years old. Although he was already married with two children, and was twice her age, she fell hopelessly in love.

Shortly before Trini met Chico, her father, who worked as a day laborer on a farm in Agua Verde, decided to return to Nayarit, and he took his family with him. Then, only a few months after Trini had met Chico, her father's employer sent people to find him and persuade him to come back to work with them in Agua Verde. Trini did not want to go, and she secretly sent a letter to Chico, asking him to please come get her and take her with him. The messenger with whom she sent the letter could not find Chico because, that very day, he had left for the hills to work cutting wood. Saddened and dejected, Trini was forced to go back to Agua Verde with her parents.

From Agua Verde, Trini wrote Chico letters, which she sent with a woman who went each weekend to visit her relatives in Nayarit. The letters that Chico sent back to her were not exactly the love letters that she had anticipated. Instead, they were dry and unemotional, which didn't make much sense to her. In time, Trini discovered that her letters to Chico had never been delivered, and that the letters he supposedly wrote in return were secretly written by the woman's brother. Trini lost all hope of ever seeing Chico again. She resigned herself to destiny and married another man with whom she had two children.

A few years later, her parents decided to return to live in Nayarit, and Trini left her husband, took her children, and went with them. Life there was not easy. With her two small children to support, she had to do whatever kind of work she could find. She began selling *bolis* (flavored ice) and *pozole* (stew made with hominy, beef, or pork) from the house that she shared with her parents. Next, she washed and ironed clothes for people; at times, she worked as a cook in homes of wealthy families. Washing and ironing until her nails wore away made it possible to support her children. Washing and ironing was also how she came to see Chico once again.

Chico, whose wife had died several years before, now lived alone with his two children. Because he had no one to wash and iron for them, he paid Trini to do it. One day, he and Trini suddenly decided to get married. He asked permission from her parents, and they accepted. The couple lived for a time in Nayarit until Trini suggested that they visit Agua Verde, where her aunt still lived. She and Chico stayed for a month, living with the aunt, and Chico liked Agua Verde so much that he did not want to return to Nayarit. They stayed on, in a house of palm leaves that Chico built.

While they lived in Agua Verde, at the beginning of the 1960s, the agrarian struggles in Sinaloa had reemerged, and the conflicts over land were frequent and intense. The ideals of agrarianism and the clamor for land once again echoed into even the remotest corners of Sinaloa. Landowners protected their fields, and campesinos demanded that the state give them land to organize ejidos.

To survive, Chico and another group of men who lived in Agua Verde but were not ejidatarios rented small parcels of land to cultivate that were part of a private property. The owner was a woman from Rosario, who is remembered today for only two things: Her last name was Senaide, and she had gunmen who killed people. Because the farmers didn't have money, they paid the woman's foreman, Maximiliano, with a sack of corn from each harvest. However, the foreman never gave the corn to the woman, so she believed that they were not paying her, and she decided to take back the parcels. Chico and the others went to Rosario, to the woman's house, to talk personally with her. They explained that they had given the corn to the foreman, and they didn't know why she hadn't received it. She didn't believe them, and she threw them out of her house, insulting them and saying they were a "pack of rats and lazy men." When they left the woman's house, they went to talk to the director of the Agrarian Reform Office ejido in Rosario, and they asked his advice, because they needed the land to survive. The director explained that the only option they had was to organize an ejido on the land that belonged to Señora Senaide, and he urged them to unite to petition for it.

Upon returning from Rosario, they called a meeting in Agua Verde to begin the paperwork to apply for the lands. Chico recounted this process of organizing the future members of the ejido in his own words:

> One day, I said to a man from Agua Verde, to Salomé Figueroa, "Let's do something; let's put in an application to the government to ask that they give us land, because we want to work for ourselves." It was dangerous because they were wealthy people. In those times, they killed anybody who wanted to start an ejido. I was beginning to get scared, but I didn't let them frighten me. Hunger makes one think things. Then, because I knew that I wasn't going to spend the rest of my life living like a peon, I said, "Well, even if they kill me, I'm going to do it." At night, I went out and rounded up the men, and I asked them, "Hey, you there, do you want to join this ejido group?" Some answered that they didn't, because they didn't want to end up shot dead. But I continued, until I had gotten together 116 men.

Chico rallied together the men, and they began the formal paperwork to organize the ejido. On April 15, 1967, they went to Culiacán to submit the official application for the lands that Senaide had claimed as her own (Gobierno del Estado de Sinaloa 1968). Leopoldo Sánchez Celis, the governor of Sinaloa at that time, supported them and approved the ejido provisionally. On May 27, 1967, the official newspaper of the state of Sinaloa notified all the landowners who would be affected by the formation of the ejido, and on June 23, the first general and agricultural census was conducted in El Cerro. Thus, the long and slow process of requesting and legally receiving the land finally ended.

The ejido of El Cerro was officially constituted with 346 inhabitants, of which 116 men were transformed from peones into ejidatarios (Gobierno del Estado de Sinaloa 1968). Finally, on March 23, 1968, the official newspaper of the state government publicly announced the state's official approval of the formation of El Cerro as an ejido. That announcement included the names of the 116 ejidatarios who formed the ejido, the details of the official grant, and how the land would be distributed.[1]

With the ejido legally approved, Chico and the other ejidatarios now had the task of measuring and distributing the parcels. Using hatchets and machetes, they also had to clear the hillsides for space to build houses and sow their crops. They built their mud houses hastily, with roofs made of palm leaves, but they had no electricity or running water. Within a few months, the presidente municipal sent them a teacher to start a rural school and begin educating the children. The ejido's first board of directors consisted of a president, a man named Valentín, and a treasurer, Chico.

Despite the approval for the formation of the ejido and the official government opinion that no one owned the land where it was to be established, Senaide continued claiming the property. Her gunmen watched the ejidatarios day and night until, one day, the ejidatarios decided to confront them. Having hidden their own weapons in their knapsacks, bags, and hats, they demanded to know why the gunmen were watching them and what they wanted. Even though it was not the truth, the gunmen answered that they represented Senaide, and they wanted to make "an arrangement" with Valentín. The gunmen explained that Senaide had nothing against them, and she had decided to let them work in peace. The ejidatarios, incredulous, answered that they thought that Senaide had sent the gunmen to kill them. The gunmen answered by saying that the ejidatarios shouldn't believe "those stories," because they weren't going to harm them. Chico and Valentín thanked them for their good "intentions," and they all shook hands in a sign of peace and said goodbye, but it was apparent that they were not rid of that gang.

Two years later, in 1970, an ejidatario of El Cerro turned up dead. Someone had killed him with a pistol. Even though the reasons and circumstances for his death were never entirely clarified, El Cerro's *comisario* (commissary) was blamed. Knowing that the community blamed him for the death and that Senaide's gunmen were watching him, he decided to leave town and went to live in another state. Chico and the other ejidatarios, even though the gunmen continued to watch them, did not want to give up the ejido in light of all the work they had invested in organizing it. They stayed on, and with great efforts and sacrifices, they built and formed a community.

Trini and Chico lived together in El Cerro for twenty-four years, until the day he died. Here were born eight of their children and most of their grandchildren. Trini's parents and brothers and sisters also came to live in El Cerro.

When I went to see Trini at her home during my return to El Cerro and she told me the details of Chico's death, I noted that she had changed somewhat. She was sixty-three years old, but she did not look it. She seemed younger and more relaxed, but also very thoughtful. I found her sitting in her rocking chair, on the balcony of her house, with her gaze lost in the hills that surround the ranchito. It was the beginning of the rainy season, and El Cerro was transforming its appearance from a lugubrious and gray ranchito into a happier and more animated place, decorated with the green leaves of the trees that grow on the hills and the fuchsia bougainvillea that adorn the houses. Trini, dressed in a long flowered skirt and huaraches, with her long hair showing only a few white hairs, her rosary hanging at her neck, remained a moment looking fixedly at the hills. When she came out of her rapture, she said to me, "The hills are blooming. First, the yellow flowers come out, and then the white ones, and the last to bloom are the pink ones." I asked her, "How do you know that the flowers come out in that order?" She answered, very seriously, "Every year it is the same. Always around this time, the hills begin to bloom. That is the signal God sends us so that we know that he is always thinking of this ranchito and of us, the poor people who live in it. Besides, for many years, I have been watching how the hills change. Ever since we came to live here, around this rainy season, I'm in the habit of sitting here to contemplate the hills. I see them change from dry and bald, as if they were dead during the dry season, to a green jungle during the rains."

Then she looked at me, smiled, and said, "Mariluz, I have something to tell you." "What?" I asked her. "I'm in love," she responded. "With whom?" I asked her incredulously. She did not answer. She got up quickly from the rocker, and she said, "I'll be right back."

When she returned, she had something with her, which she held tightly in her hands. It was a piece of paper, carefully folded over. She sat again in her rocker, looked me in the eyes, and asked, "Do you want to see him?" "Who?" I asked her. "Well, the man," she answered. She didn't even wait for me to respond. Trini, looking around as if she wanted to be certain that no one saw her, opened the palm of her hand, and she began to unfold the piece of paper. Hidden within it were two 2" x 4" black-and-white photographs, which she jealously guarded.

Trini's new love, Efrén, was ten years younger than she, and he was a *curandero* (native healer) by profession. He arrived in El Cerro suddenly one day, during the rainy season, with the idea of joining one of Agua Verde's fishing cooperatives. In the small town in Nayarit where he had lived, he had heard that the shrimp fishing in the Caimanero Lagoon has always been excellent and one could make good money that way. One day, he just got up and left Nayarit and came to live in El Cerro, which has a fishing cooperative with a fishing ground on the Caimanero Lagoon. No one in El Cerro knows the details of how Efrén came to stay in El Cerro or how he ended up living in Trini's house. What is a known fact is that when Efrén arrived in El Cerro, Chico was already very ill. He had lost all hope that the doctors would cure him, but when he heard that a curandero had come to the ranchito, he asked Trini to go find the man to see if he could save him. The curandero was Chico's last hope.

Efrén brought all his equipment, his herbal medicines, and his cards for reading the future, and moved into Chico and Trini's house. From the moment that he arrived, he started trying to cure Chico. However, Chico showed no signs of getting better. A few months later, he died. The people of El Cerro still comment that "instead of curing him, the curandero killed him dead." Many say that, from the beginning, Efrén saw an opportunity to get his hands on Chico's lands and his wife, and that was why he must have given him a potion to make him die quicker. The fact that even after Chico died Trini continued living alone in the house with Efrén reinforced this rumor.

Trini's children also resented that their mother continued to live with Efrén. They got so angry about it that they stopped visiting her, and some would not even speak to her. For her children, a strange man, who had just appeared in the ranchito, wanting to take the place of their deceased father was bothersome. But what most bothered and hurt Trini's children was that Efrén was living in their father's house, which he had built with his own hands. They believed that if it was true that Efrén loved their mother, he had an obligation to build another house, where the couple could live and start a new life together.

The situation between Trini and her children was so tense that she and Efrén decided to move to Nayarit. He went first, and she followed him. Trini returned occasionally to look after her lands and house, but she always quickly returned to Nayarit. This went on for several years until she finally returned to El Cerro to live. A few months afterward, Efrén joined her, so they were living together once again in Chico's house, and the children continued to disapprove.

When Trini and Efrén began living together in 1994, the reform of Article 27 of the Mexican Constitution had already been promulgated. The revision of the law brought to a close the era of agrarian distribution. One of the principal components of this reform was the privatization of the ejido sector. This amendment meant that land, which had once been held communally, was legally deeded to individual ejidatarios through the Programa de Certificación de Derechos Ejidales y Titulación de Solares Urbanos (Program for the Certification of Ejido Land Rights and the Titling of Urban House Plots, or PROCEDE). The goal of this program was to deliver the title of the land to ejidatarios, which would make it possible for them to rent the land, sell it, or use it as collateral for loans.

Participation in PROCEDE was voluntary, and the ejidos had to hold several assemblies to decide if the majority of ejidatarios were willing to join the program. The people of El Cerro remember in the beginning of the program when the land surveyors came for the first time to measure the land and give the maps for the ejidatarios' parcels to each of them. In El Cerro, uncertainty and their lack of knowledge about the program's concrete objectives influenced the response of the ejidatarios at the start of PROCEDE. Many ejidatarios doubted that the program would benefit them in any way. Some, especially those who were involved in the initial struggle to acquire the land, believed that the reform of Article 27 was a way of motivating them to sell their lands. They reasoned that if this were true, then the land would return to the control of the latifundistas because they were the only people with enough money to buy large tracts of land. Some believed that it was ironic, after all the sacrifices that they had made to obtain their land, that they were now being encouraged to sell it. Others thought that once they had the title to the land, it would make it much easier to sell or rent a part of the parcel in order to provide for the needs of the household. By 1997, 95 percent of the ejidatarios of El Cerro had received the titles to their lands.

Even though most of the ejidatarios have the deeds to their property, Trini found herself among the small number who, even as late as 1999, have been unable to acquire titles. Her situation is odd because it is influenced by the fact that Chico died without a legally valid will. It seems that the directors of the ejido took advantage of Chico's failure to designate an heir, and they dropped him from the ejido. The only will that he left was a letter written by hand eight months before he passed away.[2]

Even though Trini showed this letter to the board of directors, they ignored her. The letter was only an informal document, because the Agrarian Reform Bureau in Culiacán did not have any document showing that Trini was legally the heir of the lands belonging to Chico. When the children learned that their father had left the land to Trini, the fact that she was living with the curandero was even more upsetting to them. According to Trini, Chico decided to leave everything to her because there were so many children, and he could not divide the lands among them because each would have received a piece so small it would have been useless. He also did not want to leave the lands to some of them, but not to others, because this would have led to conflicts among them. He left the land to Trini, on the condition that she would decide if the two younger sons truly needed parcels, which she would then give to them. Trini wanted to wait to see which of her children would help her to farm the land so that she could give those parcels to the ones who did. All her sons, except the two youngest, already had their own land, and they devoted all their time to tending and planting it. The two youngest sons, both married with children, were fishermen and day laborers, but they helped their mother when they could. Trini and Chico's daughters did not inherit their father's land. As is the custom in El Cerro, the daughters inherit only when there are no sons in the family. The daughters thought that this was very unjust because many of them had also helped their father work the land, and they believed that it was their right to inherit something, even if it were only a piece for a household vegetable garden.

Trini demanded her rights as a widow to inherit the lands belonging to her deceased husband, and she began to attend the meetings that the ejido held. At the time of Chico's death, she became an ejidataria and, as such, she had the obligation to attend to matters relating to the management of those lands as well as to issues relating to the organization and functioning of the ejido. Initially, she made every effort that she could to comply formally with her duties. Nevertheless, it was not an easy thing because the ejido consisted, for the most part, of men who did not take ejidatarias very seriously. Aside from Trini, there were only nine other ejidatarias, all of whom had inherited the titles to the land from their deceased husbands. Attending the meetings also took away from the time that she spent doing housework and looking after Efrén. She stopped attending the meetings and sent one of her younger children instead.

Her situation was made more complicated because Efrén did not have a steady job. His reputation as a curandero in El Cerro was dubious; people had lost a lot of confidence in him when Chico died. Efrén's few clients came only occasionally, from other communities far from El Cerro, and many stayed to live with Trini during the time that Efrén was treating them, which could take from a few days to a few weeks. This meant that the household expenses increased because Trini had to make sure there was enough not only for her and Efrén to eat but also for the patients.

Efrén worked on and off as an independent fisherman during the shrimp fishing season. Sometimes he also worked as a day laborer, cutting chilies and broomcorn. His participation in these activities was sporadic, however, and the little bit of money that he earned did not cover household expenses. All the responsibility of maintaining the household fell on the shoulders of doña Trini, who planted the corn and beans each summer, applied for loans from Programa Nacional de Solidaridad (National Solidarity Program, or PRONASOL) to buy seeds and fertilizers, and scraped together money to buy flour to make the tortillas each day and to buy others things that a household requires.

Seeing that their economic situation was not getting better, Efrén proposed to Trini that she sell part of her property and give him a portion of the profits to buy a membership in one of the area's fishing cooperatives. Trini tried to sell a piece of the land, but no one in El Cerro wanted to buy it because they felt that Chico had struggled and sacrificed to get this property, so she was not entitled to sell it. Efrén then suggested that she sell the house, and she accepted on the condition that her children also agree that she should do so. In exchange for their permission, she would divide part of the profits among all of them. The children refused because they knew that some of the money would go to Efrén. However, the asthma from which she had suffered for many years had recently gotten worse, and she needed to go frequently to the doctor and to buy the medicines that he prescribed. Finally, because she needed the money to treat her illness, the children agreed to let Trini sell a small piece of the land. She sold it to her own daughter, and so the property stayed in the family.

Despite her illness, Trini still had to look after the house and maintain Efrén. This situation bothered her children so much that they asked Trini to live with one of them so that they could give her the care she needed. Several months later, her illness worsened so much that Efrén finally agreed to leave, but not before asking Trini's children if they would give him the money to buy his bus ticket back to Nayarit. The children, who wanted him to go once and for all and to leave their mother in peace, gave him the money, and one of the daughters took Trini in to live with her. Her youngest children finished the paperwork for the transfer of the land, which was finally awarded to her in 1999.

The history of El Cerro, from its founding as an ejido and a community up until today, is marred with social struggles and local conflicts over control of natural resources. Without doubt, land is one of the natural resources that have always been the focus of these struggles and conflicts. However, the struggle for land is only one of the many battles that people in El Cerro have had to face since the time when the first families founded the community. Another is that which they must fight daily as they try to survive in an ecological context marked by aridity, low levels of land productivity, a short rainy season, scant economic alternatives, and a declining natural resource base.

The Ecology of El Cerro

The impression that one forms of El Cerro is influenced largely by the two climatic periods that characterize southern Sinaloa: the dry season and the rainy season. If one visits the community for the first time during the dry season, or *la seca*, as the people call it, one cannot avoid posing the question: How is it possible for a human community to exist in this place? During this season, the dust and the heat, the lack of vegetation, and the grayness of the hills are the most noticeable characteristics of the countryside that surrounds El Cerro. At first glance, the dryness of the land in this season makes it unimaginable that anything could ever grow here. During the dry season, which lasts between November and June, the main concern of the people has always been having enough water stored up to satisfy the demands of the households and the needs of the animals.

It is not a coincidence that the community is named El Cerro because it is located literally on the top of a hill. Because of the community's elevation and the topographic characteristics of the area, the groundwater level is very deep. That is why El Cerro has no wells. The first time that I did fieldwork in the community, in 1989, potable water was not yet available in any of the homes. At that time, this was a principal complaint of the residents. Water had to be transported in containers from Agua Verde, and twice a week, the presidente municipal sent a truck from Rosario to deliver water. In some cases, women had to haul water from a channel that bordered the community and connected the Río Baluarte with the marshes, where a shrimp farm had been built. Several families collected water during the rainy season and stored it in containers to use during the dry season. The women of the town also washed their clothes in the channel, and everyone in the community had to bathe in it.

Because most of the responsibility for collecting and transporting water for home use fell to the women, a group of them organized in 1989 to seek a solution to the lack of potable water. This group of women, led by Lupe, attended the meetings of the ejidatarios to explain their concerns about the lack of water. The meetings, which at that time were held in one of the schoolrooms, always ended up being interesting events. The ejidatarios all sat inside the schoolroom, while the women stood outside. Nevertheless, as soon as the ejidatarios took up the water issue, the women, standing in the doorways or with their heads sticking through the windows, voiced their complaints and concerns. Lupe and this group of women collected signatures in the community and took the list to the presidencia municipal to prove to the municipal authorities that the lack of water presented a huge need. On several occasions, they also invited the legislative representatives from the municipio to visit so that they could ascertain for themselves the impact that the lack of potable water had on the community.

When I returned to El Cerro in 1993, it had drinking water. I could not be certain if this was due to the campaign that the women had carried out or because of a cholera outbreak, which occurred in the community in 1991. It may have been a combination of both factors. What is clear is that, beginning then, people were able to bathe in their homes, and the women no longer had to haul water from the river. The water reached El Cerro through a system of pipes, from a dam built in Agua Verde.

Even though most of the agriculture practiced is seasonal, that is, planting occurs during the rainy season, several homes cultivate corn and beans during the dry season. These households require a constant flow of water to irrigate their crops. A system of pumps built by the household members connected to the channel transports the water to the fields.

When one sees El Cerro during the rainy season, the image that one forms of it is entirely different from the impression one gets during the dry season, the so-called *tiempo triste*. During the rainy season, the ejido transforms into a small jungle. The shrubs and vegetation adorning the hills seem to resuscitate from a long lethargy, to offer the ranchito a renewed sense of life, and the town fills with joy and fresh hope. Even the spirits of the people seem to change when the rainy season begins. The careworn, exhausted, and worried faces that people wear throughout the dry season suddenly become smiling and relaxed. Around the beginning of June, the people begin to predict the exact arrival date for the rains.

People recognize the extreme importance that the rain has for agriculture and fishing. Based on the quantity of precipitation, they predict whether the fishing and the crops will be abundant. When the first rains fall, people quickly focus on preparing themselves for the new agricultural and fishing seasons. A typical scene at this time of year is represented by fishermen seated in the patios of their houses, repairing or making fishing nets to use in the harvesting of shrimp. The farmers, for their part, begin to clean their fields and mend their fences.

During the dry season, the scarcity of water is the most pressing problem, but during the rainy season, the abundance of water also poses a problem. When there is a high level of precipitation, or when it rains consecutively for many days, water saturates the land, turning El Cerro into a bog. Because the streets are unpaved, huge pools of water and mud form, making them impassable. The roads that lead to the fields, and even the fields themselves, turn into large bogs, which forces the ejidatarios to stop working the land in order to give the soil a little time to dry out. The quantity of rain also reduces the levels of salinity in the lagoons and estuaries, which affects the migratory cycle of the shrimp, with major repercussions for fishing.

Besides water, land continues to be one of the natural resources that residents are most concerned about. At the founding of the ejido, all available land was distributed among the first families that established the community. As the land parcels were being officially awarded, no one considered the long-term population growth of the ejido. This population growth results from two primary factors. The first is the natural growth of the original population that founded the ejido, that is, the children and grandchildren of the first ejidatarios and their families. The second factor is the periodic immigration of people from other parts of Sinaloa or from other states within Mexico. Both factors have greatly contributed to increasing the pressure on the small amount of available land. The demand for land has grown as the new generations establish their households. Many young couples are forced to live with their parents, while others must build their homes on their parents' lots.

The ejidatarios recognized that land is scarce and, in the face of that scarcity and the need to expand the community, they petitioned the mayor of Rosario to enlarge the ejido. The petition was denied. In 1991, a group of residents, among them the children of ejidatarios, invaded part of a mango farm that belonged to a private-property owner from the town of

Rosario. The fields of the farm lay right on the edge of the ejido and constituted the only land that was appropriate for building houses in the area that surrounds El Cerro. It was flat land that did not require clearing, and it provided a natural geographic continuity with the community. After the people invaded the land, the owner agreed to sell them the lots where they had built their houses, and they paid him on credit. Several non-ejidatarios also took advantage of the opportunity to acquire land to build new houses.

Fields or cultivable plots are also in short supply. The people who came to live in the community after it formed as an ejido did not manage to get land to farm. Because of the high cost of land, very few non-ejidatarios have been able to acquire their own parcels. Others think that it is not worthwhile to buy farmland in El Cerro because it is of poor quality and requires a high level of input to make it productive.

In addition to farm fields or smallholdings, and the land for housing, a third kind of land in El Cerro is *agostadero,* or summer pasture for cattle grazing. El Cerro has two summer grazing areas that were incorporated into the original endowment. The grazing lands, like the community's other natural resources, must be used communally, shared among the ejidatarios. Nevertheless, because only a few have cattle, the lands were often invaded by cattlemen from other communities, who brought their livestock to graze in the pastures without the ejido's permission. After 1992, and because of the new agrarian law, the government transferred to the ejidal assembly full rights to manage its lands. This new state policy has allowed the ejidatarios to rent part of the pasturelands to private ranchers who are not members of El Cerro. It has also encouraged several ejidatarios, whose lands are not productive enough to raise corn or beans, to sow feed grains. By converting that land into pasture, they can also rent to ranchers from nearby communities. The pasturelands are rented during the rainy season, at a price that fluctuates between one hundred and three hundred dollars per season.

The last type of land found in the ejido is the marshland. This is the damp area located on the outskirts of the ejido at the edge of the Huizache-Caimanero Lagoon Complex. These salt-laden and swampy lands were unusable just a short time ago. In the mid-1980s, with the development of the government-sponsored Shrimp Aquaculture Program, this area gained tremendous commercial value. In the 1980s, these lands also belonged to the state, and thus they could not be sold or rented. Then, in the mid-1990s, the neoliberal policies and agrarian reforms made it possible to rent or sell land for aquaculture projects, and the assembly rented a portion of its marshes to a private company. That company is entirely responsible for operating and managing the shrimp farm, and the ejidatarios do not play any direct role in decision making. In exchange, the company pays rent annually to the assembly.

Apart from land, El Cerro has few natural resources that are of any use to its residents. There are no large forested areas because the ecological characteristics of the region are not propitious for the growth and development of woodlands. There are, nevertheless, patches of land within the ejido where valuable lumber trees grow. The ejido assembly is responsible for regulating the harvesting of timber, and members who want to cut wood to build homes must request permission to do so. The assembly has designated an ejidatario to be in charge of regulating the cutting of the trees. Nevertheless, this is not always done consistently.

Even though it is illegal to cut timber to sell, lumber poachers occasionally encroach on El Cerro. When this has happened, it has frequently been because someone, almost always from another community, has bribed the person in charge of monitoring the use of the trees. Men from other communities have also entered the ejido, usually at night, to cut the trees and take the wood without permission. The ejidatarios do not get wind of these activities until they take a tour around their parcels, and when that happens, it is usually too late to catch the culprits.

A stone quarry, located at the end of its main street, is another natural resource that El Cerro counts among its assets. People use the rock to construct houses and as filler in the community's streets. People from other communities also buy the rock. The presidente de vigilancia of the ejido assembly is usually responsible for monitoring and regulating the extraction of rock from the quarry. Even though the profits supposedly go to the community chest, in reality few people benefit.

Ironically, the community's most important asset, the resources offered by fishing, does not lie within the geographic boundaries of the community but, instead, is spread throughout the nearby lagoons and estuaries. For the residents of El Cerro, most fishing-related activity occurs in the Huizache-Caimanero Lagoon Complex because it is so close by. However, the people must share the right to exploit this ecosystem with the residents of other communities that neighbor the Huizache-Caimanero Lagoon.

Conclusion

Political ecology, as a theoretical approach, places special emphasis on local and regional history. Specifically, it uses history to shed light on the various processes that, over time, contribute to shaping how people access and use natural resources within a particular setting. The history of the rise of El Cerro as an ejido and community—as is true for most of the ejidos in southern Sinaloa—is directly connected to a series of political and social struggles. The demand for land has always been at the heart of this conflict. However, the end of the agrarian struggle in southern Sinaloa in no way represents the achievement of a utopia for the people of El Cerro. Not even the neoliberal policies and the reform to the agrarian legal framework can offer a happy ending to the history of struggles, conflicts, and uncertainty that characterizes the daily lives of the residents of this community. As the case of the family of Trini and Chico illustrates, these struggles, conflicts, and uncertainties continue at the local level, thus marking the daily rhythms of the people of El Cerro.

To understand the origin of these conflicts, we must ask ourselves an important question: Who really controls the natural resources of the community? As we have seen in this chapter, three principal sectors exercise different levels of control over the natural resources of El Cerro: the state, the ejidatarios, and other communities in the area. State control manifests itself mostly through management and development policies for natural resources. The control that other communities exercise is determined, in many cases, by the relationships that have developed between individuals from El Cerro and individuals in those other communities. In other cases, it is determined simply by the risk that certain individuals take in coming to poach the natural resources that belong to the people of El Cerro. And the control that ejidatarios exercise? It relates directly to the structure and organization of the ejido.

4

On Top of a Hill

The Structure and Organization of a Mexican Ejido

> Life is calm. One who doesn't work, doesn't eat. In the mango and
> chili season, there is lots of work. One isn't accustomed to luxuries
> or conveniences. The land doesn't grow enough these days to live
> off. It is hard to build a house. People earn very little, just enough to
> eat.
>
> —María Félix, 1995 (my translation)

When I met Patricio Morales in 1989, he, like most of the ejidatarios of El
Cerro, divided his time between farming his parcel and fishing. Patricio
was the president of El Cerro's fishing cooperative, and three years earlier
he had served as president of the ejido's Surveillance Committee. Catching shrimp provided him with an income that was much greater than what
he made selling corn and beans that he grew on his land, and it was through
his work as a fisherman that he saved money to build his house. When I
saw him again in 1993, he had stopped fishing, even though he continued
to be a member of the cooperative. Instead, he had sown pasture and transformed his parcel into summer grazing lands, which he rented to cattlemen from other communities. Finally, in 1999, he stopped being a
fisherman and a farmer to become a taxi driver. With the money that he
had saved from his fishing income, he bought an *auriga* to transport people
between Agua Verde and Rosario. When I asked him why he had become a
taxi driver, he answered that neither farming nor fishing was producing
enough money to maintain his family. Moreover, he was thinking about
his children's future. Patricio wanted to give them an education so that
their lives would not be as difficult and filled with hard work as his own
life had been.

Like Patricio, life for most people in El Cerro is very difficult, and like the main street, it is incomplete, twisted, and full of rocks and puddles. In this community, economic impoverishment has intensified over time, and therefore, households must daily seek out immediate solutions to combat this uncertainty. Indeed the economic uncertainty that permeates the daily lives of El Cerro's residents is a theme that stands out in my interviews and conversations each time I return to conduct fieldwork in the community.

This uncertainty is clearly reflected in the residents' ongoing preoccupation with subsisting, day to day, without being able to count on permanent employment or knowing whether the rainy season will be good. It is also reflected in the lack of adequate information that would allow them to know for certain if the government loans will arrive in time to buy the seeds and fertilizer needed to make the land, eroded and unfertile after so much use over a long period, productive. In other cases, people's perception about the deterioration of ecological conditions in the Caimanero Lagoon and the decline in shrimp production also produces uncertainty because it is always doubtful that the next fishing season will be better than the previous one. Throughout the community, the lack of disclosure and explanation about the potential real effects of various policies and programs the government implements is another area filled with uncertainty.

This constant uncertainty with which the residents of El Cerro live might not seem surprising until one analyzes and understands in detail the local history of El Cerro's origin as an ejido and community. As the previous chapter illustrates, an important fact that we can infer from this history is that the community was founded precisely to combat economic uncertainty in the lives of the first families that came to live here. That shared uncertainty resulted in a community whose structure and organization are influenced by aspects such as the community's relationship to the government, the social relations among its members, the organization of local institutions, the relationship of its members with other communities, and the variation in the levels of access that the residents of the community or the members of the household have to available natural resources. This chapter presents a physical, demographic, political, economic, and social profile of the community of El Cerro.

Community Settlement and Formation

When one asks someone what motivated them to come to live in El Cerro, the most frequent response is that they came in search of better economic and social opportunities. For many families, such as that of Chico and Trini, El Cerro was one more step in the migratory process that began in the state of Nayarit. For some, El Cerro was the last step in this process, but for others, that process has begun again. The first inhabitants of El Cerro came from various places, including communities within the municipio of Rosario, other municipios in Sinaloa, or from other Mexican states. The organization of ejidos, such as El Cerro, created geographic spaces within which a group of people united, even though they often lacked any kinship whatsoever. These people, coming from different communities and regions in the country, shared a common goal of getting their own piece of land to farm and, thereby, improving the quality of their lives. Many, such as Trini and Chico, migrated first to Agua Verde, the community closest to El Cerro.

The case of another family, that of Manuel and his wife, Rita, also illustrates this migratory process and the way in which El Cerro was settled. Manuel was born in El Verde, a rancho in the municipio of Concordia. His father, a farmer, bought a piece of land in another rancho called El Chapote, also located in Concordia, and he took his family to live there. Manuel grew up in El Chapote, where he and Rita subsequently met, married, and raised seven children. Manuel worked as a peon, tending cattle and planting corn on the property belonging to a man from El Chapote. Even though their lives were peaceful enough, Manuel was worried about educating his children because there were no schools in El Chapote. One day, he said to his wife, "Rita, I think that we are going to have to leave here. There is no school for the children. You don't know anything, and me and the children, we know even less! We are all going to end up being just a bunch of donkeys. Let's go live some place that has a school."

When Semana Santa (Holy Week vacation) arrived, Manuel went to Rosario to visit a friend with whom he had grown up in El Chapote. His friend offered to lend him money for a pair of mules so that he could grow corn on his friend's lands during the rainy season, but he put as a condition that they divide the harvest fifty-fifty. The friend's lands were located in a rancho in the municipio of Rosario. Even though Manuel did not like the idea of continuing to work for someone else, he decided to accept the proposition because he thought that this would be a good place for his family to live. This arrangement did not last long, because the soil was infertile and produced very little. Farming this land required a lot of work, and don Manuel needed to earn money to maintain his family.

On the returning bus to El Chapote, Manuel met a man, José, who turned out to be a friend of one of his relatives from El Verde. José told Manuel that he would recommend him to his son, who happened to have lands in Agua Verde. One Sunday, on a trip Manuel made to El Verde's market to buy food, he met a man who told him that José's son would give him a job as a peon, planting his fields, and that he would send someone to help move the family to Agua Verde. Manuel went home and told Rita what had happened. They packed up their belongings, put the things on the backs of three mules, and, at midday, the employees of the son of José came to pick them up.

In Agua Verde, Manuel and his family lived during the dry season in a small house that belonged to José. This was a crude structure made of mud, and because it did not even have a roof, at night, they could see the stars. With the first drops of rain during the rainy season, the house flooded and Manuel asked José to help him find another house. José got them a house made of concrete, with a thatched roof.

Because his salary as a peon was not sufficient to support the family, Manuel became a pescador libre. However, because he was not a fisherman, he first had to learn how to fish. He bought a net and went to the river to practice. Afterwards, he began shrimp fishing in the Caimanero Lagoon, selling his catch to the only local fishing cooperative (Alvaro Obregón). The cooperative paid him very little money, and he began selling the shrimp to a *changuero* (shrimp smuggler). Manuel had to sell the shrimp behind the back of the cooperative because if the members found out, they would never again buy shrimp from him and they would not let him fish in the lagoon. To conceal what he was doing, Manuel sold half of the shrimp to the changuero and the other half to the cooperative. In this way, he was able to save up enough money so that when he and his family moved to El Cerro, they could build their first house.

Being a peon and a pescador libre, without having anything to call his own, were the two conditions that motivated Manuel and the other ejidatarios of El Cerro to organize and to fight for lands on which to establish an ejido. When the state legally granted them the land and approved the founding of the ejido, they were transformed into campesinos. The state supported them, granting them legitimacy as authentic campesinos and ejidatarios.

Once they settled in El Cerro and began to work their fields, it was not long before they realized that the lands for which they had fought and sacrificed had very poor quality soil. Making them productive would require capital and a lot of hard work. The government, through loans and credits, gave them the capital needed to purchase seeds, fertilizer, and tractors. Nevertheless, due to the aridity and lack of irrigation systems, the farmers could plant their fields only during the rainy season. The most that the ejidatarios could expect were two harvests of corn and beans per year, and the yield was destined primarily to satisfy the alimentary needs of household members. Once again, the ejidatarios turned their attention to catching shrimp. They again became pescadores libres, and they continued selling their output to the Alvaro Obregón fishing cooperative.

Understanding that their status as pescadores libres was not particularly favorable to them, and motivated by the commercial importance of shrimp and the Caimanero Lagoon's tremendous productivity, the ejidatarios decided to unite once again, this time to organize their own fishing cooperative. At the outset, the fight was uphill, because the Alvaro Obregón cooperative would not let them organize, and they lacked government support. Finally, in 1975, the government intervened with the formulation of a law that allowed ejidos whose lands were adjacent to lagoons or estuaries to organize cooperatives. The ejidatarios of El Cerro could now legally register their cooperative, transforming themselves from pescadores libres into pescadores auténticos, with the help of the government, which again granted them legitimacy.

Today El Cerro is a mixture of several processes that have contributed to molding and consolidating a geographic, demographic, social, cultural, and economic space, where there previously existed only a hill, covered by brush during the rains and dust during the dry season. El Cerro is, in every sense of the word, a rural community, which exists within a clearly demarcated geographic space. However, a series of local social, economic, and political processes, which transcend this space, also define the community, creating on the hill's edge a cultural mosaic decorated with complexity, contradiction, and meaning.

The Physical Layout of El Cerro

At first glance, El Cerro seems to be nothing more than a small village formed by two rows of houses built on both sides of a dirt road. As is true for most ejidos in southern Sinaloa, El Cerro consists of two principal areas: the town and fields. The town constitutes the space where the community's social, cultural, political, and economic life takes place. The ejidatarios' fields give the community its sense of identity as an ejido and symbolize the fruit of a struggle over many years to obtain land. These parcels are located on the outskirts of the town, near the road that leads to the marshes. Some are so far away that the ejidatarios must ride mules, burros, horses, or bicycles to get to them.

Traveling by car or bus from Rosario, the main highway connects to a dirt road that leads to El Cerro. This road, twisted, full of rocks, dusty during the dry season, and full of puddles and mud during the rains, is also the community's main street. At the road's main entrance, there is a store, belonging to an ejidatario from El Cerro and managed by his grand-daughter. The store sells sodas, candy, and fruit. It is also where many of El Cerro's young men gather to play dominoes, and where people wait for the bus to Rosario.

Down the road, on the right-hand side, is the community's only tortillería, owned by the son of an ejidatario from Agua Verde. The community also has two small cement buildings that house the offices of the ejido's assembly and the fishing cooperative. There is only one school, where first through sixth grade is taught. Nevertheless, its four rooms are insufficient to accommodate the school-age population, and the teachers have improvised a classroom under a tree so that when one passes near the school, one can hear the teacher shouting to the children, or giving them their daily lesson.

Near the school are the foundations of a church, whose construction started in 1998, but which is unfinished because the community has run out of money. Immediately behind the church is a mango farm, which belongs to a landowner from Rosario. Lying next to it are lands that, at one time, formed part of the farm, but that a group of families from El Cerro invaded to build their houses. Locally, the people call this area La Colonia. The only other salient physical features are a kindergarten built on higher land and a wooden, palm-thatched house where Alcoholics Anonymous meets at night.

El Cerro has experienced a series of improvements since I lived there in 1989. At that time very few homes had electricity. By 1993, 90 percent of them had been connected to the power grid and pipes had been installed to supply drinking water to the community. Another important change was the construction of latrines in each of the homes, as a result of a cholera outbreak that had occurred. In 1995, the first telephone in the community was installed, and by 2001, the community had eighteen telephones in all. El Cerro's physical structure, however, is constantly challenged by immigration and demographic change.

Demographic Structure, 1989–2001

El Cerro has no fixed pattern of settlement except that which is somewhat limited by the physical ecology of the area. However, the older people can identify exactly the first houses built in the community. The ejidatarios who founded the community built their houses on flatlands skirting the hillsides. As the community continued to grow, the residents cleared brush on the higher parts of the hill to make space to construct new houses. The people who live in the highest parts of El Cerro are the people who arrived after the end of the land distribution. Whether people live up high or down on the flats serves locally to distinguish the founders of El Cerro from the newcomers.

Generally, the population of El Cerro is distributed in the community's highest areas and its flatlands. In 1989, when I conducted the first census of the community, 657 inhabitants lived in 113 households. The population in El Cerro in 1989 was relatively young, with 57 percent of the population under twenty years of age (see figure 4.1). The population sixty-five years of age or older was small, comprising only 2.3 percent of the overall population. The low number of people in this category is due to El Cerro's relatively recent establishment. When I carried out the census in 1989, the community had existed for only twenty-one years.

Since the 1989 census, the population of El Cerro has grown. According to the census I took in 2001, there are 1182 inhabitants, almost double the population in 1989. Similarly, the number of households has more than doubled, growing to 257 in 2001. This population increase is due to two primary factors. The first is the natural population growth resulting from the reproductive cycle of the first families who established the community. The second factor is immigration. People from other parts of the

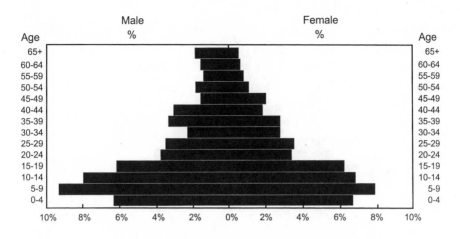

Figure 4.1
Age-sex structure of El Cerro's population, 1989

municipio and the state in general are continuing to arrive in the region in search of work in agriculture and in fishing. Although the majority comes to work only during the agricultural cycle and in the shrimp season, returning to the communities of origin at the end of the season, others remain permanently in the area. Since the 1990s, there has been a migratory flow of people from the mountains of Rosario. Although some come looking for work in fishing or agriculture, many are fleeing the drug trafficking that has invaded many of the communities in the mountains.

According to the 2001 census, the population of El Cerro continues to be young, with 81 percent being thirty-nine years of age or younger, and only 11 percent fifty years of age or older (see figure 4.2). The number of people who are older than sixty-five years of age has increased somewhat (by 2 percent), because the community's original population is beginning to age.

The continuing youthfulness of El Cerro's population has various implications. First, as this young population grows, the demand for income-generating economic activities also increases. Second, if the deterioration of natural resources continues, this future generation will continue living under the same, or worse, conditions than the current generation experiences. Third, given the lack of economic opportunities, and the continuing degradation of natural resources, the only viable economic alternative that this youthful population will have is to emigrate, a process that is

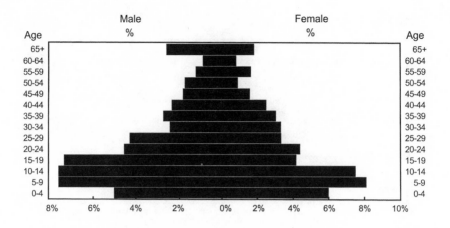

Figure 4.2
Age-sex structure of El Cerro's population, 2001

already occurring in El Cerro. Yet, regardless of such dynamics, El Cerro has developed a political structure, similar to other ejidos, that attempts to provide the inhabitants with some degree of order and organization, and in contrast to the physical and demographic structure, it has undergone few changes.

Political Structure-Local Government:
The Asamblea Ejidal and the Comisario

One unique characteristic of the Mexican ejido is its political organization. Ejidos are organized as units of production, whose highest political level is the group of people who make the economic decisions concerning the use and distribution of the land and other natural resources under the control of the ejido. This group of people (all men)—who form the asamblea ejidal, which is composed of a president, treasurer, secretary, and Consejo de Vigilancia (Surveillance Committee)—govern the ejido politically. These officials, whom the ejidatarios elect during a special meeting, change every four years. Only the ejidatarios can vote. The rest of the community has neither voice nor vote in the election of the asamblea ejidal.

The ejido is the entity that controls natural resources that are within the boundaries that form the community. The asamblea ejidal makes the decisions about selling rock from the quarry or renting agostaderos to people from other communities. The money obtained from both the rent of the summer pasturelands as well as the rent of fields or the sale of rock remains in the hands of the asamblea ejidal, and they determine how to use these funds. Even though the ejidatarios can sell their lands and ejidal rights, in the end, the asamblea ejidal has the final word in approving or denying the transfer of ejidal rights to another person.

By 2001, El Cerro had fifty ejidatarios, sixty-six fewer than the number who originally founded the ejido. Because there are so few ejidatarios, most have sat on the asamblea ejidal at some point in their lives. All ejidatarios must attend the monthly meetings. Even though most ejidatarios are men, ten women have ejidal rights, which they inherited from their deceased husbands or bought from relatives. Nevertheless, despite the existence of ejidatarias, their participation in the assembly is still very limited. As of 2001, no woman has ever sat on the governing board, and women's participation in the ejido is limited to attending the various meetings that are held.

The world of the ejidatarios is a world of men. It is a world that is always driven by suspicion, secretiveness, and discretion. Few people who are not from the ejido can penetrate this world and few know with certainty what its real functions are. Even though the community knows who sits on the asamblea ejidal, the issues the ejidatarios face are considered separate from those faced by the rest of the community. Many people in the community believe that the asamblea ejidal represents an opportunity for the ejidatarios to make money because the assembly controls the use of El Cerro's most important natural resources. This belief is reinforced because the income from the sale or rental of these natural resources is not shared with the community.

While the asamblea ejidal manages the natural resources, the comisario is the person in charge of monitoring order and peace in the community. Over the many years that I did fieldwork in El Cerro, I had the opportunity to know several of its comisarios and to converse with them about their experiences. In the past, the ejidatarios elected the comisario, but today, Rosario's mayor appoints him. The comisario receives a letter from the mayor, formalizing his appointment and explaining the duties. He also receives a credential that identifies him as comisario for the community. The comisario is appointed every three years, after the election to select the mayor, and he acts as liaison between the community and the municipal town hall. It is the duty of the comisario to attend the meetings that are held for the municipio comisarios in the town hall of Rosario, and in most cases, the town hall provides a subvention for the cost of the trip. It is the comisario's responsibility to report to the *regidores* (magistrates) of the town hall about the problems that exist within the community. It is also his responsibility to grant permits for the holding of dances or other fiestas in the community, as well as to intervene in fights or in matters of domestic violence. Further, the comisario has responsibility for regulating the admission of people who want to move into the community. The following case illustrates some of the duties of the comisario.

Pablo remembers with emotion his period as comisario in El Cerro. Sitting in a rocking chair under the palapa that he had built at the side of his house, and now with white hair and wrinkled skin, he told me, smiling, about the biggest incident that occurred during his time in office, which was from 1982 to 1985. It involved a woman in the community who held a dance without a permit. When Pablo went to complain, the woman insulted him and told him that she'd have a dance if she darned well felt like it. She then grabbed an ice pick, threatened him, and chased him all through El Cerro. Pablo also remembers that it was his daughter who helped him write the reports and complete the forms sent from Rosario. Because he did not know how to read or write, he depended completely on the help of his daughter in order to comply fully with his commitments as comisario.

In my conversations with the various men who had been comisarios, it was always apparent that the most difficult task they faced was intervening in domestic-violence incidents. Many thought that this is something that should be resolved only within the marriage itself, and they felt uncomfortable when they had to struggle with such situations. Others chose to look the other way, and they acted insensitively to the abuses that women suffered at the hands of their husbands. The following case illustrates how one comisario reacted to one situation of domestic violence.

In the summer of 2001, there was a case of domestic violence in which Patricio Morales, the current comisario, mediated. According to the version that circulated in the community, it seems that a husband arrived home drunk and began to beat his wife. She complained to Patricio and asked him to please take her to Agua Verde, where there was a judge with whom she could file a formal complaint. Because Patricio was also a taxicab driver, he saw this as an opportunity to make some money off this woman, and he agreed to take her on the condition that she pay him the cost of the fare from El Cerro to Agua Verde. Patricio took her and left her in front of the courthouse. When he returned home, the woman's husband was waiting for him to complain that Patricio had given his wife a ride to Agua Verde. Patricio advised him to give her another good beating so that she wouldn't be such a tattletale. When some members of the community talked to Patricio about the incident and blamed him for not resolving it himself, personally, he defended himself by saying, "I don't even govern in my house, much less in this rancho."

Although the responsibility for maintaining peace and order in the community theoretically falls on the shoulders of the comisario, many people think that most of the comisarios accept the job for personal interests and not to work for the well-being and smooth functioning of the community. For many people, El Cerro "will never progress if they do not take the initiative." This is why different work committees have formed, which contribute to a sense of order, solidarity, and cooperation among the households of the community.

Community Committees

The various committees in El Cerro were organized by the residents alone or with the government's encouragement and support. These are the Church Committee (el Comité de la Iglesia), the Health Committee (el Comité de Salud), the School Committee (el Comité de la Escuela), and the Public Works Committee (el Comité de Obras Públicas).

The Church Committee was formed by the initiative of the residents of El Cerro. It was organized by two young women who took charge of raising money to buy materials and of organizing people to provide labor in the building process. Every Sunday, starting very early in the morning, these two women worked, shoulder-to-shoulder with groups of men who rotated in and out, throughout the day to provide manual labor and to assist the bricklayer who was constructing the church. The young women took charge of ensuring that, at one point or another, all the men in the community who were fit to work contributed their labor. The Church Committee consists of a president, vice president, secretary, treasurer, and two members-at-large, all of whom are women.

Another successful committee deals with health issues. With government support, the Health Committee formed to avoid the propagation of illnesses, such as dengue, cholera, and malaria. A woman also heads this committee, and she is in charge of organizing community members in groups so that, at least twice a month, the neighborhood is cleaned and trash is picked up. The organized groups also take charge of retrieving and discarding any containers that may hold rainwater, because these serve as a breeding ground for mosquitoes.

The community has also established a School Committee, which is in charge of raising money for various school activities that the teachers undertake, such as graduations, Christmas parties, and Mother's Day celebrations. It is also in charge of monitoring parents to ensure that they send their children to school and motivating the parents to attend the meetings that the teachers hold throughout the school year. This committee also comprises only women.

The Public Works Committee ensures that the town's streets are passable throughout the rainy season. To achieve this, men have to work together to extract the stone from the quarry and deposit it in the rain puddles. This committee also keeps the edges of the roads clean and clears the weeds that grow in them.

Such political structure supports the scaffolding upon which rests the economic cycle of the community. Moreover, like its political structure, local, regional, national, and global processes influence its economic structure.

The Economic Structure

The set of economic activities in which the households of El Cerro participate constitutes an annual cycle. Some people participate in all phases of the cycle, while others do not, depending, partly, upon a household's immediate need for income, the number of members, and the development stage through which a given household is passing, among other things. One can expect that households with the greatest economic need take advantage of the various available activities, so long as household conditions are propitious for members' participation. Those households that have a greater number of members have a greater need for income, but the household's stage of development is going to determine how many of its members can participate in the available activities. If there were many small children, then one would expect that only the members who are considered old enough to work would be involved in income-generating activities. Factors outside the control of the household's members are also influential. These include such things as environmental conditions; demand from local and global markets for specific commodities and for the labor associated with their production; and government intervention in creating new economic opportunities.

Because most people continuously rotate among a variety of economic activities, it is very difficult to know with precision the main occupation of each inhabitant. How a person defines his or her occupation depends primarily on the economic activity in which he or she is involved at any given moment. The first interviews in which I asked people for their principal occupation did not produce satisfactory results. Almost all the men answered that they were farmers or fishermen, and few answered that they were day laborers. It was not until I changed the questions to "How many occupations do you have, and what are they?" that the gamut of economic activities in which these households are involved was revealed. This was crucial in my interviews with women, because most had previously responded that their occupation was housewife. They had not considered their work as day laborers or domestic employees to be an occupation. The seasonal nature of the activities in which people participate also significantly influences the definition of occupational structure in El Cerro. Only ejidatarios who can farm their own fields year after year consider agriculture to be a steady occupation, even though they may not necessarily consider it their principal occupation.

El Cerro's occupational structure, based on a 1995 survey I took, reveals that most households in El Cerro (38 percent) have one or more members who practice fishing. Agricultural day labor is the second most common economic activity (32 percent), followed by subsistence agriculture (16 percent) and shrimp aquaculture (9 percent). The category of "other," represented by jobs such as taxi driver, domestic employee, or mechanic, accounted for only 3 percent of the households, and work in construction, for only 2 percent.

This occupational structure influences how the rest of southern Sinaloa views the community of El Cerro. From the time of its founding, subsistence agriculture and El Cerro's status as an ejido gave the town its identity as a campesino community. Years later, with the organization of the cooperative and the ejidatarios' involvement in catching shrimp, El Cerro took on an identity as a fishing community. In both cases, nevertheless, the ejidatarios were the owners of their own labor, and they sold only what they produced on their plots or the shrimp that they caught. This situation changed during the 1990s because availability of fishing resources

Figure 4.3
The economic cycle of El Cerro

diminished and cultivable land deteriorated. The development of commercial agriculture in the region has transformed communities like El Cerro, which had been considered a community of producers, into suppliers of a labor force that serves as the motor of that type of agriculture.

Today, El Cerro's households take advantage of the jobs that are available almost year round in commercial agriculture. The various seasons of commercial farming and shrimp fishing, known locally as *frascas*, characterize the economic cycle in which these households participate (see figure 4.3).

The agricultural frasca consists of the chili, mango, and broomcorn crops. Of these, the longest is the cultivation of chili, which extends from September to May. The frasca for broomcorn (*sorgo escobero*, or just *escoba*, as the residents of El Cerro call it) runs from March to May. This frasca involves only the harvesting of plants. The mango frasca is the shortest of the agricultural seasons. The residents of El Cerro work only in the harvest, which usually lasts through May and June.

The agricultural frascas provide the households of El Cerro with a minimum income, but the community recognizes the shrimp frasca as the most important economically. Its economic importance lies in the fact that in previous years, during a good fishing season, the fishermen could earn enough to maintain their families for almost the entire year. Today, residents of El Cerro, Agua Verde, and other communities in the region are aware that the shrimp production in the Caimanero Lagoon keeps diminishing from season to season. Nevertheless, for many of them, fishing for shrimp continues to be the economic activity that renders the highest income. However, income from catching shrimp varies greatly, depending on how productive a season is, the price of shrimp in the local and international markets, and how much any individual is able to catch.[1]

Once the shrimp season starts, people try to catch as much as they can because they have no guarantee of how many weeks the shrimp will last. Even though Mexican law regulates shrimp fishing, in practice, people exploit this resource as common property, and at the beginning of the shrimp season, fishing reaches its highest level. As the season advances and the shrimp catch begins to diminish, effort falls off as well. For many of the households in El Cerro, catching shrimp is a year-round activity. In addition to catching shrimp, members of some households in El Cerro fish for *peces de escamas* (scale fish) and crabs. A local demand exists for fish, such as *mojarra* and *lisa,* which fishermen sell to the restaurants of Agua Verde. The crab (*jaiba*) catch is destined mostly for home consumption. Some fishermen have a contract to sell all the jaiba they can catch to the cantinas in Agua Verde, which steam them to serve as appetizers with beer.

Work in local and nearby shrimp farms and hatcheries also provides people with year-round employment. In shrimp farms, men are usually hired as guards, while women are hired as cooks. In the hatcheries, men are hired to clean up the tanks where the shrimp larvae reproduce, and are employed as cooks. In 2001, only six men and four women from El Cerro were employed in the shrimp farming industry.

The yearly economic cycle also includes a transitional period, between the agricultural frascas and the start of the shrimp season, in which there is little available work for the community. The residents of El Cerro refer to this time, which usually occurs during August, as the *piojillo*. When you ask residents what piojillo means, the two answers are that it refers to the lack of economic resources for the household or that it refers to the lack of an income source as a result of the shortage of work. For many, this is the period when hunger and necessity strike, like a *piojo* (louse) that constantly bothers someone. For others, the piojillo represents the fact that one "scrapes and scrapes, without finding anything." In this context, the piojo is a metaphor to imply that the people try to find money wherever they can, but their efforts are in vain.

In general, the households of El Cerro survive by continuously rotating through the agricultural frascas and shrimp fishing. During the piojillo, many households catch shrimp in the off-season, or dedicate themselves to selling food and other articles. In El Cerro, few households can survive solely from fishing or paid labor in the agricultural frascas. The most common pattern is that households try to take advantage of every available economic opportunity.

While participation in this economic cycle allows some households only to stay afloat, others manage to accumulate enough money to invest in material goods, to make improvements to the home, and to purchase and maintain livestock. This inequality in access to productive resources between homes is precisely what contributes to social and economic stratification in the community.

Socioeconomic Stratification

At first glance, El Cerro seems to be a uniformly poor community. When one arrives there for the first time and asks if some households are better off economically than the rest, the initial response is, "Here we are all the same. We are all poor." Nevertheless, this shared poverty, like the relative calm that the visitor perceives, is only a passing illusion. Although there is great economic poverty in El Cerro compared to Agua Verde or other communities in the area, this poverty is not distributed equally among all the community's households.

For many years, anthropologists studying rural communities in Mexico and Central America have repeated the importance of analyzing the socioeconomic differences existing among households.[2] Their recognition of the great range of socioeconomic variation that characterizes rural Latin

American communities has contributed to demolishing the myth about the homogeneity of these communities, which had persisted for many years in ethnographic and development studies. To demonstrate socioeconomic variation in households, these anthropologists have employed a variety of techniques, ranging from designing and administering questionnaires (for example, the socioeconomic survey that Guarnaccia and others [1988] designed) through the collection of socioeconomic indicators to measure the distribution of wealth and the use of key informants to learn how the community is structured, from the point of view of its own residents.

Sheridan (1988) and Guarnaccia and co-authors (1988) agree that a relationship exists between socioeconomic status for households and differences in the level of control that those households exercise over the economic resources that they generate and over natural resources available in the community. They suggest that this relationship can be determined by examining the differences in wealth that exist among the households instead of the income that those households generate. The reasoning behind this assumption is that, due to the nature of work available in rural communities, it is difficult to calculate the real income of each household for a specific period. Nevertheless, one can expect that people invest most of their income in home improvements, material goods, and livestock. In rural Mexican communities, such as El Cerro, the difficulty in determining income for each household is influenced not only by the seasonal nature of many economic activities, but also by the fluctuation in the value of the peso and the lack of a fixed salary for many of these activities. Even though it would be fairly easy to determine how much an agricultural day laborer might earn during a week of work, it would be much more difficult to determine how much a fisherman might earn, due to the great uncertainty that surrounds that economic activity.

However, what must be noted once more is that the natural resources of land, fishing, wood, and quarry are specifically the province of ejidatarios who also established the fishing cooperatives. Thus, socioeconomic stratification in El Cerro is constructed by that differential access, and contrary to many of the arguments that generally assume the failure of the Mexican ejido, the organization of El Cerro as an ejido actually produced positive results for the ejidatarios. According to this argument, then, one would expect that the households of the ejidatarios would have a higher economic standing than those of the non-ejidatarios.

Although this hypothesis is broad, and there could exist an endless number of variables that might contribute to the economic success of the ejidatarios, the variable that I am interested in exploring is the socioeconomic level of the households, reflected in the distribution of wealth. Specifically, this analysis focuses on the relationship between being an ejidatario and level of accumulated wealth. A first step in investigating this relationship is determining the distribution of this wealth among households in the community. This procedure requires designing an instrument to compile information relating to factors that contribute to the accumulation of wealth in the community. For this, I used a socioeconomic survey similar to that designed by Guarnaccia and co-authors (1988). That survey, adapted to the circumstances in El Cerro, compiles information on the characteristics of the houses and the possession of goods and livestock. The survey took place in 1989, just before the amendment of Article 27 of the constitution and the transformation of the legal framework that governed the ejidal system.

I administered this survey to a random sample of forty-three ejidatario households and fifty-three non-ejidatario households.[3] Once the information was gathered, the next step was to compare the levels of wealth among the households to determine whether ejidatario households were wealthier than non-ejidatario households.

I based the comparison of house types on construction material and number of rooms. According to community residents, the best houses are those that have two or more rooms, are built of adobe or concrete, and have a concrete floor. The analysis of house types reveals that more non-ejidatarios have poorer housing than ejidatarios. Thus, 38 percent of the non-ejidatario families, compared to 21 percent of the ejidatario families, live in dirt-floored one-room houses made of *barro* (mud), wood, or adobe. Most houses belonging to ejidatarios are also made of adobe but are larger than those of the non-ejidatarios. In comparing which of the two groups lives in the best houses (defined as the biggest houses, made of adobe or concrete, with a concrete floor), we see that 56 percent are ejidatario families. Only 28 percent of the non-ejidatario families live in the best homes in El Cerro.

In analyzing data on consumer goods, we find a similar pattern. The people of El Cerro view a refrigerator or a car as a social-status symbol and a sign that the household is relatively well off financially. Refrigerators and cars are the most valuable economic goods in the community, and the hardest to acquire. The homes of the ejidatarios contain more con-

Table 4.1
Ejidatarios and non-ejidatarios wealth compared, 1989

House Type

17% more non-ejidatarios than ejidatarios live in the poorest quality houses (mud, wood, or adobe walls; dirt floor; with one room).

28% more ejidatarios than non-ejidatarios live in the best quality houses (adobe or concrete walls; concrete floor; with two or more rooms).

Consumer Goods

22% more ejidatarios than non-ejidatarios own stoves.

27% more ejidatarios than non-ejidatarios own televisions.

18% more ejidatarios than non-ejidatarios own radios.

6% more ejidatarios than non-ejidatarios own cassette players.

6% more ejidatarios than non-ejidatarios own CD players.

21% more ejidatarios than non-ejidatarios own blenders.

13% more ejidatarios than non-ejidatarios own irons.

35% more ejidatarios than non-ejidatarios own sewing machines.

38% more ejidatarios than non-ejidatarios own wardrobes.

18% more ejidatarios than non-ejidatarios own dining sets.

27% more ejidatarios than non-ejidatarios own china cabinets.

10% more ejidatarios than non-ejidatarios own electric fans.

14% more ejidatarios than non-ejidatarios own refrigerators.

12% more ejidatarios than non-ejidatarios own cars or trucks.

Animals

5% more ejidatarios than non-ejidatarios own mules.

6% more ejidatarios than non-ejidatarios own cows.

18% more ejidatarios than non-ejidatarios own horses.

21% more ejidatarios than non-ejidatarios own pigs.

5% more ejidatarios than non-ejidatarios own donkeys.

2% more ejidatarios than non-ejidatarios own chickens.

Source: Author's household survey, random sample of 43 ejidatarios and 53 non-ejidatarios, 1989

sumer goods than the homes of non-ejidatarios. Notably, only ejidatario households own a car or truck.

The analysis of livestock ownership between the two groups also reveals that ejidatarios own more livestock, such as mules, cows, horses, and burros, than non-ejidatarios own. More ejidatario households invest part of their monetary resources in these costly animals. Chickens are the most common, least valuable animals, but they are the animals that people most often eat, and this may be why non-ejidatario households are more likely than ejidatario households to raise chickens.

A comparative summary of the differences in wealth between ejidatario and non-ejidatario households (see table 4.1) supports the argument that ejidatario households are less poor than the rest of the community. The ejidatarios live in better houses and have more material goods and livestock. This difference in wealth between the ejidatarios and the non-ejidatarios can be explained by the fact that the ejidatarios have greater access to the natural and economic resources of the community. The ejidatarios have land to farm, constitute the majority of the fishing cooperative membership, and make decisions about, and receive the income from, renting pasturelands or marshes. The ejidatarios also receive financial aid from the government, such as PRONASOL loans.

Although most of the ejidatario and non-ejidatario households fit well in this analysis, there are exceptions. Some ejidatario households have much less wealth than those of the non-ejidatarios. The case of Pedro López, a married, fifty-nine-year-old ejidatario, with a two-year-old daughter, illustrates this. This family lives in a one-room, dirt-floored, cardboard house, one of the least desirable houses in the community. The home has neither water nor electricity. The only material good that the family owns is a gas stove, and the only livestock are chickens. Pedro works as an agricultural day laborer, and he is a member of the ejido's fishing cooperative. Although he owns land, he does not farm it because the soil is of such poor quality.

Some non-ejidatario households also are exceptions in that they have a higher level of wealth than many ejidatario households. An example of a non-ejidatario who is better off than many of the ejidatarios is Miguel Rivera. Miguel and his wife, Ana, have five children and live in a two-room concrete house, with a concrete floor. Among their material possessions are a stove, television, iron, and cassette player. They also own pigs. Miguel works as an agricultural day laborer and an independent fisherman, and Ana works as a day laborer in the chili harvest. Their high level of wealth may be explained by the fact that they both work outside the home.

These cases, although exceptions, are important because they do not fit within the wealth model I developed. These cases are, as the others discussed here, from information I compiled during 1989, two years before the reform of Article 27 and the privatization of the ejido. With the re-

forms to constitutional Article 27, and the promulgation of the New Agrarian Law, it was anticipated that the economic and social situation for
ejidatario households would remain the same or improve. This premise is
based on the following changes established as a result of the reforms
(Cornelius and Myhre 1998; Procuraduría Agraria 1993): (1) The state
granted more autonomy to the ejidal assembly to make decisions concerning the use and distribution of the natural and economic resources belonging to the ejido; (2) the ejidatarios were given full legal rights to sell,
rent, sharecrop, or mortgage their lands to use them as collateral in obtaining loans; and (3) ejidatarios were allowed to enter into joint ventures
with outside investors or to form associations among themselves or with
outsiders. If we continue with this line of thinking, then, a reasonable
hypothesis would be that these new changes contributed to increasing the
socioeconomic gap that already existed in 1989 between the households
belonging to the ejidatarios and those belonging to the non-ejidatarios.
This hypothesis is based on the argument that these new changes gave
ejidatarios greater control over the resources of the ejido and the legal
right to use the lands to generate income through renting or mortgage
loans. This argument is also based on the fact that even in 2001, the
ejidatarios continued to be the majority members of the fishing cooperative.

In that context, and to continue this wealth analysis, I will argue that
there were more changes in wealth between ejidatarios and non-ejidatarios
after the implementation of the reforms. That is, the wealth gap between
ejidatario and non-ejidatario households continued to increase after the
reforms. To test this hypothesis, I conducted a household survey using
the same socioeconomic survey that I had used in 1989. I administered
this survey to a 50 percent random sample of 124 households in El Cerro,
25 of which belonged to ejidatarios.

The results indicate that, as was the case in 1989, a greater percentage
of ejidatarios compared to non-ejidatarios continued to live in the best
houses. As in 1989, a greater percentage of non-ejidatarios than ejidatarios
lived in the most humble homes, but this percentage had declined by 4
percent in 2001. In terms of consumer goods, we can see that since 1989,
the gap in consumer goods ownership between ejidatario and non-ejidatario
households declined considerably. We can see that the acquisition of these
goods by non-ejidatario households grew in 2001. For example, a larger
percentage of non-ejidatario households had televisions, stoves, blenders,

electric fans, cars, CD players, and refrigerators than in 1989. The ejidatarios continued to have more livestock, especially pigs and horses.

In summary, even after the reforms of Article 27 and the formulation of the New Agrarian Law, the households of the ejidatarios continued to have the best houses and more animals than the non-ejidatario households. Today, however, there is little difference between the two types of households when one compares them in terms of consumer goods that they possess. Definitively, since 1989, the non-ejidatarios have acquired more of these goods. Nevertheless, this is not necessarily indicative of the non-ejidatarios having more money to invest in the purchase of such things. Rather it means that the non-ejidatarios are much more in debt today than they were in 1989. The acquisition of these goods by the residents of rural communities became easier following the implementation of NAFTA. Prior to the implementation of this treaty, people had to travel to Rosario or even to Mazatlán to buy a television, stove, or refrigerator, and the prices for these items were very high. Today, many of the furniture stores and pharmacies in Agua Verde have a supply of these goods, and moreover, they sell them on credit, which makes the purchase easier for people who do not have the full amount in cash. Additionally, during recent years, one can observe traveling salesmen who come to the community daily in trucks, selling furniture and electrical appliances, and the people of El Cerro buy from them on credit. Another factor that contributes to the acquisition of these items in the community is the emigration that has increased in the last decade of the twentieth century. The migratory process influences the acquisition of these material goods in two ways. The first is through remittances, sent by relatives who have migrated, which El Cerro's residents directly use to buy electrical appliances, such as refrigerators or stoves. The other way is through the introduction of these goods by relatives who come to visit, bringing them as gifts.

Factors influencing the increase in consumer goods in El Cerro's households make one think that the criterion of whether or not these households possess such goods as a wealth indicator may not be the most appropriate choice. A more precise wealth indicator could be to assess the ownership of fixed property, such as houses. In that case, then the ejidatario households have more wealth because, for the most part, they still possess the best houses and the most livestock, as well as owning land. When we compare the quality of the houses inhabited by the ejidatarios in 1989 with those in 2001 (see table 4.2), we find that during this period, the number of

Table 4.2

Ejidatarios and non-ejidatarios wealth compared, 2001

House Type

13% more non-ejidatarios than ejidatarios live in the poorest quality houses (mud, wood, or adobe walls; dirt floor; with one room).

28% more ejidatarios than non-ejidatarios live in the best quality houses (adobe or concrete walls; concrete floor; with two or more rooms).

Consumer Goods

5% more ejidatarios than non-ejidatarios own stoves.

3% more ejidatarios than non-ejidatarios own televisions.

7% more ejidatarios than non-ejidatarios own radios.

1% more ejidatarios than non-ejidatarios own cassette players.

17% more non-ejidatarios than ejidatarios own CD players.

15% more ejidatarios than non-ejidatarios own blenders.

16% more ejidatarios than non-ejidatarios own irons.

27% more ejidatarios than non-ejidatarios own sewing machines.

14% more ejidatarios than non-ejidatarios own wardrobes.

16% more ejidatarios than non-ejidatarios own dining sets.

5% more ejidatarios than non-ejidatarios own china cabinets.

14% more non-ejidatarios than ejidatarios own electric fans.

24% more ejidatarios than non-ejidatarios own refrigerators.

7% more ejidatarios than non-ejidatarios own cars or trucks.

Animals

4% more ejidatarios than non-ejidatarios own mules.

10% more ejidatarios than non-ejidatarios own cows.

26% more ejidatarios than non-ejidatarios own horses.

27% more ejidatarios than non-ejidatarios own pigs.

2% more non-ejidatarios than ejidatarios own donkeys.

10% more ejidatarios than non-ejidatarios own chickens.

Source: Author's household survey, 50 percent random sample, 2001

ejidatarios who lived in the better houses in the community increased 32 percent. In contrast, the number of ejidatarios who lived in poorer houses dropped by 17 percent during this period. Concerning the ownership of livestock, the percentage declined in most cases, but not significantly.

Of the three categories used as wealth indicators, the only one that supports the hypothesis that the socioeconomic stratification in the community should have increased after the reforms is the one measuring the type of house that El Cerro's ejidatarios and non-ejidatarios inhabit. The other two indicators, consumer goods and livestock, refute the hypothesis. If we analyze the results aggregately, however, we can infer that even though the socioeconomic gap between the groups has declined since 1989, it continues to be the ejidatarios who have the socioeconomic advantage in the community. Nevertheless, this situation is likely to change as the ejidatarios sell their lands and their ejidal rights. This pattern has already begun to appear, and indeed, there have already been cases of ejidatarios who have sold their lands and ejidal rights in exchange for a truck or to ejidatarios from Agua Verde, who cultivate the lands with pasture and convert them into pasturelands for their livestock.

To supplement my wealth analysis, I also used an emic approach by asking the people of the community, themselves, to categorize households using their own measures of wealth. I also asked people to provide me with other criteria they use to categorize the households in the community.

Local Models of Economic and Class Structure

To determine the manner in which the people of the community explain socioeconomic stratification among households, I used a methodology similar to that Lynn Stephen (1991) used. I asked six informants (three men and three women), who know all the residents of the community well, to rank El Cerro's households in different groups based on their perceived socioeconomic differences.

According to the informants, the households that are better off economically are those that have the most wealth. For the informants, wealthy households are those that have a good house, material possessions, and livestock. For them, a "good" house is built of adobe or concrete with a concrete floor and has more than two rooms.

Four of the informants grouped households in three more or less equivalent categories because they distinguished three different levels of wealth accumulation. The other two informants grouped them into only two categories, one for households at the peak of the socioeconomic scale and one for those located lower down. The categories that all the informants used to group the households as better or worse off coincided. The first category that they used comprised households that had a higher socioeconomic position or more wealth. They called this category "those who live better" or "those who are less poor." The second category, "those who do not live so badly" or "those who have neither a lot nor a little," comprised the households that had a middle socioeconomic position within the community. The third category, "the poor people," "those who are really badly off," or "those who don't have money to pay the gravedigger," comprised the households that had the least wealth in the community. According to the ranking that the informants gave, the households that had the most wealth in the community belonged to the ejidatarios. Nevertheless, of the fifty ejidatarios who live in El Cerro, only six fell into the category of "least poor." On the other hand, none of the households belonging to non-ejidatarios fell into this category. The great majority (80 percent) of the ejidatario households fell into the category of "those who do not live so badly," but only 46 percent of the non-ejidatario households fell into this category. The households in the "poorest" category included the majority (54 percent) of the non-ejidatarios and only 8 percent of the ejidatarios.

All the informants agreed that the wealthiest household in El Cerro is that of Esteban, an ejidatario, and his family. Their three-room concrete house, with its concrete floor, is one of the best in the community. They also own livestock, including cows and horses, and land. The informants also ranked as having a high level of wealth those households that include a store or tortillería, or those that have, at minimum, one person in the family who is a member of the fishing cooperative. The poorest households, according to the informants, are those where the household head is female, the parents are already old and live alone, or the family has recently immigrated to the community.

When I asked the informants why some households had been able to accumulate more wealth than others had, they gave two interesting responses. The men said that the heads of these households are *codos* (tightwads), and they do not like to spend money. Concerning one of the community's wealthiest heads of household, a male informant said, "There are people who can afford to eat well, but they don't eat so that they won't have to spend money. The husband has cattle and money in the bank, but they don't eat well at his house. He is really tight-fisted. If his wife needs a tomato or an onion, she has to go door to door looking for it."

The women informants believed that Esteban and the other heads of wealthy households are "careful men, who don't throw their money around." According to these women, the economic success of a household depends on how careful the head of household is with his money. From the perspective of the women, if a man does not drink or have vices, then he knows how to take care of the little that he has and is concerned for the future of his children. When I asked Esteban how he had gotten his wealth, he told me that it did not happen overnight, but it took him many years and great sacrifices to accumulate what he had. Esteban emphasized that never going to the cantinas helped him to save money; if he had frequented them, today he would have nothing. He also commented that he had saved all the money that he earned catching shrimp, and with a part of it, he bought three cows and a tractor. With the profit from the sale of the three cows, he bought six. Then he bought even more, and today, with eighty head, he has the biggest herd of any ejidatario in El Cerro.

Esteban's son also believed that his family was one of the best off economically. He attributed this to his father having no vices and investing the money that he makes wisely. The son said that other ejidatarios could be as well off as his father if they did not spend their money in the cantinas.

The women informants also differentiated between households whose male heads are *responsables* (responsible men) and household heads who are *perdidos* (losers). According to them, the responsible men in El Cerro are rare, and to that they attributed the community's widespread poverty. Even though the categories of responsables and perdidos are intimately tied to whether a man drinks alcohol and wastes money in the cantinas in Agua Verde, this is not always the case. According to the informants, Ramiro is a responsible man even though "he is a drunk, but he brings his wife money and food for the family. If one of his children is sick, he takes the child to the hospital. He is very responsible. He gets a loan when they don't have money to buy food instead of sending his wife to do that, as do most of the men around here. He drinks, and spends time in the cantinas in Agua Verde watching the women dance." According to the women informants, "Ramiro is very perdido, but he is also responsable."

Although level of wealth is an important factor influencing how the residents themselves classify households, it is not the only expression of social and economic differences among the community's households. Another common form used to indicate these differences is with the categories of *auténticos* (real ones) and *forasteros* (outsiders), a categorization based on the origin of the resident. The term "auténtico" refers to the families of the ejidatarios who founded El Cerro and who, according to themselves, have the most right to live there. The term "forastero" refers to the families that have recently come to live in the community and have no kinship relation to the auténticos. The use of this categorization of auténticos and forasteros goes in only one direction. The forasteros never use this term to refer to their position in the community nor do they use the term auténtico to refer to the ejidatarios. For the most part, the people who are considered to be forasteros are entirely unaware that there are people in the community who use that term to refer to them.

Who, in reality, are the forasteros, and what makes them different from the rest of the inhabitants of El Cerro? For the most part, the forasteros are people who have migrated from the sierra in the municipio of Rosario. They are looking for agricultural or fishing work, and they end up living in El Cerro. In the view of the auténticos, the forasteros have distinct characteristics that set them apart. One thing is how they dress, with long-sleeved checkered shirts and cowboy boots. The forasteros bring with them this kind of clothing used in the mountains, where the climate is much colder than along the coast. The auténticos also attribute a kind of speech to the forasteros that is different from that of the rural population along Rosario's coast. One woman expressed the generally held—and somewhat contemptuous—view that auténticos have about forasteros: "The forasteros, for the most part, come from the sierra. They only get together with those from the sierra. They mix with their own kind. They are not ejidatarios. They fight with people in the sierra, and then they flee. They grow marijuana in the sierra."

This view of the forasteros makes them the scapegoat for many problems that beset the community. When I talked with older people, they always mentioned the tranquility that had existed in the community before the forasteros arrived. According to them, a level of confidence among the community's households, which existed when everyone knew everyone else, has disappeared. In earlier times, the people told me, one could sleep outdoors on a cot. Today, many are afraid to do that because someone might rob or harm them. During the past five years, the quality of life in El Cerro had deteriorated, and violence and the sale of drugs had increased, due to the growing economic impoverishment. Many people make a connection between the social deterioration in the community and the arrival of people from the mountains. The idea that many of these new immigrants work by farming marijuana in the mountains helps to reinforce that perception.

When one talks with various families that came from the sierra, one notices that they came for the same reasons that the community's founders came: in search of a better life. They came to work as agricultural day laborers or independent fishermen, and they came to live in El Cerro because they knew people here, and because it was easier to rent a house here than in Agua Verde. During my conversations with them, I have never mentioned the topic of marijuana out of fear that someone might accuse me of working for a government agency combating drug trafficking, and that something might happen to me. Even though most people in the community are aware of the importance that drug trafficking has in Sinaloa's economy, this is not a topic that people discuss openly in the community.

Both the socioeconomic differences as well those of class contribute to the heterogeneity in El Cerro. These differences, real or perceived, also influence how social relations unfold among the various households in the community. However, as the following section illustrates, socioeconomic stratification is organically associated not just with the economic stability and uncertainty of members of the community but with the actual physical health that members of the community suffer and enjoy.

Health, Illness, and Uncertainty

In El Cerro, most households, at one point or another, have had to invest their scant economic resources to cure a family member who has fallen ill. The stories that mothers and fathers tell about the sacrifices that they made to cure a child are common. Leticia and Martín lived through this experience when their eldest daughter was ill. The girl was fainting and had stomach pains, fever, and a lack of appetite. Leticia took her to the doctor, who diagnosed the girl as having both typhoid fever and amoebas. The doctor based his diagnosis on results from blood and urine tests done in a private laboratory, tests that cost ten thousand pesos. The doctor told the parents to boil the water that they gave the girl to drink and not let her eat food sold by street vendors. That season Martín earned thirty thousand pesos catching shrimp, but he had to spend twenty thousand pesos on laboratory tests and medications that the doctor had prescribed. Martín was lucky that he made a lot of money during that fishing season so that he did not have to get a loan to help cure his daughter. Even though he had planned to invest his earnings in adding another room to his house and buying a motor for his boat, he was satisfied that the money could be used to cure his daughter.

Another, more extreme case also illustrates the economic vulnerability and uncertainty that households in El Cerro suffer. One afternoon in November 1991, Rodrigo Quintero's wife and some other women were frying pork rinds in a bonfire improvised in the patio of the house. The family's eldest son, a four-year-old, was running around, playing with the other children, when he suddenly tripped and fell into the pot where the food was frying. He was seriously burned, and his parents took him immediately to the hospital in Rosario. The burns were so serious that the doctors sent the boy to the medical center in Culiacán. All the money that Rodrigo had saved from working as a fisherman and at the shrimp farm went to pay for the hospitalization and treatment of his son. The boy was hospitalized for three months in Culiacán, and when they released him, his face and arms were deeply scarred. His parents, desperate and without money, decided to migrate to Tijuana in the hope that their son could receive treatments to help erase the scarring in one of the city's hospitals. To make the trip to Tijuana, Rodrigo borrowed money from his family and went by bus from Mazatlán to Tijuana. In summer 2001, I met the boy for the first time, when he came with his mother to visit relatives in El Cerro. He was now fourteen years old, and although he still had scars, they were no longer so prominent. Three plastic surgeons had operated on him in a Tijuana hospital, and as soon as he returned from El Cerro, another surgeon would perform yet another operation.

These two cases, apart from illustrating the economic pressure on households when someone becomes ill or experiences a medical emergency, also show that residents have no choice but to take sick relatives to hospitals and clinics in other communities because there are none in El Cerro. These cases also illustrate the path, or different steps, that people must take to procure adequate health care. El Cerro does not have any basic health-care services. Its residents must go instead to the clinic in Agua Verde, which offers services focused on nutrition, first aid, and natural childbirth. These services are free for the members of the households that participate in the Programa de Educación, Salud, y Alimentación (Program for Education, Health, and Nutrition, or PROGRESA), which the Mexican government sponsors. In El Cerro, 147 families participate. Although they do not have to pay for medical consultations, they must pay the costs of the laboratory tests and medications. The people who do not belong to PROGRESA must pay twenty-five pesos for each visit to the clinic, pay for laboratory tests, and purchase the prescribed medications. In emergencies, patients are sent to the hospital in Rosario, Escuinapa, or, in some cases, Mazatlán.

El Cerro does not even have curanderos, although the people use their services. A curandero is, nevertheless, a last resort, to which people turn only when they have lost confidence and hope in modern medicine and in the doctors that have treated them. To get the services of a curandero, sick people travel as far as the municipio of Rosario or the city of Escuinapa. Residents of El Cerro hear by word of mouth about the existence and reputation of a curandero and where he lives, and then they decide if they will go to see if this person can provide a cure. When Cirilo fell ill, he decided to consult a well-known private doctor in Escuinapa. The doctor diagnosed him as having both an enlarged liver and an enlarged heart. He told him that he needed immediate treatment. He hospitalized him for several days, after which Cirilo felt much better. Two weeks after returning home, however, he became sick again, with fainting and nausea, so his wife took him back to the doctor in Escuinapa. He continued under that physician's care for three years, but he did not improve. Cirilo finally decided to see a curandero, who lived in the mountains of the municipio of Rosario. This man recommended that Cirilo buy various medicinal herbs and teas. The next year, when I returned to El Cerro, Concha, his wife, told me that he had passed away five months before. They never knew for certain what was wrong with him.

These cases show some of the types of medical problems from which the residents of El Cerro suffer. To evaluate the health conditions of the residents of El Cerro was no easy matter because of the lack of specific studies on the health of the community. However, a 1994 study in the community found that the most common childhood illnesses are coughs, the common cold, diarrhea, and parasites (Iribe Fonseca 1994). The Agua Verde clinic treats those illnesses. The same study also found that alcoholism was one of the most common ailments from which men suffer. The results of the 1994 study showed that eighty men in the community suffered from problems relating to alcoholism. In El Cerro, there is an Alcoholics Anonymous chapter, but no one knows for certain how many men attend the meetings.

Because of the lack of concrete studies, I asked the doctor in charge of the Agua Verde clinic to show me on a diagnostic sheet which illnesses the residents of El Cerro contract. According to the doctor, the diseases that they suffer from relate directly to the hygienic conditions in the community, such as the use of latrines, the poor quality of drinking water, and the abundance of dogs living with the people. Betraying a classist and paternalistic attitude, he commented that many of these illnesses are related to the high levels of promiscuity that, according to him, exist in the community. For example, in his view, sexually transmitted diseases occur because most of the population lives out of wedlock and the women change husbands frequently. Although his argument is certainly debatable, his assessment gives us an idea of the general health conditions in the community.

According to his diagnosis, the most common illnesses in the community are gastrointestinal ones, such as intestinal amebiasis, roundworm, and pinworm; infectious respiratory diseases, such as acute otitis media (middle-ear infection) and angina; sexually transmitted diseases, such as urogenital candidiasis; and other illnesses such as ulcers, gastritis, slight malnutrition, and the effects of domestic violence. The doctor is currently treating a patient who, he believes, may be the first case of AIDS in El Cerro.

Despite the existence of all these illnesses, the only available health services in El Cerro are offered by the *promotora de salud* (health promoter), who is elected from among the women in the community and trained by the Desarrollo Integral de la Familia (Family Development Programs, or DIF, a government agency). This woman is charged primarily with offering women family-planning information. In 1993, the promotora de salud was María Félix, one of Trini's daughters, who was elected through PRONASOL to be the rural health worker in El Cerro. Her job consisted of going door to door to talk with women about the contraceptive methods available to them, and to awaken their interest in using contraceptives. According to her, the most popular contraceptives among the women in the community were the pill and the injection. As part of her job, María Félix had to monitor that the women used the birth-control methods correctly and that they did not suffer any negative consequences from their use. The government gave María Félix pills, injection medicines, and syringes, which she distributed to women of the community.

In addition to providing family-planning education, the woman who is the promotora de salud is also charged with sharing information about sexually transmitted diseases, such as AIDS and venereal disease. As part of the sex education that she offers, she distributes condoms to the young

Table 4.3
Male and female education levels in El Cerro, 1989

Level	Total	%	Males	% of total	Females	% of total
No schooling	77	14	51	9	26	5
Elementary	386	71	214	40	172	32
Middle school	57	11	26	5	31	6
High school	16	3	5	1	11	2
University	4	<1	1	0	3	<1
Total	540	100	297	55	243	46*

Source: Author's household survey, 100 percent sample, 1989
*Rounding numbers may cause final percentage totals to vary by a percentage point.

men in the community. Some even come directly to her home to ask for condoms.

Yet, despite these community health promoters, the long-term prognosis for many, if not most, community members is one based on who can get available health care that is not only affordable but does not lead to greater catastrophic economic results because of the scarcity of income and resources. For many, such a possibility is beyond the adult members of the community, but hope lies in their children's education.

Changes in Education and Literacy

The people of El Cerro consider education to be the main weapon to combat poverty. Parents are always encouraging their children to go to school because they want them to have better opportunities than they had. Most parents, when asked, say they would like to see their children obtain a university degree and get a job in a company or a bank. However, getting an education beyond the elementary level is often very expensive and difficult. In El Cerro there is only an elementary school. The young people who want to continue their education beyond elementary school have a few options but are also constrained by the economic needs of their families. Those who are able to go to junior high or even to high school can attend the schools in Agua Verde or in the city of Rosario. Those who have the economic means to attend the university must travel to Mazatlán; but

Table 4.4

Male and female education levels in El Cerro, 2001

Level	Total	%	Males	% of total	Females	% of total
No schooling	96	10	59	6	37	4
Elementary	598	60	314	31	284	28
Middle school	229	23	120	12	109	11
High school	60	6	30	3	30	3
University	16	2	5	<1	11	1
Total	999	101	528	53	471	47

Source: Author's household survey, 50 percent random sample, 2001
*Rounding numbers may cause final percentage totals to vary by a percentage point.

the economic need of most households is such that this is highly problematic.

Yet, there have been improvements in educational attainment between 1989 and 2001 (see tables 4.3 and 4.4). In 1989 only 13 percent of the population had completed middle school or high school in comparison to almost 30 percent twelve years later. Similarly, 1.6 percent had completed the university in 2001, while twelve years earlier only 0.7 percent had done so. As well, the no-schooling rates had decreased from 14 percent to 10 percent in those ensuing years. In large part, such improvements are due to adult literacy programs and a greater emphasis on educational attainment within the community.

Conclusion

This chapter provides background on how the community of El Cerro formed and how it is currently structured and organized. Among the processes that contributed to its formation are migration, the agrarian struggle and formation of ejidos, and the development of a local economy largely influenced by the production of export commodities.

El Cerro, as is true for most Sinaloan rural communities, has a basic structure and infrastructure that emerged and developed as the result of its residents' constant struggle with state policies, and a changing environment and economy. Clearly, El Cerro has struggled in the midst of population growth, a highly constrained physical environment, and a political organization that is intimately tied to its status as an ejido.

In economic terms, its inhabitants survive by farming the land as ejidatarios, by hiring themselves out as agricultural day laborers, and by catching shrimp and other species that inhabit the lagoons and marshes near the community. The participation of households in these economic activities, and principally, if a household has a member who is an ejidatario, contributes greatly to the socioeconomic stratification of the community. This stratification will continue deepening to the extent that people continue to migrate to the community without economic resources and with little probability of having access to land or to the few other natural resources of the community.

However, despite its socioeconomic stratification, its lack of health-care facilities, and its scarce educational facilities, the community of El Cerro continues to survive. The case of El Cerro suggests that rural communities in southern Sinaloa struggle to survive despite state policies, the scarce economic alternatives, and ongoing environmental change. As I will discuss in chapter 8, it is at the household level that the various resistance strategies are constantly being created to confront the changes that these communities are undergoing.

From Hacienda to Community

A Political Ecology of Celaya

Everyone who lives here is very poor. The crisis is so severe that at times people don't even have food to eat. But despite everything, life here is good because we live peacefully. We pass our days, eating and surviving from our work. Both the man and the woman must work. Right now, we're very hard up because there isn't any work.
—Victoria, 1997

According to the people of Celaya, the first time that they saw the gringos was in December 1997, two weeks before Christmas. Even though the dry season had already begun, the lagoons that surround the community were still full. Their water was so crystal clear that it seemed like great mirrors reflecting even the least conspicuous contours of the landscape. The white clouds decorating the sky with their designs, the open wings of the birds in full flight, and the branches of the trees with their large tapering leaves were all painted like a mural on the beautiful, quiet lagoons.

Very early on a Friday morning, before the rays of sun had gathered enough strength to penetrate everything in their path with unbearable heat, the gringos arrived unannounced. They entered Celaya down the middle street, in a small white trailer, pulled by a red car. They parked it in the middle of the sandy roadway, under the curious gazes of the people and amid a chorus of barking dogs. From their houses, people fixed steady gazes on the trailer, waiting in silence for someone to step out. Everyone was expectant, worrying that some unforeseen event might occur, something that they had never before witnessed in their lives. A few were afraid.

After about five minutes, which to the people of Celaya seemed an eternity, two men and two women stepped out of the trailer. The four were blond with blue eyes, tall and robust. The women wore shorts and t-shirts, and the men, jeans and t-shirts. With the little bit of Spanish that they knew, the gringos began talking to the Celayans, who—still astonished—were staring at them as if they were watching an apparition of a ghost or a long-suffering specter. The gringos were saying, "Come here, please, we have something for you." The Celayans, immobile and thoughtful, tried in vain to understand the mirage they were seeing, and no one dared to move closer for fear that they would be shoved into the trailer and taken far away, to some unknown destination, from which they would never return.

It took more than half an hour before a pair of shirtless and shoeless kids, overcome by curiosity, drew closer and asked the strangers whom they had come to visit. One of the female visitors took a shirt from a bag, and giving it to one of the children, said, "That's for you. I hope you can use it." Very excited, he ran to his parents and told them that the gringos had given him the shirt, and that they had a lot more clothing to give away. When the people saw that the children had come out of their encounter with the strangers unharmed, many began to move closer and stand around the trailer. The strangers then brought out more bags with clothes, toys, and school supplies that they had brought as gifts, and using sign language, they asked the people to get into a line.

While the Celayans, amid a lot of laughter, waited patiently for their turns, the two women passed out hot dogs and Coca-Cola. They asked the name of each person and in turn introduced themselves. The people didn't care that the clothes and toys that they gave them were not new; instead, delighted with the event, they calmly accepted what they were given, even when the clothes were not their size. It had been so long since anyone had given them anything that, in a sign of their gratitude, the Celayans remained in the middle of the street to talk with the gringos. The last time they had received something had been when the various candidates for Escuinapa's presidente municipal had come to visit, bringing with them packages of basic foodstuffs to exchange for votes. Once the election was over, however, the winner never gave them another thought, much less returned to visit.

When the gringos had finished distributing the things that they had brought, they said goodbye to everyone, promising that they would return the following year around the same time. They got in their trailer and drove out of Celaya, leaving the barking dogs that ran behind the trailer covered in a wave of dust. Since the visit by the gringos, more than four years have passed, and they have yet to fulfill their promise to return. The people still remember the visit, and the event has become part of the oral history of the community. They use the story as a reference point for other things that occurred before or after. Many times in daily conversation, people ask, "Do you remember when the gringos came? What do you suppose became of them?" Some Celayans comment that when they see Americans on the highway that goes to the tourist spot of Teacapán, they always wonder whether or not they are the same people who came to visit that day.

When visiting Celaya for the first time, one forms an impression, similar to what the Americans must have thought, that it is a poor village, but picturesque and happy, surrounded by lagoons full of crystal-clear water, and lying in the midst of fields of mango, coconut, and lime trees. Yet as its history illustrates, Celaya's political ecology is much more complicated and dynamic. Among Celaya's most notable traits are its tall and slender coconut palms, waving in time with the wind, whose long, green branches seem to touch the indigo sky. With the green of the coconut palms is the verdure of the mango, guava, and papaya leaves that grow wild in the patios of the houses, giving the sensation that this town is an oasis lost in the midst of a wave of dust and heat.

Walking down its dusty, unpaved streets, the sandy texture of the soil is so unavoidably noticeable that it seems that, somewhere in the past, the land on which this hamlet was built must have been a beach. The children, running and playing freely in the streets under the full sun, and the people talking, as they stand in the doorways of their houses or in the middle of the street, suggest that Celaya is a close-knit community. People coming and going at all hours of the day, year round, makes it appear that Celaya, like El Cerro, is a dynamic geographic and social space, in which the contact between the households and the outside world is so frequent that it all seems natural. This may be due to its geographic proximity to the town of Escuinapa or the ejidos and haciendas in the area, or because the highway that goes to Teacapán passes near the edge of the community. Whatever the reason, Celaya is not an isolated community. To the contrary, the relationships between the inhabitants of Celaya and people from the outside are so imminent that, at times, it seems impossible to distinguish who really lives or does not live in the community.

People come and go, some with haste and others without, as if this could mold the passage of time that marks the routine of their lives, whether to make it last longer or pass more quickly. Early in the morning, the trucks arrive to pick up the jornaleros who work cutting wood or in the coconut or mango harvests. Other trucks and cars arrive, and they park in front of the community's only cantina. People also leave in the early hours to work on their parcels of land or at the haciendas near the community. The women wait for the bus to go to Escuinapa's municipal market or the Tienda Ley, to take their children to the clinic, or to visit relatives living in other communities. Others leave to work in the chili fields or in the coconut plantations. In the afternoon, the trucks return, bringing home the jornaleros, now tired and sweat-soaked after an arduous day of dusty, hot labor. The cars also return to initiate a second round of visits to the cantina. During the day, traveling salespeople arrive, selling clothes and household electrical appliances or collecting for goods bought on credit. The owners of nearby haciendas also arrive to hire men to care for their animals or women to clean house or cook for them. On Sunday mornings, the Jehovah's Witnesses arrive to persuade the population to convert to their religion, and the priest from Escuinapa comes to preside over the Catholic mass. During the Christmas season, people return from Louisiana to visit their relatives, and during the summer, others return from California. At any point throughout the year, relatives arrive from Tijuana or Rosarito to spend their vacations, but others also leave to look for work in those same places. Some, such as the Americans, come only once in a lifetime, stopping just by chance in Celaya on their annual trip from Oregon to Teacapán. And on weekends, people arrive from nearby villages to attend weddings, baptisms, or *quinceañeras* (girls' fifteenth birthday celebrations).

When I went to Celaya for the first time, the rainy season had begun, and the lagoons that surround the community seemed to overflow their banks from the huge quantity of water they were holding. The vegetation was so green that it made me think, for a moment at least, that I was on a tropical island. My fieldwork was ending in El Cerro, and I wanted to come to the municipio of Escuinapa to carry out a preliminary visit to the second community that I was planning to study. In Mazatlán's Fisheries Office, as well as in El Cerro, they suggested various other places as possible sites where I could do my study on the social and environmental impact of shrimp aquaculture. Celaya was one of the suggested communities because its extensive system of shrimp aquaculture, which had developed there, contrasted greatly with the semi-intensive type in El Cerro. I arrived in Celaya on a Saturday morning, after taking three different buses, from El Cerro to Rosario, from Rosario to Escuinapa, and from Escuinapa to Celaya.

The first thing I did upon my arrival was to ask some children where I could find members of the aquaculture cooperative. They told me that they were meeting in one of the schoolrooms, and I went and introduced myself. One member, perhaps in a friendly gesture, told me, "Come in, biologist, we were expecting you!" Without understanding why they said they were expecting me, I asked how they knew that I was coming. The man answered that the word had already spread that a young woman, who was carrying out her social service on the cultivation of shrimp, was visiting various communities in the area where these types of projects had been developed, and the Celayans had assumed that eventually I would visit them. Before I had gotten over my astonishment of realizing how fast the news traveled in the region, the members invited me to go with them to see the lagoon where they were raising shrimp. Called locally Las Palapitas, this lagoon is only a short distance from Celaya, and on its banks, one could still see the now empty plastic bags that had been used to transport shrimp larvae. There was also a panga floating at the lagoon's edge, and a wooden structure with a cardboard roof, which the members used as shelter from the sun when they were standing guard over the shrimp to ensure that no one would poach them and none of the wild birds that nest in the area would eat them. After visiting the lagoon and touring the community, I said goodbye, but not before I promised them that I would return the following week, to live in Celaya. This first visit gave me a sense of the physical layout of the community and the impression that its residents were very hospitable and united.

When I returned the next week by bus, hauling my luggage through the street, the cooperative's members were waiting for me. They had found a place for me to live, in the home of Alfonso, his wife, Angelita, and their four children, who kindly took me in. From that moment, they became my adoptive family. Alfonso is one of Celaya's founders, and his experiences both at the hacienda, where his father worked as a peon, and with the process of forming the community have contributed invaluably to the oral reconstruction of the history of Celaya as a human settlement. Both Alfonso and Angelita, thanks to their incredible memories and their conversational gifts, proved to be excellent informants, not only about what takes place in Celaya but also about what happens in nearby locales. On many occasions I sat in a hammock on the patio of their house, where nopales and guava trees grow, sharing with them my interpretations of what I had observed in the community.

For many people, the family of Alfonso and Angelita would not represent the prototype of the campesino family that one would expect to find in a rural community such as Celaya. Alfonso does not cultivate land nor does he depend on the land for his livelihood; instead, he is a salaried employee of Escuinapa's town hall, where he operates heavy machinery. Angelita has never had to work outside the home, but she participates actively in several of the committees organized in the community. When I met them for the first time in 1989, their eldest daughter, Miros, was studying to become a teacher of learning-disabled children. One of their sons, Hugo, was an aquaculture-cooperative member, and the two youngest children were finishing secondary school.

In addition to their own children, Alfonso and Angelita raised her niece and nephew, who are now living in Louisiana and Arizona, but they come home whenever they can to visit them. It was through this family that I was able to gain a better understanding of the interrelationships among the community's households, and how these households' relationships with other communities influenced the form in which daily life unfolded for the Celayans.

One thing I noticed immediately during my first week in Celaya was that my first impression of Celaya as a space filled with a mist of peace and tranquillity was slowly evaporating, like the *agua fresca* of a recently opened coconut that had been abandoned in the sun. During the time that had elapsed since my initial visit until I returned, only a week later, an event occurred that had caused that cloud of calm to darken until it finally exploded in sparks that dispersed to every corner of the community. There were two main versions of this event circulating through Celaya during 1989. The most widespread was as follows:

One night, while the treasurer of the aquaculture cooperative was guarding the lagoon they had seeded with shrimp, two masked men attacked him. They threatened to kill him if he did not immediately turn over the money that the bank had lent the cooperative to begin the cultivation cycle in the lagoon. Fearing for his life and the lives of his family members, the treasurer agreed to go with the assailants to his house to get the money. Once he had given them the money, the assailants brought him back to the lagoon, where they tied him to a tree with a rope and gagged him with a kerchief. The next day, when the treasurer did not come home, his brother went to look for him and found him tied up and unable to call for help. The treasurer described what had happened, and also admitted that one of the assailants had said that the cooperative's former president had sent them to steal the money.

When the other members learned what had happened, they went to the police in Escuinapa. Based on the treasurer's written complaint, the police arrested and jailed the former president. After holding him for a week, the judge ruled that there was insufficient evidence, and he set the former president free.

While this was taking place, the community fragmented into two factions: One, consisting of a minority of the cooperative members and their families, sided with the treasurer and believed his version of the events. The other, composed of the majority of members and their families, believed that the treasurer was lying and that the former president was innocent of the charges brought against him. The members of the two factions would not speak to each other out of fear of appearing to betray their loyalty to either the treasurer or the former president. Even the families in the two factions stopped interacting and talking to each other, which created a very tense atmosphere in the community.

In addition to the impact that this incident had on Celaya, it also affected the professional and personal relationship between the two biologists who were the cooperative's advisors. One of the biologists was confident that the treasurer's version of events was accurate, while the other expressed solidarity with the jailed former president. They felt so strongly about it that they became estranged, and both decided to quit their jobs and leave Celaya. The members of the cooperative, even without its biologists, were confident that they would be able to get another loan from the bank to continue raising shrimp. Nevertheless, when the bank officials learned of the incident, they not only refused to lend more money, but also proceeded to confiscate the cooperative's only truck along with other equipment acquired with the original loan. The cooperative members, without money, equipment, or biologists, and in conflict among themselves, decided to give up shrimp cultivation and return to their traditional occupations. Some went back to working as day laborers in the coconut and mango groves. Others continued to fish for shrimp, and others went to work as peones on the nearby haciendas.

In general terms, this was the predominant climate in the community when I formally began my fieldwork. The relations among the Celayans had become so tense that I often felt as if they were watching me to determine if I interacted more with one faction or the other. This forced me to take a neutral position and to be very cautious in talking with people in order to avoid giving a false impression that I had aligned myself with one of the groups. Despite this, in comparison to El Cerro, my entrance into and initial fieldwork in the community was relatively easy and without obstacles. This was largely because the two biologists who had been consulting with the cooperative were women, and the cooperative's members as well as the rest of the community had become accustomed to seeing women working in occupations that are considered nontraditional within rural communities.

During the time that passed while I was doing my fieldwork, I began to learn, little by little, the details of the controversial event. People, when they grew to know me better, talked about which version was the right one, according to them. Nevertheless, when I finally left Celaya, I remained uncertain whether it was the treasurer or the former president who had stolen the money.

In 1993, when I returned to Celaya to continue my fieldwork, I found the community more united than it had been in 1989. The members of the cooperative, which had recently been reorganized, were preparing to harvest shrimp that they had raised in the lagoon. This time, however, they had not had to depend on the bank to lend them money to buy the larvae; instead, Mother Nature had done her part. During the rainy season, the lagoons filled with water, connecting it to the ocean through various natural channels. With the flow of seawater, the shrimp larvae entered the lagoon where the cooperative had once cultivated shrimp, and these wild specimens began to grow, living on the natural nutrients found in the lagoon. The members, seeing shrimp in the lagoon, reunited and organized themselves into shifts so that they could guard the lagoon night and day. The harvest for that year was so good that they were even able to buy a truck, which they used not only for the needs of the cooperative but also to provide services to the community. For example, when the school needed to have a fence built, the members organized themselves with others from Celaya, and they went in the truck to the hills to cut wood. When one resident became gravely ill and had to be rushed to the emergency room of the hospital in Escuinapa, the truck was used to transport the patient.

The unity and solidarity that I witnessed upon my return in 1993 contrasted greatly with what I had seen in 1989. It was apparent that the bitterness and rivalries that had developed because of the theft of the money had been smoothed over. When asked about the theft, people commented on it as a thing of the past, something so removed from the present that now it existed only as part of the community's collective memory. Everyone in Celaya now talked openly about it, with the kind of big sense of humor they exhibit when telling stories about storms that have battered the community or their experiences trying to cross the U.S.–Mexico border. This theft, like the visit by the Americans, had become part of Celaya's oral history and is today a reference point to mark the passing of time and to locate other events that occurred before or after the theft.

Over the years in which I did fieldwork in Celaya, I came to realize that it is a relatively well-united community, in which trust, kinship and gender relations, and the relations among the households constitute the principal threads from which are woven the bonds of that unity. The solidarity and unity perceptible in the community is reflected in the daily visits that members of households make to each other's homes; in the fiestas, such as the birthday of the community's patron saint or the Día de la Virgen de Guadalupe; in the parties that the women celebrate yearly during the Christmas season; in the excursions that they organize to visit other states in Mexico; in the collection of signatures on a petition to close the cantina; and in the trips that they organize during the summer to collect clams at the beach.

But I have also come to understand that the bonds of trust that give rise to this unity are so fragile that all it takes is a small misunderstanding among the members of a few households, or any minor incident, however insignificant, to make this unity decay like a corn tortilla left out in the sun. Nevertheless, not all the links of trust or kinship that unite the Celayan households are local or recent. Some transcend the community's boundaries and extend to other rural settlements in the area, the town of Escuinapa, and even the U.S.–Mexico border. Others, the great majority, have their roots buried in the foundations of the hacienda that was the silent witness to the lives of sacrifice and servitude suffered for many years by the first inhabitants of Celaya, who struggled to earn their daily bread with dignity, by the sweat of their brows, working as peones from sunup to sundown. A greater understanding of the origins and formation of these linkages thus requires reconstructing the local history of Celaya from its origin as a human settlement and its evolution as a community. In order to do this, I lay out the history of a founding family of Celaya, who had a major influence in its development and evolution as a community.

A Revolt for a Mexican Village: A Tale of Love, Loss, and Struggle

Socorro and Arturo met for the first time at a fiesta in the town of Escuinapa, more than forty years ago. Shortly after, they fell deeply in love. Socorro had already been married once and had two children from that first union. This did not bother Arturo, however, who asked her to elope with him. From the outset, Socorro's mother opposed the courtship, and she went so far as to dump a bucket of urine on Arturo one night when he came to serenade her daughter. The only choice that Socorro had was to leave her children with her mother and run off with Arturo.

Socorro and Arturo went to live in the Hacienda Las Cabras, where Arturo had been living and working as a peon for more than seven years. In the 1960s, Las Cabras was one of the most prosperous and largest haciendas in southern Sinaloa. It raised pigs, for meat, and dairy cows. It also had extensive fields of corn, coconut groves, and bean fields, which supplied primarily local and regional markets. Its first owners were Spaniards, but later some Americans bought it, and after that, it became the property of Natividad Toledo, the father of Antonio Toledo Corro, the governor of Sinaloa from 1981 to 1986. With the resurgence of agrarian struggles in the region during the 1960s, much of the hacienda's property was expropriated and distributed as ejidal grants to the rural population that had fought tenaciously for a piece of land to farm and live on. Indeed, some of the largest ejidos in the municipio of Escuinapa were established on the properties expropriated from the Hacienda Las Cabras.[1]

Most of the peones who worked at Las Cabras came originally from the ranchos or villages near the hacienda, as was the case with Arturo. Many, like him, ended up living at Las Cabras when their parents, searching for work, became *peones acasillados* (resident laborers on a hacienda). Here their children grew up, and here the peones grew old. Life at Las Cabras, for both the parents and children, was anything but easy, and according to Arturo, it was "nothing but work, and more work, from the time I was old enough to hold a machete." The peones and their families lived in a world separate from the rest of the hacienda. They lived in one-room, floorless houses with mud walls and roofs made from palm branches. These houses were built in the area surrounding the main house of the hacienda. They had neither electricity nor running water, and the peones used candles or oil lamps for light. The women cooked the food with wood-fueled fires. There were so many mosquitoes that they had to sleep with netting to avoid being bitten.

The owner of Las Cabras, at that time Natividad Toledo, lived with his wife and children in the "big house." An enormous bronze bell, which began to ring at five in the morning, jealously guarded the rhythms of the passage of time and the routine of work on the premises of the hacienda. At that hour, the hacienda's four foremen arrived to assign people the work they would do that day. The peones labored cleaning the coconut groves and planting corn, beans, squash, watermelon, cucumber, and melons. The women did housework, but they also helped their husbands with planting, fishing, and opening the coconuts in the process of converting it to copra.

The peones could not support their families on the salary they received (twelve pesos per day), and they had many unmet needs. According to Arturo, "We often awoke in a terrible mood because cornmeal was so scarce that we didn't even have a tortilla to eat." The foremen paid them for their work, but food and household expenses were the responsibility of each family. Many ended up in debt to the stores operating on the hacienda, which sold food and other basic necessities on credit.

Some families fed themselves on the abundant wild animals—deer, rabbits, *chachalacas* (wild chickens), and armadillos—that they trapped in the nearby hills. The armadillos, in particular, were so abundant that people bumped into them at night as they went into the hills to take care of their biological necessities. Shrimp, which was also abundant in the lagoons and marshes near the hacienda, complemented the peon's diet and was an important source of income.

At that time, however, only a few people fished for shrimp. The peones working at Las Cabras were among those few, and they fished in the lagoons adjacent to the hacienda. The shrimp were so abundant that people could fill bags and baskets, and only with the largest specimens. Because there was no refrigeration, the peones preserved the shrimp by drying it in the sun for several days and salting it with salt from the lagoons. They sold this preserved shrimp directly from their houses to buyers who came to the hacienda in search of it.[2]

Life for the peones on the hacienda was generally hard. Nevertheless, Arturo and others believed that their situation was a little bit better while Natividad Toledo owned Las Cabras because he treated them all equally, without showing preferences for certain individuals. After Natividad Toledo's death, their situation worsened when the hacienda passed to his son, José "Chepe" Toledo, who formed a partnership with the Coppel family of Mazatlán.

The death of the elder Toledo coincided with the resurgence of the agrarian struggles in Sinaloa, and many of the landless peones at the hacienda organized to fight for the formation of ejidos. In the face of this situation, the new owners of the hacienda chose to hire an administrator to put matters in order. Héctor Escutia ruled with an iron fist and fought tirelessly to avoid an expropriation that would result in the conversion of the hacienda's lands to ejidos. One of the first things that he did upon taking possession of the hacienda was to expel most of the peones who worked there. Under the pretext that the hacienda now had new owners, Escutia used a thick chain to lock the main gate to keep the original peones out, and he brought in outsiders, from other communities, to replace the hacienda workers.

The original peones were left without work and without housing. Seeing that their economic and social situation was not going to improve, the peones chose to organize. They began little by little, with a small group of ten men, who met together clandestinely at night. They also went to Mexico City, to the offices of agrarian reform and the Liga Campesina to formalize and legalize their petition.

There is little written documentation of the efforts to organize and request an ejidal land grant, with the exception of a telegram and a letter, in which the peones complained of the unjust treatment that they received from Señor Escutia.[3] The telegram, dated March 23, 1962, from the *procurador de asuntos agrarios* (attorney for agrarian matters) to the mayor of Escuinapa, explains a complaint from a group of peones, claiming that Escutia refused to give them work in reprisal for the workers having filed the in-progress petition for a land grant. In a response, dated March 26, 1962, Pedro Zamudio, the mayor, assures the attorney that he was already aware of the problem confronting the peones of Hacienda Las Cabras. Only a few days earlier, a group of ten had come to his office to explain the situation and to ask him to take part in this issue so that they would get their jobs back, independent of the processing of the land grant.

While the peones were launching their fight to obtain land, the hacienda fell into decay. The new owners decided that it was to their economic benefit to use the land that remained to grow high-value commodities, such as corn, beans, and coconut. Consequently, they undertook the painful task of deforesting the remaining woods surrounding the hacienda. The clear-cutting of the brush is one of the events best remembered by the people, like Arturo, who lived on the hacienda. They were silent witnesses to this rapid and abrupt process.

The deforestation of the hills around the hacienda was not a costly process in an economic sense, but it required extensive manual labor, which was mostly provided by men from the neighboring rural communities, who were hired specifically to clear-cut the brush. Because the peones were only hired for a short period, they did not have houses in which to live, and they had to improvise camps on the hillsides, where they ate, slept, and took care of their biological necessities. The wage that they received for this work was twenty pesos per week, but compared to the few other jobs available at that time, it was a lot of money. They used the *roza-tumba-quema* (slash-and-burn) method to clear the trees, cutting them with axes and machetes, leaving thousands of black trunks, still alive and with their roots buried in the earth, which were then pulled down with tractors. Working around the clock, the workers were able to complete their task of destroying a large part of the area's natural vegetation in a very short time. The final step in the deforestation process consisted of setting fire to the now-dry remains of the cut vegetation.

One of the most vivid memories that Arturo has of this period at the hacienda was of that great blaze. When the workers set fire to the dry vegetation, the animals that had survived the first stages of the clear-cutting began to come out of their hiding places. The flames were so high that, according to Arturo, they seemed to touch the sky. The frightened deer ran from their hiding places, trying in vain to escape the fierce flames. When the fire reached them, they came out burning in a ball of fire, running as fast as the wind, trying to find refuge in the lukewarm waters of the lagoons. Some of the peones took the opportunity to hunt the animals and eat them. Nevertheless, very few creatures survived the ferocious violence of the fire. When it died down, the countryside around the hacienda was desolated. Bones from the skeletons of deer, javelinas, rabbits, armadillos, and jaguars that had died in the fire covered the ground. According to Arturo's estimate, more than one hundred hectares of forest were slashed and burned.

While they prepared the new fields for planting, the ex-peones from the hacienda continued to demand their right to a piece of land. Finally, Escutia agreed to give them land. However, he gave it in the form of individual smallholdings rather than organized as an ejido, as the peones had wanted. Why he chose to do that is not entirely clear. When one asks the Celayans about it, their answer is that they received the land as indemnification for all the years that they worked on the hacienda. My speculation is that the owners felt that it would be more to their benefit to give land as private property to a few families than to let the government expropriate a large tract for an ejido.

The land was divided among twenty peones and their families. However, it was not the property that they had requested within the hacienda. Instead, they received some salt-soaked land, poor quality soil, on the outskirts of the hacienda near the lagoons. Each peon received twenty hectares to farm and a forty-square-meter lot on which to build a house. Escutia took charge of arranging to have a house built for each of the twenty families, consisting of only one room, adobe walls, palm-leaf roofs, and a dirt floor. They were so small that the whole family could not fit inside at the same time. During the dry, hot season, almost everyone slept outdoors on cots in the patio. In the rainy season, they had to pluck up their courage and curl up tightly together inside the house, hoping that the rain would stop. There was no electricity or water.

Life for these twenty families who founded Celaya was very difficult. Their transformation from peones acasillados to campesinos meant that they had no other option than to farm for a living on the salty soil. To survive, they used the experience and knowledge they had acquired farming on the hacienda. They began the long, tiring process of clearing the lands, little by little, to create fields where they could plant their crops. They used a simple method for sowing, consisting basically of digging a hole in the ground with a machete and putting in the seed. They used no fertilizers or pesticides. They raised cucumbers, watermelon, beans, and corn, which they harvested themselves. Most of the harvest was for home consumption. The corn and beans were stored for several months in structures called *chapiles*, with wooden walls and palm-leaf roofs. Before storing the crop, they added lime to the corn to keep the weevils from eating it.

Celaya's first families lived in extreme poverty. Besides using the food they harvested to feed themselves, they also fished for shrimp in the nearby lagoons. With the passage of time, things improved somewhat. The clearing of larger tracts of hillside enabled the Celayans to expand the area available for planting. With earnings from the sale of agricultural products, Celayans were able to buy a pair of mules and a hand hoe to make the work easier. With time, the economic situation of the community improved, as people started to invest part of their earnings from agriculture in the development of the community's infrastructure. They built their own wells, called *tiros*, in the patios of the homes. They also greatly improved their houses by adding concrete floors, kitchens, and latrines. The Celayans built the first school in the community, made with adobe walls and a palm roof. Five days a week, a teacher from Escuinapa came to Celaya to give classes to the children in first through third grade.

The economic situation for the Arturo and Socorro's family improved when they began to plant mangoes on their land. This occurred just as there was an increase in demand for that fruit, in both regional and international markets. Arturo sold his entire mango crop to buyers from Escuinapa, who took charge of processing and marketing it. With the income generated from the sale of the mangoes, they built a better, much larger house, made of concrete, with a concrete floor, two bedrooms, a living room, and a kitchen. They also bought a tractor to work the land.

With the passage of time, some things in Celaya have changed but others have stayed the same. The changes have not been uniform, nor have they affected all the households in the same way. Some homes are economically better off than others. Some suffer from a higher incidence of domestic violence and alcoholism than others. The community has potable water and electricity. There is a Catholic church, a kindergarten, and a CONASUPO store (Comisión Nacional de Subsistencias Populares, or National Commission of Popular Subsistence, a national food staples company). Despite these changes, Celaya continues to be a geographic and social space characterized by heterogeneity and inequality. Something that has not changed much in the community, which the residents still retain, is the thing that impressed me from the first moment that I visited Celaya: their sense of unity. The daily interaction among the members of the households, the cooperation and reciprocity, the confidence and help that they give one another are qualities that still survive in the community from the days when the founding families knew each other from working together on the Hacienda Las Cabras.

Since those days, these families, along with the new ones that have formed, have had a direct connection with the ecological environment that surrounds them. Their use of the available natural resources has contributed to the subsistence of the various generations that today make up the community. Despite the rapid ecological changes this region has experienced, the residents of Celaya continue to transmit their knowledge of the environment from one generation to another.

Of Mangoes, Lagoons, and Coconuts: The Ecology of Celaya

The countryside that surrounds Celaya has two principal components: the lagoons and the mango and coconut fields. These two characteristics of the landscape are so obvious at first glance that one does not need to enter the community or live with its residents to notice it. Nevertheless, only people who travel through the area can really appreciate or disparage these aspects of the landscape. Whether appreciation or disparagement depends on one's understanding of the region's history, of the importance and impact of the development and expansion of commercial agriculture, and of the relationship between the lagoons and the residents of the area's rural communities. To obtain a detailed understanding of how this landscape, which provides the setting for Celaya, relates to its residents, however, it is necessary to have a profound understanding of the dynamic of the processes that contribute to making it a community.

Many people in the town of Escuinapa have never visited Celaya, and some have never even heard of it, even though the communities are only fifteen minutes apart by bus. Celaya sits on the right-hand side of the highway from Escuinapa to Teacapán, but it is not exactly the kind of place people go to visit or even just to see. Its poverty, rural nature, and lack of amenities combine to create an impression that this community has been left behind and marginalized, far from the "progress" and economic development that brought with it the boom and growth in commercial agriculture in the municipio of Escuinapa. Not even the tourists, who come from Mazatlán to take boat rides through the lagoon systems and mangrove forests, bother to stop there. Anyone who enters Celaya has a definite reason for being there. Some come to visit relatives, others to see a sweetheart, to try to win votes during an election for the presidente municipal, to hire workers for copra processing or chili or mango harvests, or, for the Americans, to do charity work.

When one asks Celayans about the community, the most common answer is that it is a ranchito that changes greatly depending on the hour of day or the season. People from outside the community who come to visit very early in the morning leave with the impression that it is a ranchito full of noise. The noise comes from children playing in the street or walking to school and the footsteps and conversations of the men going to work. It comes from women washing dishes and tidying up houses, dogs barking at any little thing that moves, and pigs squealing for food. And it comes from the radios, whose music disperses to every corner of the community. There comes a moment in the morning when one feels that all the sounds on earth are present there. Often it seems that all the noises join to form one big sound, which paralyzes one upon hearing it.

Those who visit the community around ten in the morning leave with an idea that this is a village of women. At that hour, the children are in school, the men working outside the community, and the only people in the streets and in the homes doing housework are the women. One can hear their voices while they wash clothes in the tubs behind their houses and chat with one another, or when they go to the little stores that are inside homes or visit a neighbor to borrow sugar or rice.

For those who visit around two in the afternoon, Celaya can seem like a ghost town. At that hour, the sounds of the morning have fallen silent, and the men and children have returned from work and school. The whole family is reunited inside the house, eating or resting, and not a soul is seen on the streets of the ranchito. There is such pervasive silence that one cannot avoid thinking that one is in a small town much like Comala, "the town without noises," which Juan Rulfo describes in his novel *Pedro Páramo*. Even the squeals of the pigs and the barks of the dogs have stopped while they quietly sleep in the mud holes or under a tree or chair.

When twilight begins to fall, around six in the evening, you can again hear the morning sounds. The children play in the street. The people take chairs or rockers outside and sit in front of their houses or under trees, chatting about the events of the day. Some women prepare frijoles and tortillas for the evening meal, while others prepare sandwiches and tacos to sell. At this time, the music from the cantina can also be heard everywhere, and one can see the men going in and out of the bar. The squeals and barking of the pigs and dogs join the sounds of the crickets, the frogs, and the chickens that cluck in chorus while they try to get up in a tree to sleep. All the sounds come together again to make one sound until around ten at night, when the inhabitants have all fallen asleep to rest tranquilly until another hectic day begins.

Only the Celayans and other people who live there for a long period can

The main street of Celaya.

truly appreciate the diversity and dynamism of this community. Even though these different facets of Celaya now form an integral part of the daily routine of their lives, the different sounds, the comings and goings of the people, and even the silence never pass unperceived. Entirely to the contrary, the Celayans are always alert to everything and everyone. They know not only everything that happens in their community but also what happens in other communities and in the town of Escuinapa. They always know who is working outside the community, where they go to work, at what time they leave, and when they come back. They also know which relatives visit the members of the various households and where these people come from. The Celayans are well aware of when the dogs bark, and at whom, or what, they are barking. They know if the pigs squeal because they are hungry or thirsty or if they sleep because they are tired. Nothing and no one can ever pass unperceived through this community.

For many people, Celaya seems to be a rural community just like so many others in the region, but when one lives with the residents for a long period, one easily notices that this place has certain characteristics that make it unique. One of these is the story of the founding of Celaya. It has been more than forty years since the first families established themselves there, but one can still find traces of that history. It exists in the houses built for the first residents after they were expelled from Las Cabras and relocated there. All the people in Celaya, both the children and adults, know how many of those houses remain standing, having survived storms, torrential rains, and unbearable heat. They also know to whom these houses, built with adobe walls and palm-leaf roofs, belonged or still belong.

Another characteristic of Celaya that contributes to its uniqueness, perhaps the most visible at first sight, is its ecological environment. Built in a sandy valley, surrounded by lagoons, Celaya is notable for its residents' close relationship with and deep understanding of the environment and the available natural resources. The lagoons that encircle the community are major food sources for the residents. They fish there for shrimp and the peces de escamas that the households consume, but that they also sell and give away, both within and outside the community. Shrimp, for example, is eaten in the homes, sold to changueras in the community, or sent with visiting relatives to feed family members living in Tijuana. The lagoons are also used to raise shrimp because they provide the needed nutrients for the shrimp to grow without having to add fertilizers or food supplements.

The Celayans also know the basic characteristics of the vegetation that borders the shores of the lagoons. They categorize as mangroves all tree-like vegetation that grows bordering the lagoons or next to the coast. However, they distinguish among three types of mangroves. For the Celayans, the best known, and easiest to identify, is the red mangrove, or *candelón*. They are well aware that clusters of large oysters, which are favorites to eat, grow in the roots of this mangrove. They also know the tree's value as lumber; they use it in building houses because of its great durability. The other type of mangrove that the Celayans use, especially for building fences for their fields, is the *Laguncularia racemosa*, known locally as mangle. The third type that abounds in the area is the *Avicennia nitida*, known locally as the *botoncagüi*, or black mangrove.

In addition to the importance of the mangrove trees bordering the lagoons, salt produced there until recently was also extremely important for the nutrition and economy of the residents of Celaya. Until the mid 1990s, these lagoons were mined for salt. Just as the Totorames had done, the inhabitants of the region mined the salt from these lagoons for many years. The Cooperativa Salinera, based in the town of Escuinapa, was in charge and had the legal rights to exploit these deposits. The members of the cooperative mined the salt. What they gathered was left to dry in the sun for several days in square wooden molds. It was then taken in cloth bags to the cooperative's warehouse in Escuinapa. From there the salt was sold locally and exported to Mazatlán. The people of Celaya benefited because the cooperative gave them permission to collect it for household consumption even though they did not have the right to mine it commercially. The Celayans used the salt not only to cook but also for processing and conserving shrimp and meat.

The residents of Celaya and other communities in the region use the lagoons communally as a natural resource. Even though the lagoons have been awarded legally as a fishing concession to specific cooperatives in the municipio, the Celayans have always found a way to fish them without the cooperative members finding out.[4] The significance of these lagoons for the Celayans is reflected in the fact that everyone knows their names.

Celayans are also attentive to the changes that have occurred to the lagoons surrounding the community. For the most part, these changes resulted from the construction of the shrimp farms built around the edges of them. For example, in one of the largest lagoons, which is very near Celaya, five shrimp aquaculture farms have been built. This has accelerated the environmental deterioration of the lagoon system. The construction of the tanks has altered the hydrological processes of the lagoons because the water no longer flows freely but remains contained within them for long periods.

Another factor that influences the alteration of the hydrological cycle of the lagoons is the pumping of water from them to the tanks, leaving certain seasonal lagoons now permanently dry. Moreover, because of the construction of a channel to guarantee a permanent supply of water to the lagoons, they remain flooded year round. Consequently, the lagoons that were previously used during the dry season for salt mining no longer produce salt. The Cooperativa Salinera had to cease operations as a result of the permanent flooding of the lagoons, leaving 150 members without a source of income.

Another effect of the construction of shrimp farms in the area relates to the transformation of the lagoons from a communal resource into a private one. The areas surrounding the shrimp farms are legally under concession to the owners of the companies or cooperatives that constructed them. The Celayans, who before would fish in these lagoons, no longer can do so because the lagoons are now private property.

In addition to the evident changes that have transformed the lagoon ecosystems, the Celayans, along with the residents of the other rural communities in the area, have observed how commercial agriculture is day by day proliferating more. The expansion of both the agricultural boundary and the various agricultural products grown in the area is a frequent topic of conversation among the Celayans. This is a topic they talk about when lying in a hammock trying to rest, or when washing clothes in the tubs, and even when friends and relatives come to visit. For the Celayans, the accelerated development of commercial agriculture in the area is one aspect that greatly concerns them for two principal reasons. The first is that they have witnessed the processes by which the valley that forms part of the community has lost its native vegetation, only to see it replaced by crops with a great commercial value in local, regional, and even international markets. The second is that they themselves have participated in this transformation. For most of the households in Celaya, the employment of its members as day laborers in the commercial export–oriented agriculture, such as the mango and coconut farms, constitutes their main source of income. These mango and coconut farms, belonging for the most part to doctors, politicians, and businesspeople from the town of Escuinapa, can be seen all along the highway that goes from Escuinapa to Teacapán. Because they are irrigated frequently, they give a green hue to the rural countryside, even during the dry season. The brilliant red and yellow of the mangoes when they are mature contrasts with the green of the coconuts, to melt into the landscape framed by the indigo sky and the clearness of the waters in the lagoons. The influence and acquisitive power of commercial agriculture in the region is so great that many Celayans have sold their parcels to doctors and farmers from the town of Escuinapa, who convert it to agricultural groves raising mango and coconut palm trees.

The community of Celaya, as such, does not have within it a great variety of natural resources. Not even the lagoons that its inhabitants exploit belong legally to the community. The only natural resource available to the households is land. Nevertheless, this also has been the object of transformation. The Celayans estimate that 80 percent of the cultivable lands awarded to the founding families was sold, mostly to people from outside the community, including doctors and farmers from Escuinapa. For those families who still have their land grants, the fact that these are day by day becoming saltier and more degraded—making the task of planting ever more difficult—is one more dimension of their daily struggle for survival in a rapidly changing ecological context.

Even though Celaya was physically structured as an ejido, this community, unlike El Cerro, does not have any communal pasturelands. The people who have cattle must graze them on their own fields. Celaya, like El Cerro, faces serious problems of scarcity of lands onto which it can expand. Not even the owners of Las Cabras, who ceded the land, nor the government, which obliged them to give it to peones, took into account the community's long-term population growth. This growth, like that which is occurring in El Cerro, is caused by two principal factors: the natural growth of the founding families and the immigration of families from other states, especially Michoacán. Celaya, like El Cerro, was not immune to the migratory wave that battered southern Sinaloa during the 1970s. Indeed, very close to Celaya is a community called Cristo Rey, which is made up entirely of *Cristero* families that migrated from Michoacán.

Celayans understand that the scarcity of land is one of the most pressing problems for their community. In 1997 they began measures in the presidencia municipal to expand the boundaries of the community. These actions, however, were not fruitful because the lands adjacent to the community, which could have been incorporated, belonged to private owners. For Celayans, the only option to be able to expand the community was to buy part of that land. This also proved to be impossible because the owners refused to sell it. The only land that Celayans were able to buy was a ten-square-meter lot where they built a church.

While land is a natural resource that is becoming ever more scarce, water is an abundant natural resource. The valley where Celaya is located is at sea level. For that reason, the water table is close to the surface. Indeed, when the first families came to live there, they all sank wells to supply themselves with water. Today, many of these families still have wells, but they are no longer in use because Celaya now can count on a permanent source of potable water that comes by aqueduct from the town of Escuinapa. The water from the wells is too salty, and to be drinkable, one would need to treat it with chemicals. The only use for the wells today is to give water to animals and plants. The owners of parcels also have wells from which they pump water to their fields during the dry season.

Contrary to what occurs in El Cerro, water is not a limiting factor in Celaya. Even during the dry season, people can count on having potable water, and the owners of fields use water from their wells to irrigate their crops. In Celaya, as in El Cerro, people are always searching the skies for the first signs that the rainy season is about to begin. They understand

and recognize the great importance that water has for maintaining the ecological balance of the lagoons, especially in regulating salinity. They also understand that the relationship between the physical and chemical conditions of the lagoons and the production of shrimp is both close and fragile.

However, the Celayans' preoccupation at the start of each rainy season is not with whether there will be sufficient rain to fill the lagoons and feed the mango and coconut groves, but whether there might be too much water, to the point of flooding the valley or submerging the bridge that connects Celaya to the town of Escuinapa. Indeed, because Celaya lies at sea level and is surrounded by lagoons, it floods whenever it rains hard. Its streets become impassable, mined with deep potholes filled with water. The fields also flood after the strong rains, and in most cases, people lose their crops entirely. With the rains, swarms of flies and mosquitoes also arrive, which like a black, dense cloth slowly spread across the ranchito's streets and houses.

Conclusion

The political ecology of Celaya I discuss in this chapter emphasizes the history of its founding as a human settlement and community and the ecological characteristics of the area. From that history come two important themes: the struggle of the residents to achieve a better life, and the town's placement on hacienda lands. These factors are similar to the history of the origin of El Cerro. The struggle for land was the primary factor that impelled the formation of both communities. Nevertheless, in the case of Celaya, these struggles resulted in a community with a private-property landholding system, and not an ejido, as occurred in El Cerro.

The political ecology of Celaya also reveals that since its founding, the community's ecological environment has suffered various transformative processes. The deforestation of the lands that belonged to the Hacienda Las Cabras was a process that rapidly eliminated much of the area's vegetation in order to convert the deforested tracts to coconut and mango plantations and pastureland for cattle. The transformation of the ecological environment that surrounds Celaya did not end with the deforestation of the hacienda's lands. The deforestation continued, although on a smaller scale, as the early groundwork was laid for the creation of Celaya. To build their houses and lay out agricultural fields, the families that established the community had to clear the brush from the lands that they had received.

The environmental transformation continues in the area. The lagoons, which for so long served as a food source for the people in Celaya and other nearby communities, today face environmental degradation. This is partly due to the production of one of southern Sinaloa's most important commodities: shrimp. To see how these lagoons have changed, one only has to tour the area to quickly see that where, only seven years ago, there had been a crystal-clear lagoon bordered by mangrove trees, today there is a shrimp farm with earthen embankments and a large main gate, guarded night and day by a watchman.

The founding of Celaya did not mean that the peones who had been working at Hacienda Las Cabras immediately achieved utopia. They did not even succeed in getting the lands for which they had really fought. For most of the founding families, their life continued to be permeated with struggle, uncertainty, and sacrifice, just as it had been at the hacienda. Their struggles are reflected in how they have organized and structured their community, in the work that they do to earn income, and in the unity that continues to characterize their households.

6

In the Shade of the Coconut Trees

The Structure and Organization of Celaya

Residents of Celaya expressed their discontent over a marisquería [seafood restaurant], operating as a cantina, which opened eight months ago. Almost 80 people signed and presented a petition that claims the music continues past 4 a.m. without regard for a diabetic woman who lives next door. "The owners have already been told to turn down the volume, even if the drinking continues, but all we get in response is frustration," the document claims. It also says the petitioners are seeking the closure of the marisquería-cantina, which has been operating for eight months. Despite appeals to the Presidente Municipal, no action has occurred. Given the urgency to close the locale, the signers demand that the document be forwarded to the state government and the Office of Alcohol Inspection.

—Héctor Castro, "Molesta a Vecinos de Celaya Instalación de Una Marisquería" (my translation)

The story in this epigraph, bearing the headline "Celaya's Seafood Restaurant Disturbs Neighbors," appeared in the Sunday edition of a local Mazatlán newspaper. The residents of Celaya hoped that this newspaper story would publicize the source of a difficulty that had bedeviled them for some time. By denouncing this problem, which was interfering with the daily routine in the community, the Celayans were attempting to end a cold war between them and the owners of the marisquería, a restaurant specializing in seafood. The women in the community developed the idea of organizing to write a petition and collect signatures. As one of them, Graciela, explained to me, they took action because, "We are the ones who are the most affected by this problem."

Long before the newspaper published the story about the community's problem with the marisquería, I had already heard about the women's struggles and frustrations as they tried to close the establishment. In July 1997, when I returned to Celaya to continue my fieldwork, I noticed that the women in the community were more united than they had ever been before. Gone were the petty quarrels and rivalries that had existed between several of the Catholic women and Natalia and her daughters, who had converted to Pentecostalism, much to the surprise of the entire community. Now, the main topic of conversation among the Celayan women was the marisquería and the enormous threat that this represented to their households.

During this period of fieldwork, while I walked the sandy streets of Celaya, I saw that someone had put a sign on the roof of one of the houses on the first street. "Tecate," written in big red and black capital letters, jumped out from it. Under the word "Tecate," also in capital letters, but written a little smaller, appeared the name of the marisquería, "Restaurante El Papayito." I admit I was surprised that someone in the community had decided to open a restaurant, but I did not pay much attention in light of the pressing economic circumstances that most households were facing. I continued tranquilly on down the street, under the hot noonday sun, moving along with the rhythm of the breathing of the dogs that slept curled up under the coconut palms. I arrived at the house of Angelita and Alfonso, who were sitting and chatting in the patio behind their home. When I commented that a restaurant had opened in a house on their street, Angelita exclaimed, "It's a restaurant in name only! In reality, it's a clandestine cantina, disguised as a restaurant only to keep up appearances."

The other residents confirmed what she said. However, only while visiting the home of Natalia and Rafael did I really grasp the impact that the establishment of this clandestine cantina had had on the community's households. When I arrived at their house, Natalia was preparing lunch in her dirt-floored kitchen, where she cooked with wood. While she warmed the tortillas on the *comal* (griddle), she talked with three Pentecostal women who had come to visit her from Isla del Bosque. Natalia had converted three years before, and she no longer wore pants, as she had when I first met her in 1989, while she sowed chili in the fields that a man from Escuinapa had lent to her husband, Rafael.

That day, she, her daughters, and the visiting women were all dressed in long skirts and long-sleeved shirts, and they all had long hair, tied in ponytails. Natalia introduced me to the women, whom she called her sisters of the church, and then she invited me to eat lunch with them. She led us to her other kitchen, one inside her house, with concrete walls, roof, and floor, as well as a gas stove and a dining table seating six. While I was at the table, I noticed that the picture of the Virgin of Guadalupe, which used to hang on the wall, was no longer there. I asked Natalia about this, and she told me that she had removed it because her new religion prohibits the adoration of the Virgin.

As she served the shrimp soup, refried beans, and corn tortillas that she had prepared, she asked me if I had heard that a cantina was operating in the community. When I told her that I had learned about it at Angelita's house, she proceeded to unburden herself to me, expressing her frustration and rage at seeing that a family from her own community had had the nerve to open a cantina.

For Natalia, as well as for the other women in the community, the central problem was not that someone had suddenly decided to open a moneymaking enterprise. The issue was the kind of business: a bar that sold alcoholic beverages. The cantina constituted an ongoing threat to their husbands' wallets and to their household economies. Natalia explained that her husband, like most men in the community, spent all his time at the cantina, wasting the little money that he earned, while she and her children lacked basic necessities.

Natalia and the other women in Celaya had forceful arguments as to why the community should shut it down. For example, in the past, if the men in Celaya had wanted a beer, they had to go all the way to Escuinapa or Isla del Bosque to buy it. This meant taking a bus or getting someone to drive them, which was a big effort that required time and money. With the establishment of the clandestine cantina in Celaya, the men no longer had to work so hard to get their beer. They did not even have to leave home. The ability to buy and consume beer right in their own community has contributed to an increase in the consumption of alcoholic beverages in the homes themselves. Another woman complained that the cantina sells beer and other alcoholic beverages to minors. Most women in the community also agreed that when their husbands or children return from work as jornaleros, the first thing they do is stop at the cantina, whereas before they came straight home to eat or rest. This particularly bothers the women on paydays, because the men spend a large portion of their earnings at the bar, and then, when they arrive home, there's not enough left to give the wives the money they need to cover the family's basic necessities.

Another argument is that the bar has upset the community's daily routine because strangers—mostly men—come and go at all hours. Celayans expressed mistrust of these outsiders because they do not know these men or what kind of intentions they may have. The women fear that the drunks will disrespect them or their daughters, or will start fights and beat up their husbands or sons. Indeed, several shootings have already occurred in the cantina, and men have been injured, but, so far, no one from Celaya has been hurt. Yet another argument is that the noise and the music from the bar continue far into the night, disturbing people's sleep and interrupting the peace and tranquillity of the community.

The establishment of the clandestine cantina has contributed to raising the level of economic uncertainty for families because money destined for household expenditures now goes for beer or tequila. Especially for the women, not having the security of being able to count on income from their husbands and sons causes a lot of tension and worry as well as aggravating the uncertainty that permeates their daily lives.

While I did fieldwork there, an ongoing topic—emphasized particularly in conversations with women—was the concern about the progressively worsening economic situation. The women shoulder the brunt of the responsibility for ensuring that their households possess the economic resources to cover the costs for food, health, and educational needs of their families. When I interviewed him in 2001, Daniel, the community's *síndico* (sheriff), aptly expressed the Celayans' view of the repercussions of the local and regional economic deterioration: "The community's economic situation is very serious. I see friends, neighbors, who at times can't even turn on the stove."

What Daniel is saying is that the economy in Celaya is so bad that households sometimes do not have enough money even to buy the flour to make tortillas. Edmundo, the manager of the only CONASUPO grocery store in the community, shares the same view. The deterioration of Celaya's economy has affected him because he often has to sell on credit to the women when neither they nor their husbands can pay in cash for the food they need. To help families stay afloat, he has even had to raffle off basic foodstuffs during the piojillo season, when work and money are scarce in the community.

Their economic situation led the women to take up arms in this matter. Before gathering signatures and denouncing the situation publicly in the newspaper, a group of them went to speak to the owners of the cantina to ask that they close it and open, instead, some other kind of business, such as a grocery or stationery store, which the community lacks. The owners would not agree, and the women then decided to complain in person to the mayor. However, the only answer they got was that he could do nothing because the owner of the cantina is a compadre of the man in charge of distributing beer in the region. In light of their public denunciation of the cantina, the women expected that the bar would be closed and their problem thus resolved. Nevertheless, that did not occur, and it is very unlikely that they will succeed. The women as well as others in the community have had to resign themselves, and there is no alternative but to watch the cantina owners making more money with every passing day as their own households grow poorer.

For Celayans, the opening of a cantina is one of several signs of change that reflect the passage of time and various processes that have influenced Celaya's evolution from a settlement into a community. Indeed, when one asks residents if they believe their community has changed, most answer with a resounding "yes." For them, many changes can be seen visually, such as the presence of a church and school, concrete houses, furniture and electrical appliances, the bar, drinking water, and electricity. However, they are also aware of other, less readily visible, changes, which are a consequence of a variety of social, political, and economic processes that southern Sinaloa has experienced since the middle of the twentieth century. These changes are related to migratory processes, the expansion of commercial agriculture, environmental deterioration, and economic transformation at both the local and regional levels.

Immigration, for example, is one process that has greatly influenced the formation of southern Sinaloan communities. For Celaya, immigration has not reached the same levels nor has it had such an impact as it has had in El Cerro and other of the region's communities. However, in Celaya, it has also played a significant role in the creation of new social networks that transcend the community's geographic boundaries. The case of the family of Victoria and Lorenzo, discussed below, illustrates this process.

From Peasants to Wage Laborers: The Migration Experience of a Celayan Family

Whenever I did fieldwork in Celaya, I visited Victoria. Because she'd always had the urge to write about her life, she had asked me to get her a diary. On the day I went to deliver it, she was alone, seated in a rocking chair, contemplating the colorful birds she kept in various cages. On several occasions, she had said that she wanted to tell me her life story, but only when we could be alone so that no one would interrupt us. One day, when we had started to talk, her mother arrived to visit, and we had to postpone our conversation because, Victoria confessed, her mother did not like her talking about the past. On the afternoon I dropped by to bring her the diary, she told me that it was a good time to talk because her husband was away working and her children were in school. I sat in a chair at her side, and we began to talk about her life. Victoria, enraptured, looked at the pink bougainvilleas that adorned the arches of her house while she dug deep into her memories. She began to reminisce about her decision to leave her hometown and about her life in general: "My life has been a heavy cross to bear, from the moment that we left our home. I look at the people who live here, and no one has suffered more than I have suffered."

Born in 1954, Victoria grew up in a rural community in a municipio in Jalisco. She arrived in Celaya when she was fifteen years old. She recalled her childhood as one filled with need and limitation because of the poverty in which her family lived: "We were very poor. We were always struggling, and, worse yet, my father was a drunk. Sometimes he had to go to town to sell firewood or charcoal, but he often got drunk and would spend the few pesos that he had earned."

Even though her father drank, Victoria remembers him with nostalgia and affection. The memories that she still has of her father return each time that she watches the rain fall on the trees and plants that she herself planted in the patio of her house:

> I really like the rain. Each time that it rains, the memories come back. It makes me sad and happy, too. I remember when I was helping my father work in his cornfield . . . it would rain, and he would put on a cape and sit on a rock. Like baby chicks, we would sit tucked beneath that cape. My father would fall asleep, and we would come out very carefully so as not to awaken him, and we would go and play.

While she was still a child, she met her husband, Lorenzo. They would marry when she was barely fourteen years old and he was only fifteen. Only a few months after their marriage, an incident happened in the rancho in Jalisco that forever changed the course of their lives. Victoria refers to this event as something "very momentous and very private." Even though she never told me the specific details, she did explain that they had to flee because people in the community wanted to kill her husband. I never knew the reason. Nevertheless, Victoria did tell me that during an attack on her husband, a cattleman accidentally shot her father. Three days later, they buried him, and Victoria and her husband escaped that night, escorted by a police officer, who was her father's brother. They went to live in Teacapán, a coastal ejido near Celaya, in the municipio of Escuinapa. Here Lorenzo's brother, Paco, lived.

They lived in Teacapán for five months until Lorenzo got work as a guard in a hacienda near Celaya that belonged to a physician from Escuinapa. His job required that he tend the livestock and fields, night and day, and the doctor gave him a small house where he and Victoria could live. Two years later, they had saved enough to buy the land they own today in Celaya. They began to build their house, little by little, room by room. Living in Celaya was very hard on Victoria at first because she could not get accustomed to the new community.

Years passed and with the birth of her four children, Victoria finally got used to living in Celaya. Both she and her husband had to work hard to bring up the family right. For fifteen years, Victoria worked for the physician for whom her husband also worked. Her job consisted of organizing the group of women who harvested lemons from the fruit trees the physician had planted in fields that he had bought from one of Celaya's founders. They invested a large part of their income in enlarging their house. They built a kitchen, bath, porch, and three bedrooms.

For a while, it seemed that finally her life was on a more tranquil course. Then, suddenly, one of her children died. The boy was working on the same ranch as his father, and it seems that he was cleaning a pistol when it accidentally went off and killed him. Both Victoria and Lorenzo were devastated by the death of their son. When I last saw them during the summer of 2001, they were barely beginning to recover from the enormous loss that his death meant for them.

Victoria and Lorenzo's story reveals important aspects about the migration to southern Sinaloa and the settlement of people in rural communities in the region. Like them, most who settled in Celaya and in other rural communities in the municipio of Escuinapa came from rural communities, primarily in the states of Jalisco and Michoacán. Also, most immigrants came in search of better economic opportunities. As is true with El Cerro, many immigrants arrived first at other communities in Escuinapa before finally settling where they reside today. In Celaya, as in many other southern Sinaloan settlements, the migratory process was influenced by social networks of relatives and friends already living in the community and by government policies, such as the Agrarian Reform Law, which encouraged the formation of many of these communities in the first place.

As the case of Victoria and Lorenzo shows, the migratory flow to southern Sinaloa also reveals individual motives that encourage migration, its regional character, its gender dimensions, and the social and economic conditions that influence migrants' lives. As was the case for the original inhabitants of the rural southern Sinaloa communities, these migrants depend on the availability of work in commercial agriculture and fishing to survive. However, in contrast to El Cerro and other ejidos in the region, immigration into the community has been limited by Celaya's lack of available land and the requirement that people purchase their property.

As is happening in other rural communities in Escuinapa, Celaya is changing. Today, this community is a geographic and social space with its own physical characteristics that emerged as a result of the processes that led to its development as a community.

The Physical Layout of Celaya

The community's physical layout seems, at first glance, similar to that of other communities and ejidos in the area. Celaya, like El Cerro, has two principal sections, a residential area and the agricultural fields. The residential area consists of fifty-four houses, lined up one next to the other, on three horizontal streets and two vertical unpaved streets. Unlike El Cerro, the three horizontal streets have names. But because there are no street signs, only the members of the community know these names. When you travel to Celaya by car, the driver will usually ask if you want to be dropped off on the first, second, or third street, referring to the horizontal streets.

All the social, political, and economic life of the community's households occur in the residential area. Here one may observe with greater clarity the physical changes that Celaya has undergone since its beginnings as a human settlement. However, the settlement does not have a complex infrastructure.

Celaya has a kindergarten and an elementary school. There is also a Catholic church, where a priest from the town of Escuinapa says mass once a week and where certain religious rites are celebrated, such as baptisms, quinceañeras, and the Día de la Virgen, so important to the Celayans.

The community's store, located on the first street, was the CONASUPO many years ago, but today it bears the name DIFCONSA. It sells basic goods, such as rice, beans, oil, onions, potatoes, soda, candy, and chips. Additionally, various households sell candy, chips, and sodas, and two even have video game machines, to which the children of Celaya seem to be continuously glued.

In addition to the church, store, and schools, there is also the cantina, disguised as a restaurant, which opened in 1997. It operates out of one of the homes. Its owners, nevertheless, refuse to admit that their "restaurant" is really a bar. They defend their position by saying that the people, especially the women, are envious of the business because it is making money for its owners (Castro 1998).

The community's other section consists of agricultural fields sprinkled among the coconut palms, lagoons, and mango groves that surround the town. Some of these fields were sold to businesspeople and physicians from Escuinapa so that they could grow mangoes, chilies, and lemons. Depending on the distance, the Celayans who still own their parcels and cultivate them usually come and go on foot or by horse. At least two families use tractors to get to their land. The fields and their crops give Celaya its character as an agricultural community. They also function as a living symbol of the founders' struggle to obtain this land.

Political Structure

If, on one hand, the community's physical structure is a symbol of change, on the other hand, its political organization has not changed since its founding. That organization is based on the appointment of a síndico, a man from the community who has a good reputation and can maintain law and order.

Local Government: The Síndico

While I was doing fieldwork in Celaya in June 1998, an incident occurred that has now become part of the community's oral history. A young man, Mauricio, was visiting the community, as he was accustomed to doing every Sunday to see his boyfriend. That Sunday, he arrived very early in the morning dressed in a white *guayabera* (loose shirt), white pants, and white shoes. When he arrived at his boyfriend's house, a relative told him that the man was not home because he had gone to Isla del Bosque. Mauricio, despite being angry, decided to wait for him to return, and to pass the time, he went for a drink at the cantina. When he left the cantina, he went again to the man's house to see if he had returned. The man's parents, along with two of their other children, had brought chairs out to the street and were sitting and chatting among themselves. They failed to notice when Mauricio went inside through the backdoor. Mauricio, being drunk, climbed under the mother's bed and fell asleep.

At nightfall, the woman went to her room to go to bed, and, as she did every night, she took off her shoes to place them under the bed. On lifting up the coverlet, she was understandably startled to see under her bed a white bundle, immobile and of indefinite form. She was so frightened that she started screaming, and her husband and children ran into the room. The woman thought that the white mass was a ghost of a man who had died in Celaya a few weeks before. The children and husband tried to calm her, saying that it was just some sheets bunched up together. To prove it, one child took a broomstick and began to poke the bundle. Mauricio, feeling the jabs, awoke from his profound sleep, opened his eyes, and moved his hands and legs. With that, everyone began to scream in chorus. Mauricio, perhaps the most frightened of all, scrambled out from under the bed and ran out of the house. The mother, when she saw who it was, chased him down the street with the broom.

They failed to catch Mauricio, so they went to complain to Daniel, who, at the time, was the síndico of Celaya. Daniel, quite against his will, had no choice but to notify the police in Escuinapa's town hall. After a few hours, two police officers arrived, went to the woman's house, and mentioned that they had met a man going to the cantina who told them he didn't know anything about the incident. The woman asked the police officers to describe the man physically, and when she confirmed that he was Mauricio, the policemen ran out in pursuit of him. Mauricio saw them coming, began to run, and, jumping the barbed wire fences, he hid in the mango groves. The police officers ran after him, but they could not find him.

Hours passed, and Mauricio was nowhere to be found. The police officers, tired of waiting, returned to Escuinapa. The residents of Celaya began to grow concerned for him, and many feared that something bad might have happened to him because he was known to have a heart condition. At dawn, the townspeople sent some children to find him, which they did, asleep under a mango tree. Mauricio awoke and soon he was seen going down one of the towns' streets, and, without saying goodbye to anyone, he got on a bus and left. Since then, he has never returned.

This anecdote not only gives a glimpse of daily life in Celaya but it also reflects some of the paradoxes that the síndico faces: ensuring peace and order while leaving personal sentiments aside. One day, seated in a hammock in the patio of his house, Daniel confessed to me that he had felt terrible having to call the police to search for Mauricio. He did not want to do it, but he had to because his duties as síndico require it. For Daniel, calling the police felt like a betrayal of the friendship and trust that Mauricio had placed in him and the community. Mauricio was well known there, and the people liked him a lot and respected him because he made contributions to community events. Mauricio had organized dances to raise money for the school, and one of Daniel's biggest concerns was not knowing who would take Mauricio's place now that he had detached himself from the community.

When I interviewed Daniel in 1997, he had been in the position for two years, having been elected in 1995. Seated in his sister Raquel's kitchen, while she busied herself making tacos to sell, Daniel reflected on his experiences and his role as síndico. "It is *un carguito trabajosillo* (a tough little job) that requires a lot of patience," he told me. Moreover, "One has to know how to control people and, at the same time, live with them," he added. When people from Escuinapa's presidencia municipal came to ask him to run for síndico, Daniel had doubts about it. He was uncertain how he would avoid neglecting his agricultural fields if he fulfilled all the duties that he would have as síndico. However, he convinced himself to run, saying, "I'm going to throw my hat in the ring, and if I can't do the job, well, they can remove me."

I asked him how things were going with his duties as síndico. He told me it was going well because he had not failed in the eyes of anyone in the community. According to him, the key to success in this post is to avoid conceit or the belief that you are better than the rest. As Daniel put it, "One must do whatever it takes to be certain that the post doesn't go to one's head." I also asked him about the most difficult situations that he has encountered as síndico. He told me that there were three types of issues in which he involved himself that were very difficult to resolve.

The most frequent is domestic violence, which usually occurs because the husband has been tippling and is drunk, and then he beats his wife. In these cases, the foremost responsibility of the síndico is to go to the house and talk to the couple. Daniel always tries to talk with them, especially the husbands, to make them see that what they did was wrong. He tells husbands, "You shouldn't argue. That isn't how you treat your family; you mustn't let the alcohol take over. I know what it feels like when you are walking around in a mood from the alcohol, but in half an hour, it's over. Then you can't even look at your wife for the shame you feel." If after this chat, the husband continues drinking and beating his wife, Daniel reports him to the Office for Public Safety in the city hall. But that is not always a solution, according to Daniel. There have been many cases, he claims, in which he presses charges against the husband, who is called to appear at the presidencia municipal. However, in front of the director, the wife usually changes her story to protect her husband. That is why Daniel prefers to try to resolve these cases within the community and to achieve *por las buenas*—through persuasion—that the husband respect his wife.

Another situation in which Daniel intervenes arises when livestock stray into someone's fields and eat the crops. Many of these cases end in fights, and the injured party comes personally to lodge a complaint with the síndico. Daniel tries to resolve the situation by going in person to see the owner of the livestock at his home and to persuade him to take responsibility for the damages. Daniel estimates the cost of the damage, and he draws up an agreement for the owner of the livestock to sign, in which he promises to pay the injured party, whether in cash or in installment payments, for the losses caused by his livestock. If, after several weeks, the injured party does not begin to receive payments, the síndico has no choice but to report it to the Office for Public Safety.

The third situation in which Daniel involves himself, and the one that is perhaps the most difficult to resolve, are complaints relating to the operation of the cantina. He personally supported the community and helped write the petition to close the place. Daniel agreed that the cantina has contributed to disturbing the peace and to increasing the consumption of alcohol, especially among young men.

Celayans view the post of síndico as a *cargo,* or burden. This view is influenced by the situations in which the síndico intervenes and his duty to negotiate a fair solution. However, in Celaya, the term "cargo" does not carry the same connotation that it has in indigenous Mexican communities. In rural southern Sinaloa communities, the post of síndico does not have any religious function or meaning. It is, instead, a political post to which the community's adult men, mostly married, aspire. The post represents an opportunity for men to offer their services to the community. Nevertheless, not all the men in the community have to be síndico at some point in their lives. Moreover, contrary to what happens in the cargo system in Mesoamérica, a man can refuse to accept the duties of síndico without suffering any political or social repercussion.

The síndico in Celaya is chosen in the same way as in the other rural communities in Escuinapa. During the electoral campaigns for presidente municipal, each candidate selects a candidate for síndico in each of the rural communities. If the candidate wins the position of presidente municipal, the man that he picked for síndico is automatically installed in the post. Years ago, before Daniel was nominated, the mayor directly elected the síndico, based on two principal criteria: residence in the community and a willingness to attend the monthly meetings held in the city hall. Very little importance was placed on personal qualities or the capacity of the person to fulfill the role. Today in Celaya, a vote is taken to select the síndico. The mayor sends a representative, a bureaucrat (*licenciado*), to organize the elections and count the votes of the members of the community.

Nowadays, to be a candidate for síndico, a man has to fulfill the following prerequisites: residence in the community, no criminal record, and submission of a resume that lists all the activities in which he has participated and the different positions he has held in the community. The appointment letter from the presidencia municipal formally lays out the general duties of síndico. At a local level, these responsibilities consist of guarding the public order and issuing permits for fiestas and celebrations. At a regional level, the síndico acts as a liaison between the community and the larger political organization in the municipio because he must report directly to the presidencia municipal about the problems that arise in the community as well as the social events that occur there.

The material benefits that the síndico receives in compensation are few. The presidencia municipal pays a monthly salary, around twenty-five dollars. It also issues him a firearm and written permit to carry it. Very few men make the decision to accept the síndico nomination based on the material benefits that they would receive. For Daniel, as for many others, the main attraction of holding the post of síndico is related to the respect, power, and prestige it brings. The community considers the síndico a leader who has the top authority for ensuring order and that the residents live in peace and harmony.

Celayans are aware of the duties that the síndico must perform and of the qualities that he should possess to be a good leader. For the Celayans, the síndico must have character traits that reflect his capacity to resolve problems that the community faces. If he were a weak man, without a good character, he would be considered someone who is inattentive to the community's life and consequently, he would not merit the respect nor admiration that he would otherwise earn through his concern with the community's issues.

Outside the physical boundaries of the community, the síndico also has an opportunity to develop new social and political relationships that benefit him. The post of síndico lasts only three years, and after a term ends, the presidencia municipal may recruit him, or agricultural businesspeople may contact him to organize *cuadrillas* to work in their fields. Although it is an effective and recognized means of serving and of exercising leadership in the community, the position of síndico is open only to men.

In Celaya, another common means of achieving leadership is by volunteering. These services, incorporated for the most part within the structure and organization of various committees, serve to support the participation and promote the cooperation of Celayans on issues that concern them as a community. The involvement of the Celayans, primarily women, nourishes these committees. Celayans organize along gender lines in programs or initiatives on health, education, and religion.

Local Committees: Service and Cooperation within the Community

In Celaya, as in El Cerro, two kinds of committees operate: those related to government programs, and those initiated by the Celayans themselves. The first type organizes as a way of repaying the services that the government provides residents of rural settlements. Participation in this type of committee is, in most cases, mandatory in order to receive specific benefits, such as, for example, health care or education. In this type of committee, the members function principally to serve their community as payment for the government-provided services.

The committees that Celayans organize address community needs. The success or failure in achieving the set objectives depends on two primary factors: leadership and cooperation.

To explain the functioning of these committees in detail, I have chosen to focus on two that have operated in Celaya for more than ten years. The Comité de Salud (Health Committee) represents the type of committee supported by the government, while the Comité de la Iglesia (Church Committee) arose as a community initiative.

El Comité de Salud: The IMSS–Solidaridad Program in the Local Context The Instituto Mexicano del Seguro Social–Solidaridad (IMSSS) program is under the Programa Nacional de Desarrollo (National Development Program) and the Programa de Reforma del Sector Salud (Program on Health Care Reform) for 1995–2000. The IMSSS began in 1979, when the Mexican government combined the Instituto Mexicano del Seguro Social (IMSS) with the main office for the Coordinación General del Plan Nacional de Zonas Deprimidas y Grupos Marginados (General Coordination of the National Plan for Depressed Zones and Marginal Groups, or COPLAMAR). This fusion resulted in the Programa IMSS–COPLAMAR. Ten years later, in 1989, during the presidency of Carlos Salinas de Gortari, the program's infrastructure increased, and the name changed to IMSS–Solidaridad (Gobierno del Estado 2000).

The program's main goals are to offer medical services and to involve communities in promoting the health care of their residents. The program focuses on communities considered marginal because of high poverty levels, and it operates in seventeen Mexican states, including Sinaloa, and in 16,858 communities (Gobierno del Estado 2000).

A major component of the program is the Health Committee, which operates at the community level. This committee functions as a liaison between the community and the rural medical unit that delivers basic health care to the residents. It usually consists of three to six residents of the settlement, one of whom is selected as president and the rest as the spokespeople for health, sanitation, nutrition, and education. The people who work in the rural medical unit usually provide the committee members with training and advice.

Celaya's Health Committee consists of six members: a president and five spokespeople. All are women who were born and raised in Celaya. The community does not have a rural medical unit because it has fewer than five hundred inhabitants. Consequently, the committee receives help from the unit operating in the ejido of Isla del Bosque. The president of the committee, Adela, received basic training in first aid and in diagnosis and treatment of common, easily treated diseases.[1]

People who receive medical care under this program must do community service. Adela, as committee president, is responsible for organizing people to perform their community service, which usually consists of cleaning up the settlement. It is common on Sunday morning before mass to see men and women cutting trees, clearing, and cleaning the area around the settlement, especially the area that separates Celaya from the main highway. Others are in charge of picking up trash in the streets and placing it in a receptacle for burning. People are also responsible for cleaning their yards.

Each week, Adela and the spokespeople organize a brigade responsible for fulfilling community service. They are also responsible for ensuring that people turn out to participate. If someone does not attend, they find out why and remind the person that his or her presence is important because it benefits the community. Even though her duty requires her to report nonparticipants to the rural medical unit, Adela usually gives them a second chance. She reports only those who have received services through the program and yet repeatedly do not show up and have no valid excuse.

The participation in the Health Committee is mandatory, required by the government in exchange for free health services for the community. A person is a member of the committee throughout the time in which he or she may use the health services that the IMSSS program offers.

El Comité de la Iglesia: Religion as a Basis for Cooperation Unlike the Health Committee, participation in the Church Committee is entirely voluntary. It consists of six women: a president, a treasurer, a secretary, and three members-at-large. It formed because of the community's decision to build a Catholic church—in Celaya, most of the households are Catholic.[2] People who wanted to hear mass had to travel to Escuinapa or Isla del Bosque. The Celayans believed that to become a true community, they should have a church where they could celebrate mass and the rites that form part of the life cycle. The committee from the outset was always composed of women because, as Victoria pointed out, "Men don't have a head for religious matters; they are very inattentive."

Victoria and the other committee members had to work hard to build the church. They raised most of the money selling food and organizing raffles. The rest was a gift from the presidencia municipal. The committee was responsible for ensuring that the priest came every Sunday to give mass. They also took responsibility for decorating the church and helping to organize baptisms and other events held there. For example, July 4, the Día de la Virgen del Refugio, Celaya's patron saint, is an important religious celebration for the community. The preparation starts several months in advance, as the committee enlists the help of all the residents. The event requires extensive organization and planning as well as money to cover the costs. The committee is in charge of collecting funds and asking the presidente municipal for his help in making the event possible. The celebration lasts the entire day, from early morning until late at night. To mark its opening, the committee hires a mariachi band that arrives at dawn to sing "Las Mañanitas" to the Virgin. The celebration continues throughout the day with a series of events, provided by the presidente municipal, that include bicycle races, dances, and even poetry readings and fireworks. Along with the committee, the rest of the women in the community are deeply involved in putting on this annual event.

In addition to these two committees, where women are clearly the major participants, others require everyone's cooperation. For example, the Comité de Debates (Storm Committee) is made up solely of men. They are responsible for assuring that the homes and community infrastructure are not seriously damaged during hurricanes and storms. The Comité de la Escuela (School Committee), made up of both men and women, is organized by teachers and requires the participation of the parents whose children study in the community's elementary school.

The organization and participation of the Celayans in the various committees is only one reflection of their involvement and solidarity at the community level. One reason solidarity and cooperation is possible is that Celaya still remains a small settlement. This is reflected in the community's demographic structure.

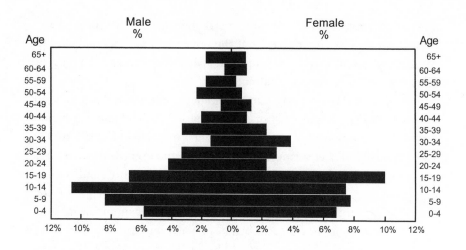

Figure 6.1
Age-sex structure of Celaya's population, 1989

Changes in Demographic Structure, 1989–2001

Even though Celaya does not have a fixed settlement pattern, the residents know exactly which of the houses were built first in the community and where they are located. These buildings are scattered, and originally, the space between them was far more extensive than it is today. Now, the number of houses has increased, and it is common to find two or more built on the same lot.

When I took my first community census in 1989, Celaya had 311 inhabitants, distributed in fifty-three households. The average household had six members. The number of children per household varied between three and eleven, with the average being five. In 1989, the male population was slightly larger than the female population (52 percent and 48 percent, respectively).

In 1989, Celaya's population was also relatively young, with 63 percent under twenty years of age, split equally between men and women (see figure 6.1). The segment sixty-five years of age or older was very small and constituted 2.6 percent of the population. Like El Cerro, Celaya is a community that formed relatively recently, which explains the low numbers of older people. Indeed, when I conducted fieldwork in 1989, the community had existed for only twenty-six years.

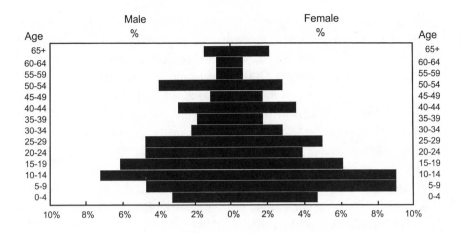

Figure 6.2
Age-sex structure of Celaya's population, 2001

Unlike El Cerro, Celaya has lost population. According to the census I took in 2001, there were 277 inhabitants, 34 fewer than in 1989. Although the number of households increased from 53 in 1989 to 59 in 2001, that is not significant growth.

The decline in population is the outcome of two factors: increase in emigration and death. During the last five years, emigration rates have risen. In at least three cases, entire families have left to live in Tijuana or Rosarito in Baja California. In other cases, individual family members who appeared in the 1989 census no longer live in the community. Some have migrated to Tijuana or the United States and others have gone to live in Mazatlán, the town of Escuinapa, or other rural communities, such as Teacapán or Isla del Bosque. Land scarcity along with economic considerations lead especially young married people to go to live in the town of Escuinapa or other rural communities in the area. The scarcity of land and the system of landholding based on small properties has also contributed to limiting immigration to the community. Unlike what occurs in El Cerro, in Celaya, no houses are available for rent, and everyone who wants to live in the community has to buy, at minimum, a lot on which they can build a house.

Another factor, mortality rates, although not terribly significant, must also be considered in explaining the decline in the number of inhabitants in Celaya. Since I took the first census in Celaya in 1989, at least ten people who were included have died. Of these, only one was a woman. Only three died of old age, and the rest died in work-related accidents.

In spite of the deaths of mostly young people and the aging of its founders, Celaya continues to be composed primarily of young people (see figure 6.2). According to my 2001 census, 83 percent of the population is thirty-nine years old or younger, and only 13 percent is fifty years or older. The gender composition of the overall population has also changed since 1989, with the female portion (54 percent) now larger than the male portion (46 percent). Again, this can be attributed to emigration and the death of males. The number of people who are sixty-five years of age or older has increased slightly (1 percent) because of the aging of the original population, as is the case in El Cerro.

The fact that Celaya continues to comprise primarily young people has important implications. One of the challenges confronting Celayans is how to maintain a population balance to ensure the community's effective functioning and structure. It is hard to meet this challenge because of the lack of viable economic opportunities, the degradation of natural resources—especially the lagoons and marshes—and the scarcity of land within the community. These factors, together, contribute to making the future fate of Celayans not that much different from what is in store for the people of El Cerro. As in El Cerro, one of the viable alternatives is emigration, and that process is beginning in Celaya. In Celaya, the factors mentioned above affect the community's households to different degrees, depending, in part, on the makeup of the household.

Las Temporadas y el Piojillo:
The Economic Cycle of Celayans

In July 1999, while I was in Celaya doing fieldwork, Carlos, my husband, and I went to see a parcel of land that Alfonso's brother was planting. Even though we had arrived early in the morning with the intention of talking with several farmers and visiting their fields, no one was out cultivating his land at the time. When we arrived in the community at 9 a.m., almost all the men had already left for work at jobs outside the community. Celaya had turned into a town of women. The only voices that could be heard were those of the women talking or scolding their children while they did their domestic chores. We visited several houses, asking if they knew of people who were planting their fields so that we could talk with them. The women said that there were only four or five men in the community who still cultivated their fields. Of these, only one, Alfonso's brother, was working that day on his land. We went to his house, and his wife told us that he had gone to his field. The woman asked Azucena, her ten-year-old granddaughter, to take us there. With Azucena as our guide, the three of us left on foot under the beating sun, bordering the lagoons in whose mangrove trees nested hundreds of migratory birds.

Nearing the field we met Jesús, a man from Isla del Bosque, who was plowing a field with a tractor so that he could plant watermelons. We stopped to chat with him, and he told us that a man from Escuinapa owned the field where he was working. Jesús told us that he had an arrangement with the owner to receive 25 percent of the harvest in exchange for clearing and planting the land.

The parcel of Roberto, Alfonso's brother, bordered the field belonging to the Escuinapan, and in comparison, it looked like a dirt pile. While Jesús plowed the Escuinapan's field with a tractor, Roberto used a horse-drawn plow, and his brother-in-law, Pepe, walked behind him, planting the watermelon seeds by hand and covering them with earth that he kicked over the top. They were planting the field *a medias*; that is, each would receive half of the harvest produced. Because they did not have any irrigation pumps, they were taking advantage of the start of the rainy season to be able to sow the crop.

As we sat together to eat, Carlos, Azucena, and I eating the flour tortillas we had bought in the Tienda Ley in Escuinapa while the men ate the lunch that their wives had prepared, Pepe told us about his experiences trying to migrate to El Norte, the United States. With a great sense of humor, he told us how he had failed three times as he tried to cross the border that separates Mexico from the United States so that he could go to live with an American woman he had met in Teacapán. After eating, Carlos, Azucena, and I returned to Celaya, and Roberto and Pepe continued plowing and planting the fields. When we passed the field where Jesús was working, he had finished, and he offered us a ride back to Celaya.

This vignette illustrates three important aspects of the Celayan economy. First, even though subsistence agriculture is still practiced in the community, fewer and fewer households depend entirely upon it for survival. Sec-

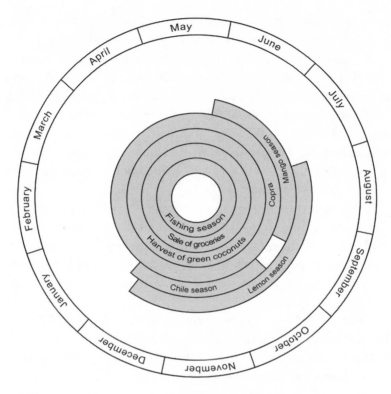

Figure 6.3
The economic cycle of Celaya

ond, commercial agriculture continues as time passes to acquire greater importance. Third, migration is gaining importance as an economic alternative both within Celaya and within the region generally.

When one asks why agriculture is no longer as important as it was when the community formed in the 1960s, one of the answers is that most of the founders have sold their fields. Some sold them to other Celayans or to people coming from other states, but most sold them to the agricultural businesspeople from the town of Escuinapa. When asked about the circumstances that motivated people to sell their land, many said they believed that most sold for economic reasons. When Celayans first arrived from Las Cabras to establish the community, the available economic alternatives were very limited. They hoped to be able to live off the land, but reality proved different. Residents soon discovered that to make their fields produce, they needed a minimum of capital to invest in seed, fertilizers, tools, and other farm-related items that most lacked at the time. Therefore they opted to sell the land and invest part of the money they made in improving their houses. Many Celayans agree that "in those days, one could make more money selling land than farming it." Others believe that some sold their parcels because they didn't want to be farmers. And some thought certain people sold simply because they wanted to have money to spend on drink and other wasteful pastimes.

The reasons that the Celayans have for selling their lands vary, but taken together they demonstrate that the land stopped being a symbol of a shared struggle and turned into a commodity. While in the past, having land to farm was a symbol of triumph achieved by thousands of peones in southern Sinaloa who struggled against the state and the local and regional bourgeoisie who exercised control in the area, today for the Celayans, land symbolizes only one more aspect of the history of the development and evolution of their rancho as a community. For the founding Celayans, land was a status symbol and a source of prestige, a way of measuring socioeconomic differences that existed among the households. Nowadays, land symbolizes the past as coconut, mango, and chili plantations continue to proliferate in the region.

The coconut palms in the patios of the Celayan homes do not easily let one forget that this is a community linked to a regional market. The mango and chili plantations lying next to the community serve as a perennial reminder that Celaya has also joined the global marketplace. As subsistence agriculture continues to decline, the plantations that produce agricultural export commodities are increasing.

As in El Cerro, most households survive because members participate in a cycle of economic and productive activities, which includes subsistence agriculture, wage labor in commercial agriculture, fishing in the lagoons and marshes, working as domestics, and, in several instances, selling food, candy, sodas, and alcoholic beverages from small stores located inside homes (see figure 6.3).

Celaya's founding families stayed afloat by farming their parcels and fishing for shrimp and other aquatic life abundant in the nearby lagoons or marshes. Like subsistence agriculture, shrimp fishing is declining in importance with each passing day, but it continues to be a main aquatic resource, both because of its commercial value and the ease with which it is caught. Other aquatic resources with economic importance for the

Celayans are jaiba and lagoon fish, such as lisa and mojarra. Because Celaya lacks an organized fishing cooperative, the volume of shrimp that Celayans produce is minimal; unlike the cooperatives, they lack the needed infrastructure and equipment to fish for, store, and process shrimp.

In Celaya, most households have members who fish for shrimp, but most Celayans do not perceive themselves as fishermen. Indeed, in my 1989 census, not one household indicated that any member dedicated himself or herself to fishing. In reality, the Celayans do not consider fishing to be a primary economic activity because of its low productivity and the sporadic way in which it is pursued. Generally, households complement their incomes with earnings from shrimp fishing. Faced with a financial emergency, some family members will fish for shrimp to sell within the community or in the town of Escuinapa. In this context, shrimp can be viewed as a secret bank account that is used to cover urgent needs that arise in the household.

If neither fishing nor agriculture are the primary economic activities through which Celayan households now survive, then what do the Celayans live on? Celaya is one of many rural communities in southern Sinaloa that provides the labor force that is the motor for the area's commercial agriculture. The participation of members of Celayan households in agricultural wage labor has increased from 1989 to 2001. According to my 1989 survey, only 32 percent of the households had one or more members who worked as agricultural wage laborers, but by 2001, that figure reached 82 percent for the households that depend on income generated in commercial agriculture. Most Celayan households currently have one or more members who earn their living as agricultural day laborers on the nearby coconut, mango, or chili plantations, which reflects two important changes that have occurred at the local and regional level. First, in 1989, 38 percent of the households had a member who belonged to the shrimp cooperative that the community established in 1986. When the shrimp aquaculture project failed due to internal conflicts within the cooperative that ran it, its members returned to working as agricultural wage laborers or jornaleros. At the regional level, the growth in commercial agriculture reflects the neoliberal policies implemented at the end of the 1980s and favoring the model of export-led economic development.

Chilies are one of the most important crops that the municipio produces. Their cultivation is concentrated in the Isla del Bosque, Palmito El Verde, and Cristo Rey ejidos, located in one of the municipio's largest valleys, very close to Celaya. Chili production starts in October, when the land is prepared for planting, and it closes at the end of December with the harvest, which is taken in trucks to the processing plants in Escuinapa for packing and exportation.

Coconut is another cash crop with which the Celayans work. During the administration of Antonio Toledo Corro, an ex-governor of Sinaloa, the idea arose to build a processing plant for coconut, and the coastal areas of Escuinapa were planted with coconut palms. In Escuinapa, coconut is harvested in both its stages: green (that is, unripe) and dry. Both the green coconut and the copra seasons run year round.

The Celayans refer to the harvest or cutting of the mango as the *temporada del mango,* which begins at the start of June and concludes around the end of August or early September. It is a task that involves heavy manual labor. Celaya supplies part of the workforce each season, when the owners of the plantations come directly to the community to hire workers.

The lemon harvest is yet another agricultural job in which the Celayans are employed as wage workers. Most Celayans, both men and women, work in the harvest, which starts at the beginning of August and continues until the end of December. The lemons are packed for exportation in packing plants in Escuinapa.

Almost 80 percent of the Celayan households have at least one member who works as an agricultural day laborer. Although commercial agriculture provides a large part of the overall income for households, other economic activities also generate income for Celayans. One of these is domestic housework, which some Celayan women perform. The Hacienda Las Cabras employs one Celayan, Sonia, as a cook. Sonia has worked as cook there for more than twenty years. Other women, especially young ones, get work as domestic employees in the houses of professional people or politicians in Escuinapa.

Even though Celaya is a small community with a limited range of economic activities for its households, it is highly stratified, both socially and economically. This stratification is reflected in the variation in structure and makeup of the houses and in material possessions, including household items and livestock. It is also reflected in how Celayans view each other.

Unos Tenemos Menos que Otros:
The Socioeconomic Stratification of Households

The first impression that one forms of Celaya is that there is an equally shared poverty, but this quickly vanishes when one visits each of the households in the community. When observing houses in detail, whether watching the pigs and chickens running around the patios, or noticing the furniture and electrical appliances in the living rooms and kitchens, one can see substantial economic inequalities. The Celayans themselves recognize the existence and the causes of these inequalities. Daily conversations often turn to discussions about which family is well off or which scarcely has enough to eat.

One criterion that Celayans use to categorize households socioeconomically is the wealth that each possesses. The unequal distribution of wealth among the households is visible in the houses themselves, and in the furniture, electrical appliances, and animals that families own. For the Celayans, a family that possesses a good house with nice furniture and modern electrical appliances is well off economically. If, on the contrary, a family lives in a poor house, with little furniture, and a dirt floor, the Celayans interpret that as a sign that the family is poorly off economically.

Celayan houses vary in size, architecture, and building material. Indeed, the range in the types of houses in the community varies from those built with palm-frond walls and roofs to those built from concrete block. One of the greatest aspirations that the Celayans have is to be able to own a big, well-built house, and they are very proud when they achieve this. Thus, when one asks the Celayans how they constructed their houses, behind their answer is usually hidden a story of sacrifices made to be able to build it.

Once, while I was doing fieldwork in the community in 1998, I went to visit Victoria, and the first thing that I noticed was that her kitchen was very clean and well organized. She had the glasses, all the same color, placed on a shelf on the wall, and the pots and pans were hanging from the ceiling. I mentioned that I really liked her house, especially the arches that adorned the main entrance. She proceeded to tell me in great detail how they had built the house, little by little, until it was its current shape and size. Her story underlines the fact that her house began as only a one-room habitation with adobe walls and no floor. The one room served as a living room, kitchen, and bedroom. Later, with assistance from her husband's boss, who lent them money, they were able to begin enlarging the house, adding walls and a concrete roof. It is now one of Celaya's largest and best built homes, with four bedrooms, a living room, a dining room, a kitchen, two bathrooms, and a terrace adorned with arches.

Not all houses in Celaya have the amenities that Victoria's house has, however. At the other extreme are the poorest houses in the community, which are floorless, one-room habitations with adobe blocks or mud walls and palm-frond roofs. Most were among the first homes built in Celaya, and they have managed to survive the inclemencies of time and use. Some of the founding families or their children still live in these houses.

In addition to the houses, possession of material goods and animals represents another criterion Celayans use to rank their households in terms of wealth. The types of consumer goods owned include stoves, televisions, refrigerators, CD players, electric fans, and cars. Animals include those that are eaten or sold, such as pigs, chickens, and turkeys, and work animals, such as horses, burros, and mules.

One of the main arguments of this book is that the economic impoverishment of southern Sinaloa's rural communities has gotten worse, beginning in the 1990s, as a consequence of political changes in the government (especially those putting high priority on the development of commercial agriculture) and environmental damage (especially to the coastal ecosystems). These changes have also had economic repercussions for the households, which is reflected in the quality of housing and in a diminishment in acquisition of consumer goods and animals. To be able to prove this, in 1989 and again in 2001, I compiled information on wealth, using the same socioeconomic survey that I administered to the households in El Cerro. Because Celaya is not an ejido, the households' socioeconomic differences are not based on the control that certain households might exercise over the natural resources available to members of the community.

In 1989, I administered the survey to forty-seven of the community's fifty-three households. In terms of house quality, most (55 percent) had "better" homes, that is, buildings of two or more rooms, made of concrete or adobe, and having a non-dirt floor. Only 11 percent lived in the poorer houses, that is, one-room dirt-floor buildings made of clay.

In 2001, the percentage of families that lived in the better houses had increased to 81 percent, an increase of 26 percent compared to 1989. The percentage of the families that lived in the poorest households had dropped to 7 percent, a reduction of more than 4 percent compared to 1989.

The most commonly owned consumer goods in 1989 were the wardrobe and the sewing machine. All homes had at least a wardrobe, and 79 percent had a sewing machine. The least common were a motor vehicle (6 percent) and a CD player or CD discs (23 percent). In 2001, the most common consumer goods in the households were televisions and electric fans (both 96 percent). Vehicles continued to be the least common, with only 15 percent of the households owning one in 2001. Another of the least common consumer goods in 2001 was the sewing machine—only 15 percent of the homes had one.

The difference in possession of consumer goods between 1989 and 2001 shows that there was an increase of 56 percent in the number of homes that had at least an electric fan. This was the most common household good in the community in 2001. In general terms, the possession of consumer goods in Celayan households increased by 2001. Nevertheless, as in El Cerro, this increase does not necessarily mean that the Celayans had more money to invest in consumer goods in 2001 than they had had in 1989. Instead, many goods are more easily available as a result of NAFTA. Before the agreement, the Celayans had to travel to Mazatlán or Culiacán to buy televisions or CD players. Today, they can buy these things in the store in Escuinapa or through traveling salesmen who routinely come to the community. Celayans also get these goods from relatives and friends living on the border or in the United States, who bring them as gifts when they come to visit.

The most common animals in most Celayan households in 1989 were chickens and pigs. In 2001, these animals were still the most abundant in the community besides horses. Nevertheless, the percentage of households that had pigs and chickens diminished by 31 and 49 percent, respectively. In general terms, the number of animals that Celayans owned had diminished by 2001. This reduction is due in part to the price for some of these animals, especially horses and pigs, which increased in recent years. Moreover, many households complain of the high cost of maintaining chickens and pigs, which keeps them from buying them because they don't have the resources to feed them.

The information presented above represents the etic approach that I used to determine the socioeconomic differences among the Celayan households. Another of my interests was to determine how the households themselves perceived and categorized these differences.

Local Models of Economic and Class Structure

To research how the households themselves explain the socioeconomic differences that exist among them, I used an emic approach, just as I did for El Cerro. Following the same methodology, which is also the methodology that Lynn Stephen (1991) used, I asked four key informants (two men and two women) to rank Celaya's households in groups based on the socioeconomic differences they believe exist among them.

The Celayans believe that the socioeconomic differences that exist in the households are reflected in the wealth that each has. According to the key informants, the differences in wealth, in turn, are reflected in the type of house in which a family lives. According to these informants, socioeconomic differences are also expressed in the economic activities of the members and in the material goods that they own. The least common consumer good in Celaya is the motor vehicle. The four key informants agreed that whether or not a household has one is a significant indicator of how well off that household is. Based on these characteristics, these informants placed Celayan households in three categories: *los pobres* (the poor), those who are *ni bien ni mal* (neither good nor bad, in other words, neither well nor badly off) and *los superiores* (well-to-do).

Los Pobres

According to the key informants, 11 percent of the Celayan households fell into the "poor" category. Of these six households, four are female-headed, in which only the mother works and the children are young or in early adolescence. The other two households have both parents, but the father cannot work due to illness (in one case, the man suffers from rheumatic arthritis and is disabled). These households also comprise members without stable jobs or who earn a very low salary. These families do not own a vehicle, and they live in the poorest houses, built of clay or adobe, floorless, with only one room, and lacking electricity and drinking water. One example from this category is the family of Lorena and her three children, who live in a one-room, floorless adobe house. Since she was widowed ten years ago, she has had to take responsibility for supporting her three children, and most of her income from working as a domestic employee at the Hacienda Las Cabras goes to feeding and educating her children.

Ni Bien ni Mal

The key informants categorized the majority of the households (83 percent) as being those that *"no tienen mucho ni poco"* ("do not have very much nor very little"), or who *"no viven ni bien ni mal"* ("do not live particularly well nor particularly badly"). Although their members work, these households earn only enough to cover the basic costs of living, including food, health care, and education. These households are unable to save enough money to purchase a vehicle or construct a large, well-built house. The family of Delia, her husband Tito, and their three children is an example of this type of household. They have a two-room house, with concrete walls and floor. They also own some electrical appliances, such as a refrigerator, a blender, an iron, and a fan, as well as animals, such as pigs and chickens. However, Tito is the only member of the family who works, and his entire salary goes to supporting the family.

Los Superiores

The four key informants placed only four of all the households in Celaya, that is, 8 percent, in the "superior" category. These households have the largest and best built houses, and, additionally, one or more of the family members has at least one stable, year-round, well-paying job. These households also have one or more vehicles. The four key informants consider don Alfonso's and Angelita's household to be among the most well off. Alfonso has stable work, as a heavy machinery operator for Escuinapa's presidencia municipal, that pays a fixed salary. His children are married and the household expenses are minimal. His house is built with concrete walls and floor, and it consists of a living room, kitchen, bathroom, and three bedrooms.

The classification of the households in Celaya also reflects the gender differences of the four key informants. In classifying the households in terms of wealth, the men always used the criteria of house quality and size, whether or not a family owned a vehicle, and the quantity and type of livestock. For the two women informants, household wealth was also an important indicator, but wealth alone was not the most important indicator. For these women, the process of wealth accumulation was also connected to other factors, such as domestic violence, alcoholism, and infidelity. The two women informants classified the households in terms of the behavior of the male head of the household. According to them, the households of Celaya are divided into those whose male heads are *borrachos y viejeros* (drunks and womanizers) and those who are *hombres de su casa* (family men).

The women informants indicated that 90 percent of the households had male heads who were drunks and womanizers. According to these key informants, the households in which the male heads are womanizers or drunks are worse off economically than the rest of the households because these men waste money on women and drink, which would otherwise be spent on household necessities.

The Celayan households that are best off are those in which the head of household does not drink nor womanize; in other words, someone who is a family man. These are the men who work very hard to support their families and who do not go to bars or waste money going out with women. These are men who invest money in a large, well-built house, with many amenities, such as a refrigerator, CD player, and car. According to the women, family men are scarce in Celaya. The two women key informants, as well as many other women I interviewed in the community, agree that the most admired family men among all of them is Alfonso. According to the Celayans, Alfonso comes straight home from work, does not like to drink or waste money, and helps his children a lot.

Celayans also categorize the households in their community in terms of the provenance of a family. As in El Cerro, where founders are distinguished from newcomers, when a family can trace its descent from the Hacienda Las Cabras peones who founded the community, it is a clear indication of their "authenticity" as members of the community. These families are known locally as "the founders." If, on the other hand, a family arrived in Celaya after the community was founded, it is considered to be one of the *chútaros* (newcomers). However, unlike El Cerro, where the category *gente de la sierra* (people from the hills) has a pejorative connotation, the term chútaro is not disrespectful. To the contrary, when someone says to someone else, *"oye, chútaro!"* ("hey there, chútaro!"), it is done in a joking way and is not meant to offend.

In general terms, Celaya is a fairly diverse community characterized by the socioeconomic differences that exist among the households it comprises. It is also differentiated by the level of access that households have to basic services, such as education and health care.

Curanderos y Médicos: Access to Health Care

Once while I was talking with Daniel, in his sister Raquel's kitchen, she confessed to me that she was a curandera. I had finished my interview with Daniel about his experiences as síndico in the community, and he had said goodbye, put on his white hat, mounted his white horse, and left to take a turn around his fields. As soon as he left, Raquel began to talk to me about her work as a curandera and the different medicinal plants that she used to cure certain illnesses. Her reputation as a curandera extended beyond the borders of Celaya, and women from Escuinapa, Tecapán, and Isla del Bosque came to see her, bringing their children for her to cure them. While Raquel prepared *churros* (flour fritters) to sell that night, she told me that she massaged children to cure them of indigestion. In her own words, Raquel told me, "I rub their little bellies for three days, then I give them a medicine called Greta," an orange powder that is sold in the pharmacies in Escuinapa, which is mixed with water to cure indigestion in children. Raquel also uses various medicinal plants to cure indigestion, in particular the leaves of *epazote, estafiate,* lime, and guava. Raquel also cures children using cigar smoke to raise the crown of the head, which can cave in when a child has diarrhea or suffers a fright. Depending on the treatment the patient needs and the type of medicine that is used, Raquel charges between twenty and thirty pesos per visit. When people cannot pay with money, they sometimes give her a few kilos of shrimp or chicken.

Even though Raquel is the only curandera in Celaya, many people in the community use the services of curanderos who live in other rural communities or in the town of Escuinapa. For example, the Celayans frequently see *sobadores* (traditional massage therapists) or *hueseros* (traditional chiropractors). The Celayans alternate regularly between physicians and curanderos, depending on the type of illness and their belief about which type of doctor is most suited to treat it. Usually, they see a physician first, but if they are not satisfied with the diagnosis or the treatment, they will then see a curandero. If, on the contrary, after having consulted a curandero, they do not see any improvement, then they go to see a physician.

There are no clinics or hospitals in Celaya. The residents have basically three options for medical treatment: They can go to Isla del Bosque to the Unidad Médica Rural (rural clinic), to Escuinapa to the IMSS, or to the town's private practitioners. The Celayans usually go first to Isla del Bosque because it is only two kilometers away. The rural clinic has on its perma-

Table 6.1
Male and female education levels in Celaya, 1989

Level	Total	%	Males	% of total	Females	% of total
No schooling	37	15	22	9	15	6
Elementary	137	56	58	24	79	32
Middle school	54	22	30	12	24	10
High school	16	7	5	2	11	5
University	0	0	0	0	0	0
Total	244	100	115	47	129	53

Source: Author's household survey, 100 percent sample, 1989

nent staff a physician and nurse assistant, and it includes a consultation room, pharmacy, hospital beds, waiting room, and a place for the doctor to sleep. The clinic services include childbirth, first aid, and treatment of minor illnesses, such as respiratory infections, stomach upset, and urinary tract infections. The Celayans who participate in PROGRESA can go to the clinic free of charge, but they must pay for medicine and laboratory examinations. In Celaya, thirty families participate in this program. In exchange for the benefits they receive, they must attend presentations that the health advocates organize in the community and participate in the Clean Up Committee, which is responsible for keeping the area around the community free from trash (IMSS 2001). They are also required to participate in various educational programs, such as on water treatment and the hygienic handling of food.

When the illness from which someone suffers cannot be cured in the clinic, then the alternative is to go to Escuinapa. The services of the IMSS are free, but the laboratory exams and the medicines are not. Only as a final recourse will they see one of the private doctors in the town, who specialize in gynecology, general medicine, pediatrics, cardiology, psychiatry, and optometry. The cost per consultation is relatively high, approximately 150 to 200 pesos. To cover the costs of the visit and treatment, families will borrow money from relatives, friends, or their employers. The Celayans know a doctor's reputation from others in the community who have been treated by him or her. The reputation of a doctor extends beyond the confines of Escuinapa and spreads to all the rural communi-

Table 6.2
Male and female education levels in Celaya, 2001

Level	Total	%	Males	% of total	Females	% of total
No schooling	17	9	10	5	7	4
Elementary	150	75	62	31	88	44
Middle school	22	11	8	4	14	7
High school	4	2	1	<1	3	2
University	6	3	2	1	4	2
Total	199	100	83	42	116	59*

Source: Author's household survey, 50 percent random sample, 2001
*Rounding numbers may cause final percentage totals to vary by a percentage point.

ties where there are people who have been patients of the doctor. Women, especially, share information on female gynecologists because there are few women gynecologists, and the women prefer to see a female doctor rather than a male one.

In order to have a more exact idea of Celayans' general health, in addition to talking with families and with the health advocates, I also visited the rural clinic in Isla del Bosque and interviewed the doctor in charge. The doctor was kind enough to present me with a copy of the community record, which provides a general overview of the health of the Celayans. According to this record, the most common illnesses that the Celayans suffer are amebiasis, tonsillitis, acute respiratory infections, urinary tract infections, vaginitis, poor nutrition, diarrhea, diabetes, arterial hypertension, and pulmonary tuberculosis (IMSS 2001). In addition to these ailments, alcoholism and domestic violence have increased over the years. According to an estimate made by Angelita, 85 percent of the households experience domestic violence and 90 percent, alcoholism.

Changes in Education and Literacy

As in El Cerro, education is very important in Celaya. Most parents would like their children to obtain a university degree, but because of the precarious economic conditions of most households, this is often difficult to achieve. Despite this, as in El Cerro, there have been improvements in educational attainment in Celaya.

The Celayan children attend grade school in the community itself. However, those who wish to go on to secondary school must travel to the town of Escuinapa. In Teacapán, near Celaya, there is a technical school offering courses on fisheries management, and the students graduate with a degree equivalent to an associate's degree in aquaculture. As is the case for the residents of El Cerro, Celayans who want to attend college must go to Mazatlán or Culiacán. There are very few Celayans who pursue college work, and as of 2001, only six had graduated from college.

In 1989, 56 percent of the Celayans over the age of six were enrolled in or had completed primary school. The majority, 32 percent, were women. On the other hand, no one in Celaya was studying or had studied at the university level. Of the entire population, 15 percent had no schooling, of which the majority (9 percent) were men (see table 6.1).

By 2001, the number of people in Celaya with no schooling had dropped by almost one half, to 9 percent (see table 6.2). Of this segment, most (5 percent) were men. On the other hand, the number of people who were studying in or who had completed primary school had grown by 19 percent, with women in the majority. The number of Celayans who had attended or were attending the university had increased, and the majority, 2 percent, were women.

Conclusion

The information discussed in this chapter provides an overview of how the community of Celaya is structured and how it functions. It details the social, political, and economic features that contribute to making Celaya a rural community. Among the most salient features are the election and appointment of a síndico, people's incorporation and participation within the local economic cycle, the participation of its residents in various committees, and people's access to health services and education. These features, however, are not unique to Celaya; El Cerro and other rural communities in southern Sinaloa share them.

Celaya, nonetheless, has three main characteristics that in combination make it unique: (1) its system of land tenure, based on private property; (2) a strong presence and influence of commercial agriculture; and (3) a slowly declining population rate. These characteristics are interrelated. The development of a commercial agriculture industry attracts people from other areas who come to work during the agricultural cycle but in many cases end up staying permanently in the region. As a result immigration to the municipio of Escuinapa and in southern Sinaloa, in general, has increased. Immigration, however, has not increased in Celaya because its land-tenure system makes it more difficult for new people to move into the community. This in turn helps to maintain a low population rate.

Despite these characteristics, Celaya, like El Cerro, is a heterogeneous community, and this is partly reflected in its class and socioeconomic stratification. As natural resources become scarcer and as economic impoverishment grows, class and economic stratification will likely continue to increase.

Part III

Households, Gender, and Resistance

Culminating Struggles at the Intersection of Economy,

Production, and Natural Resources

Julieta Mora and Miguelina Campos working in the El Cerro tortilla factory.

Introduction to Part III

A primary concern of political ecology is how human-environment relationships play out at the local level; particularly, how patterns of natural resource use relate to households and their struggles and conflicts (Grossman 1998). One question addressed in the following two chapters is, What are the local-level responses to environmental degradation and the economic impoverishment of southern Sinaloa's rural population?

Scholars examining this question for other populations note that these responses, which they label "survival strategies," "adaptive strategies," or "resistance," initially emerge at the household level. For example, Bonnie J. McCay (1978), in her study of Fogo Islanders, points out that the initial responses to fishery declines emerged at the level of individuals and households. She identifies two main adaptive strategies developed by local households, which she terms "intensification" and "diversification." Intensification refers to the expansion of alternatives within the fishing industry, such as investing in gear to fish species that are not in decline. Diversification refers to an increased commitment to another economic activity, such as wage labor or the decision to migrate.

Susan Stonich (1993, 151) points out that "families are not merely victims of economic misfortune but have conceived innovative strategies to cope with deteriorating circumstances." In her research in southern Honduras, she found that responses to environmental degradation usually emerge at the household level. These strategies for survival, as she terms them, include the diversification of income-generating activities, increased participation in the informal economic sector, increased participation of women in the labor force, transformation of agricultural systems, and migration.

Studies on the effect of the Mexican economic crisis on the poor have also shown that responses and coping strategies usually emerge at the household level (González de la Rocha and Escobar Latapí 1991; Grindle 1991; Benería 1992) and include an increase in the number of workers per household, increased participation of women in income-generating activities, and migration.

In southern Sinaloa, the household level is where people do battle with decreased provisions and the social and economic constraints imposed by environmental degradation. The household is the strongest thread of the rope that ties together the structure and the organization of the communities of El Cerro and Celaya. Households in these communities represent a dynamic space within which, on a daily basis, people make important decisions, negotiate roles and responsibilities, develop relationships with other households beyond the community, celebrate rites, transfer knowledge from one generation to another, and develop resistance strategies to help members survive periods of crisis.

As the following chapters will demonstrate, households in rural southern Sinaloa have developed similar responses to those discussed above. However, because rural women play a key role in assuring the daily survival of their families, the further economic impoverishment of their households, as a result of natural resource degradation, affects them differentially. For rural women, natural resource degradation creates further burdens and responsibilities to which they must respond. Thus, the following two chapters examine how rural households in El Cerro and Celaya resist the effects of economic impoverishment and environmental degradation.

Global Economies, Local Livelihoods

Gender and Labor in Rural Communities

Charity begins at home, and the first thing that we Latin Americans must ask ourselves is what resources do we have available with which to cement a development that, beginning at the local village, would allow us to become active participants instead of passive victims of the swift global movement of the twenty-first century?
—Carlos Fuentes, *En esto Creo*

In August 2000, el piojillo was so severe that the people of El Cerro could not save enough money to buy school supplies for their children. The mango and broomcorn harvests were over, and the shrimp fishing season had not yet begun. To make money, people had only one option: To go to the marshes to *changuear,* that is, to poach shrimp. As they had done every year at this time, the fishing cooperatives were hiring Marines, from the Mexican Navy's infantry, to guard their fishing zones in the lagoons and marshes, making it very risky to changuear. The men of El Cerro were afraid of being caught by these Marines, or *Marinos,* as they are called locally, who would confiscate their fishing nets and punish them by forcing them to do pushups or eat Purina.

Maguey was very troubled because her daughters had started their studies at the university and they didn't have the money for tuition. A little sadly, she told her husband, Rosalío, about her worries, and she said, "Let's go catch shrimp. Look, my fishing net's over there . . . Let's go. I'm willing to do pushups, or whatever it takes, but I want money so that the girls can study." Rosalío, trying to make up his mind, answered, "If I go, because I'm a man, they'll beat me up and take the shrimp. But they don't do anything to women. Still, it's an embarrassment when women go alone to the marsh." This made Maguey angry, and she answered, "Who cares about embarrassments! I want the girls to study, and I'm going to do whatever it takes to make it possible."

Filled with courage, Maguey got together with six other women from the community. She took her fishing net, and tying it around her belt as tightly as possible, she hid it under her loose blouse so that no one would notice it. The women arrived at the marsh, and they told a little six-year-old boy who had come along to keep an eye out and warn them if he saw the Marines coming. Maguey gave him a red shirt, and she told him to wave it as a signal if he saw a car coming so that the women could run and hide in the underbrush. Once they were certain that the boy understood what he had to do, they began to fish. The shrimp were plentiful, and the women were concentrating so hard on catching them that no one noticed that the boy had fallen asleep. Suddenly, a truck full of Marines arrived, and the women shouted, "Los Marinos!" and ran to hide. They sprinted into the mangrove swamp and buried themselves in the mud, placing aquatic plants on their heads as camouflage so that they would blend in with the vegetation.

The Marines got out of the truck and began to search everywhere they thought the women might be hiding. The men were armed with submachine guns, which they fired now and again to frighten the women in the hope of making them come out of hiding. One of the women got frightened, and she came out of the water. When the Marine spotted her, he immediately demanded her fishing net. The woman, terrified, answered, "Here it is." The Marine, seeing the net empty, asked, "And the shrimp? Where are they?" Pointing to the few that remained tangled in the netting, she said, "These are all I got." Maguey, realizing that the Marine was going to continue harassing the woman and that he intended to take away these few shrimp, came out of the water. She courageously said to him, "Look, do you think that this woman and the rest of us came here because we like it or because we enjoy suffering? We came out of necessity, because our children are studying and because we have to help them get ahead. And what's it to you? You have enough to eat, and a regular paycheck—a check you can count on—but not us! Why don't you take the shrimp from people who catch them so they can go on a drunken spree? Take it from them, but not from us, who come here because we have to feed our children! We are women—we don't want the money so that we can waste it."

The Marine, by now enraged, said to Maguey, "Hey, just who are you? Are you the ringleader of these changueras?" Maguey, looking him right in the eye, answered, "No, I'm only a poor woman, just like them." Nastily, the man grabbed the net out of the hands of the other woman, but Maguey, in turn, grabbed it from him. Losing his patience, he went for his pistol. Maguey, now furious herself, reacted rapidly. With a machete in hand, she said, "You shoot me, and I'll crack open your skull." The man was so enraged that he could barely speak, but through clenched teeth he said, "Señora, this had better be the first and last time that I see you around these lagoons because the next time I catch you, I'm going to put you in my truck and take you and deposit you in the Caimanero Lagoon. Then your husband will have to come to retrieve you and get the hell of a lecture he deserves so that he won't be letting you come here ever again." Maguey, calmly but courageously answered, "Well, may God prevent you from doing something to me because you have superiors and rules to follow. If something happens to us, you are not alone or acting freely, but have people who lead you around by the nose." The man, seeing that Maguey wasn't going to give up, said, "From now, when we catch a woman poaching, we're going to rape her so she won't be coming around here anymore." Maguey, still refusing to give in, said, "If we wanted you to rape us, then we should go where we might at least catch more shrimp. If we are here, struggling, it is because we came to get food not so that you would abuse us."

The Marines, tired of arguing, decided to leave the women in peace, but only on the condition that they would go home and never poach again. Still frightened, the women courageously continued fishing until they filled their buckets. Then, walking rapidly, they went home.

This true story, about a group of women from El Cerro who fished for shrimp during the off-season, is indicative of the injustices suffered by residents who fish "illegally" in a struggle that has existed for years in southern Sinaloa. It is also a story of resistance against state policies that continue to promote the commercial exploitation of shrimp for global markets, with little regard for the needs of local communities. By "breaking the law," the women portrayed in the story are not only resisting the state policies, but in doing so, they become aware of the abuses against the rural population and courageously defend themselves in every possible way.

This chapter discusses the manner in which the people of El Cerro and

Celaya use their labor to resist the changes suffered by their households and communities as a result of environmental degradation and economic impoverishment. It focuses on how both men and women have been incorporated into a global economy, while struggling to support their households and local economies. The chapter also examines the traditional and emerging gender division of labor within the subsistence, formal, and informal economies of the communities.

Economy, Labor, and Production

Today, the economic uncertainty that reigns in southern Sinaloa means that one of the greatest challenges rural households face is obtaining a regular income to cover their basic necessities. In Celaya and El Cerro, 90 percent of the households would lack sufficient income to meet daily needs if they did not develop other strategies. To this end, households combine resources generated through work in the various economic activities available within, and beyond the limits of, their communities. As discussed in previous chapters, members' participation in these economic activities is cyclical, and it is the household members themselves who, based on their immediate needs, decide in which and in how many activities to participate at any given moment. Today, in both communities, households combine work in the subsistence, informal, and formal economies. Among these activities are fishing, agriculture, livestock raising, agricultural day labor, and work—as laborers or members—on the shrimp farms. Emigration has also begun to appear as an option in both communities. In both communities, household participation in the three economic sectors and the recent migratory process are significant factors to consider when attempting to explain how southern Sinaloa's rural population resists the local effects of environmental degradation and economic impoverishment.

The Subsistence Economy and the Local Production
of Rural Households

In both communities the daily struggle to ensure the well-being of household members is intensifying. The communities' residents describe this daily challenge as an attempt to *hacer de tripas corazones* (make hearts from guts), in reference to their having to make do with whatever they have available. Thus, in both communities, most households are strongly linked to the subsistence economy, which enables them to stay afloat even at times of crisis. In Celaya and El Cerro, the subsistence economy covers everything from raising livestock, gathering wood and water, and preparing food, to planting one's own field. Within this economy, well-established gender patterns dictate which tasks should be or, it is hoped, will be done by women and which will be done by men.

Livestock raising, for example, is organized along gender lines. Women take charge of breeding and caring for domestic animals, such as pigs, chickens, and turkeys. Raising these animals requires dedication and money. Chickens, for example, must be fed with rice when they are small, and twice a day with corn and Purina when they are mature.[1] For the most part, households eat the chickens they raise. A chicken is slaughtered when a family member is sick and needs a little chicken soup to recover, or when the family is celebrating a rite, such as a baptism or a birthday. Chickens are also exchanged or used to pay for services or favors, such as childcare, help with agricultural chores, consultations with curanderos, and to repay loans. People also view chickens as a source of savings because they can be sold when there is an emergency (for example, during an illness, when a member of the family needs to see a doctor or to purchase medicines). The economic value of a chicken depends largely on its size.[2]

In both communities, pigs are almost always used as a "savings account," a reserve to cover emergencies or basic household necessities, such as school tuition for the children or medical costs. Households rarely slaughter the pigs they raise unless it is to celebrate a major rite, such as a wedding or a quinceañera. In both communities, people prefer to raise pigs until the animals are old enough to sell, thus subsidizing a portion of the household expenses.[3]

Raising pigs can be a burden on a household because it costs money to feed them.[4] Nevertheless, despite the work that women must do to raise pigs, they do it because, in the words of one Celayan, "it is a savings that one has in reserve in case one needs money for whatever emergency may arise."

Men are responsible for caring for beasts of burden or work animals. The most common in both communities are burros, horses, and mules, which are usually owned by households whose members also own agricultural fields or livestock. Burros are used primarily for traveling to the fields or for transporting firewood or water. Horses are used primarily for transportation to the fields or to visit relatives or friends in other communities.

Mules are generally used to plow land or to transport sacks of cement, bricks, or fertilizer. Such animals also serve as a savings account because they can be sold when there is an emergency, such as an illness, or when someone in the family must subsidize the cost of a trip to Tijuana. In households that own cattle, men are responsible for taking them to the waterholes and to graze in the pastures.

Besides raising animals, many households survive by eating fruit that the trees in their patios produce. Almost all homes have some kind of fruit tree nearby. Men or women may have planted these trees, but in some cases, a tree has sprouted after someone tossed away a seed after having eaten a piece of fruit. In these cases, the plant has taken root and grown without fertilizer or water. The most common fruit trees in Celaya and El Cerro are guava, papaya, coconut palm, avocado, mango, fig, lemon, and tamarind. Household members consume most of the fruit, but sometimes an excess harvest is shared with, or exchanged or sold to, others in the community.

Collecting firewood for cooking is another of the tasks that women must undertake in various households. Although most households in both Celaya and El Cerro have gas stoves, several do not. Those homes depend on firewood for cooking. Most women who use wood must haul it from the hillsides, far from the community. Collecting wood can take between three hours and an entire day, depending on how far a woman has to travel to and from her home and how much wood she needs. Women usually gather wood between one to three times per week, going together in groups or accompanied by adolescent daughters.

Women are also responsible for food preparation. In both Celaya and El Cerro, this means that women often have to get the food, for example, by going to the market or the store to buy it or to their husbands' fields, where they pick corn, beans, or chilies. Food preparation takes a lot of time. In both communities, meals are eaten at least three times a day. People rise early, around 5 or 6 a.m. While the men get ready to go to work, the women are in the kitchen preparing breakfast. After 2 p.m., when the main meal of the day is eaten, the women return to cook. What this meal consists of usually depends on what food is available in the house or what can be acquired in the community or in nearby communities. Women often spend two to three hours preparing a meal, including the time it takes to go to the store to buy tortillas, cook the beans, and fry or cook the meat.

Besides subsistence activities, agriculture provides certain foods for the households that farm. Nevertheless, as I already mentioned, subsistence agriculture is declining in importance with the passage of time.

Subsistence Farming, Households, and the Environment

Each year at the beginning of June, the residents of southern Sinaloa's rural communities focus their gaze on the sky, searching for a sign promising the arrival of the rainy season. When one lives here at this time of year, events in the rest of the country and the region seem relegated to secondary status and high priority is given to predictions people make about when the first raindrops will fall and whether it will rain too little or too much that year. As the rainy season approaches, it is as if reality stops indefinitely to make room so that those who live here can form new hopes and plans. In the streets, one no longer hears mundane conversations about current telenovelas, drug trafficking, municipal politics, and local events, such as births, deaths, clandestine love affairs, and migrations. Conversations turn around the anxiousness people feel to see the season's first raindrops, and the memories and experiences of previous seasons revive. Farmers gather in the street to talk and share their uncertainty over the likelihood of getting loans from the PRONASOL, which will make it possible for them to buy the seeds and fertilizer that they need to plant their plots of land. They also share the uncertainty of not knowing if the bean or corn crops they will grow in the coming season will sell for a good price. Despite uncertainty, farmers begin to make plans to plant their land in the hope that this season will be better than the last one.

The great importance that rain plays in the lives of the campesinos of southern Sinaloa lies in the nature of their agricultural practices, which are seasonal, requiring them to plant during the rainy season. Most campesinos do not have irrigation systems in the plots, so rain is critical for their crops and the subsistence of their households.

The people in the communities usually predict that the rainy season will begin around June 24, the Día de San Juan (St. John's Day). They base this on years of observing and noting in the collective memory when previous rainy seasons have begun. The Día de San Juan is celebrated in these rural communities with water; that is, people throw buckets of water on each other. Children, especially, run through the streets with pails, trying to splash each other. Indeed, any visitor or resident who walks the streets on that day runs a risk of having a bucket of water dumped on him or her. This regional tradition is so deeply rooted that even when traveling in an auriga from the town to the rural communities, one runs a risk that at a stop to let off a passenger, a group of young women with their buckets hidden in the bushes will suddenly appear to splash all the passengers.

Farmers in El Cerro and Celaya begin to clear their fields at the end of June. They take advantage of the time before the arrival of the rains to repair fences, pull dried vegetation, and plow and rake. They begin to think about what and how much to plant in the upcoming season. They also take advantage of this time to clear the *cuamil,* or high hillsides, which will give them more area to plant.

Following the first rains, farmers do not immediately plant but wait, instead, until after the first nine days of July, which they call the *sangre de Cristo* (blood of Christ). During this nine-day period, which symbolizes the nine months during a woman's pregnancy, it is said that the earth, like a woman, is pregnant. With the first raindrops, grass begins to sprout and the dry vegetation turns green once again, and the people of southern Sinaloa's rural communities believe that the earth begins to give birth. For them, the arrival of the first rains symbolizes man's close-knit relationship to nature. They believe that human beings and plants are interrelated, and everything that happens to the earth affects mankind, too. Thus, before it rains, a person can become weak from stepping on the pregnant earth. Because they have walked on the ground, people insist that they are without strength or the desire to do anything. When the rainy season starts, the pains go away, and the people are cured. For them, the rain is like the blood of Christ because it has the power of (re)birth and healing. After the nine days, when the grass has grown, it is said that the earth has given birth, and because of all the water it has absorbed, it is sufficiently fertile to plant.

The farmers, with family members, decide what crops to plant based on the type and quantity of seed they have stored up or on the amount of money they can use to buy seed. They also consider the immediate needs of household members and the relevance the different crops have for feeding the family.

Another factor that farmers consider when deciding what to plant is the type of soil in their fields. This determines what crops are most likely to grow. Based on experience from years of trying different crops, the farmers can recognize which are best suited for their particular fields. They are aware that soil types in their fields vary. Soil quality is defined using criteria such as color, texture, moisture, and workability. According to the farmers, most common in Celaya is sandy, or third-class, soil, which retains little moisture because water filters through it. The most appropriate crops for this soil type are corn, beans, watermelons, and jícama. According to the farmers, approximately 85 percent of Celaya's soils fall in this category. Another type, locally called *tierra firme* (hard soil), is characteristic of the low-lying areas. This is harder, compact ground that retains moisture. Beans, corn, and cucumbers grow well in this type. Most farmers agree that the least common soil in Celaya is that which is called *tierra negra* (black soil). This is the most fertile, but it is distributed only sporadically among Celaya's fields. Almost anything grows in this soil, including corn, chili, cucumber, and squash.

In El Cerro, the farmers classify their lands based on the two types of soil most commonly found there: *tierra barreal* and *tierra lama*. According to the farmers, the first is a clay soil that becomes sticky when wet and extremely hard when dry. It is the most common soil in El Cerro, and it is good for growing watermelons, tomatoes, chilies, and beans, but to plant those seeds, farmers must wait until it rains so that the soil becomes damp and soft. The tierra lama is black soil, generally soft, which, when wet, is like a sponge, absorbing and retaining the water. The farmers prefer tierra lama because it is more fertile than the clay soil and "with a little bit of digging, one can grow anything in it."

Although soil types partly determine what can be planted, in both communities the most important crops are corn and beans. Both are destined for home consumption, even though a few farmers sell excess supply to other households or to buyers who come to the community. Generally, farmers in both Celaya and El Cerro sow corn and beans in an intercropping scheme. Sometimes a farmer will take advantage of whatever space is available on his land to plant watermelons or chilies, intermixed with bean and corn plants. Some people plant coconut palm or mango trees, which help to shade the other crops.

The technology used to cultivate these crops is minimal and it often reflects a household's economic condition. Those households that are better off economically can afford to buy or rent a tractor to plow the fields before planting. Those who hire someone with a tractor to plow for them must pay approximately twenty-five dollars per hectare. The farmers who cannot afford to own or rent a tractor must plow with mules or use pickaxes and hoes. Fertilizer and pesticide use also reflects the economic status of a household. Very few farmers use commercially produced fertilizers or pesticides. Instead, most fertilize with chicken or cattle manure, which they can get in their community or buy from the chicken farms in Rosario or the dairies in Mazatlán.

Household members provide the manual labor needed to prepare the land for planting crops for home consumption. Age and gender determine each individual's job. The agricultural cycle begins with the *taspanar*, or clearing of the parcels of land. Men perform this chore. They also do the work in the next phase, the *escardar*, or plowing of the fields. Both women and men sow the corn and beans, and everyone in the household is involved in caring for the crop as it grows. After the seeds sprout, family members apply manure and weed to the area around the seedlings. Everyone in the family works during *el corte*, the harvest, of the corn and beans. Following the harvest, everyone helps to clean and separate the corn and beans. They scatter the corncobs and the seedpods on the floor, and then beat them with a rod so that the corn and beans will fall out. The final stage, in which the entire family participates, consists of bagging the corn and beans so that it can be stored in their houses.

Ecological factors, such as the type of soil, and the economic condition of a family strongly determine a farmer's ability to grow commercially valuable crops. In El Cerro, the land is much drier than in Celaya, and most of what is grown is destined for home consumption. Chili is the only commercially valuable crop that is planted, and it requires extensive labor and fertilizers, pesticides, and irrigation. Celaya's lands are well suited to growing coconuts, which are in great demand and have significant commercial value in the region. Other Celayan farmers use part of their lands to grow chilies or mangoes.

Many farmers in both communities complain that it is becoming harder every year to plant their fields either because they lack money or because of the land's environmental deterioration. As a result of the Mexican government's neoliberal policies, the financial funds available to farmers who primarily plant crops for home consumption were drastically reduced in order to give preference to commercial agriculture. In addition to financial difficulties, most farmers also have to struggle with environmental degradation, which is increasing with the passage of time. Farmers in both Celaya and El Cerro are aware of the environmental damage to their fields, and it is a prominent and frequent topic in conversations. They believe that *la tierra está cansada* (the land is worn out), and that is why it no longer produces. Indeed, scientific studies in the region show that soil erosion is one of the gravest environmental problems (Perales Rivas and Fregoso Tirado 1994). Consequently, many farmers annually face a dilemma of whether or not to plant. Those who plant are in agreement that, as time passes, it will become increasingly difficult to get a good harvest from their lands, and to make the land produce, they will need money and technology. In their opinion, the land must be hoed and fertilized to heal it.

In the face of this dilemma, the farmers have two options. One, more common in El Cerro than in Celaya, is to convert plots into pastureland by planting them with grass. These fields are then rented to people, who live in the community or are from somewhere else, and who have cattle but do not have anywhere to graze them. Another option is to work the land a medias. The owner of a parcel who chooses this option lends his or her land to another farmer to plant, under the condition that they share the harvest equally. Parcels are also rented for a fixed sum. Usually, the person interested in renting the land approaches the owner and makes an offer, "I'll give you so much for so many hectares." The number of hectares and the quality of the land determine the amount of the rent.

The inhabitants of both Celaya and El Cerro live with a constant concern about their ability to find viable alternatives that will get them the income they need to cover their household expenses. To have enough to cover these expenses, the households combine the incomes from all the economic strategies in which the household members participate. Shrimp fishing, legal and illegal, is one of the strategies that have helped many households survive during economic crises.

Pescadores y Changueros: Fishing for Shrimp

In July 1998, Emilio and his nephew went to the marsh to changuear, even though it was still the off-season. They stopped by a canal running near the marsh that was filled with lots of shrimp. After tossing in Purina to attract them, Emilio and his nephew began catching the shrimp with their nets. They were so busy that they did not notice when the Marinos, hired by the cooperatives to guard the fishing areas during the off-season, surrounded them. Even though Emilio and his nephew would have had a chance to toss the shrimp back and run, they stayed where they were. They had heard rumors that the Marines would become angry and violent when changueros tried to run. So, to avoid getting beaten up, they stayed put. When the Marines approached, they asked the two men what they were doing with their nets, and, instead of lying, Emilio and his nephew told the truth: They were fishing for shrimp. The Marines misinterpreted this as arrogance, and one of them nastily asked Emilio, *"Que muy machito, no, cabrón?"* ("So, a very tough guy, no, son of a bitch?") The Marine kicked Emilio and threw him to the ground, and then he ordered him to get up. Angry, Emilio said, "Why are you hitting me?" And he added, "That's why I didn't run. I could have run, but I stayed put and waited for you because you guys get mad whenever someone runs, and then you beat us up, and not because *'tenga huevos o sea muy machito.'"* ("I have balls or am a tough guy.") The Marine kicked him again, grabbed him by the arm, and, dragging him, hid him in some brush while the Marinos went after other poachers who were also fishing in the area. Even though they ran after them, however, they could not catch them. They returned, frustrated and aggravated, to continue interrogating Emilio and his nephew. They asked them their names, and then they ordered them to do fifty pushups each. When they were done, the soldiers put a foot on their backs to add extra weight and ordered them to do twenty more.

When they were finally done, one of the Marines asked Emilio and his nephew if they knew what it felt like to be shot. They answered no, and the men warned them that if they did not want to find out, they'd better not run the next time they were caught poaching. Just as the Marines were ready to go, another arrived, and he asked them why they had the Purina. After answering that they tossed it in to attract the shrimp, the Marines made them eat it and drink salt water from the marsh. At last, the Marines let them go, but the damage from the combination of the Purina and the salt water gave them stomachaches and diarrhea for several days.

There are many stories like this in the rural communities of the region. These accounts, while sprinkled with the characteristic good humor of the Sinaloan people, are also interspersed with tales of the abuse and injustices suffered by the men and women who poach shrimp. These stories illustrate the social and economic struggle the residents must suffer in order to gain access to the shrimp. This struggle pits the co-op members against the "independent," or unorganized, fishermen. The government considers the first group to be *legítimos y auténticos* (legitimate and entitled) and the latter to be illegal and poachers.

The issue of entitlement and illegality has political and economic ramifications, which influence how both categories of fishermen are perceived and treated by state agencies and local residents. In southern Sinaloa, the entitlement of the fishermen has been an ongoing motive for social struggles. The government has had to intervene in order to resolve the fights. The contempt the government has for independent fishermen is revealed in its use of terms such as changueros or *pescadores furtivos*, which implies that they are poaching shrimp. Because this resource is part of the patrimony of the Mexican people, the use of these terms converts the fishermen into thieves robbing their fellow countrymen.

Locally in southern Sinaloa, *changuerismo* refers to the clandestine act of fishing and selling shrimp. It is considered a social, political, and economic phenomenon that has its roots precisely in the exclusion of some groups in favor of others, who are allowed to exploit the shrimp resource. For some, especially those who are in power, changuerismo is "a terrible phenomenon, which has grown like a cancer along Mexico's Pacific coast" (Gaxiola Aldana 1999, 2). For the disempowered, who fight for the right to commercially exploit shrimp, changuerismo is "an everyday act of resistance" (Scott 1985) that excluded groups have created to actively contest the government's policies. Changueros operate outside the law, and thus they are accused of committing a crime against nature and their fellow citizens.

During the off-season, which runs from approximately March to September, the co-op fishermen and the government are prepared to defend the shrimp tooth and nail from poachers. Assigning members of the Infantería de Marina, or the Mexican Navy's infantry, to act as police to guard the lagoons and estuaries is one of the ways the government helps co-op fishermen at the expense of other community members. During the final months of the off-season, July and August (el piojillo in the rural communities), one of the few ways in which locals can survive is by poaching shrimp. The confrontations between co-op members and changueros— the former trying to protect the shrimp, the latter trying to catch it— reaches its most fevered pitch during this time. The co-op members and local officials hope that the government will support them unconditionally in protecting the shrimp from the changueros.

The government also supports the organized fishermen by setting up roadblocks in southern Sinaloa to prevent contraband shrimp from being shipped to the interior of Mexico. The members of the Infantería de Marina or officials from the Procuraduría Federal para la Defensa del Medio

Enrique Díaz Rodríguez fishing with his atarraya in a lagoon near El Cerro.

Ambiente (Office of the Attorney for Environmental Defense, PROFEPA) are charged with inspecting vehicles that travel on the region's main highways. In southern Sinaloa, there are two principal roadblocks, one in the town of Villa Unión, near Mazatlán, and the other in La Concha, in the municipio of Escuinapa. All vehicles, including buses that are going to Mazatlán or Nayarit, must pass through one of these two inspections. When the military personnel are running them, they stop the vehicles and ask the drivers where they are coming from and their destination. If they notice anything suspicious about the occupants or the vehicle, the soldiers order them to park so that they can be searched.

In addition to the roadblocks established by the government, the fishermen themselves have created strategies to prevent people from "robbing" them of the shrimp. The fishermen who work in the open ocean, for example, block the mouths of the rivers at the shoreline to prevent the entrance of fishing trawlers. The co-op members who take their catches from the coastline block the roads to the lagoons and marshes where they fish. The start of the shrimp *zafra* (season) marks the end of the piojillo. The local economy revives once money begins to flow again, when the fishermen and their families can buy with cash instead of on credit.

The inshore fishermen of El Cerro and Celaya, whether organized in a cooperative or independent operators, follow the same routine to prepare for each new shrimp fishing season. This work begins in early July and continues until the government proclaims the start of the season. During this period, a typical scene in both communities is a group of men under a tree, mending nets. Most fishermen weave their own nets, and this takes almost two months. If they are co-op members, they can get on credit the cord and other materials needed to make a net. If they are independent fishermen, however, they must buy the material at stores in Agua Verde or Rosario. After a net is made, it has to be ironed. The net is stretched tightly from point to point in a tree. Very hot water is thrown on it so that the knots in the weave will smooth out. It is left tied to the tree for however long it takes for the knots to be sufficiently smooth, or ironed, usually at least overnight.

Besides readying his net for the start of the fishing season, a fisherman, particularly one who is a co-op member, must repair his panga and the boat's motor. The organized fishermen have an advantage in that the co-operative lends them the panga and all the equipment they need to fish. In contrast, an independent fisherman must buy his own panga and motor, or at least borrow them from relatives or friends.

When the government declares the end of the ban, the shrimp harvest officially begins in the bays and estuaries of southern Sinaloa. In rural communities, both the co-op fishermen and the independent ones await this moment anxiously to undertake the tenacious race that is characteristic of the struggle to catch the greatest quantity of shrimp possible. Although by law the shrimp are a resource that can be fished only by co-op members, in practice this resource is exploited communally. The fishermen are determined to fish as much as possible during the season, until the supply of shrimp disappears. Nevertheless, on some occasions—in particular when the shrimp in the fishing grounds are still very small—the co-op members decide to postpone the date to begin to fish. This self-imposed ban by the cooperatives is intended primarily to give the shrimp more time to grow so that they can reach the size that has the greatest commercial value.

Shrimp fishing usually occurs at night. Co-op members, with their equipment ready, go in groups to the lagoons and estuaries, where they pick their fishing ground. There on the shore, they build a palapa from bits and pieces of wood and cardboard. Here they will sleep and spend several weeks, without returning home. Wives or relatives send food to them every day with whomever in the community is going out to the fishing grounds. In general, these places are relatively remote and peaceful, and many fishermen rest and relax while they are there. The fishing is done in groups of three or four men, who are relatives, compadres, or, at least, friends. They take turns during the night, with some sleeping while others guard the equipment or fish. The shrimp is stored in coolers packed with ice before being delivered to the cooperative's leadership. All expenses—maintaining the pangas, repairing nets or weaving new ones, and gasoline—are subtracted from the earnings, which are divided equally among the group. Often, without letting the leadership know, the fishermen sell part of the shrimp to changueros, who buy it at a higher price. The men remain at their fishing grounds until the quantity of shrimp diminishes or those that are caught prove too small to sell to the export market. During this phase of the season, which the fishermen call *la quiliada*, the two or three kilos of shrimp that they are able to catch, they sell to changueras, and the earnings are destined solely for the subsistence of their households.

Unlike the co-op fishermen, the changueros do not have a fixed place at which to fish. Because they operate outside the law, they must fish on the banks of the lagoons and estuaries, hidden among the mangrove thickets. The changueros generally fish during the early morning hours when the estuaries and lagoons are mostly empty of legal fishermen. Very few changueros have pangas because they cannot risk being seen by co-op members, but those who do have them hide them with care in their homes or in the bushes surrounding the lagoons. A changuero's equipment consists simply of a net and bicycle. He goes out to fish at night, in total darkness, and cannot risk taking a lantern or anything to light his way that might alert the co-op members or the soldiers who are hired to guard the fishing grounds. The changueros go out to fish in groups, and when they are fishing, they have a peculiar and secret way of communicating so that they cannot be identified. They never use their names. When they see a soldier coming, they usually say "je" or "ah" to warn other changueros. When they see the soldiers coming, they drop everything where it is and run so as not to be caught. If the changueros are caught, besides the danger of physical assault, the soldiers may confiscate their nets, shrimp, and bicycles. To get the net and bicycle back, a changuero has to go directly to the cooperative that confiscated them and pay a fine. By doing this, however, he will come face to face with the cooperative members, which would reveal his identity. Most changueros, to avoid being identified, give their confiscated nets and bicycles up for lost. Sometimes changueros send their wives to retrieve the things.

The changueros, as independent fishermen, have an advantage that they can sell the shrimp to whoever offers the best price. They usually sell it to women in their community, locally called changueras. The changueras operate within a system of social and economic networks that connect women in communities like El Cerro and Celaya with other changueras in the towns of Escuinapa, Rosario, and Mazatlán. All the residents of these rural communities or small towns know which women are changueras. Even the co-op members and Marines know because they see them selling the shrimp in the municipal markets, on street corners in the towns, or on Aquiles Serdán Street in Mazatlán.

It is difficult to know with any scientific accuracy how many women in both communities sell shrimp. One of the reasons is that it is a seasonal occupation. Some women do it for a short time, only to save enough money to send their children to school or to buy something they need for their homes. The more established changueras, who have been able to develop social and economic networks with other changueras, have turned changuerismo into a profession that brings them a sufficient income, as well as a certain prestige, respect, and status within their communities. Well-established changueras train younger women. They take the younger ones along to learn to bargain and sell the shrimp, and to establish networks. The work is not easy because one must travel long distances and sometimes suffer harassment by soldiers, co-op members, or game wardens. One can also spend long hours in the hot sun or in the crowded marketplace trying to sell the shrimp, only to return home without having made a sale.

Undoubtedly, for changueras, changueros, and the co-op members, shrimp generate most of the income for their households. In comparison with other economic activities that are available to the residents of both communities, shrimp fishing, despite all the risks, offers the advantage that one can easily make money in a short time. In the past ten years, nevertheless, the stocks of shrimp have declined. Manuel remembers with joy those times when shrimp were abundant, "Before, fishing was better than now. There was a lot of shrimp. A person could catch two hundred to three hundred kilos in a single night. I once caught four hundred kilos in one night! Now a man spends all night fishing, and he only catches ten kilos. Fishing is dead as an occupation." For Manuel, as well as for other fishermen, the reasons for the decline in the shrimp stocks are many, but one is declining rainfall over a span of many years. According to Manuel, "The rains have changed a lot. Before, it rained nicely, the river swelled, the arroyos here were running, and all that water ran off into the marsh. Now, it won't rain. The marsh is dry, and it has to rain if it is going to be possible for the ocean waters to bring the shrimp in." Other fishermen think that the decline in productivity is the result of aquaculture farms that discharge contaminated water into the lagoons, killing the shrimp. Other factors that have contributed to lower production during the last decade of the twentieth century are the El Niño phenomenon; population growth, and with it, the increase in the number of fishermen; and the contamination of the coastal ecosystems.

The scarcity of shrimp means that the fishing season grows shorter with each passing year. The season used to last eight months; today, the bulk of the catch occurs in the first two months. Faced with this decline, the residents of El Cerro and Celaya have had to seek out economic alternatives to earn income. One of these is employment as jornaleros in the agricultural plantations near the communities.

Jornaleros: Working in Other People's Fields

Very early in the morning, before the sun is up, the main street in El Cerro fills with the hubbub of people. Men and women, mostly jornaleros, preparing to face a new day of work, gather on one side of the street or sit on the ground, waiting for a ride. They all know each other, and while waiting, they take advantage of the time to chat and catch up on the events that have happened in the community. Some, as they pass houses where other jornaleros live, call out to them, saying, "Let's go!" and then they wait for their companions so that they can walk together. Almost everyone has plastic gallon jugs or bottles of water slung across their backs with a rope. Both the men and the women are dressed in long pants, long-sleeved shirts, and hats. Only the youngest men go shirtless, as if they wanted to challenge the potent rays of the sun that will soon enter triumphantly between the white clouds that decorate the sky this hot June morning. These people make up the cuadrillas of jornaleros that form daily in El Cerro to go to work on the chili, mango, or broomcorn plantations in the nearby ejidos.

This scene is typical not only of El Cerro but also of Celaya and other rural communities in southern Sinaloa. Working in fields belonging to someone else has become one of the principal economic activities by which a broad sector of the population earns income. Work as a jornalero is not new in the region but began with the appearance of commercial agriculture in southern Sinaloa, in the 1950s in the municipio of Rosario and in the 1980s in the municipio of Escuinapa (CAADES 1987). Nevertheless, the number of people who seek work as jornaleros has increased yearly. A household survey I conducted in El Cerro in 1989 showed that 45 percent of the community's households had at least one male member engaged in agricultural wage labor. By 1998, this figure had risen to 76 percent. Similarly, the 1989 survey showed that 23 percent of Celaya's households had at least one male member engaged in agricultural wage labor. By 1998, this figure had risen to 65 percent.

Like rural women elsewhere, those in Celaya and El Cerro have been able to augment household income by joining the agricultural wage-labor workforce.[5] Although women's employment in agriculture is neither a new nor even a recent phenomenon in Mexico, the increased number of women who work as jornaleras is new. The 1989 household survey showed that in El Cerro, 21 percent of the women aged fourteen and older were working as jornaleras, and in Celaya, 9 percent were. However, the 1998 survey showed that in El Cerro, 72 percent of all women age fourteen and older and earning cash were jornaleras. In Celaya, the figure was 55 percent.

Agricultural wage labor, for men and women both, is seasonal and affected by climate, global market demand for agricultural commodities, and the demand for manual labor on individual plantations. A common characteristic of day labor is the organization of cuadrillas, usually formed by people from the same community. The number of cuadrillas that are organized in each community depends directly on the demand for manual labor that the plantation owners make. The cuadrillas are organized according to the agricultural cycle, taking into account the seasons for each agricultural commodity. The work teams on the chili and broomcorn plantations organize for planting and again for the harvest. The coconut work teams also form twice, first to harvest the green coconut and then to harvest dry coconut. The mango and lemon plantations require workers only during the harvest.

The plantation owner selects one individual to organize the cuadrilla and oversee the members as they work. In southern Sinaloa, this person is called the *caporal,* and she or he acts as a mediator between the workers and the crop owners. The caporal is someone who has worked for many years on the plantations, and thus has a broad knowledge of the various stages involved in this kind of manual labor. The caporal is also a person that the plantation owner knows well and trusts fully.

The caporal is responsible for going from house to house asking if people want to join the cuadrilla. In some cases, people come directly to the caporal's home to see if he or she can use them. Caporales select members based on several criteria, but primarily kin relationships and trust determine who is selected. One of the teams that Maguey organized in 2001 serves as an example. Of the thirty-five members, thirty are relatives on her mother's side. Of these, four are brothers, eight are cousins, six are nephews, and twelve are second or third cousins, with the remaining four being comadres or compadres. The kinship and trust that exist between the caporal and members of his or her cuadrilla and among the members themselves facilitate work so that it can be performed as rapidly and easily as possible. It also reduces the number of employees who fail to meet their work obligations or who quit before the job is over. Because caporales have a close relationship with their workers, they persuade them not to miss work and to do a good job. If someone does not work hard, it breaks the sense of trust and friendship that exists. This trust also lets caporales lend money to workers until payday. If someone doesn't show up to work, or if someone performs the job poorly, the caporales will no longer lend that person money and will not invite him or her to join future teams.

In addition to trust and kin relationships, another aspect that helps ensure that workers do a good job is the training they get when young. Children as young as twelve years of age are allowed to work as jornaleros. Many accompany their mothers and fathers so that they can learn what the job requires. While children learn, they also earn wages, but these are much lower than what is paid to more experienced laborers. The wages vary depending on the type of plantations, but in 2001, the average wage was approximately sixty pesos for an eight-hour day. Children who come with their parents get between twenty and thirty pesos per day. The caporales receive an additional fifty pesos daily for managing the cuadrillas. It normally takes two or three seasons of work to learn to do the work involved in day-labor jobs.

When one asks the people of El Cerro and Celaya what day-labor jobs are like, most agree that it is very hard work, even harder than fishing. A day in the fields is at least eight hours long, from sunup to sundown, for a miserable wage. The jornaleros do not have any health or social security benefits, only the payment they get for the work. While the region's residents consider day labor in general to be among the worst of possible occupations, they still distinguish among the work that is done for different types of crops.

El Cerro's jornaleros consider work on the broomcorn plantations to be the hardest. They call it the "broom work," to denote that the salary is based on what is harvested by *tarea* (section) and that the plant is used to make brooms. The broomcorn plantations lie all along the highway between Rosario and El Cerro. The deep-green plants stand out from other vegetation, but they are hard to distinguish from corn plants because the large leaves, supple stalk, and shape of the flower are similar in both. Broomcorn, however, is smaller than regular corn. The owners of these plantations are farmers from Rosario or ejidatarios from Agua Verde, who export their harvest to Sonora and Arizona for broom manufacturing. The work of the jornaleros is to harvest the plants. The teams arrive at the plantations around 7 a.m., either by foot or on bus, depending on the distance from El Cerro. When they arrive, they break into groups of three or four people. Each group is assigned a tarea to harvest, which consists of two or three furrows of planted land measuring approximately two hundred meters in length. (When the furrow measures less than two hundred meters, then the group is assigned four or five.) The jornaleros take between three and four hours to harvest each tarea, and the maximum number they can finish in a day are two. In 2001, the plantations paid thirty pesos per tarea.

Work on broomcorn plantations is divided into daily periods. The jornaleros begin working at 7 a.m., and around 11 a.m., they return home to eat and rest. They then return to the fields, to work from 2 to 6 p.m. One of the biggest complaints that jornaleros have is that the plant leaves cut their hands and the ear spikes give off *alguate* that causes their bodies to itch and irritates their eyes. To avoid this, many jornaleros dress in long-sleeved shirts and cover their heads and mouths with towels and kerchiefs. Despite these measures, many return home at the end of the day *alguatados*, itchy and with red eyes. Many jornaleros think that working in the broomcorn harvest is "dangerous, because when there is wind, the alguate is blown all around us."

Work in the chili fields, according to the residents of both communities, is considered hard and a little dangerous. The jornaleros work in two phases: planting and harvesting. The chili plantings are made with plants that are produced in nurseries or *planteros* grown from seeds. A seed usually takes about forty days to germinate, and once the plant has a strong stalk and enough leaves, it is taken from the nursery and planted in the fields. Bending over at the waist, the jornaleros plant the chilies using their hands, placing them in holes that one of the workers has dug with a tractor, and then covering the chilies with earth. Being bent over or stooping for many hours on end produces backaches. The harvest commences when the chili reaches approximately the size of a fist. The cuadrillas arrive early in the morning, and each worker is given a furrow to harvest. To harvest the chilies, the day laborers must bend over and remain this way for long periods of time, which also hurts their backs and upper legs. Each chili that is picked is deposited in a large basket that the men carry on their shoulders and the women carry on their heads. When they fill a basket, they deposit it in a truck that transports the crop to processing plants in the towns of Escuinapa and Rosario. The first harvest that occurs is called *la limpiada* (the cleaning) because it consists of picking the chilies that have ripened early and are past their prime. This crop is sold locally in the municipal market of Rosario and to the stores in Agua Verde, or it is given to the workers. The better chilies are exported, because according to a chili farmer in Agua Verde, "The best quality goes to the United States and the worst stays here in Mexico."

One of the biggest problems that jornaleros working in the chili harvest face is pesticide contamination. No other agricultural commodity in southern Sinaloa depends as much on pesticides. In my conversations with jornaleros, I could deduce that very few know about the harmful effects of pesticides or the ways to protect against contamination. The little knowledge jornaleros have about pesticides was apparent once when I visited one of the chili fields that is near El Cerro and one of the workers, in short pants and shirtless, was spraying the plants with pesticide. He was using Agrimex, and the label on the container read: "Danger: Highly Toxic." Very few owners of the chili plantations warn their workers that they are going to spray with pesticides. In most cases, people find out that spraying is occurring when they see the plane flying above them and they feel the drops of pesticides falling on their heads. Many complain that while spraying is happening, they have headaches. There are even cases of people who have become poisoned or intoxicated from the spray.

The chili farmers or local people, such as ejidatarios or small-scale farmers who plant chilies, buy the pesticides from stores selling agricultural products. These are locally called agroquímicas, and their owners are mostly engineers or agronomists, who have training in the technology that is used in agricultural parts of Sinaloa, such as in Culiacán. These professionals advise the chili farmers on the type of pesticide to use according to the type of infestation that they need to eradicate. They also introduced drip-irrigation technology, which is used to irrigate the chili fields in Agua Verde.

Work in the mango plantations, for many jornaleros, is also dangerous because the unripe fruit gives off a substance that irritates the skin. Others workers claim that the dry branches of the trees cut them, and sometimes rats or snakes are hiding in them. The jornaleros protect themselves from these dangers by dressing in long pants, long-sleeved shirts, and hats such as *cachuchas* (baseball caps). As soon as the cuadrillas arrive at the mango plantation, they disperse among the trees and begin harvesting the fruit that is not too green nor overripe. In the harvest, they use a *characa*, a rod with netting on the tip so that the mango will not fall to the ground and break. A mango cuadrilla usually consists of thirty-five people. Working together, they put the harvested mangoes into *jabas*, or wooden boxes, which they then load on a truck. Once the truck is fully loaded, the jornaleros receive a fixed amount of pay, regardless of how long they worked. In 2001, the wage was seven dollars.

In Celaya, most jornaleros work in the harvest, or *corte*, of green coconut and in the collection of dried coconut for copra production. For both jobs, jornaleros organize in cuadrillas. Because harvesting green coconut requires climbing the palm tree, these cuadrillas consist solely of men, most of them young. They use a tool, called a *vacote*, made of a dried bamboo shoot, which is lengthened by attaching an aluminum pole tipped with a razor. Cutting coconut is dangerous work because the palm trees are so high. Indeed, in Celaya there have been several cases in which boys have fallen from the palm trees and been injured. As the coconut is cut, men on the ground collect the fruit and load the truck. The buyer, the owner of the coconut grove, and the cuadrilla organizer negotiate in advance to set the wages that the jornaleros will receive. The price is usually based on the number of full trucks that the buyer requires. The organizer divides the money equally among all the workers, but, because he puts together the cuadrilla and must ensure that it completes the work satisfactorily, he receives additional pay. The length of the workday depends on

María Cruz-Torres, her friend Olga, and Olga's
daughter, Jareth, in Celaya.

two factors: the number of trucks to fill and the number of workers in the
cuadrilla.

Coconuts that are not harvested when green are allowed to dry for use
in copra production. The job performed by the copra jornaleros consists
primarily of extracting the coconut pulp. Women, men, and children are
driven in a pickup truck to the coconut plantations, where they spend
most of the day. An initial task, performed by men, women, and children
alike, is the collection of coconuts that have fallen to the ground, which
they carry to where everyone will sit to extract the pulp. The men open
the coconuts with an axe, and the women and the children spread them on
the floor to let them dry. Once dry, both men and women extract the pulp

and load it on the truck. Brokers pay the jornaleros based on the amount of coconuts each processes. For example, in 2001, the wage was ten dollars for one thousand coconuts. Many women feel reluctant to work in the copra production because they do not want to be away from their homes for long periods each day. Because of this the organizers of the cuadrillas began bringing the dried coconuts directly to families so that they could extract the pulp when they had the time. Today in Celaya, it is common to see the front yards, backyards, and roofs of houses covered with drying coconuts.

Undoubtedly, agricultural wage labor provides many families in El Cerro and Celaya with some income to cover their household expenses. In both communities, the growing presence of women in the workforce is widely recognized, but the incorporation of women into the agricultural workforce has posed new challenges. One is a constant attempt to reach a balance between domestic chores and participation in agricultural wage labor and other day-labor jobs, which has further burdened women's already busy lives. Even when women are earning cash outside the home, they still need to perform household tasks and care for husbands and children. Many men in rural Sinaloa do not participate in household chores and rarely help to take care of the children. Childcare facilities in these communities do not exist, and for the most part, while they work in the fields, women have to rely on their older daughters, comadres, neighbors, and relatives for help with the children.

Another challenge is related to the new power struggles within the household. The participation of women in agricultural labor has distorted the image of the man as the family's breadwinner and decision maker. Women's control over income has reduced their economic dependence on men and given women the power and ability to make decisions within the household and spend their income on things that are important to them, such as purchasing land of their own or improving their houses. Their husbands often resent this power, and in both communities, the new power struggle within the household has reached its maximum expression in incidents of domestic violence.

Working outside the home poses difficulties, and agricultural wage labor is arduous, factors that have strongly influenced women to seek economic alternatives within their communities that would allow them to spend more time at home. This would give them some flexibility in how they allocate their time to work, childcare, and household chores. Many

Claudia Preciado Cruz, a high school student, making tortillas for lunch.

women find the most effective means of generating income and achieving flexibility within the informal economy.

Women in the Informal Economy

There are many ways to define the informal sector of the economy. Jennifer Abbassi and Sheryl Lutjens (2002, 29) define it as something that can be "recognized by low income and low productivity; by self-employment or small enterprises with few employees, limited capital, and access to credit; and by instability and a lack of protection afforded to formal sector workers." Citing Patrice Franko (1999), they assert that three categories make up the informal sector: domestic work, self-employment, and microenterprise. In El Cerro and Celaya, the most common are microenterprises and domestic work. Nevertheless, as we shall see below, these are not the only categories within the informal economies of these communities.

The sale of goods is one of the main activities by which women generate cash. In both communities, women operate small grocery stores out of their homes, where they sell candies, sodas, and *artículos de primera necesidad* (commonly consumed food items), such as beans, rice, flour, vegetables, and canned food. Women also spend much time preparing food to sell in the evening or during special celebrations, such as *posadas*, quinceañeras, weddings, and baptisms. The preparation of food is a long process that usually begins very early in the morning, with women traveling by bus to the town's market to purchase the needed ingredients. Other women peddle food, especially tostadas and tacos, in front of schools or outside of their own houses.

Making and selling handicrafts is another source of income for many women. In both communities, women spend their little bit of leisure time knitting, embroidering, and making paper flowers. The most common craft is the *servilleta* (cloth napkin), a piece of fabric embroidered with bright-colored thread and used to wrap warm tortillas. Tablecloths and pillows are also embroidered, and doilies are knitted, even though this requires more time than embroidering. A few women also earn cash by making crepe-paper flowers; however, they do so on a demand-only basis for special celebrations, such as weddings, baptisms, or the Day of the Virgin of Guadalupe. Because the communities do not have a marketplace and most women find traveling to market towns too difficult, handicrafts are made to be sold locally among the households, at the request of relatives, neighbors, or friends.

Women also sell clothes from their homes or by going door to door in their communities and the other nearby settlements. They purchase the clothes in bigger towns, even Mazatlán, Guadalajara, or Tijuana, where merchandise is cheap. Most women sell on credit to their customers and collect the payments weekly.

A relatively small segment of women have found jobs as domestic workers in nearby haciendas or in the houses of the urban elite. They generally go to these jobs daily, rather than staying overnight, and the work consists mostly of cleaning, cooking, shopping for groceries, and caring for the elderly.

It has recently become apparent that women are participating in two activities that are uncommon in these communities. Working in cantinas is one. Celaya's sole cantina employs the members of the family that owns it. The work of the wife and daughters is limited to cooking and selling food, soft drinks, and beer. The husband and sons sell liquor such as tequila and brandy. El Cerro does not have a cantina, but some young women work in bars in Agua Verde. In addition to selling alcoholic beverages, a few also work as dancers. Prostitution, although common in the region, is usually concentrated in the red–light districts of Escuinapa and Rosario. There are no prostitutes in Celaya, but a part-time prostitute recently arrived in El Cerro. Everyone knows about her, and it has become a pastime to see how many of the men buy her services.

Although women's participation in the various activities discussed above offers them more flexibility than day-labor work, it is worth noting that these activities also add to their daily burden. Many women spend their days constantly switching between domestic chores and managing their *tiendas* (in-home stores) or spending part of their time going to the market to buy the ingredients to make food that they will sell. Domestic servants must take time to travel daily to the towns or other communities where they have found work. Nevertheless, most women in Celaya and El Cerro are convinced that the income that they earn is crucial in satisfying a part of their households' economic needs. Without their participation in the agricultural workforce or informal sector activities, their households would be in an even worse economic situation than the one in which they currently find themselves.

In general terms, subsistence agriculture, shrimp fishing, agricultural work, and participation of women in the informal economy are strategies or mechanisms that many households in both communities use to survive. In some sense, these strategies are linked to government policies and local and global processes, but—with the exception of shrimp fishing—the state did not create these activities with the intention of directly benefiting the inhabitants of Celaya and El Cerro. Both communities have experienced the government's development programs, which, in theory at least, aim to expand the economic activities available to the rural population. One of these programs is shrimp aquaculture, implemented in some rural coastal communities during the late 1980s. One of the main objectives behind the Mexican government's support for the development of a shrimp aquaculture industry was job creation to promote regional and community development by improving the standard of living and nutrition of the rural poor (Lobato 1988; Secretaría de Pesca 1989). Other objectives were to increase shrimp production and generate profits from shrimp exports.

The Experience with Shrimp Farming and Rural Development

Even though it has been almost twelve years since El Cerro's shrimp farm stopped operating, memories of it are still alive for those who worked there. People remember with anger when they worked on the farm and the way in which the biologists and the company managing the farm treated them. They refer to their work on the shrimp farm, or *viveros,* as an anguish (*una angustia*), a time of suffering they had to endure.

Their experience with shrimp aquaculture occurred during the first stage of the industry's development, in which only cooperatives comprising the rural working population were allowed to participate. The shrimp aquaculture cooperative of El Cerro was organized in 1987, and one of the main problems facing members in starting the shrimp farm was lack of capital. The cooperative addressed this problem by entering into a partnership with a private company. A large construction firm from Mexico City, interested in shrimp farming, came to southern Sinaloa to find a partner. The company proceeded to build the shrimp farm with its own construction workers and a few additional workers from the local community. Eventually the company hired the members of the cooperative as wageworkers for the farm. The company also agreed to a profit-sharing arrangement with cooperative members and promised that 19 percent of the profits would go directly to the ejido itself.

The type of shrimp aquaculture system developed in El Cerro was semi-intensive and relied upon the harvest of wild stocks of shrimp larvae to meet its production needs. The shrimp larvae were harvested from the wild by the biologists and some of the cooperative members. Water was pumped from an estuary to the ponds and its basic parameters (oxygen, ph, salinity, temperature) were monitored on a constant basis. The juvenile shrimp were transferred from one pond to another until they reached marketable proportions. The farm had 207 hectares on federal (government) land and 69 hectares on the ejido's land.

The shrimp aquaculture cooperative of Celaya was organized in 1986. In this community, the extensive type of shrimp aquaculture system was introduced. The system was located in two adjacent lagoons in which cooperative members built sluices to block the exit. Juvenile shrimp were brought from the ocean, stocked in the lagoons, and left there to grow, without additional fertilizer or food, until they reached a marketable size. This system produced one harvest per year. Shrimp culture was limited to the rainy season, from July to January, when the lagoons filled with water. This extensive system, although technologically simple, required funds to pay for wages and biologists' salaries, and to buy technical equipment (such as that used to monitor water parameters), office equipment, a pickup truck, oxygen tanks, nets to build the gear used in the capture of the shrimp larvae, a small boat, and fiberglass boxes to transport the larvae. Also, money was required to build the sluices in the lagoons and to pay for cooperative representatives to travel to Mexico City to deal with bureaucratic matters.

The members applied for bank loans, but this was problematic because of their lack of collateral. They solved this problem by building sluices in the lagoon that were then used as collateral for a loan of approximately 66 million pesos (approximately seven thousand dollars). The cooperative cultivated shrimp for two years, producing only enough to pay for members' salaries and to repay the bank's loan.

In both communities, a series of labor, managerial, and technological conflicts unfolded that caused the disintegration of the cooperatives.[6] Looking back at their experiences, people still contrast the positive and the negative impact of shrimp aquaculture upon their communities, their households, and themselves.

In El Cerro the only direct benefit was that the main road was repaired because it was needed to gain access to the shrimp farm. Another benefit to the community was that the cooperative contributed money that was used to repair the community's school. Otherwise, most people knew that it had existed but most of them were not aware of what was going on within the cooperative or the shrimp farm. Many inhabitants thought of cooperative members as being slaves at the shrimp farm and often felt sorry for them. The only real direct benefit that shrimp aquaculture provided the members of the cooperative in El Cerro was that it guaranteed a steady salary from a more or less secure job, although the income was low.

Among the negative effects of shrimp aquaculture in El Cerro were the impacts on members' health and time allocation. Members of the cooperative were constantly complaining about getting sick after they started working at the shrimp farm. For most members, especially those who were ejidatarios or worked as wage laborers, it was hard to get used to working all night, isolated and cold, during certain periods of the cycle. The shrimp farm lacked adequate facilities such as a kitchen or bathroom to help workers cope with the hardships of the environment.

In Celaya, the initial benefits included the purchase of a pickup truck and the legal allocation of two lagoons in which members of the cooperatives cultivated the shrimp. The major unintended consequence of shrimp aquaculture was the division of this community into two politically charged segments.

In 1993, when I returned to the communities, the Mexican fishing law had been amended to allow the participation of private entrepreneurs in shrimp aquaculture. As a result, the construction company purchased the shrimp farm from the members of the cooperative of El Cerro. The members agreed because they believed it was a good opportunity to free themselves from the kind of forced labor they were required to do and because they were better off economically working on something else. The company gave 10 million pesos (approximately one thousand dollars) to each member, acquired the sole rights to the shrimp farm, and brought in people from other communities to work. In Celaya the cooperative has attempted several times to start up with a new shrimp aquaculture project, but these attempts have failed because they lack the money to invest in shrimp larvae and equipment.

When I completed my fieldwork in the communities in the summer of 2002, a few people from El Cerro were employed as day laborers in some of the shrimp farms and hatcheries built in Agua Verde. The men were hired mostly to clean up the ponds and work as guards, and the women were hired as cooks. In Celaya, no one worked at a shrimp farm or hatchery.

Although shrimp cultivation may have been considered one more strategy within the array of available economic activities for the inhabitants of El Cerro and Celaya, it did not produce the desired results. The economy for those households that participated did not improve, and the family members had to return to a dependence on their traditional occupations. Instead shrimp aquaculture did contribute to exacerbating the problems of environmental degradation and to social conflict over fishing for the region's existing stock of shrimp. Because people can no longer continue to live as they did years ago, mostly from fishing and farming, they keep searching for alternatives that can provide them with better economic opportunities, such as migration.

Indeed, migration is becoming another important strategy for many households in both communities. Migration, within Mexico and internationally, has alleviated pressure that the communities would otherwise face as the result of the need to support people unable to find work. Migration has also meant additional income through remittances migrants send back to their household.

The Migration Experience

In southern Sinaloa's rural communities, stories abound about people from the region who have emigrated to the northern border region or into the United States. In both El Cerro and Celaya, most people, even those who have never migrated, know a story or two about a relative, friend, compadre, or someone from another community who has gone away. These stories, spiced with the typical Sinaloan sense of humor, tell the vicissitudes of those who have taken a risk by trying their luck on the "other side" in an attempt to improve their economic situation. Many of these stories describe the way of life along the border, work in *maquiladoras* (assembly plants), border crossings, *coyotes* (immigrant smugglers), *La Migra* (Border Patrol), deportations to Mexico, life in El Norte, and the return to the rural community. Having heard stories based on the experiences of those who left and have returned home, most of the communities' residents know about the economic opportunities available in the border states and the United States.

The following vignettes highlight the migration experience of the people of El Cerro and Celaya. I collected these narratives over a six-year period, while conducting fieldwork in the communities. As a collection, these stories represent the range of experiences for the communities' residents who have migrated, and they provide the social and human context needed to understand the national and international migration process in rural southern Sinaloa.

Case 1: Cyclical Migration to California

Fernando, the son of Manuel, went to Napa Valley, California, during five consecutive years. The first time was in 1995, when he was barely eighteen years old. His brother-in-law, who had been working in the California vineyards for fifteen years, convinced him to come in search of work in Napa Valley. The brother-in-law told him that it was a nice area, and that Fernando would earn good money working in the grape harvest. The first time that Fernando went to California, he was accompanied by three boys from Agua Verde. They arrived in Tijuana, where a coyote, to whom his brother-in-law had paid one thousand dollars, was waiting to cross them over into the United States. The coyote took them to his house in San Diego, where they stayed hidden for several days until he could get them fake papers and put them on a plane and send them to other states. He took Fernando to the airport to catch a plane to San Francisco. Once on board, Fernando felt frightened because he had never flown before. He was lucky, however, because he sat next to a Chicano, who spoke Spanish. The man, noticing that Fernando was very nervous, asked him where he was going. When he realized that both he and Fernando were going to San Francisco, he told him not to worry because he would help him so that he wouldn't get lost. When they arrived in San Francisco, the Chicano helped him to find his way throughout the airport and to locate his brother-in-law, who was waiting for him at the exit gate. Within two weeks, Fernando began to work, and even though he had to get up every day at 5 a.m., he was earning four hundred dollars per week. Out of this money, he paid one hundred dollars for rent, and the rest he saved. He sent money to his parents in El Cerro, particularly when they were sick or needed to buy something for the house. He worked in Napa Valley usually from March until October, and during those seven months, he would save about four thousand dollars, which he brought with him when he returned to El Cerro. With that money, he bought a car and built a bathroom and a new kitchen in his parents' house. On one of his trips home, he fell in love with a girl from the community and got married. With the money that he had saved, they built a house so that they could stay in El Cerro.

Case 2: Permanent Migration to California

Alejandro, Victoria's younger brother, went to the United States while he was still very young. He was living with Victoria in Celaya and working as a day laborer harvesting mango and coconut. The work was difficult, and he hated the heat and mosquitoes, so he and his older brother, Rodrigo, decided to go to the United States in search of better jobs. Their employer lent them money to pay for the trip. They took a bus from Escuinapa to Tijuana, and once there, they hired a coyote to take them into California. When they arrived, La Migra, the Border Patrol, pursued them and arrested Rodrigo. Alejandro escaped with two other men and continued on his way. They incarcerated Rodrigo for a week before deporting him to

Tijuana. After this experience, Rodrigo vowed he would never try crossing the border again, and he returned to Celaya. He traveled for more than a month—enduring hunger and sleeping under trees—until he finally arrived home. Alejandro spent some time wandering from place to place throughout California, accompanied by some men from other states in Mexico whom he had met and who, like him, had recently arrived. In San Diego, he worked in the strawberry harvest; in Los Angeles, in the construction industry; and, finally, in Anaheim, he found a more permanent job as a guard at a newspaper plant. He fell in love with the manager, an American, and married her, but the woman was much older than he and could not have children. Alejandro wanted a family, so he divorced her. He then met a Chicana, another co-worker at the plant. They married and had two children, and they currently live in Santa Ana. During the summer of 1998, after a ten-year absence, Alejandro went back to Celaya, taking his wife and children with him.

Case 3: Family Migration to Tijuana

Mariana moved to Tijuana with her husband, Antonio, and their six children. Antonio was a fisherman, but he had not been able to make enough to support the family. The couple saved up for the bus fare from Mazatlán to Tijuana, and once there, they stayed with Antonio's sister. Mariana and Antonio worked for two years in a Tijuana dairy processing plant called Baja Foods. After that, both got jobs working in Bolsas y Polietilenos de la Frontera, an Asian-owned plastics factory, where they worked for three and a half years. Mariana's entire family lived in a single room in the sister-in-law's house, paying a monthly rent of two hundred dollars. Their life in Tijuana was filled with continual hard work and family conflict. It was also costly because all their income went to pay for rent, food, and schooling for their children. Their situation was made more complicated when Antonio's mother came to Tijuana to live with them in the same house. The woman, who had never been happy that Antonio had married Mariana, was continually trying to get them to separate. The mother-in-law lied to her son, telling him that Mariana had a lover and that the child she was expecting was not his. Antonio believed this story, and he began to mistreat Mariana, even to the point of beating her on two occasions. After six years, they returned to El Cerro and tried to readapt to living there. Their daughters, however, made a lot of trouble. They had liked living in

Tijuana because the school where they had studied was good and the climate was cooler. Mariana agreed with her daughters, and she believed that in Tijuana they had eaten better and were healthier. After six months of living in El Cerro, the family returned to Tijuana. Upon returning, the situation between the mother-in-law and Mariana changed when she told the woman that she never wanted to see her again and wanted to be left in peace. Antonio has distanced himself from his mother and treats Mariana much better than before.

Case 4: Migration of Young Single Women to Tijuana

Sujey, Raquel's daughter, wanted to go to Tijuana to live with her aunt. She was eighteen years old, and after finishing secondary school, she didn't want to continue studying. In Celaya, she worked for a while in the planting and harvesting of chilies, but her parents thought that it was a good idea to send her to her aunt so that she could try to get a better job. Only a few weeks after arriving, she found work in a maquiladora making computer parts. They paid her 150 dollars per week, and of that, she gave thirty dollars to her aunt to help with household expenses. She also sent fifty dollars monthly to her mother in Celaya, and the rest she saved. The work in the maquiladora was hard because she had the night shift, but she liked it much better than working from sunup until sundown in the fields. After two years of living in Tijuana, she returned to Celaya during the summer. While there, she met a boy from Isla del Bosque, and they married. They lived for a while in Celaya, in her parents' home, and then they moved to Tijuana, where they currently live.

These four cases illustrate the dimensions and characteristics of migration, within Mexico and internationally, as residents from southern Sinaloa's rural communities experience it. One characteristic is that the people migrate "on their own account," that is, without the assistance of a government program. Another is that migrants who visit their home communities—telling (exaggerated) tales of their new lives in the places where they have been living—influence others to migrate. The example of those who have migrated to the United States, and who return to their communities in vans and dressed in fashionable clothes, is particularly influential. This contributes to the idealization of life north of the border. Yet another characteristic is that many people migrate to places where relatives or friends are already established. On arrival, newer migrants join the already existing social and economic networks of the relatives and friends who have welcomed them. A very important dimension is that initially, only young, single men migrated. Today, the trend is for an entire family to move. In some cases, the male head of the family goes first to find a job and a place to live, and then the rest of the family follows him. Another trend is for young, single women to leave their home communities in search of work. These girls are sent to live with relatives in border cities, such as Tijuana or Nogales, where they find employment in the maquiladoras.

Migration increased during the 1990s in the two communities. In 1989, when I first conducted ethnographic research in the region, only 19 percent of all households in El Cerro had members who had migrated to other parts of Mexico, the border region, or the United States. In Celaya, none of the households reported having members who were migrants. Since then, migration has increased dramatically. The 1998 survey showed that 42 percent of a random sample of thirty-eight households in El Cerro had at least one member who had migrated. In a random sample of twenty-eight households in Celaya, the figure was 36 percent. For the most part, people migrate in search of employment, going to Mazatlán, to the northern border states, such as Sonora, or to border cities, such as Tijuana, Mexicali, Nogales, or Rosarito. This is often an intermediate step in an eventual migration to the United States, where these migrants seek employment in the industrial, agricultural, or service sectors. In households with migrants, remittances to the family account for about 10 percent of family income.

Conclusion

The people of El Cerro and Celaya have never lived in complete isolation. They are well aware of their place in the global economy and how their labor produces goods that are exported for consumption by people in other countries. They also know that they have little control over the economic development of their communities. Because of this, most of their efforts are channeled into sustaining the household's economy.

Mexican campesino economies are ever more dependent on the process of occupational diversification that has emerged within households (de Teresa Ochoa and Cortez Ruiz 1996). An increase in the number of workers and the incorporation of women and children into the workforce characterize this process. To provide their households with basic resources and income, the people of Celaya and El Cerro practice livelihoods that involve an array of subsistence and economic activities, both within and outside the communities.

Among the productive activities in both communities, subsistence agriculture stands out. It is paradoxical that in these two communities, which formed directly from the struggle for land in the region, the residents today can no longer depend on the land to cover even their minimal basic necessities.

Subsistence agriculture has been displaced by commercial agriculture. An important aspect of labor participation in commercial agriculture is the growth in the number of women who are working as day laborers. Day labor places new demands on women, who must constantly struggle to balance their work in the fields with their domestic chores. Precisely because of all the constraints that agricultural work entails, many women have created other alternatives for generating income, within their own homes and communities.

The informal economy constitutes an important link in women's labor participation. Activities like selling food, shrimp, clothing, basic goods, and handicrafts generate income and are more compatible with the time that the women of both communities must invest in order to do their domestic chores. Many of these activities offer them greater flexibility than day-labor work.

On the other hand, even though shrimp fishing has been one of the greatest supports for the regional economy, its contribution to the economies of these communities is becoming ever more limited due to the overexploitation of the resource. The fishing seasons are becoming shorter every year, which affects the annual income that fishermen earn. Due partly to overexploitation of the resource and partly to the government's proposal to generate new sources of employment for the rural population along the coast, the Mexican government implemented a national-level program for shrimp aquaculture. Rural communities, such as El Cerro and Celaya, participated in the first phase of the program, but their experience with this type of rural development was not entirely favorable. The failure of the projects in both communities was linked to a series of economic and social conflicts that have remained engraved in the memories of those who were involved.

Today, very few viable economic activities remain for the rural population in southern Sinaloa. Migration, considered as the last hope, is growing more popular among residents of El Cerro and Celaya. They view migration, primarily to the border region or into the United States, as an option that offers better job opportunities and a higher standard of living. Migration, however, has its personal and social costs because, in many cases, the migrant is cut off from relatives and friends (Cohen 1999). Changes in U.S. government policy, such as Proposition 187 and incidents such as the attacks on the Twin Towers in New York, directly affect the Mexican migration process, making it more difficult and riskier. The residents of El Cerro and Celaya are aware of changes and incidents, which they consider when analyzing the possibility of migrating.

In general terms, one of the top preoccupations for households in El Cerro and Celaya is the ability to have enough money to meet family members' basic needs. To confront this challenge, the residents undertake the array of economic activities that are available to them within their communities and the region. However, that is not enough to combat the poverty that entraps them. The people of El Cerro and Celaya are not alone in their struggle to combat poverty. According to Wayne Cornelius and David Myhre, "Mexico's poverty problem had become increasingly concentrated in its rural sector, and of the 50 percent of Mexicans whose incomes were below the officially defined poverty line, 70 percent lived in rural areas" (1998, 8). In their daily struggle with economic uncertainty and the region's environmental problems, the residents of El Cerro and Celaya resist by using mechanisms that promote cooperation and mutual help among the households.

8

La Lucha

The Dynamics of Household Relations and Resistance

No one ever dared feel sorry for her. Her toughness was so outland-
ish that people began to seek her out to ask her for help. What was
her secret? Who sheltered her from her own afflictions? Where did
she get the ability to remain standing despite the worst misfortunes?
—Angeles Mastretta, *Mujeres de Ojos Grandes*

Victoria had not yet overcome the enormous depression that followed her
son's death when she realized that her husband was seeing another woman.
Several months earlier, her son had died when a pistol he was cleaning
accidentally fired. Now, with great sadness, Victoria asked her husband if
the rumors she had heard about his having an affair were true. Lorenzo
denied it even though he did not sleep at home two or three nights out of
each week. As the rumors in Celaya grew, Victoria's suspicions turned into
an obsession to learn the other woman's identity. She asked around town
and, eventually, she learned that the woman lived in Tijuana but was currently visiting relatives in Celaya. Her name was Magdalena.

During the annual fiesta that the elementary school hosted, Victoria
could see that, indeed, Lorenzo and Magdalena were in a relationship.
Victoria was president of the School Committee, so she sat at a table with
the other committee members and the teachers while Lorenzo sat at table
with his compadres. From where she was, Victoria could observe her husband and Magdalena exchanging looks and flirting. The fiesta unfolded
without incident, and at 10 p.m., Victoria, who was by then very tired,
decided to go home.

She went to bed and fell asleep, but a few minutes later, she heard her daughter-in-law knocking at the door and calling to her. Victoria quickly got up, opened the door, and saw that the girl was in tears. "What happened?" Victoria asked her with great concern. The daughter-in-law answered, "Right in front of me, Lorenzo left with that woman in a truck!" Enraged, Victoria dressed and went to see her daughter, Teresa, in the hope of convincing her to come with her to look for Lorenzo. Teresa tried to persuade Victoria to calm down, but her mother told her angrily, "Look, daughter, even if the devil takes me, tonight I'm going to screw over your father and that woman. Tonight they are going to see what I'm capable of."

It was drizzling, but this did not stop Victoria and her daughter from waiting in the street for the pickup truck in which Lorenzo had left. After waiting half an hour, it passed by, but neither Lorenzo nor Magdalena was in it. The truck didn't stop, so the women ran after it. Each hung on to one of the side-view mirrors, but still the driver did not stop, so they grabbed him by the hair and forced him to pull over. With great irritation, he asked them what they wanted. Angrily, Teresa demanded, "Tell my mother where you dropped off my father!" The driver told them that he had not seen Lorenzo in a long time, but they did not believe him, and so they began to beat him. And Victoria, with her patience exhausted, said, "Why are you acting stupid? With me, stupid, you're screwed, you son of a bitch!" The women jumped into the back of the truck and forced the driver to take them to Lorenzo. The drizzle became a fierce downburst, but even getting soaked could not make the women drop the idea of pursuing him, even if that meant driving ten miles to the town of Escuinapa.

In the middle of the storm, they arrived at a hotel in Escuinapa. Here, the driver told Victoria, she would find her husband. The women ordered the driver, "Wait for us here, son of a bitch; you'll be sorry if you dare to leave us behind!" Inside the hotel, they asked the receptionist to give them Lorenzo's room number. The man started to refuse, but the women screamed at him, so he had little choice but to tell them. They ran up the hotel stairs, all the way to the third floor; Victoria knocked softly on the door, and, altering her voice, she said she was Magdalena's cousin and needed urgently to talk to her. Magdalena believed this, and opened the door; but when she realized that Victoria was standing there, she tried to slam it shut. Victoria stopped her by putting her foot in the door. The frightened woman ran, turned out the light, and jumped under the covers of the disheveled bed.

Victoria told Teresa to guard the door and not let anyone in. Then, she entered the room, turned on the light, and closed the door. Lorenzo, on seeing Victoria, almost died of fright, but he became so agitated that he began scolding her for following him. While the couple argued, Magdalena made a run for the bathroom with the idea of locking herself in. Seeing Magdalena naked, Victoria grabbed her by the hair and began to beat her. Lorenzo tried to stop his wife, but Victoria slapped him in the face, too. Greatly ashamed, Lorenzo dressed and left the room, and Victoria continued beating up Magdalena.

Victoria beat Magdalena for almost an hour, and then, as frosting on the cake, she grabbed the woman's clothes from her hands and warned her, "Now I'm going, you bitch, you disgraceful whore. You'll pay for this, because you're left with nothing, for being such a slut. That's my husband, and you betrayed me. You've seen the consequences just in case it ever occurs to you to try to sleep with him or another married man. This time, I won. Remember that by what you did you mocked me, and I'll never forgive you that, you whore." The woman, wailing, begged Victoria to return the clothes, but she refused.

Victoria grabbed her husband by the arm, pulled him out the door, and said to her daughter, "It's time to go," leaving Magdalena alone and naked. Lorenzo tried to return to the room to leave Magdalena some money so that she could take a taxi to Celaya, but Victoria stopped him, saying, "If you dare give her a centavo, I'll report you to the police." They got in the truck. Lorenzo did not open his mouth to say a single word, and his head hung down with shame. He looked like a dog that had just been ejected from the house, its tail between its legs.

Magdalena, filled with shame, had no choice but to ask the receptionist to lend her a sheet so she could cover herself and go home. In the wee hours of the morning, she arrived in Celaya in a taxi, wrapped only in a white sheet. Her aunt, on seeing Magdalena, was shocked and asked her what had happened, but very upset, Magdalena said only that she needed money to pay the taxi driver. She then got dressed and went to the síndico's house to make a complaint. She told him that Victoria had taken her clothes, and she asked the síndico to go with her to Victoria's house to retrieve them. He said, "Nothing of mine has been taken. Go by yourself. But I'll warn you: Victoria has a pistol, and if you go to her house at this hour of the night, she's likely to shoot you." Magdalena thought about this, and, as of today, she has never gone to retrieve her clothing.

Victoria recounted this story to me during one of my visits to Celaya. I had already heard some of what had happened because other people in the community had talked about it. When I arrived at her house, the first thing she asked was if I had heard the story. I told her that I had heard something about it, but not the details. Then she told me to get out my tape recorder because she was going to tell me the true version of what had transpired. She wanted me to tape her to include the account in my book, so that anyone who read it could understand what the community's women suffer because of their men. After taping, she said, "And in case you don't believe me, wait here a minute." She returned with a bag in her hands, and in front of me, she began to empty it out. Astonished, I watched as out of the bag came, first, a pair of pants, then a blouse, then a brassiere, and finally, some underpants. On seeing my surprised reaction and curiosity, Victoria quickly said, "Those are her clothes! I'm keeping them put away, hoping that she may come looking for them; and if she dares to, that bitch, I'll give her another round of beatings." Four years have passed since this incident, and the woman has never returned to Celaya, much less come in search of her clothing. And Lorenzo has never again been unfaithful.

When I conducted open interviews with women in southern Sinaloa, one of the most frequent topics of conversation was the hardship and uncertainty that permeate their daily lives. Most women in Celaya and El Cerro reported that there is great tension in their households, because everyone is struggling so hard to make ends meet. For many women, tension and despair are also the result of juggling all their daily responsibilities within their homes while trying to engage in income-generating activities and find time for themselves. Women refer to these tasks and pressures in their daily lives as *la lucha diaria* (the daily struggle). For the great majority of women, their lucha begins at sunrise and does not end until all household members are in bed. The lucha also consists of a woman's intermittent search for new and different ways to support her family and provision her household. In addition, for many women, their lucha involves perennial attempts at making their marriages work out in a satisfactory manner.

Women in southern Sinaloa repeat a widely known proverb: "In heaven, God has a throne waiting for the woman who was happily married during her life; as of now, it remains vacant." Women use this saying when talking among themselves about their domestic difficulties. They use this saying to imply that it is common for all marriages to have problems, but it is the women, generally, who have the greatest responsibility for meeting and resolving domestic challenges. They also use it to suggest that few women can claim to have, or have had, a happy marriage because, on top of taking care of her children and household, a woman must also look after her husband. The proverb comes up when women are comparing their domestic situations with those of other women. By invoking it, they understand that they are not alone in their daily struggle because—by the mere fact of being female—they should expect to confront similar situations. Women in rural communities are not the only ones familiar with the proverb; it is also heard in towns and larger, more cosmopolitan cities, such as Mazatlán. Most women in the communities recognize that matrimonial happiness depends not solely on the wife but on the couple, and they also understand that having domestic disagreements or quarrels, especially connected with gender relations, is very common. However, these women cannot understand or accept that they must endure physical or mental abuse by their husbands in addition to facing all the daily problems and struggles that arise in trying to ensure their children's well-being.

Life in households in rural southern Sinaloa is far from a bed of roses. The story above illustrates some aspects of the conflicts and dynamics occurring in households in Celaya and El Cerro. Many conflicts originate from how gender relations manifest in households. In most cases, women must make a major effort to get their interests and points of view taken into consideration in decision making about household management and maintenance. For many of them, a basic part of their daily struggle is to ensure that their voices are not silenced by patriarchism, gender and class inequalities, and the economic poverty that is so prevalent in rural Mexican society. Inequality and poverty have increased in recent years as a consequence of globalization. Indeed, because of globalization, the feminization of poverty has grown markedly (Abbassi and Lutjens 2002). In addition to poverty, having to struggle constantly against the subordination to which they are subjected within their own homes is a never-ending challenge for women in El Cerro and Celaya.

Notably, during the ten years I was doing fieldwork, the topic of domestic violence frequently came up in my conversations with the communities' residents.[1] Domestic violence is not always easy to document. In El Cerro and Celaya, women do not talk about it openly within the communities or even within their own homes. Nevertheless, most people are aware of incidents when they occur. The women, especially those who are married and have children, talk among themselves about their husbands' abuse, but they do so privately. The first time I heard about cases of domestic violence in the communities occurred when I returned to southern Sinaloa after a two-year absence. I arrived in El Cerro and asked for Eneida, one of the women whom I had met there while doing my doctoral dissertation fieldwork. When I asked a woman who was walking in the street for the whereabouts of Eneida, she, in turn, asked me if I was referring to la Ene whose husband beat her. I told her I was not certain if they were one and the same. The woman went on to tell me about the times when Eneida's husband had come home drunk and beat her. In one of these instances, the woman told me, Eneida grabbed her husband by the testicles, and he was so ashamed, he never hit her again.

In subsequent years, the topic of domestic violence came up in my interviews with the presidentes de vigilancia, who must intervene in such cases as part of their responsibility for maintaining order in the community. However, several years had to pass and I had to undergo changes in my own life before the women would acquire enough trust to feel comfortable telling me about their experiences with domestic violence. One of the most significant of these changes was that I ceased to be a student and a single woman without children and became, instead, a professional and a wife and mother. At that point, the women began to include me in their social networks and to talk uninhibitedly in my presence about their marriages. When I asked them why they had not talked to me about these issues years earlier, they answered that I would not have understood because I did not have a husband or children. These women believe that only a woman who has been married or has children can understand their own travails because she will be more likely to have experienced similar situations.

Initially, our discussions of domestic violence came about casually because we were talking about other topics, such as work or children's health. Only gradually did we reach the subject of abuse within the household. In other cases, certain women invited me into their homes because they wanted to talk to me about their experiences, perhaps hoping for my sympathy or advice. I saw that, in most cases, they needed to unburden themselves to someone who would listen. I may have been a worthy confidant both because I was in an ambiguous position—being part of the community, and yet apart from it—and because I was university-trained and would thus have some knowledge about domestic violence. The topic of abuse often came up when I was talking with a group of women about the difficulties they face. Most agreed that domestic violence was a major problem affecting them. In reality, and according to key informants, 80 percent of the households in Celaya and 85 percent of those in El Cerro reported incidents of domestic violence during 2001. The key informants in both communities agreed that instances of domestic violence have increased in recent years, and they attribute this to the increase in precarious economic conditions that the region is experiencing.

Many women think that the lack of adequate jobs and the pressure that the men feel as household providers sinks them in a cycle of alcohol consumption: A man spends the little bit of money that he earns on drink, and then, when he arrives home drunk, his wife scolds him, and they begin to argue and fight.[2] In other cases, the displacement of the man as the primary breadwinner changes the traditional patterns of gender relations, which creates insecurity and the need to constantly exercise the power that they believe they possess. In both communities, there are women who work and provide the greater share of household income in comparison to their husbands. In certain cases, these women are victims of mental and physical abuse from their husbands, who feel that their role as household head has been relegated to second tier. These men believe that by controlling their wives, they can regain their place within the home.

Some women believe that domestic violence is part of a cycle, with the practice being transmitted from generation to generation, and they think their husbands are abusive because the men's own fathers were also. Still other women believe that domestic violence sometimes occurs without any reason whatsoever. For example, referring to a case in which the husband beat his wife because he thought that she was ugly, a woman from El Cerro told me, "Around here, they hit you even if it is only because you're ugly." In both communities, the reasons for domestic violence are varied, and more detailed studies are needed.

However, an important fact that comes out of women's experiences with domestic violence is that they do not accept it but, instead, they always resist and struggle to combat it. Most of the women do not feel that they are responsible for the abuse they suffer or that they are the cause that sets off or encourages abuse from their husbands or fathers. The women of El Cerro and Celaya are not, in any way, passive victims, who accept with resignation the violence or poor treatment of which they are the objects.

Nor are they passive victims of globalization or patriarchy. To the contrary, most do whatever they possibly can to confront domestic violence. The problem is that they have few resources at their disposal. These rural communities do not have shelters for victims of domestic violence or clinics that offer psychological help or guidance. This situation is not unique in El Cerro or Celaya: Even in the urban areas of the municipios of Escuinapa and Rosario, no shelters or concrete assistance is available for victims of domestic violence. Although many reasons exist for the lack of adequate health services in rural communities, according to Alatorre Rico, Langer, and Lozano (1994), in Mexico one reason is the reduction in availability and quality of services for the poor as a consequence of the economic crisis and structural adjustment policies.

What are the options for women living in rural communities, such as El Cerro and Celaya? The only options they have are to seek the help of relatives and friends; report their husbands to the presidente de vigilancia, síndico, or municipal police; or defend themselves by beating their husbands. Many women agree that when they defend themselves and beat their husbands, the physical abuse ends because their husbands feel ashamed that the wives have rebelled and called their manhood into question. Some women report their husbands to the police, but others do not, not so much because of fear of the husband's reaction, but because it is expensive to do so. When the husband is jailed, a woman loses a source of income, because her husband cannot work. Many women, needing the income that their husbands usually bring in, decide to drop the charges, but to get the husband out of jail, a woman has to pay bail, which wastes the little bit of money that the couple still has. Most women recognize that reporting their husbands to the police sends a warning message, but they also know that in economic terms, it is not to their advantage, and so they choose not to file a report. In other cases (especially those involving the poorest women and those who do not have relatives in the community), the women choose not to file a report out of fear that their husbands may abandon them. These women tolerate abuse because they need their spouses' economic support to be able to feed and educate their children, and because they understand that women-headed households are among the poorest in the communities.

But domestic violence and abuse are behavioral reproductions cycled by extreme poverty, limited resources, and a degrading natural environment. Domestic violence is the end point of the tension and conflict of long-term economic and social marginalization. Yet, the women in El Cerro and Celaya, as well as most women throughout Third World countries, confront and resist the effects of globalization by creating survival strategies within and beyond their own homes. In Mexico, for example, Lynn Stephen (2002), in a study of women's social movements, shows that, in rural areas, women develop survival strategies to cope with environmental degradation and economic impoverishment.

The feminization of resistance against globalization, according to Abbassi and Lutjens (2002, 34), "finds women pursuing the survival of their families, augmenting their work inside and outside the home as they stretch scarce resources and seek more through additional labor." In the previous chapter, I discussed how, in both communities, the increase in women's participation in the formal and informal economies reflects a new strategy for generating the income needed to guarantee a household's basic existence. Another strategy, documented in Mexican urban households (González de la Rocha 2002), consists of altering nutrition patterns according to a household's economic needs. In both Celaya and El Cerro, women decide what to feed their families, and they plan and prepare the types of food that they serve daily. The basic diet consists of tortillas, beans, chicken or shrimp, and vegetables. In times of economic crisis, women make tortillas instead of buying them in the tortillería because it is less expensive to do so. A bag of Maseca, the meal from which the tortillas are prepared, lasts a household at least two or three days. During crises, household members depend more on foods they can obtain locally, such as nopales, mangoes, chilies, corn, chicken, eggs, mojarras, and other freshwater fish. Because they can grow, raise, or catch these food items themselves, these items often cost very little or even nothing. The women can invest in clothes or schooling for their children the money saved by eating such food.

These strategies—increasing the number of women involved in income-earning activities and changing the eating patterns—arise within the households themselves. Another study, done in Mexico on the strategies or responses the population has developed to confront the consequences of the economic crisis, also showed that the social responses were private, that is, produced and taking place within households, because the population was concerned with survival at the household level (González de la Rocha 2002, 68).

Nevertheless, in El Cerro and Celaya, not all the strategies or responses to economic poverty and environmental degradation are individual efforts or arise within the household itself. Other strategies exist that are based on cooperation and reciprocity among households. These strategies develop around family, friendship, or compadrazgo, and they connect the households economically and socially. A very important characteristic of these strategies is that they rest on a base of well-cemented bonds of trust, which interconnect these relationships to form a bridge for the exchange of support, ideas, resources, experiences, and solidarity. Although these strategies are not of recent invention but have existed since the communities formed, it is worth noting that their importance becomes more apparent in times of crisis because they provide the rural population, and especially the women, with a shield to protect them from uncertainty and desperation. Before discussing these strategies in detail, it is necessary to explain the way in which *parentezco* (kinship relations) functions within the communities, in particular when they involve relatives or are based on *comadrazgo* (co-maternity among women).

Bonds of Blood: La Familia

In El Cerro and Celaya, familial bonds transcend the communities' geographic boundaries by extending to the region's other rural communities, such as Agua Verde, Isla del Bosque, and Teacapán; to the towns of Escuinapa and Rosario; to Mazatlán; to border cities, such as Nogales and Tijuana; and to U.S. states, such as California and Louisiana. Despite the distance, visits, telephone calls, and messages (sent with individuals who are traveling between these places) maintain relationships among relatives.

One important characteristic of kinship relations in the communities is that in many cases, several generations of the same family reside in the community, which fosters exchanges of help, support, and cooperation among them. The households of these families function as a series of clusters, whose nucleus is, generally, the home of the grandparents or the eldest relatives. Carlos Vélez-Ibáñez (1996, 148) defines clustered households as those that are "usually centered around an ascending generation in which kin live close to children and their families of orientation, and in which exchange relations are maintained and mobilized." The proximity of the households facilitates the interaction and exchange among their members, which, in turn, promotes cohesiveness and solidarity among some family members.

The family of Benito and Regina, in El Cerro, illustrates how clustered households function. Their home is the nucleus or meeting center for all the relatives. Here, children and grandchildren gather each afternoon to tell stories and plan for the future. The daughters come here to make tortillas for the entire family, and the children play here throughout the day. The reciprocity among the family members is significant and is reflected in the exchange of small favors, such as childcare, transportation, help in the fields, lending money, and care of the sick.

Indeed, it is relatives on whom people rely during a crisis. Although harmony is certainly not a principal characteristic of these families, during crises the differences and rivalries among members seem to vanish to facilitate cooperation and assistance. For example, the illness of Trini united her children, who had become alienated from her following the death of Chico. Even the daughters who were angry with her were among those who took the best care of Trini until she passed away. All the children contributed money and time to try to help their mother recover.

Assistance and cooperation among women is very important for a family's maintenance. The case of my compadres demonstrates this. When the husband lost his job in the shrimp larvae laboratory, my comadre decided to try her hand at selling shrimp for a while. She had never done this before, but her mother, who had been a changuera for many years, helped her. The mother lent my comadre money to buy shrimp, and she also took her along to sell it in the town of Rosario. Thus, her mother trained her, little by little, so that my comadre could be a changuera too.

In other instances, the kinship relations provide networks to help people find jobs or to migrate. When someone learns of a job opening or that an employer is recruiting workers, people usually tell their relatives first before spreading the word any further. Similarly, when someone decides to migrate, they initially go to the family to tell them of their decision. They may ask for a loan to cover trip expenses or take steps to start the process of establishing contacts with relatives or friends who already are living in the location to which they plan to migrate.

Although it is true that the kinship relations are important, especially for families with few economic resources, it is also true that the relationships are fragile and can be broken easily. Blood ties uniting a family endure the passage of time, across various generations, but the social relations are severed when mutual trust among the members is, for some reason, broken. Fictive kinship relations are also important and play a similar role to blood ties. The compadrazgo system interconnects many households within the communities and with other communities in the region and in other Mexican states, and with communities in places as far away as California.

Comadrazgo: A Ritualized Kinship of Mutual Trust among Women

On Sunday, July 5, 1998, I became the comadre of one of Trini and Chico's children. My husband and I baptized Romario, son of Jorge and Carmen, in the Catholic Church in Agua Verde. The child was already three years old, but his parents had wanted us to be the *padrinos* (godparents), so they waited to baptize him until I made one of my visits to El Cerro. When we arrived that summer in Sinaloa, we went immediately to El Cerro, to the home of our future compadres, to deliver the baptism clothes for the child and to discuss when to have the baptism. The following Sunday, very early in the morning, we returned to El Cerro to pick up our compadres so that we could all go to the church in Agua Verde together. My future godchild was dressed all in white. When we arrived at the church, we sat in a small room with another family and waited for the priest to finish mass and come to get us. Before beginning the rite, he asked us if we were Catholics, and if we understood the responsibility that being godparents of a child brought with it. When I answered that I had also been baptized and had godparents, he smiled as if to let me know that he approved of me being the *madrina* (godmother). The priest then proceeded to ask Jorge and Carmen if they had been married in the church and if the child was legitimate or illegitimate. They answered that they were living in a common-law union but that they would marry in the church as soon as they were financially able to. After the questioning, the priest asked us to enter the church, and he led us before the altar to begin the rite of baptism. While he carried out the ceremony, the priest explained the significance of the baptism and our responsibility as godparents in the eventuality of the death of the child's parents. The priest then threw holy water on the child's head, while he said, "I baptize you, Cruz Romario Flores, in the name of the Father, the Son and the Holy Spirit."

When the ceremony was over, we thanked the priest and gave him money as a donation in sign of our appreciation and to help cover church expenses. On leaving, we noticed that a group of children was anxiously waiting for us to throw coins on the ground, as was the custom. According to tradition, *el bolo*, as the money given at a baptism is called, symbolizes the wish that the baptized child have a prosperous life filled with well-being. We tossed the coins, and as if a candy-filled piñata had just broken, the children launched themselves forward to grab the money, amid shouts and shoving.

We returned to El Cerro to begin the most anticipated part of the rite: the party. The entire family was already gathered and waiting in Trini's house. In the patio in front of the house were chairs and tables piled with shrimp and grilled fish. This fiesta is one of the most important phases of the baptism because it offers the opportunity to seal the bonds of compadrazgo socially while the community acknowledges the child as yet another member sharing the same religion. During this party, the godparents meet the rest of the family and begin to develop bonds of trust, which are the primary base on which the compadrazgo system rests. The entire family shares the costs so that the fiesta will be filled with merriment, music, and food. The godparents, in particular, also contribute money to cover the costs: Our compadres asked us to contribute the cake and beverages.

After that fiesta, the relationship between my compadres and me had been transformed completely, from one that was casual to one of mutual respect. The child, who had before called me Mariluz, began to call me Nina, a nickname for madrina. My compadres, who before had addressed me using the Spanish familiar form for "you" (*tu*), began to use *"usted"* (the formal form) when they spoke to me, and I had to grow accustomed to using "usted" when speaking to them. A network created through compadrazgo is built on both trust and respect, and it involves all relatives of the child's parents and of the godparents.

The compadrazgo system in Mexico has been extensively studied. Anthropologists, in particular, have written on the functions and roots of compadrazgo in the country's various regions (see Mintz and Wolf 1950; Foster 1953; Nader 1969; Lomnitz 1977; Kemper 1982; Nutini 1984; Sault 1985).[3] Compadrazgo originated in the period of Spanish conquest and colonization, although there is evidence that the Aztecs and Mayas practiced similar rites of parentezco (Stephen 1991). It functions to help preserve the social network, promote social mobility in a community, and contribute to the social, economic, and physical welfare of a community's inhabitants (Lomnitz 1977, cited in Cohen 1999).

In El Cerro and Celaya, compadrazgo serves to cement relationships among relatives and friends, because these are primarily the people invited to become godparents. The women in the communities play an important role in the compadrazgo system: They usually take the initiative in deciding who are potential compadres, inviting the selected people to become the godparents, and organizing the rites through which compadrazgo is forged. Women also prepare the food to serve and make decorations to use in the rites. Men often provide the money to cover the costs, but the women are in charge of buying whatever is needed.

In El Cerro and Celaya, comadrazgo begins with one of the rites of passage, when a woman becomes the madrina of a daughter or son of another woman. The most important of these is baptism because it is the first rite celebrated in a person's life, and it is linked to the Catholic religion. For the baptism, the godmother must be Catholic, have been baptized herself, and be married. Being a madrina represents one of the highest honors that a woman can receive, and it requires that the child respect her equally with her or his own mother. To ask a woman if she wants to baptize a child shows that the parents trust and feel respect and affection for her. Refusing to be the madrina at the baptism can have serious repercussions in the friendship between the mother of the child and the woman who was sought as the madrina. In such a case, the bonds of trust that previously existed between the two women would be broken, and in the future, other people in the community would not invite her to be a madrina.

Although baptism is one of the most important rituals in the life of the residents of Celaya and El Cerro, and one of the most respected and prestigious ways of becoming a madrina, other rites also lead to comadrazgo. Within the Catholic Church, the first communion and confirmation, when the child accepts the seven sacraments, are two other rites requiring godparents. If the rite is for a girl, the custom is for her to have a madrina; if it is a boy, a padrino (godfather, called the sponsor in English). The madrina or padrino is responsible for buying the child's outfit and accompanying her or him to the church.

Other rites of passage requiring a madrina are quinceañeras, weddings, and graduations. For quinceañeras and weddings, the madrina's main responsibility is to help cover the costs of the ceremony, and it is common to invite four or five women to be godmothers for the birthday girl or the bride. One buys the girl's dress, another the flowers, another the cake, another the food, and so on. A madrina for a graduation is primarily responsible for buying a gift and attending the ceremony. These rituals are based on cooperation and reciprocity: It is expected that someone who has been a godmother will not have difficulties in finding a godmother for her daughter or son when the time comes. However, unlike baptism, these rites do not carry future responsibilities: The function of the madrina is limited only to that particular event. In contrast, the baptismal madrina is expected to show concern for the child's development and look out for his or her well-being, including assuming the mother's place if she were to die. The godmother often must help cover the costs of the child's education, and, although it is not required, people expect that she will give gifts on the child's birthday and at Christmas.

The relations of comadrazgo keep women connected both within and beyond the communities. Comadres get together to visit and chat, support each other, share events in their lives, and offer mutual assistance in times of crisis. Cooperation and reciprocity develop within a context permeated with trust and respect. In both communities, the presence of social and kin networks greatly influences the strategies or responses created to combat poverty. Relationships that are consanguineal, affinal, or fictive (such as compadrazgo) offer households a glimmer of hope at the end of the dark tunnel created by their daily struggle for survival.

The Resistance Strategies of Rural Women

Lynn Stephen (2002) has documented the creation of survival strategies among rural women in Mexico in the face of ecological and economic impoverishment. These strategies, for the most part, are based on collective action and involve women's organization and participation in popular social movements. In rural southern Sinaloa, no social movements have emerged yet. However, women have united to better the social conditions of their households. In at least two instances, women in both communities have joined forces to demand better living conditions. The women from El Cerro organized a group to protest the lack of potable water in their community. In Celaya, women organized and collected signatures to demand the closure of the cantina that was consuming a large portion of their husbands' salaries. However, most responses develop at the household level, with women from various households joining forces. Women's strategies and responses are designed mostly to relieve economic uncertainty in the short term. Four strategies are common to all households in both communities: *cundinas*, food pooling, childcare, and labor exchange.

Cundinas: A Local Rotating Credit System

One of the greatest concerns for women in these communities is being able to have money available when they need it. To save money is not an option when one does not have any surplus. The local banks make it very difficult for a person from a rural community to get a loan without collateral. Frequently, a woman's relatives do not have money to lend her when she needs it. And sometimes remittances, sent by husbands or other relatives living in the United States or Tijuana, fail to arrive in time to cover the household expenses. Whatever the case may be, pressing economic need in the communities drives women to seek a way to have money available to help cover household needs. Participation in Asociaciones Rotativas de Crédito (Rotating Credit Associations, or RCAs), called cundinas in southern Sinaloa, provide a viable alternative for obtaining a sum of money in a short time.

Cundinas did not originate in El Cerro or Celaya or even in southern Sinaloa. Nor do they exist only among people with few economic resources. Throughout Mexico, cundinas operate, and even middle-class people and professionals participate in them. Carlos Vélez-Ibáñez (1983) describes RCAs as a cultural invention prevalent among Mexicans in Mexico and in the southwestern United States. In Mexico, a cundina may also be called a *tanda, rol, rifa, bolita, mutualista, quiniela, quincela, vaca, vaquita, el ahorro,* or *redonda.*

RCAs share the characteristics of being based in an informal group connected by mutual trust and lasting for a predetermined period. The group members each agree to contribute an equal sum of money at regular intervals. The number of people involved can vary, depending on the amount that must be contributed, how often a contribution is required, and the length of time the association will last. Each time the participants make their regular contribution, one member receives all the money. The cundina ends once each participant has had her turn receiving the pooled money. The money rotates among the members of the association.

People's motives for joining RCAs also vary. A principal reason is the need to obtain a sum of money in a short period, whether to cover expenses or to buy something needed. Many women join cundinas when they want things for their home, such as a television, bed, stove, set of dishes, or dining room table. Women may also join cundinas because they want to save money to buy their children toys at Christmas or clothes and books for school.

In El Cerro and Celaya, the cundinas are always organized by women because, according to Inés, one organizer, "Men are responsible for other things." People are more willing to participate in a cundina when a woman organizes it because they have greater confidence that she will not spend the money on alcohol. For most women, a cundina can get them out of a tight spot in an emergency, or it can provide money to help pay debts. Many women consider cundinas to be a form of a savings account, which they pay into regularly. To join a cundina, according to them, forces them to save money, which otherwise they might easily spend on necessities.

Cundinas are organized when a woman takes the initiative to create one, or when a group asks a woman to organize one. When someone decides to organize it on her own, she usually goes door to door, asking people if they want to "enter," or join the cundina. When a group is interested in finding an organizer, they usually go directly to the woman they want to ask her to take charge. Before deciding to participate in a cundina, a potential member needs certain information: the amount of payment that will be received (two hundred, three hundred, or five hundred pesos); how often a contribution must be made (weekly, bimonthly, or monthly); and the identity of the other participants. Members must have confianza so that they will fully comply with their obligation to contribute money until each person has received her respective payment. The organizer usually provides this information.

How do cundinas function? Once the organizer has formed the group, she may assign a number to each member depending on when she joined, or the numbers will be given based on those who ask for the first turns, depending on when they need the money. Normally, cundinas consist of ten numbers. In El Cerro and Celaya, however, most cundinas consist of ten people and an organizer. According to Vélez-Ibáñez (1983), if the organizer takes a free turn as her fee, then this is classified as a *cundina muerta* (dead cundina) because this is a charge for the association's execution and correct functioning. If a person fails to contribute the sum that corresponds to her, the organizer is responsible for providing the missing money. In contrast, in *cundinas vivas* (live cundinas), the organizer does not charge a turn and default is avoided by pure social pressure that ensures payment. The major difference between viva or muerta versions lies in the

Table 8.1
Kinship relations in a cundina

Turn	Relationship to Organizer
0	organizer
1	cousin's wife
2	comadre
3	cousin
4	cousin
5	cousin's wife
6	comadre
7	comadre
8	cousin
9	comadre
10	cousin's wife

degree of confianza that exists among the people who make up the association. In cundinas vivas, there is greater confianza among the group that no member will default.

In cundinas muertas, the organizer always takes the number 0. The other members can choose whatever number they like, depending on whether they have immediate need for money. The organizer records in a notebook the names and the turns of each participant. In a cundina with the goal of saving 550 pesos in eleven weeks, each participant must provide 50 pesos weekly, until each person has contributed a total of 550 pesos. The first 550 pesos go to the organizer, who will save them to cover any instance in which someone cannot pay. Then, each person receives the money as it is her turn. The main goal is that at the end of eleven weeks, each person will have received her 550 pesos. Participants can trade turns if they choose to do so. For example, a person who has taken one of the last turns may trade with someone who has an earlier turn if there arises an unforeseen need for money.

In both communities, few cundinas have failed. When one fails, it is because someone could not meet her obligation to contribute or because the organizer took most of the money. In Celaya, I know of only one case in which a cundina cycle was not completed, and that was due to the organizer running off with the money. When a cundina fails because someone did not meet her obligation, people's trust in that person is destroyed. They will never again invite her to participate in another cundina, and in some cases, people may even stop speaking to her. One way of guaranteeing that cundinas do not fail is to allow only those people in whom one has complete confianza to join. Generally, members of a cundina are kin, friends, or comadres, because great trust exists among such individuals. Cundina members in the two communities are usually relatives or people who know each other well. In one of the cundinas organized in 1997, six of the ten members were relatives of the organizer (see table 8.1).

Food Pooling

Once, I went to see my comadre at her house, but she was not there. The neighbors told me she was at her mother's fixing something to eat. Later, when I saw her, my comadre explained that she, her sisters, and some comadres had decided to cook together in order to share the costs of the food, because the economic conditions in their households were worse than they had been in previous years.

When the households in these communities do not have sufficient money to buy food, the women unite to share all the cooking for their families among themselves. Each one contributes food to cook. For example, one woman will make tortillas, another frijoles, another lemonade or *horchata* (rice beverage), and another, rice. The women are usually sisters, cousins, or comadres. There are cases in which the women collect money and buy chickens or a pig to slaughter and share. Sometimes they take turns preparing food for their families. For example, one day it will be the turn of one to cook and everyone will meet at her house, another day they will meet at another house, and so on. Usually, the woman of the house in which they meet provides all the food. It is also common for several daughters to get together at their mother's home to cook for all their families.

Childcare and Labor Exchange

There are no childcare centers in these communities. The children under five years of age, who are not old enough to attend kindergarten, must remain at home with their parents or relatives. In the communities, it is common to visit a house and see many children playing there together, giving the impression that they all live under the same roof. However,

Cande babysitting her and her neighbor's children.

when one asks, it is quickly apparent that the children are being babysat while their mothers work or do some other chore. Childcare is a labor that requires the cooperation of the entire family, neighbors, and friends. In particular, women who work outside the home and have small children must rely on the members of their kin and social networks to care for those children. In a random survey of eleven women, 82 percent said they rely on adolescent daughters, grandmothers, their own mothers, and comadres for help with childcare while they work. In El Cerro, a survey of seventy-eight women showed that 77 percent relied on their female relatives and neighbors to care for their children while they work.

Usually, the adolescent daughters are responsible for caring for younger brothers and sisters while the mother works. When there are no adolescent daughters or adults in the house, then mothers ask for help from relatives, such as grandmothers, their own mothers, nieces, sisters-in-law, neighbors, or comadres. In most cases, payment for childcare is not made with money but with gifts, such as clothes; shrimp; vegetables; plants; beauty products; chickens; other birds; electrical appliances, such as blenders or irons; and kitchen utensils, such as dinnerware or pots and pans.

At other times, favors are returned with favors. These favors are usually paid for with exchange of labor that can range from going to the pharmacy to buy medicine, going to the tortillería, helping carry wood, buying food at the store, looking for a taxi to take a family member to the hospital, cooking for the family while a woman recovers from childbirth, and helping to prepare food to sell.

Overall, reliance among women for childcare and other exchanges has developed into a cluster of economic and social transactions that engage households in a series of reciprocal relations through which flow services, income, and goods. In addition, women constantly visit each other to exchange information on prices of goods and services, available work and level of wages paid, or medical care and the reputation of curanderos and physicians. In these communities, women's networks act like counseling services to deal with issues ranging from how to cope with wayward husbands and the care of sick children to sundry other topics of mutual interest.

Conclusion

Life has never been easy for the rural population of southern Sinaloa. However, life is harder now because Mexico's economic conditions are declining. Globalization, seen by some as the integration of world markets and the elimination of economic barriers, has certainly had a very different repercussion on the rural population in Mexico. In southern Sinaloa, the process of globalization is visible in the growth of commercial agriculture resulting from the demand for agricultural commodities in global markets. Globalization is also visible in the increasing importance of fishing-based commodities, particularly shrimp, in regional, national, and global markets. Despite the region's economic importance as a producer of these commodities and the large profits it realizes from them, life for most of the rural population continues to be precarious. Poverty assails them day and night, like a ghost that is not resigned to becoming a mere shadow. The feminization of poverty, according to Abbassi and Lutjens (2002), is one of the consequences of globalization.

In southern Sinaloa, women are not sitting with their arms crossed, bemoaning their fate, hoping for divine intervention. They take the initiative to do everything they possibly can to keep their households afloat. To achieve this, they create, reuse, and reinvent strategies that, in the short term, will allow them to confront honorably the economic poverty in these communities. In the long term, these same strategies reinforce the social fabric from which the communities are formed.

Creating these strategies is not unique or specific to El Cerro and Celaya. Other studies have documented the various strategies rural households use to combat economic uncertainty. Susan Stonich (1993), for example, discusses a variety of economic strategies rural households in southern Honduras developed to help cope with economic impoverishment that they suffer because of the region's environmental deterioration. These strategies include diversification of the household's economic strategies, growth of participation in the informal economy, women's increased workforce participation, and alteration and intensification of the agricultural systems. Soledad González Montes (1997) documents the creation of strategies among the rural population in Mexico that are very similar to those Stonich discusses for southern Honduras. The migration, toward urban centers as well as border cities, the increase in the number of day laborers, and the participation of women in the informal economy are some of the strategies households in various regions of Mexico have developed to confront the havoc wreaked on them by poverty. That poverty, according to Stephen (2002, 91), is reflected in "the lack of access to water, shortages of firewood, landlessness, under- and unemployment, deteriorating health conditions, a general lack of urban and rural infrastructure, and cutbacks in social services," which in turn "has forced women to develop survival strategies related to their traditional gender roles in reproducing the labor force."

As I discussed in the previous chapter, the strategies created in southern Sinaloa at the household level are similar to those that Stonich and González Montes have noted. In addition to these economic strategies, women also rely on social and family networks to ensure the maintenance and social reproduction of their households. For the women of El Cerro and Celaya, life undoubtedly continues being a daily struggle for survival both within and outside of their households. Given the prevalent economic conditions and continuing degradation of the natural resource base on which they depend, their situation is anything but improving.

Conclusion

The Political Ecology of Change and Resistance

in Northwestern Mexico

The residents of El Cerro still have not come to terms with El Profe's death, three years ago. For most, this incident is still very strong in their memories. For others, El Profe's death made them realize that they too are vulnerable to whatever happens in southern Sinaloa. Yet, residents agree that El Profe's death is a symbol of change, because they remember no other incident similar to this taking place so close to their community. Many now realize that their community no longer seems like an isolated ranchito, alienated from the broader changes that are taking place in southern Sinaloa, in Mexico, and in the world. In reality, El Cerro and Celaya have always been part of much larger processes, and their creations are in fact part of nonlocal, national historical processes, as I have shown. Many in the communities clearly understand that their lives are linked to a global economy that is constantly demanding the production of shrimp, mangoes, chilies, or cocaine, and that their labor is sold and bought like the fruits and aquatic life they grow, harvest, and gather. They also realize that their community is facing the exacerbated challenge that other rural communities in northwestern Mexico face: their increasing inability to cope with the aftermath of so many events and relations that they cannot control. They seem to be beset with so many daily ambushes, from so many directions, that the real one suffered by El Profe and his entire family may seem like a welcome relief at times.

Yet, in the thirteen years that I had the opportunity to observe and witness the vibrant and courageous residents of El Cerro and Celaya, they have built and developed new schools, constructed churches, demanded and succeeded in getting electricity and potable water in their houses, and organized groups to improve the medical and material conditions of both communities. They have been willing to experiment with an entire exotic process in the building of shrimp aquaculture farms and their subsequent failure, and they have created little pockets of entrepreneurship without capital except that afforded by the assistance of their relatives by opening small stores, making tortillas, and selling from their home kitchens.

For most people, however, these attempts are local responses to the profound alterations of the economic and social fabric of their communities, and as I have shown, what has affected them most are those alterations related to the degradation of their natural resources and to the growing impoverishment of their communities. As a metaphor, the introduction of the cantina in Celaya with its extractive and degrading effects on the men of the village seems very much like the impacts suffered by the surrounding environments by the imposition of national and global market policies and pressures. And as in the case of the cantina, it is the women and families of the communities who have to cope with the resulting consequences of failing and deteriorating resources.

I have shown that the economic restructuring of Mexico and the implementation of state policies favoring a neoliberal economy have supported and promoted the globalization of the agriculture and shrimp aquaculture industries. This globalization, in turn, has increased the production of agricultural and fishing commodities, which in turn, has contributed to the degradation of natural resources in southern Sinaloa. From the introduction of high levels of pesticides through the increase of waste from shrimp ponds, such practices have negatively affected the region's coastal ecosystems. Moreover, the creation of shrimp ponds has encroached on and destroyed mangrove forests. Combined with such degradation is the effect of overfishing by commercially oriented fishing ventures that accelerated the depletion of the coastal and marine resource. These conditions, when combined with Mexico's economic crises, which are themselves linked to global processes, result in extreme poverty for much of rural southern Sinaloa. For most of the rural coastal population of southern Sinaloa, environmental decline has greatly reduced their ability to secure a decent existence and livelihood.

However, as I have shown, the rural people of southern Sinaloa are not merely passive victims of national policies and a global economy. In their daily struggle to survive within deteriorating economic and environmental contexts, they create and use a variety of resistance techniques and practices. Because it is at the level of the household where these conditions strike hardest, all household members, but especially women, have tried hard to develop the means and mechanisms by which to offset partially and mitigate these effects.

These range from women increasing their participation in agricultural wage labor to the creation of cottage industries that sell food and handicrafts. They pool their labor between households, participate in RCAs, and share scarcity through exchange of limited resources. They assist each other in childcare and the making of food in complex exchanges that are tied to emotive and instrumental relations of kinship and friendship. When illness or death strikes, they are present. All of these are glued together by the cultural expectations of confianza and are given life by people's daily discourse, conversations, tale telling, gossip, and simple nods of good morning.

However, it is highly unlikely that these responses and practices will be able to keep up with the continuing levels of environmental degradation and economic impoverishment. As I have shown, migration will continue to be an important strategy and ultimately the choice of last resort. But even this is only a short-term response to the long-term process of continuous degradation of the environment and of the livelihoods of those people who depend the most on their natural environment: the rural people of southern Sinaloa.

From a broad anthropological point of view, of which the political ecology approach is one, this work of southern Sinaloa shows that stressing only community dynamics without revealing their extra local, regional, national, and global dimensions is methodologically not defensible. In a sense, the political ecology of southern Sinaloa is distributed in thousands of niches like those of Celaya and El Cerro, but each of those is related to a series of economic and political links from the communities to the municipio, to the regions, and on to national and global markets and political fields. For the most part these more complex links are masked from local niches, but their environmental impacts and economic impoverishment are not.

This understanding, however, was one I acquired over time and learned in trying to lift the fog of reality before me on a daily basis. For me, anthropology as a discipline has and will change much more as our own visions expand beyond local boundaries. However, without the localities, without our approximating the lives, desires, histories, and all their consequences "on the ground," the humanity and the fullness of the struggles and resistance to causes much beyond people's control cannot be fully comprehended and, even more important, appreciated.

Afterword

Al Paso del Tiempo

More than thirteen years have passed since I began my fieldwork in southern Sinaloa. I last visited there in September 2002. I arrived as the first raindrops of the season began to caress the earth, and the vegetation that had managed to survive the havoc of the dry season was now turning green and exuberant, decorating the hills that bordered the area around Mazatlán's international airport. Throughout Mexico, preparations were under way to celebrate the Día del Grito, or the Las Fiestas Patrias, as Mexico's Independence Day, September 16, is popularly called. The Mexican flag decorated display cases in the stores and the public plazas, and recalling the days of the revolution, mannequins were dressed as *soldaderas* (women soldiers of the Mexican Revolution) and Pancho Villa.

In Mazatlán's golden zone a few tourists, baking their souls in the warmth of the midday sun as they walked the streets, were assailed by peddlers, who, in their zeal to get someone's attention, made wild gestures as they tried to sell silver jewelry or excursions to Old Mazatlán or trips through Teacapán's mangrove swamps. Oaxacan Indian women, selling gum or begging, sat on the sidewalks with their children, while others approached tourists, offering to braid their hair for fifty pesos. Downtown, daily life went on just as it had thirteen years ago, when I visited Mazatlán for the first time. The deafening noise of the traffic, the comings and goings of the Mazatlecos, and the changueras on Aquiles Serdán Street selling shrimp all continued to reflect the dynamism and diversity that characterizes Mexican cities.

Along the road from Mazatlán to Escuinapa, the cows and burros were happily eating the green pasture that had sprung up with the first rains.

Little seemed to have changed in all these years. The ejido entrances still had metal signs with their names inscribed on them, and the mango and plum orchards on each side of the road still lent a green coolness to the rural landscape. Very little had changed in the area's topography. The only visible alteration was the destruction of several hills in order to build a new highway connecting Mazatlán with Rosario and Escuinapa.

I arrived in Escuinapa on a Saturday afternoon when the mango harvest had ended and the shrimp fishing season had yet to begin. At the entrance to the town, the changueras, seated in front of their houses, were selling *camarón seco apastillado* (dried salted shrimp) in plastic bags on a table. Others had signs hanging on their walls that read, "Fresh Shrimp for Sale." People passed on the street in the heat, some on foot, and others on bicycles. A group was picketing in front of the offices of the electric utility to protest the high cost of their bills. The plaza's adornment with small red, white, and green flags was a sign that the city hall had already begun the preparations for the celebration of the Fiestas Patrias. Businesspeople complained that their sales were down, and they attributed it to the year's small mango crop, and the fact that the shrimp in the estuaries were still too small to market.

I intended to stay at Nachita's house, as I had done so many times during my fieldwork for this book. From there, I would make day trips to El Cerro and Celaya. When I arrived, I was surprised she was not at home. I learned that she had been hospitalized in Mazatlán, and her son, Rubén, was there looking after her. Her daughter, Olivia, whose house is next door, invited me to stay with her. Seeing Nachita's house, nevertheless, brought to mind memories of my last years living in southern Sinaloa. It was in this house where I would sit in a rocking chair under the mango tree, thinking about my fieldwork, while Nachita assisted customers who had come from nearby villages to buy tennis shoes and blue jeans. After finishing an arduous day of fieldwork, I would sit there at dusk to write my notes and organize my thoughts. It was strange not seeing Nachita, not hearing more of her stories about beauty queens, priests in love, statues of saints paraded through the streets to summon the rain, and *parranderos*, unfaithful men. Although she was not home, during this short visit, I sat in the rocker, gazing at the mango tree—just as I had done at other times— while I wrote this afterword. In making this trip, I hoped to get closure on this important period in my life and to learn what had transpired since last year in El Cerro and Celaya.

That night, Escuinapa's sky foretold the arrival of a fierce storm. Lightning bolts set it aglow, and the sound of thunder silenced the nocturnal conversations and the chirping of the crickets. The noise of the thunder, in turn, intermixed with the music of narco-corridos, which came from the cantinas and told about the lives of Sinaloa's most infamous drug traffickers. *"La traición y el contrabanado acaban con muchas vidas"* ("Betrayal and contraband end many lives"), one of the songs goes. The thunder also mixed into words floating out of a nearby house, "We don't need no education, we don't need no thought control," from "The Wall," sung by Pink Floyd, the British rock group. That night it rained tremendously hard. It rained as if it would never stop. The weeping of the rain overcame everything, until no other sound was audible. It seemed as if all the prayers of the people in unison had finally been heard, forming a collective plea to St. Francis of Assisi, the patron saint of Escuinapa, asking him to make it rain. The next morning, the people of Escuinapa awoke to flooded streets, but they were happy for the rain and began their day with great optimism, hoping it would make the shrimp grow and that the fishing season would soon start. Unfortunately, with the rain came the mosquitoes and the cases of dengue, *el trancazo* or *la rompehuesos* (breakbone fever), as it is popularly called in the region.[1]

Early that morning, a Sunday, I took a bus to Celaya. On one side of the highway, you could see lagoons that had been mutilated to build shrimp farms. On the other side were lagoons still intact and filled with water that reflected the white clouds, blue sky, and the green of the vegetation surrounding them. As always, the palm trees stood out because of their height and broad branches, swaying to the beat of the wind. When I got off the bus, the first thing I noticed was a big sign hanging at the entrance to the third street that read, "Welcome to Celaya." When I came closer, I saw that underneath, in white letters, were the words, "Marisquería el Papayito." This was, as the residents described it, the clandestine cantina disguised as a restaurant. I noted that it had grown since last year. The place now had a big patio with round tables, white plastic chairs, and an even bigger bar. Parked next to it were various cars, and people, mostly men, were already sitting there, eating and drinking.

When I arrived at the home of Angelita and Alfonso, their son, Luis, told me that they were out shopping in Escuinapa, but he expected them back shortly. He and his wife, Araceli, were having breakfast, and she offered me a warm tortilla with cheese. While we ate, they brought me up to date about Celaya's recent events. The biggest complaint they had was the lack of available work for the Celayans. The harvest of green coconuts had not yet begun, and the mango season had ended earlier than usual. The only thing that they could do was to wait for work to come available in the nearby haciendas. Meanwhile, Luis was helping Araceli look after the children. We sat around remembering when I first lived in Celaya, and the many times that I woke up in the morning to the rhythm of the Puerto Rican song "In My Old San Juan."[2] Now, to the rhythm of Sinaloan corridos, especially one that told the story of Camelia la Tejana, we talked about the time that I lived in Teacapán and a man tried to break into my house at night. The man apparently now lives in Los Angeles.

I continued my trip around Celaya and went to visit Natalia and Rafael. I found her, her daughters, and her sister seated in the kitchen talking. They told me that Rafael was away working in his field, but they invited me to sit in the hammock. They talked about their disapproval of and frustration about the cantina, and they voiced their regret over having failed to close it. Her daughter, who was widowed last year when the truck in which her husband was riding flipped over near Celaya, was making corn tortillas on the comal and boiling a chicken for the *comida* (lunch). Natalia told me that the first case of AIDS had appeared in Celaya. The doctor at the rural clinic in Isla del Bosque had told them about it during a meeting for the participants in PROGRESA. The physician indicated that it was a woman who had fallen ill, but he refused to identify her. Natalia took advantage of the occasion to talk to me about her religion, and to ask me about my faith. This was the first time that we had talked about this so openly. She said that it was a woman from Nayarit, who came to buy green coconuts with her son, who had convinced her to convert to evangelical Christianity. This woman lived in Natalia's home for five months. During that time, she would read the Bible to Natalia every afternoon, while teaching her to interpret it for herself so that she could see the contradictions that, according to the woman, existed in Catholicism. When Rafael arrived, he was very surprised to see me there, chatting calmly while I lay in the hammock. He asked me when I had arrived, and if I had finished the book. Then he opened up a green coconut, and he gave it to me so that I could drink the milk. He is still organizing cuadrillas of jornaleros to harvest green coconuts, but he was waiting for a buyer to arrive and ask him to fill up a truckload.

Leaving Natalia's house, I met Victoria, who was washing clothes in front of her house. She told me she had just returned from church. In front of her house, on the ground, were two stalks with green coconut, which her husband had cut for a physician from Escuinapa, who was going to stop by that afternoon to pick them up so that he could give them to a friend. Victoria invited me to sit and talk with her for a while. She had always regretted that she had never told me her whole life story. Each time she tried, her mother was visiting, and Victoria did not want to talk about it in front of her. This time she did not want to talk about the past but instead told me about her plans for the future. She had decided to get a group of women together to teach them how to weave handbags, something she was expert in, in order to market them and make money for their households. She sent two little girls to the homes of her daughters and daughters-in-law to get the bags she had made for them so that she could show them to me. She asked me to help her sell them in California and to chip in by buying at least one. I agreed, and she promised that she would have it ready in two days. She then told me a little about the various activities she was involved in at church and the scant help the members of the committee have to accomplish their tasks. Finally, she told me that she was still interested in having me write the story of her life, and she said that I could interview her during one of my other trips to Celaya.

That same afternoon, I went to Raquel's house. She was not there, but her sisters, Luz, Julia, and Gloria, were making tamales. They invited me to eat chicken and shrimp tamales, and sit in the patio of the house. Raquel was the only sister not there. I very much missed seeing her and being able to enjoy her stories, which were always embellished by her great sense of humor. She is still living in Rosarito, Baja California, with her whole family, and even though she came home for a visit last summer, this year she could not come because her diabetes was worse. Gloria's oldest daughter, Marisela, and her husband, had also moved to Rosarito. Luz continued to be involved in the church committee and selling candy and potato chips in her little store, which she rents to Coca-Cola. I asked about Mauricio, the young man who used to help them organize fund-raisers to collect money for the school. They told me that since the day the police had chased him, he rarely comes to Celaya. He is working as a cook on one of the shrimp boats that puts out from Teacapán.

I returned to Escuinapa with Julia and her husband. They plan to save enough money to visit me in California and to take their son to Disneyland. That night, it rained again, with thunder and lightning, and the streets of Escuinapa flooded anew.

The following morning was damp when I took the bus from Escuinapa to return to Rosario. I waited for the bus to Agua Verde at the *chalata,* or bus station. Rosario continues to be the town it always was: small, without big stores or buildings, with twisting cobblestone streets, and with unbearable heat. I already knew that Pancho, the bus driver, had died years before, but when the bus arrived, I was somehow still surprised to see a different, much younger, driver. I was even more surprised when I saw on the front of the bus, written in big letters, the words "Párate Pancho" ("Pancho, Stop!") in honor of what the people shouted every time Pancho drove by with his bus. Traveling by bus, I could again contemplate the greenness of the mango orchards and the imposing San Ignacio Hill, which rose majestically with its perfect outline like a pyramid. In silence, I contemplated its beauty, and I could not stop thinking of all the stories and myths people had told me about statues that disappear in front of one's eyes and the field for playing hulama that supposedly once existed on its crest.

In El Cerro, the streets were still wet but less muddy than in earlier years because stones had been scattered down the main road to prevent more puddles from forming. Nevertheless, a small lake had formed in one of the streets from the water that had flowed out of the arroyos on the hillsides, and the dogs and burros were drinking from its clear waters.

Upon arriving in El Cerro, one of the first things I noticed was that its surrounding hills had turned green again and the pink flowers had already bloomed. Like faithful friends, these blooms returned each year to add their color and freshness to this piece of the Sinaloan landscape. I thought immediately of Trini, and how much she had enjoyed contemplating the hills as they began turning green. My thoughts were interrupted by my compadres, who were standing in front of the school, talking with other parents. The children were at morning recess, and their laughter and shouts filled all the corners of the town. My compadres gave me big hugs, and when I smiled at them, I noticed a profoundly sad look. I understood that something had happened. *"Se nos fue comadre"* ("She's gone"), my comadre told me pensively, as if she were aware of what I had been thinking before seeing them. On the way to her house, she explained some of the details of Trini's death. My comadre had been with Trini when she died. She revealed that Trini sent for each one of her children before dying, and she individually asked each for forgiveness. Afterwards, when she was finally ready to die, she asked them to bring the priest from Agua Verde so that he could give her the sacrament of the holy unction.

My comadre told me that she is working in a new tortillería that had opened in El Cerro. A man from Agua Verde owns it. My comadre and another woman from El Cerro are in charge of putting the Maseca flour into the machine and ensuring that the tortillas come out correctly. She is also responsible for selling them to the people who come to buy them directly from the factory. A kilo of tortillas sells for 5.70 pesos, and the women receive 80 pesos per day each in wages. My comadre works from 7:00 to 9:00 in the morning, and from 11:30 to 2:30 in the afternoon; in the interim, she goes home. According to what she told me, this job arrived at just the right moment, because my compadre is unemployed. The mango season finished earlier than ever this year because, according to my compadre, many people from the sierra worked in the harvest this season. He attributes the increase in the number of jornaleros coming from the sierra to the difficulty these people now have in finding work in the marijuana fields due to the strict measures that the Mexican government is implementing to combat drug traffic.

While my comadre worked in the tortillería, I went to visit María Félix, Trini's daughter. We sat under the trees that surround the patio of her house, and she explained the details of the death of her mother. Trini died on February 23, the same month that Chico had died, eleven years earlier. She suffered greatly toward the end, and after the hospital in Escuinapa released her, she was in constant pain. She could not move, nor could she talk or see. She died on a Saturday, at 9 a.m., and they held the wake in her house and buried her in the Agua Verde cemetery. María Félix, crying, told me how she and her brothers and sisters had done everything possible to cure her, taking her from doctor to doctor and buying all the prescribed medicines. In trying to cure her, the family spent the few resources that they had, and they even had to sell the land that Chico had bequeathed to them. They sold it to people from El Cerro and Agua Verde, for much less than it was worth, to get money to cover their mother's medical expenses. In their eyes, it is terribly ironic and very unfortunate that in their zeal to try to cure their mother, they ended up selling the land that their father fought so hard to get. It is as if destiny were mocking them or as if the cycle that Chico, with his struggle to win land to establish an ejido, had begun were coming to a close: The family started without land, and they were ending up without land. The only thing that remains of their parents' inheritance is the house, and they are debating what to do with it. They are of a divided opinion: Some think it should be given to the younger brothers, others think they should hold on to it for everyone's use, and still others believe they should sell it, dividing the profits equally among themselves. Despite having sold the land, they are nevertheless satisfied that they did everything they could to try to save their mother's life.

According to Trini's death certificate, she died from the effects of the bone cancer that she had suffered for several years. For many of the community's residents and for Trini's children, however, it was Efrén, the curandero and Trini's lover, who killed her, little by little. According to one of her daughters, a physician, who examined Trini before she died, had said that her body was full of toxins. The children filtered their interpretation of this through their recollection of the many times that they saw Trini drinking the concoctions that Efrén prepared for her. This led them to assume that he was the one who had poisoned her, just as he had done years before to Chico. He had motives, the children say, because he had always wanted the house and the land. I learned that no one ever saw him again once he left El Cerro. He was not at her side during her final days nor did he come to Trini's funeral.

Because of the few available jobs, the people of El Cerro think that the economic situation for the households is worsening with each passing year. People cannot even afford to buy new clothes anymore, and instead have to purchase *ropa de segunda* (secondhand clothes), sold by street vendors who come to the community every other day. Many of these people, like my compadres, believe that the only possible alternative is to move away from El Cerro and to try their luck somewhere else, perhaps along the border. My compadre told me about a friend from Agua Verde, who just returned from Utah, having converted to Mormonism. His friend told him that the Mormons will help a Mexican find work, as long as he or she is willing to convert. My compadre asked me about this religion. I told him that I did not know much, except that it allows a man to have more than one wife. He laughed. Then he told me that he was thinking seriously about going for a time to Tijuana, to live with his sister and try to find work. He would go first, and later send for my comadre and the children.

We spent a long time at María Félix's house talking about the past and about how, depending on how you choose to interpret things, those memories can bring pain or they can fill one with laughter and good feeling. My friends made me laugh with the stories about Efrén's cures, and how, in most cases, he could not figure out what was wrong with his patients. They told me that sometimes he made the women strip naked and lie on their backs on the floor so that he could rub a raw egg all over their bodies before placing it in a glass in order to read their fortunes. "Someone cast a spell on you," he would tell them with concern. The perturbed patients did not skimp on the money they would pay Efrén to learn who was wishing them bad luck, and what they could do to put a stop to it. At other times, he himself prepared the bath of herbs that he gave to the ill people. Several got sicker as soon as they left the house and were drenched by the downpour on the way home. In one of the cases, the wife came to complain that her husband was worse and she did not know what to do for him. Efrén answered, "Well, what are you waiting for? Are you going to take him to the doctor, or are you going to let him die?" We screamed with laughter at the irony of his response.

When I ended my stay in southern Sinaloa, I could reaffirm that the two factors always present in the rural communities—those things that make it possible for the people to confront and resist with courage and fortitude the vicissitudes that life presents them—are their fine sense of humor and their sincere concern for the well-being of others. In the stories the people of El Cerro and Celaya tell, a sense of humor and laughter are two spices that are never lacking. Laughter, even at oneself, is what, according to them, "gives life its flavor and makes it more bearable." The concern for others was reflected on this occasion in their interest in the situation in the United States following the 2001 terrorist attacks. People are convinced that whatever happens in El Norte will eventually affect them. "If things turn bad there, please, come here to live with us," people in both communities told me. Others added, "Here we do not have terrorists, only drug traffickers." And to prove to me that not all Sinaloan corridos talk only about the drug traffic and that there exists a true concern for the highly unstable situation that the United States is experiencing, they played a corrido that was issued last year, entitled "Tragedy in New York."[3]

While I listened to the song, I thought that life in the rural communities of southern Sinaloa is a lot like a corrido. In it, there abound stories of animals, local heroes, border crossings, illicit love affairs, widows, curanderos, changueros, *guachos* (policemen), *federales* (federal marshals), unfaithful husbands, clandestine cantinas, strong uppity women, Gypsies, gringos, shrimp, chilies, and hurricanes. To these stories, one more can be added: that of a Puerto Rican anthropologist who once visited the region with the idea of spending only a year there, but who stayed thirteen years, attracted, perhaps, by a curiosity to know more about all those other stories. My story, according to the residents of the communities, begins: "When the rains arrive, Mariluz won't be far behind. She always comes with the raindrops, appearing suddenly, without warning, just like the *angelitos*, those little red insects that come out of the ground at the start of each rainy season."

As my fieldwork in southern Sinaloa comes to an end, I ask myself, who will take charge of composing the corridos based on the new stories that will appear in these communities? Without any doubt, it must be someone with tremendous admiration, respect, and affection for these people. In the end, those are the three essential ingredients that motivate one to write what anthropologists term ethnography.

Appendix

Research Methodology

This book is based on long-term anthropological fieldwork conducted on the northwest Pacific Coast of Mexico during a thirteen-year period. I carried out initial fieldwork in the southern region of the state of Sinaloa in 1989 as a graduate student studying the social, economic, and environmental impact of shrimp aquaculture development on the social and economic structure and the environment of rural communities. At that time I chose two communities in which to conduct the bulk of the fieldwork. These were chosen primarily because of the types of shrimp aquaculture systems that were developed in them. In El Cerro, the type of system developed was semi-intensive, whereas in Celaya it was extensive. I have returned to the region since 1993 and have spent part of every year until September 2003 in the two communities and the region.

Research Methods and Sources of Data

I compiled the data and information through various quantitative and qualitative research methods. These include intensive and extensive participant observation, interviews, extensive life and oral histories, focus groups, archival research, the use of economic-ranking techniques, and randomly sampled and 100 percent sampled household questionnaires.

Participant Observation

I lived with families in the towns of the municipios of Rosario and Escuinapa as well as in El Cerro and Celaya. This experience provided me with the basis for a comparative understanding of the structural relations between urban centers and rural communities, and the various issues related to class and identity in both sectors.

I participated in meetings, agricultural and household production activities, religious rituals, and fiestas—including weddings, funerals, quinceañeras, communions, baptisms, children's birthday parties, school parties, and family reunions—and simply sat out under the palapas, enjoying the coolness of fresh milk straight from the coconut with many of the families. I went fishing with families, traveled with them to visit relatives in the towns or in other communities, and shopped for food and clothes with many women. I learned how to make corn tortillas, plant chilies, harvest mangoes, extract copra, cook nopales, embroider, classify shrimp, and harvest shrimp larvae in the beach. I even went to church. Over the last ten years I became a godmother in one community, and I was considered an aunt in the other.

Interviews

I systematically interviewed more than five hundred persons within different contexts. My background in marine biology enabled me to observe closely two shrimp aquaculture cooperatives and shrimp farms developed in the two studied communities. Interviews covered the history of the fishing industry, conflicts among the various users of marine resources, state-developed management policies, local systems of resource use and allocation, biological and ecological characteristics of marine resources, processing and marketing of commercially exploited marine resources, the social organization of production, and the impact of shrimp aquaculture upon the environment. I conducted oral histories in all households in both communities to learn more about the history of the communities, the various economic and productive activities performed by a household's members, gender relations and division of labor within households and communities, conflicts over access to communal resources, environmental problems, and migration experience. As well, I interviewed local ethnohistorians to learn more about the history of the towns and patterns of natural resource use.

Life Histories

I collected and tape-recorded life histories of twenty-five purposive samples of women and men in each studied community. These histories reflect the distribution of various generations and the different economic occupations in each community.

Oral Histories and Focus Groups

I collected specific and focused oral histories of thirty men and women from each community, concentrating on conflicts over access to communal resources, the institution of changuerismo, the migration experience, and gender relations. These oral histories were also tape-recorded and transcribed. Fifty recorded focus groups of five persons each over a thirteen-year period treated the major themes of cooperation, spousal relations, children's socialization, migration, and sources of distress within households.

Archival Research

I conducted research at the Municipal Archives in Mazatlán, Rosario, and Escuinapa; Archivo Histórico de Mazatlán; and Oficina de Reforma Agraria Archival. I compiled information about the economic and political history of the municipios, the struggle for land, the establishment of ejidos, the formation of the fishing cooperatives, and patterns of land distribution and tenure. Over four hundred documents were photocopied, and I have indexed them according to major themes and periods.

Informant Ranking

Within each community, I selected main informants representing different generations and occupations for this exercise. They were asked to rank the households within their communities according to their wealth and socioeconomic status, and from this, I garnered insight into the stratification of each community.

Questionnaires

I administered a total of five different questionnaires to households within the two communities at different periods of time in order to capture changes and shifts of economy, ecology, stratification, gender relations and roles, and changes in material provisioning as well as physical and mental health conditions. The following describe in detail the sampling and foci of each of the instruments used.

Questionnaire 1: This questionnaire was a household survey I administered to all households in both communities. One section of the questionnaire was designed to obtain basic demographic information for each member of the household, such as occupation, age, education, number of years living in the community, land tenure, and migration experience. The other section was a socioeconomic interview designed to collect data to assess intracommunity differences in access to economic and productive resources. This socioeconomic interview consisted of four parts: The first part elicited information about the characteristics of the house; the second gathered information about the type of material goods possessed by households; the third asked about animal husbandry; and the last elicited information on the type and quantity of work implements possessed by individual households.

Questionnaire 2: This questionnaire was designed to gather information about the participation of household members in shrimp aquaculture projects. The questionnaire was administered to all members of the two shrimp aquaculture cooperatives in both communities. The questionnaire asked cooperative members information about the number of years within the cooperative, reasons to become a member of the cooperative, the type of job performed within the cooperative, the working cycle, and general views about shrimp aquaculture.

Questionnaire 3: This questionnaire was administered to a stratified random sample of households. The two variables used in selecting the sample were main occupation of female and male household heads, and wealth index of each household. This questionnaire asked about household expenditures, labor allocations, and migration remittances. In the cases in which the head of the household worked the land, questions were included to elicit information about the agricultural cycle, the organization of production, and the type of technology used. For those cases in which the head of the household was engaged in fishing, questions were asked about the social organization of production, technology used, and the problems facing the fishing industry. When the head of the household was a wageworker, questions were asked about the type of jobs or tasks performed, the months in which the jobs or tasks were performed, the locality, and the income obtained.

Questionnaire 4: The main purpose of this questionnaire was to collect information on land distribution and tenure among individual households. The questionnaire also asked about the selling and buying of parcels of land within the communities, especially after the reform to Article 27 of the Mexican Constitution.

Questionnaire 5: This questionnaire was designed to gather information about the participation of women in income-generating activities. It asked women about their motives for engaging in income-generating activities, the types of income-generating activities performed, the amount of time spent on each activity, the allocation of the income produced, and the household division of labor. Using a snowball technique and key informants within each community, the questionnaire was administered to all the women who at that time were engaged in income-producing activities.

Other Sources of Data

Local newspapers provided information on fishing, aquaculture, and agriculture; and publications from the Instituto de Estadística, Geografía, e Informática (INEGI) include the *Censos de Población y Vivienda* for the state of Sinaloa and for the municipios of Rosario and Escuinapa, the ejidal censuses for Sinaloa, and environmental statistics.

Notes

Introduction: A Journey of Many Paths

1. See Schmink and Wood 1987; Sheridan 1988; Stonich 1993, 1995; Hershkovitz 1993; Bryant, Rigg, and Stott 1993; Dedina 1995; Painter and Durham 1995; Grossman 1998; Andreatta 1998; Dodds 1998; Pezzoli 1998; Gezon 1999.

Chapter 1. El Sur de Sinaloa: A Historical Portrait of a Land and a People

1. The repartimiento was a system of forced labor.

2. The encomienda system was an award or gift of an indigenous settlement to a Spaniard, the encomendero. The Indians were required to give him service and tribute in exchange for protection. In addition to the distribution of encomiendas, land, water, and forests near the Indian settlements were also apportioned.

3. The presidio was a military post established in frontier territories to protect Spanish colonists. Presidios sometimes also served as "partial communities that were expected to become self-supporting, and in which a primary concern was the production of food and animal husbandry" (Naylor and Polzer 1986, 19). Although presidios were a very important institution in northwestern New Spain, from the scant information available it appears they played only a minor role in southern Sinaloa. This is not surprising given that so few Indian communities and Spanish settlements existed in the area. The presidio of Mazatlán, the first in the region, was founded in 1576, in what is today known as Villa Unión, near Mazatlán. Guarded by twenty-five mulattos and their families, its purpose was to protect the Spanish population from raids perpetrated by the Xiximes and to protect the coast against British and Dutch pirates (Ortega Noriega 1999). For a detailed discussion on the presidios of northern New Spain, see Naylor and Polzer 1986 and Polzer and Sheridan 1997. See also Moorhead 1975.

4. Generally, the Jesuits were most influential in the central and northern parts of Sinaloa, where they established the mission system. It was in these areas that most of the indigenous population was concentrated when the missionaries arrived. In the southern region, Jesuit activity was more sporadic because of the sparser population, which had

barely survived the slaughter of the military conquest. Southern Sinaloa was never integrated into the mission system even though the missionaries visited some of the Indian pueblos, especially those in the mountains. The scant information that exists with respect to missionary activity in the southern provinces is too limited to enable us to determine the impact that the Jesuit missionaries had on this area.

5. For example, in the central part of the state, numerous agricultural and ranching haciendas ended up in the hands of American surveying companies, such as the Sinaloa Land Company and the Bond and Water Company (Carrillo Rojas 1991). The Sinaloa Land Company was formed in 1905 in Mexico City to survey, colonize, buy, and sell lands. Its president was Albert Wallace. The first land that the company acquired was in the Culiacán Valley. The Bond and Water Company's president was Laurence E. Thompson, and it surveyed various lands that belonged to los notables.

6. The foreign presence in mining was most prevalent in the southern region of the state. For example, the Felton Brothers Company, founded in 1897, controlled several of the most productive mines in the municipio of Concordia. In 1904, this company won the legal right to exploit the mines in Copala and then established the Felton's Copala Mining Company (Carrillo Rojas 1991).

7. Such was the case with the California Powder Works, based in San Francisco, California, which supplied most of the dynamite used in Sinaloa (Carrillo Rojas 1991).

8. This event is explained in Padilla 1993, 31–32.

9. See *La Gira del General Lázaro Cárdenas,* Partido Revolucionario Institucional (PRI), 1986.

10. See INEGI's *Estadísticas Históricas de México* (1985), volume 1, for a listing of the main features of Article 27.

11. The expropriation of the United Sugar Company in Los Mochis is one of the most frequently cited cases.

12. See Padilla 1993, 53–54.

13. Letter written on November 4, 1960, to Francisco Alarcón, secretary general of the League of Agrarian Communities, Culiacán, Sinaloa. Municipal Archive of Escuinapa.

14. Letter sent to Pedro Zamudio, presidente municipal of Escuinapa, by the board of directors of Ejido Isla del Bosque, November 25, 1960. Municipal Archive of Escuinapa.

15. Petition sent to the presidente municipal of Escuinapa, November 17, 1960, by Filiberto Loera Martínez, Samuel Serna Loera, and Angel Alvarado Ramos, representatives of the campesinos from the faction José María Morelos y Pavón in Isla del Bosque.

16. Letter written on March 13, 1961, and sent to Professor Roberto Barrios, director of the Department of Agrarian and Colonization Issues, in Culiacán, from León García, head of the Office of Agrarian Reform in Escuinapa. Municipal Archive of Escuinapa.

17. Report on the land transfer sent to the comisariado ejidal of Isla del Bosque (December 13, 1960). Regional Agrarian Committee 15 of the municipality of Escuinapa. Municipal Archive of Escuinapa.

18. Minutes of the meeting held in Isla del Bosque, concerning the division and transfer of parcels to ejidatarios of that settlement. September 8, 1962. Municipal Archive of Escuinapa.

19. One of these corridos is titled "Justicia Ranchera." It tells the story of a campesino

who murdered his employer because the man refused to give him a piece of land to which he was legally entitled.

20. This conflict is explained in Secretaría de Pesca (SEPESCA) n. d., *La Problemática Pesquera en el Sur de Sinaloa*.

Chapter 2. Rosario and Escuinapa: The Globalization of Two Coastal Municipios

1. See, for example, Edwards 1977, 1978; Moore and Slinn 1984.

2. For more detailed information on the living conditions of migrant farm workers and the effects of pesticides on their health, see Guerra and Rocha Moya 1988 and Wright 1990.

3. See Hubbard 1978, 1993, 1994.

4. See Murúa 1978.

Chapter 3. Gypsies, Peones, and Ejidatarios: A Political Ecology of El Cerro

1. By means of the Dotación Provisional for ejidos, an area of 2,370 hectares of monte (uncultivated land), suitable for seasonal agriculture, was awarded and granted to the applicants. This included the lands of the property known as El Cajón, located in the municipio of Rosario. This property is presently entirely undeveloped, abandoned, and unexploited, without having any material indication of boundaries defining possession or smallholding, nor are there persons who possess or maintain those lands, nor is there any other indication showing that agricultural activities or other kinds of exploitation occur on that same land, by any company or private person. The aforementioned area has been divided into 116 parcels of twenty hectares each, thirty hectares for a township, and twenty hectares for a school (Gobierno del Estado de Sinaloa 1968, 3; my translation).

2. The letter, dated May 15, 1990, and addressed to El Cerro's board of directors, reads: "I hereby notify you, that I, C. Francisco Flores Alvarado, leave Trinidad Rodríguez Herrera as my heir to the property, which I have on the 20 hectares in the above-mentioned ejido, so that she may bequeath it to our sons, Jorge Mario Flores Rodríguez and Cornelio Flores Rodríguez. I leave the animals under her care. Sincerely, Francisco Flores Alvarado" (my translation).

Chapter 4. On Top of a Hill: The Structure and Organization of a Mexican Ejido

1. For example, Julio, who is an ejidatario and member of the fishing cooperative, has had income during the shrimp frascas ranging from a minimum of $250 to a maximum of $20,000. Generally, fishermen who are members of a cooperative earn a much higher income than the pescadores libres.

2. Cancian 1972, 1979; DeWalt 1975, 1979; Barlett 1982; Guarnaccia et al. 1988; Sheridan 1988; Stephen 1991; Stonich 1993.

3. The appendix contains the specific details of its design, implementation, and analysis.

Chapter 5. From Hacienda to Community: A Political Ecology of Celaya

1. Ejidos such as Isla del Bosque, Palmito El Verde, Colonia Morelos y Pavón, Cristo Rey, and Teacapán, all located very close to Celaya, share part of the property that once belonged to that hacienda.

2. One of these was a man nicknamed "El Pelochaca," who bought the shrimp from don Modesto to resell it in Guadalajara and Sonora.

3. Municipal Archive of Escuinapa.

4. The Secretary for the Environment, Natural Resources, and Fisheries (SEMARNAP) grants these concessions for a period of twenty-five years, after conducting an environmental-impact study. During this time, only the companies or the cooperatives to which these concessions were granted can exploit the areas, and generally, they themselves take charge of blocking access to the area so that other people cannot get in.

Chapter 6. In the Shade of the Coconut Trees: The Structure and Organization of Celaya

1. She is also very concerned with the community's welfare. She is considered the top person in charge of health in Celaya, and whenever I asked general questions about community health issues, the people did not hesitate to refer me to her.

2. Only six households in the community belong to other religions, such as the Pentecostals and the Jehovah's Witnesses.

Chapter 7. Global Economies, Local Livelihoods: Gender and Labor in Rural Communities

1. Two kilos of Purina will feed approximately seven chickens for one day. A ten-kilo bag of these pellets costs between fifteen and twenty pesos, depending on where one buys it.

2. Baby chicks are worth approximately three to five pesos, young chickens, between twenty and thirty pesos, and grown chickens, between fifty and seventy pesos because they can lay eggs before they are slaughtered and eaten.

3. In both communities, people pay about one hundred pesos for a newly born piglet. At six months of age, a pig is worth at least four hundred pesos, and at a year, between ten thousand and twelve thousand pesos.

4. Many people feed them Purina, and each pig consumes about three kilos daily. A two-week supply of Purina for a couple pigs costs about 140 pesos. In Celaya, for example, some households buy discarded food thrown in the trash at the Tienda Ley in Escuinapa and resell it for two pesos per kilo.

5. Several studies have brilliantly examined and analyzed the incorporation of rural women within the Mexican agricultural workforce (Arias 1994; González Montes 1994; Mummert 1994). In Sinaloa, studies on the incorporation of women have focused on the

central and northern regions of the state, where large-scale commercial agriculture began appearing at the start of the twentieth century. Studies on women and agricultural wage labor in these regions have addressed two very important processes: the proletarianization of mestiza and indigenous women living in the countryside, and the feminization of Sinaloa's agriculture (Roldán 1982; Lara Flores 1998).

6. Please refer to Cruz 1992 and Cruz-Torres 1996 for a detailed explanation of these conflicts and their outcome.

Chapter 8. La Lucha: The Dynamics of Household Relations and Resistance

1. Domestic violence is not unique to El Cerro and Celaya. Other scholars have examined the impact of domestic violence on women in Mexico. These scholars have looked at this issue primarily in the context of the relationship between women's health and poverty (Alatorre Rico, Langer, and Lozano 1994; Lara and Salgado de Snyder 1994). They have noted the importance of empirically documenting the cases of violence against women and its harmful effects on women's health.

2. Scholars of Latin America, particularly those working among the Maya, have also highlighted the relationship between alcohol consumption and spousal abuse (McClusky 2001). Lara and Salgado de Snyder (1994) indicate that the domestic violence associated with alcoholism has been well documented in the literature on those living in poverty. However, alcoholism is not the only precursor to domestic violence. For example, a study done in Jalisco, Mexico, found that half the women in a sample of 1,590 had suffered physical abuse from their husbands or fathers, and these women reported the principal cause as being "because the men were angry" (Alatorre Rico, Langer, and Lozano 1994, 234).

3. Anthropologists' fascination with the compadrazgo system has been so strong that Mexican academics in other disciplines now recognize that fact. Once I told a colleague, a scientist from the University of Sinaloa, that I was going to visit the communities, and he asked me if I was going alone or if I knew people there. I explained that I knew most of the residents because I had been doing fieldwork there for many years. Moreover, I said, I had compadres in one of the communities. My colleague calmly noted, "Oh, I was forgetting that anthropologists really like compadrazgo."

Afterword: Al Paso del Tiempo

1. While I wrote this afterword, I fell sick with dengue. I am certain I contracted it from one of the many mosquitoes that attacked my legs in Escuinapa.

2. Puerto Rican composer Rafael Hernández wrote this song, which tells the story of someone who emigrated from the island, but with the hope of returning one day.

3. This song is sung by El As de la Sierra (The Ace of the Mountain), and parts of it say, "Black Tuesday, everyone, at 8:15 a.m., when into the two twin towers, there smashed a plane. . . . War started with the United States, and look at how it began: Terrorism was launched with planes, sent against those towers that were so very beautiful."

Glossary of Spanish and Scientific Terms

agostaderos   grazing lands.

agraristas   activists in the agrarian reform movement.

agroquímicas   local stores specializing in the sale of agricultural products.

agua de Jamaica   herbal iced tea from Mexico, made of dried hibiscus flowers (*Hibiscus sabdariffa*).

alguatados   itchy.

alguate   something that causes itchiness.

auriga   a pickup truck used as a taxi.

ayuntamiento   town council.

barbasco   any of several Mexican plants of the genus *Dioscorea* having a large, inedible root that yields an extract used as a raw material for synthetic steroid hormones. Some contain a substance that can stun or paralyze fish.

bolis   flavored ice.

botoncillo   *Conacarpus erectus*.

cabildos   town councils.

camarón azul   blue shrimp (*Penaeus stylirostris*).

camarón blanco   white shrimp (*Penaeus vannamei*).

campesinista   an intellectual theory arguing that capitalism will not affect the status quo of Latin American campesinos.

campesinos   people of the Mexican countryside.

cardones   organ pipe cactus (*Stenocereus thurberi*).

castas   mixed races of Spanish, Indian, or African origins.

caudillos   revolutionary leaders.

changuear   to poach shrimp.

changueras   women shrimp traders in northwestern Mexico.

changuerismo   the act of poaching or smuggling shrimp in southern Sinaloa.

changuero   shrimp poacher or smuggler.

chilares   chili fields.

chiles rellenos   stuffed chili peppers.

colonias populares   working-class neighborhoods.

comadrazgo   ritual kinship; relationships through godmothers.

comadre   relationship between a child's biological parents and godmother.

comal   griddle.

comisariado ejidal   an ejido's officers, or board of governors.

compadrazgo   ritual kinship; relationships through godparents.

compadres   relationship between a child's biological parents and a godmother or godfather.

confianza   mutual trust.

cooperativas ejidales   fishing cooperatives organized in those ejidos with access to coastal ecosystems.

cooperativas tradicionales   traditional fishing cooperatives.

corridos   Mexican ballads traditionally used to narrate important events.

Cristero   supporter of the popular religious movement against the Mexican state that took place 1926–1929.

cuadrillas   groups or teams of farmworkers.

curandero   native healer.

decampesinista   an intellectual theory arguing that capitalism will transform peasants into proletarians.

ejidatarios   members of ejidos.

ejido   an area of land communally owned by a group of people. Also used to describe the community of common landholders itself. Ejidos were first introduced in 1917 through post-revolutionary land reforms designed to repossess privately held estates and return the land to the rural population.

el profe   a Spanish short name for professor.

encomienda   a grant of land and Indians.

epazote   an herb, also known as Mexican tea (*Chenopodium ambrosioides*).

estafiate   Mexican white sage (*Artemisa ludoviciana*).

estuaries   coastal ecosystems that consist of shallow, partially enclosed areas where fresh water enters the ocean.

gente de razón   people who followed a European way of life.

guayabera   a loose shirt with large pockets.

guerrillero   guerrilla fighter.

hueseros   traditional chiropractics.

jaiba   a crab (*Callinectes arcuatus*; *C. toxotes*).

jornaleros   wageworkers; farmworkers.

latifundia   large, landed estate.

lisa   a fish (*Mugil cephalus*; *M. curema*).

madrina   godmother.

mangle blanco   white mangrove (*Laguncularia racemosa*).

mangle negro   black mangrove (*Avicennia nítida*).

mangle rojo   red mangrove (*Rhizophora mangle*).

mangrove forests   marine shoreline ecosystems dominated by trees that can tolerate high salt concentrations.

menudo   aromatic soup made of tripe, hominy, and chili.

milpas   cultivated fields; intercropping systems of corn, beans, and chilies.

minifundio   small farm.

minifundistas   small-land holders.

mojarra   a fish (*Eugerres axillaris*).

municipios   a political and geographic division within Mexican states; similar to a U.S. county.

naciones   ethnic polities distinguished from the modern nation-state.

narco-corridos   Mexican ballads narrating events related to drug trafficking.

nopales   edible cacti. Green nopal (*Opuntia indica*) is eaten throughout Mexico.

norteño   from the north of Mexico; northerner.

padrino   godfather.

padrinos   godparents.

palapas   palm hut.

pangas   small wooden boats.

peninsulares   Spaniards.

peones acasillados   resident laborers on a hacienda or large estate.

pequeños propietarios   small-land holders.

pescadores libres   fishermen who do not belong to an organized fishing cooperative.

peso   the Mexican currency. In 2004 one U.S. dollar was about ten Mexican pesos.

piojillo   a dead season, when there is no work available.

pitahaya   a type of climbing cactus whose fruit is edible; dragon fruit (*Hylocerus* species).

posadas   Mexican Christmas parties.

pozole   a stew made with hominy, beef, or pork.

presidios   forts; fixed military installations.

promotoras de salud   women health promoters.

pueblos   Indian towns; also refers to modern urban centers or cities.

quelite   annual edible herb that grows wild in Sinaloa (*Amaranthus hibridus*).

quinceañeras   girls' fifteenth birthday celebrations.

ranchito   small village.

reales de minas   mining centers.

repartimiento   forced labor recruited from native villages and sent to Spanish haciendas and mines for specific periods of time.

salt marshes   areas of grasses and reeds that are either permanently flooded or are flooded for a major part of the year.

sobadores   traditional massage therapists.

sorgo escobero   broomcorn; also known as *escoba* (*Sorghum vulgare*).

tabachín   a tree with bright red flowers (*Caesalpina pulcherrima*).

tapisques   missionized Indians forced to work on haciendas and in mines.

tapos   weirs; fixed fishing gear used in the estuaries and lagoons of southern Sinaloa.

telenovela Latin American soap opera.
temporal heavy rains.
terratenientes landowners.
tierra caliente low land.
tierras de temporal dry land dependent on rainfall.
tortillerías tortilla bakeries.

References Cited

Abbassi, J., and S. Lutjens, eds. 2002. *Rereading Women in Latin America and the Caribbean: The Political Economy of Gender.* Boulder, CO: Rowman and Littlefield Publishers.

Alatorre Rico, J., A. Langer, and R. Lozano. 1994. Mujer y Salud. In *Las Mujeres en La Pobreza*, edited by J. Alatorre et al., 217–41. México, D. F., México: El Colegio de México.

Alcalá Moya, G. 1999. *Con el Agua Hasta los Aparejos: Pescadores y Pesquerías en el Soconusco, Chiapas.* México, D. F., México: Centro de Investigaciones Superiores en Antropología Social (Ciesas).

Alonso, A. M. 1995. *Thread of Blood: Colonialism, Revolution, and Gender on Mexico's Northern Frontier.* Tucson: University of Arizona Press.

Andreatta, S. 1998. Transformation of the Agro-food Sector: Lessons from the Caribbean. *Human Organization* 57(4):441–29.

Andrews, A. P. 1983. *Maya Salt Production and Trade.* Tucson: University of Arizona Press.

Arias, P. 1994. Three Microhistories of Women's Work in Rural Mexico. In *Women of the Mexican Countryside, 1850–1900*, edited by H. Fowler-Salamini and M. K. Vaughan, 159–74. Tucson: University of Arizona Press.

Barlett, P. 1982. *Agricultural Choice and Change.* New Brunswick, NJ: Rutgers University Press.

Barth, F. 1992. Towards Greater Naturalism in Conceptualizing Societies. In *Conceptualizing Society*, edited by A. Kuper, 17–33. New York: Routledge.

Beals, R. 1987. The Renaissance of Anthropological Studies in Northwestern Mexico. In *Ejidos and Regions of Refuge in Northwestern Mexico*, edited by N. R. Crumrine and P. C. Wiegand, 95–102. Anthropological Papers of the University of Arizona, No. 16. Tucson: University of Arizona Press.

Behar, R. 1993. *Translated Woman: Crossing the Border with Esperanza's Story.* Boston: Beacon Press.

Benería, L. 1992. The Mexican Debt Crisis: Restructuring the Economy and the Household. In *Unequal Burden: Economic Crisis, Persistent Poverty, and Women's Work*, edited by L. Benería and S. Feldman, 83–105. Boulder, CO: Westview Press.

Bonfil Batalla, G. 1987. *México Profundo: Una Civilización Negada*. México, D. F., México: Centro de Investigacines Superiores en Antropología Social (Ciesas).

Bryant, R. L., J. Rigg, and P. Stott. 1993. The Political Ecology of Southeast Asian Forests: Transdisciplinary Discourses. *Global Ecology and Biogeography Letters* 3:101–11.

Cancian, F. 1972. *Change and Uncertainty in a Peasant Economy*. Palo Alto, CA: Stanford University Press.

————. 1979. *The Innovator's Situation: Upper Middle Class Conservatism in Agricultural Communities*. Palo Alto, CA: Stanford University Press.

Carabias, J., E. Provencio, and C. Toledo. 1994. *Manejo de Recursos Naturales y Pobreza Rural*. México, D. F., México: Universidad Nacional Autónoma de México.

Carrillo Rojas, A. 1991. Los Principales Vínculos Económicos entre Sinaloa y los Estados Unidos durante el Porfiriato. In *El Porfiriato en Sinaloa*, edited by G. López Alanís, 17–33. Culiacán: Dirección de Investigación y Fomento de Cultura Regional del Gobierno del Estado de Sinaloa.

————. 1993. Aspectos Económicos y Políticos de la Revolución en Sinaloa. In *La Revolución en Sinaloa*, edited by A. Carrillo Rojas et al., 5–30. Culiacán: Colegio de Bachilleres del Estado de Sinaloa.

Castro, H. 1998. Molesta a Vecinos de Celaya Instalación de Una Marisquería. *El Noroeste*. Sunday, July 12.

Ceceña Cervantes, J. L., F. Burgueño Lomeli, and S. Millán Echeagaray. 1973. *Sinaloa, Crecimiento Agrícola y Desperdicio*. México, D. F., México: Instituto de Investigaciones Económicas, Universidad Nacional Autónoma de México.

Cisneros, C. A. 1988. *Ideología y Clase Obrera en el Campo*. Culiacán, Sinaloa: UAS.

Cohen, J. 1999. *Cooperation and Community: Economy and Society in Oaxaca*. Austin: University of Texas Press.

Confederación de Asociaciones Agrícolas del Estado de Sinaloa (CAADES). 1987. *Sinaloa, Agricultura y Desarrollo*. Colección Surco Abierto. Culiacán, Sinaloa: Author.

Cornelius, W., and D. Myhre, eds. 1998. *The Transformation of Rural Mexico: Reforming the Ejido Sector*. La Jolla: Center for U.S.–Mexican Studies.

Cruz, M. L. 1992. Evaluation of the Impact of Shrimp Mariculture Development upon Rural Communities in Mexico. In *Coastal Aquaculture in Developing Countries: Problems and Perspectives*, edited by Richard B. Pollnac and Priscilla Weeks, 54–72. Kingston: The University of Rhode Island.

Cruz-Torres, M. L. 1996. Shrimp Mariculture Development in Two Rural Mexican Communities. In *Aquacultural Development: Social Dimensions of an Emerging Industry*, edited by Conner Bailey, Svein Jentaft, and Peter Sinclair, 171–91. Boulder, CO: Westview Press.

————. 2001. "Pink Gold Rush": Shrimp Aquaculture, Sustainable Development and the Environment in Northwestern Mexico. *Journal of Political Ecology* 7:63–90.

Dedina, S. 1995. The Political Ecology of Transboundary Development: Land Use, Flood Control and Politics in the Tijuana River Valley. *Journal of Borderland Studies* 10(1):89–110.

De Mendizábal, M. 1930. *La Evolución del Noroeste de México*. México, D. F., México: Publicaciones del Departamento de Estadística Nacional.

de Teresa Ochoa, A., and C. Cortez Ruiz. 1996. El Agro en México: Un Futuro Incierto Después de las Reformas. In *La Sociedad Rural Mexicana Frente al Nuevo Milenio,* edited by H. de Grammont and H. Tejera Gaona, 17–34, vol. 2 of La Nueva Relación Campo-Ciudad y la Pobreza Rural, edited by A. de Teresa and C. Cortez Ruiz. México, D. F., México: Plaza y Valdés Editores.

DeWalt, B. 1975. Inequalities in Wealth, Adoption of Technology, and Production in a Mexican Ejido. *American Ethnologist* 2:149–68.

———. 1979. *Modernization in a Mexican Ejido: A Study in Economic Adaptation.* New York: Cambridge University Press.

———. 1998. The Ejido Reforms and Mexican Coastal Communities: Fomenting a Blue Revolution? In *The Transformation of Rural Mexico: Reforming the Ejido Sector,* edited by W. Cornelius and D. Myhre, 357–79. La Jolla: Center for U.S.–Mexican Studies.

Dodds, D. 1998. Lobster in the Rainforest: The Political Ecology of Miskito Wage Labor and Agricultural Deforestation. *Journal of Political Ecology* 5:83–108.

Edelman, M. 1999. *Peasants Against Globalization: Rural Social Movements in Costa Rica.* Stanford, CA: Stanford University Press.

Edwards, R. R. C. 1977. Field Experiments on Growth and Mortality of *Penaeus vannamei* in a Mexican Coastal Lagoon Complex. *Estuarine and Coastal Marine Science* 5:107–21.

———. 1978. Ecology of a Coastal Lagoon Complex in Mexico. *Estuarine and Coastal Marine Science* 6:75–92.

Eriksen, T. 1991. The Cultural Contexts of Ethnic Differences. *Man* 26:127–44.

Escobar, A. 1995. *Encountering Development: The Making and Unmaking of the Third World.* Princeton, NJ: Princeton University Press.

Feldman, S. 1992. Crises, Poverty, and Gender Inequality: Current Themes and Issues. In *Unequal Burden: Economic Crises, Persistent Poverty, and Women's Work,* edited by L. Benería and S. Feldman, 1–25. Boulder, CO: Westview Press.

Flores-Verdugo, F., F. Gonzales-Farias, M. Blanco-Correa, and A. Nuñez-Pastén. 1997. The Teacapán-Agua Brava-Marismas Nacionales Mangrove Ecosystem on the Pacific Coast of Mexico. In *Mangrove Ecosystems Studies in Latin America and Africa,* edited by B. Kjerfve et al., 35–47. Paris, France: UNESCO.

Flores-Verdugo, F., F. Gonzales-Farias, D. S. Zamorano, and P. Ramirez-Garcia. 1992. Mangrove Ecosystems of the Pacific Coast of Mexico: Distribution, Structure, Litterfall, and Detritus Dynamics. In *Coastal Plant Communities of Latin America,* edited by U. Seeliger, 269–88. San Diego, CA: Academic Press.

Foster, G. 1953. Cofradía and *Compadrazgo* in Spain and Spanish America. *Southwestern Journal of Anthropology* 9:1–28.

Franko, P. 1999. *The Puzzle of Latin American Economic Development.* Lanham, MD: Rowman and Littlefield Publishers.

Fuentes, C. 2002. *En esto Creo.* México D. F.: Editorial Planeta Mexicana.

Galeano, E. 1999. *The Open Veins of Latin America.* México, D. F., México: Siglo 21 Editores.

Galindo Reyes, J. G. 2000. *Condiciones Ambientales y de Contaminación en los Ecosistemas Costeros.* Culiacán, Sinaloa: UAS.

Galindo Reyes, J. G., J. Guillermo, M. Medina, C. Villagrana, and L. Ibarra. 1997. Environmental and Pollution Condition of the Huizache-Caimanero Lagoon in the Northwest of Mexico. *Marine Pollution Bulletin* 34(12):1072–77.

Gaxiola Aldana, Y. 1999. Impedidas Autoridades para Erradicar el "Changuerismo." *El Universal.* Friday, July 2, p. 2.

Gezon, L. 1999. From Adversary to Son: Political and Ecological Process in Northern Madagascar. *Journal of Anthropological Research* 55:71–97.

Gobierno del Estado. 2000. *Diario Oficial.* Acuerdo por el que la Coordinación General del Programa IMSS–Solidaridad: Publica las Reglas de Operación del Programa IMSS–Solidaridad. México, D. F., México: Instituto Mexicano del Seguro Social (IMSS).

Gobierno del Estado de Sinaloa. 1968. *Diario Oficial.* Sábado 23 de Marzo, Número 36. Culiacán, Sinaloa: Author.

González de la Rocha, M., and A. Escobar Latapí. 1991. *Social Responses to Mexico's Economic Crisis of the 1980's.* La Jolla, CA: Center for U.S.–Mexican Studies.

————. 2002. The Urban Family and Poverty in Latin America. In *Rereading Women in Latin America and the Caribbean: The Political Economy of Gender,* edited by J. Abbassi and S. Lutjens, 61–77. Boulder, CO: Rowman and Littlefield Publishers.

González Montes, S. 1994. Intergenerational and Gender Relations in the Transition from a Peasant Economy to a Diversified Economy. In *Women of the Mexican Countryside, 1850–1990,* edited by H. Fowler-Salamini and M. K. Vaughan, 175–91. Tucson: University of Arizona Press.

————. 1997. Mujeres, Trabajo y Pobreza en el Campo Mexicano: Una Vision Crítica de la Bibliografía Reciente. In *Las Mujeres en la Pobreza,* edited by J. Alatorre et al., 179–214. México, D. F., México: El Colegio de Mexico.

Grammont, H. 1990. *Los Empresarios Agrícolas y el Estado: Sinaloa, 1893–1984.* México, D. F., México: Universidad Autónoma de México.

Grande, C. 1998. *Sinaloa en la Historia: De la Independencia a los Preludios de la Revolución Mexicana.* Vol. 2. Culiacán, Sinaloa: UAS.

Grindle, M. 1991. The Response to Austerity: Political and Economic Strategies of Mexico's Rural Poor. In *Social Responses to Mexico's Economic Crisis of the 1980's,* edited by M. González de la Rocha and A. Escobar Latapí, 129–53. La Jolla, CA: Center for U.S–Mexican Studies.

Grossman, L. 1998. *The Political Ecology of Bananas: Contract Farming, Peasants, and Agrarian Change in the Eastern Caribbean.* Chapel Hill: University of North Carolina Press.

Guarnaccia P., P. J. Pelto, G. H. Pelto, L. Meneses, A. Chavez, and L. H. Allen. 1988. Measuring Socioeconomic Status: Assessing Intra-community Diversity. *Culture and Agriculture* 35:1–8.

Guerra, C., and R. Rocha Moya. 1988. *Tomate Amargo.* Culiacán, Sinaloa: UAS.

Heredia Trasviña, A. 1990. *Sinaloa: Un Estudio Monográfico.* Culiacán, Rosales, Sinaloa: Universidad Pedagógica Nacional.

Hernández Fujigaki, G. 1988. *75 Años de Historia de la Pesca, 1912–1987.* México, D. F., México: Secretaría de Pesca.

Hershkovitz, L. 1993. Political Ecology and Environmental Management in the Loess Plateau, China. *Human Ecology* 21(4):327–53.

Hewitt de Alcántara, C. 1984. *Anthropological Perspectives on Rural Mexico.* London: Routledge and Kegan Paul.

Himmerich y Valencia, R. 1991. *The Encomenderos of New Spain, 1521–1555.* Austin: University of Texas Press.

Hubbard, C. 1978. El Ayer de el Rosario. *Presagio* 11(1):4–5.

———. 1993. *Estampas de un Mineral.* Culiacán, Sinaloa: UAS.

———. 1994. *Cuentos de mi Rosario.* Self-published.

Ibarra Escobar, W., M. Aguilar Alvarado, and R. Valdés Aguilar. 1997. Conquista y Colonia. In *Historia de Sinaloa,* vol. 1, edited by J. Verdugo Quintero, 141–227. Culiacán: Gobierno del Estado de Sinaloa.

Instituto Mexicano del Seguro Social. 2001. *Expediente Comunitario de Celaya del Programa IMSS–Solidaridad.* Escuinapa, Sinaloa: Unidad Médica Rural de Isla del Bosque.

Instituto Nacional de Estadística, Geografía, e Informática (INEGI). 1985. *Estadísticas Históricas de México.* Vol. 1. Aguas Calientes, México: Author.

———. 1991. *Vll Censo Agropecuario. Datos por Ejido y Comunidad Agraria.* Aguas Calientes, México: Author.

———. 1993. *Escuinapa, Sinaloa. Cuaderno Estadístico Municipal.* Aguas Calientes, México: Author.

———. 1995. *Estadísticas del Medio Ambiente.* Aguas Calientes, México: Author.

———. 1999. *Anuario Estadístico del Estado de Sinaloa.* Aguas Calientes, México: Author.

———. 2000. *Censo General de Población y Vivienda de Sinaloa: Resultados Preliminares.* Aguas Calientes, México: Author.

Instituto Nacional de la Pesca. 1998. *Inicio de la Veda de Camarón en Aguas Marinas del Pacífico Mexicano en 1998.* México, D. F., México: SEMARNAP.

Kearney, M. 1995. The Local and the Global: The Anthropology of Globalization and Transnationalism. *Annual Review of Anthropology* 24:547–65.

———. 1996. *Reconceptualizing the Peasantry.* Boulder, CO: Westview Press.

Kemper, R. 1982. The *Compadrazgo* in Urban Mexico. *Anthropological Quarterly* 55:17–30.

Lara, M. A., and N. Salgado de Snyder. 1994. Mujer, Pobreza y Salud Mental. In *Las Mujeres en la Pobreza,* edited by J. Alatorre et al., 243–91. México, D. F., México: El Colegio de México.

Lara Flores, S. M. 1998. *Nuevas Experiencias Productivas y Nuevas Formas de Organización Flexible del Trabajo en la Agricultura Mexicana.* México, D. F., México: Juan Pablos Editor.

Latapí Escalante, A. 1988. La Antropología en Sinaloa. In *La Antropología en México: Panorama Histórico,* edited by Carlos García Mora, 139–53. México, D. F., México: Instituto Nacional de Antropología e Historia.

Liverman, D., and A. J. Cravey. 1992. Geographic Perspectives on Mexican Regions. In *Mexico's Regions: Comparative History and Development,* edited by E. Van Young, 39–57. La Jolla: Center for U.S.–Mexican Studies.

Lobato, P. 1988. Estudio Socioeconómico del Cultivo de Camarón Realizado por Sociedades Cooperativas en México. Apoyo a las Actividades Regionales de Acuacultura en América Latina y el Caribe (AQUILA). Organización de las Naciones Unidas para la Agricultura y la Alimentación (FAO). Secretaría de Pesca, Dirección General de Acuacultura, Mexico City, Mexico.

Lomnitz, L. A. 1977. *Networks and Marginality: Life in a Mexican Shantytown*. New York: Academic Press.

Macedo López, J. 1978. Escuinapa, o la Riqueza Olvidada. *Presagio* 1(17):20–22.

Maradiaga Ceceña, J., and E. Ancona Quiroz. 1996. *Perfil Socioeconómico del estado de Sinaloa y sus 18 Municipios*. Culiacán, Sinaloa: UAS.

Mastretta, A. 1992. *Mujeres de Ojos Grandes*. México, D. F., México: Cal y Arena.

McCay, B. J. 1978. Systems Ecology, People Ecology, and the Anthropology of Fishing Communities. *Human Ecology* 6(4):397–421.

McClusky, L. 2001. *"Here, Our Culture Is Hard": Stories of Domestic Violence from a Mayan Community in Belize*. Austin: University of Texas Press.

McGoodwin, R. 1979. Fisheries Policies and the Underdevelopment of Inshore Pacific Mexico. Technical Report. Woods Hole, MA: Woods Hole Oceanographic Institution.

———. 1980. The Human Costs of Development. *Environment* 22(1):13–24.

———. 1982. Aquaculture Development in Atomistic Societies. In *Aquaculture Development in Less Developed Countries*, edited by S. Peterson and L. J. Smith, 61–75. Boulder, CO: Westview Press.

———. 1987. Mexico's Conflictual Inshore Pacific Fisheries: Problems Analysis and Policy Recommendations. *Human Organization* 46(3):221–32.

Miller, M. 1990. Shrimp Aquaculture in Mexico. *Food Research Institute Studies* 22(1):83–107.

Mintz, S., and E. Wolf. 1950. An Analysis of Ritual Co-Parenthood (*Compadrazgo*). *Southwestern Journal of Anthropology* 6:341–67.

Moore, N. H., and D. J. Slinn. 1984. The Physical Hydrology of a Lagoon System on the Pacific Coast of Mexico. *Estuarine, Coastal and Shelf Science* 19:413–26.

Moorhead, M. 1975. *The Presidio: Bastion of the Spanish Borderlands*. Norman: University of Oklahoma Press.

Mummert, G. 1994. From Metate to Destape: Rural Mexican Women's Salaried Labor and the Redefinition of Gendered Spaces and Roles. In *Women of the Mexican Countryside, 1850–1900*, edited by H. Fowler-Salamini and M. K. Vaughan, 192–209. Tucson: University of Arizona Press.

Murúa, D. 1978. La Pesca en los Tapos. *Presagio* 1(17):6–7.

Nader, L. 1969. The Zapotec of Oaxaca. In *Handbook of Middle American Indians*, edited by R. Wauchope, 329–59. Austin: University of Texas Press.

Naylor, T., and C. Polzer, eds. 1986. *The Presidio and Militia on the Northern Frontier of New Spain: A Documentary History*. Tucson: University of Arizona Press.

Nutini, H. 1984. *Ritual Kinship: The Structure and Historical Development of the Compadrazgo System in Rural Tlaxcala*. Vol. 1. Princeton, NJ: Princeton University Press.

O'Connor, J. 1998. *Natural Causes: Essays in Ecological Marxism.* New York: Guilford Press.

Olea, H. 1964. *Breve Historia de la Revolución en Sinaloa (1910–1917).* México, D. F., México: Patronato del Instituto Nacional de Estudios Históricos de la Revolución Mexicana.

Ortega Noriega, S. 1993. *Un Ensayo de Historia Regional: El Noroeste de México, 1530–1880.* México, D. F., México: Universidad Nacional Autónoma de México.

———. 1999. *Breve Historia de Sinaloa.* México, D. F., México: Fondo de Cultura Económica.

Otero, G. 1996. *Overview in Neoliberalism Revisited: Economic Restructuring and Mexico's Political Future.* Boulder, CO: Westview Press.

Padilla, F. 1993. *Lo que el Tiempo no se Llevó: Los Conflictos Agrarios en el Sur de Sinaloa durante el Período Cardenista, 1935–1940.* Culiacán, Sinaloa: UAS.

Páez-Osuna, F., S. Guerrero-Galván, and A. Ruiz-Fernández. 1998. The Environmental Impact and the Coastal Pollution in Mexico. *Marine Pollution Bulletin* 36(1):65–75.

Painter, M. 1995. Upland-Lowland Production Linkages and Land Degradation in Bolivia. In *The Social Causes of Environmental Destruction in Latin America,* edited by M. Painter and W. Durham, 133–68. Ann Arbor: University of Michigan Press.

Painter, M., and W. Durham, eds. 1995. *The Social Causes of Environmental Destruction in Latin America.* Ann Arbor: University of Michigan Press.

Partido Revolucionario Institucional (PRI). 1986. *La Gira del General Lázaro Cárdenas.* México, D. F., México: Author.

Paz, O. 1983. *The Labyrinth of Solitude.* New York: Grove Press.

Perales Rivas, M., and L. Fregoso Tirado, eds. 1994. *Desarrollo Sostenible de los Agroecosistemas del Sur de Sinaloa.* Vol. 1. Mexico City: Universidad Autónoma de Chapingo.

Pezzoli, K. 1998. *Human Settlements and Planning for Ecological Sustainability: The Case of Mexico City.* Cambridge, MA: MIT Press.

Plan Nacional de Desarrollo. 1995. *Programa de Pesca y Acuacultura, 1995–2000.* Mexico City: Author.

Polzer, C., and T. Sheridan, eds. 1997. *The Presidio and Militia on the Northern Frontier of New Spain.* Vol. 2, part 1 of The Californias and Sinaloa-Sonora, 1700–1765. Tucson: University of Arizona Press.

Procuraduría Agraria. 1993. *Reformas al Marco Agrario Legal.* Cuernavaca, México: Impresores Profesionales Tauro.

Quezada, D., and Y. Bretón. 1987. *Antropología Marítima: Pesca y Actores Sociales.* Mérida: Universidad Autónoma de Yucatán.

Quezada Dominguez, R. 1995. *Papel y Transformación de las Unidades de Producción Pesquera Ejidales en el Sector Halieútico de Yucatán, México.* Culiacán, Sinaloa: UAS.

Ramírez Meza, B. 1993. *Economía y Sociedad en Sinaloa, 1591–1900.* Culiacán, Sinaloa: UAS.

Reff, D. 1991. *Disease, Depopulation, and Culture Change in Northwestern New Spain, 1518–1764.* Salt Lake City: University of Utah Press.

Reyes Jiménez, J., and A. Loaíza Mesa. 1996. Validación y Transferencia de Tecnología. In

Desarrollo Sostenible de los Agrosistemas del Sur de Sinaloa, vol. 2, edited by A. López Herrera and O. Palacios Velarde, 9–18. Mexico City: Universidad Autónoma de Chapingo.

Roberts, B. 1992. The Place of Regions in Mexico. In *Mexico's Regions: Comparative History and Development*, edited by Eric Van Young, 227–45. La Jolla, CA: Center for U.S.–Mexican Studies.

Rocheleau, D., B. Thomas-Slayter, and E. Wangari, eds. 1996. *Feminist Political Ecology: Global Issues and Local Experiences*. New York: Routledge.

Roldán, M. 1982. Subordinación Genérica y Proletarización Rural: Un Estudio de Caso en el Noroeste Mexicano. In *Las Trabajadoras del Agro*, edited by León Magdalena. Bogotá: Asociación Colombiana para el Estudio de la Población.

Román Alarcón, A. 1991. La Participación de Comerciantes Extranjeros de Mazatlán en la Economía Regional, 1877–1910. In *El Porfiriato en Sinaloa*, edited by G. López Alanís, 153–63. Culiacán: Dirección de Investigación y Fomento de Cultura Regional del Estado de Sinaloa.

Romero Beltrán, E., and V. González Gallardo. 2000. *Causas de Mortandad de Organismos Acuáticos en el Sistema Lagunar Laguna Grande-Canal La Estacada, Escuinapa, Sinaloa*. Instituto Nacional de la Pesca, Centro Regional de Investigaciones Pesqueras Mazatlán. Mexico City: SEMARNAP.

Romero Peña, R., ed. 1998. *Evaluación Biológica Pesquera, Laguna de Caimanero*. Sinaloa: Federación de Cooperativas Pesqueras.

Rosaldo, R. 1989. *Culture and Truth: The Remaking of Social Analysis*. Boston: Beacon Press.

Roseberry, W. 1989. *Anthropologies and Histories: Essays in Culture, History, and Political Economy*. New Brunswick, NJ: Rutgers University Press.

Rubio Ruelas, B., and J. F. Hirata Galindo. 1985. El Movimiento Campesino y las Invasiones de Tierras en Sinaloa durante 1976. In *Movimientos Sociales en el Noroeste de México*, edited by R. Burgos, 67–83. Culiacán, Sinaloa: UAS.

Ruiz-Luna, A., and C. A. Berlanga-Robles. 1999. Modifications in Coverage Patterns and Land Use around the Huizache-Caimanero Lagoon System, Sinaloa, Mexico: A Multitemporal Analysis using LANDSAT Images. *Estuarine, Coastal and Shelf Science* 49:37–44.

Sassen, S. 1998. *Globalization and its Discontents: Essays on the New Mobility of People and Money*. New York: The New Press.

Sauer, C., and D. Brand. 1932. Aztatlán: Prehistoric Mexican Frontier on the Pacific Coast. *Ibero-Americana* 1:1–92.

Schmidt, R. H., Jr. 1976. *A Geographical Survey of Sinaloa*. El Paso: Texas Western Press.

Schmink, M., and C. Wood. 1987. The "Political Ecology" of Amazonia. In *Lands at Risk in the Third World: Local-Level Perspectives*, edited by P. D. Little and M. M. Horowitz, 38–57. Boulder, CO: Westview Press.

Scott, J. 1985. *Weapons of the Week: Everyday Forms of Peasant Resistance*. New Haven, CT: Yale University Press.

Secretaría del Medio Ambiente, Recursos Naturales, y Pesca (SEMARNAP). 1997. *Informe de Autoevaluación de Actividades 1996–97 de la Delegación Federal de SEMARNAP en el Estado de Sinaloa*. Mazatlán, México: Delegación Federal de Pesca en el Estado de Sinaloa.

———. 1998. *Ordenamiento Pesquero.* Mazatlán, México: Delegación Federal de Pesca en el Estado de Sinaloa.

Secretaría de Pesca (SEPESCA). 1989. *Programa Nacional del Cultivo de Camarón (Informe de Avance).* April, Pachuca, Hidalgo.

———. n. d. *Estudio Sobre la Problemática Pesquera en la Zona de Lagunas y Esteros del Sur del Estado de Sinaloa.* México, D. F., México: Author.

———. n. d. *La Problemática Pesquera en el Sur de Sinaloa.* México, D. F., México: Dirección General de Organización y Capacitación Pesqueras, Secretaría de Pesca.

Shadle, S. 1994. *Andrés Molina Enríquez: Mexican Land Reformer of the Revolutionary Era.* Tucson: University of Arizona Press.

Sheridan, T. 1988. *Where the Dove Calls: The Political Ecology of a Corporate Peasant Community in Northwestern Mexico.* Tucson: University of Arizona Press.

Simental Beaven, H. 1990. *Primer Informe de Gobierno.* Escuinapa de Hidalgo: Ayuntamiento Municipal.

Stephen, L. 1991. *Zapotec Women.* Austin: University of Texas Press.

———. 2002. Women in Mexico's Popular Movements: Survival Strategies against Ecological and Economic Impoverishment. In *Rereading Women in Latin America and the Caribbean: The Political Economy of Gender,* edited by J. Abbassi and S. Lutjens, 91–111. Boulder, CO: Rowman and Littlefield.

Stonich, S. 1993. *"I Am Destroying the Land!": The Political Ecology of Poverty and Environmental Destruction in Honduras.* Boulder, CO: Westview Press.

———. 1995. The Environmental Quality and Social Justice Implications of Shrimp Mariculture Development in Honduras. *Human Ecology* 23(2):143–68.

Valdés Aguilar, R. 1998. *El Real de Minas de Nuestra Señora del Rosario.* Culiacán, Sinaloa: UAS.

Van Young, E. 1992. Introduction: Are Regions Good to Think? In *Mexico's Regions: Comparative History and Development,* edited by E. Van Young, 1–36. La Jolla, CA: Center for U.S.–Mexican Studies.

Vélez-Ibáñez, C. 1983. *Bonds of Mutual Trust: The Cultural Systems of Rotating Credit Associations among Urban Mexicans and Chicanos.* New Brunswick, NJ: Rutgers University Press.

———. 1996. *Border Visions: Mexican Cultures of the Southwest United States.* Tucson: University of Arizona Press.

Verdugo Quintero, J. 1997. *Historia de Sinaloa.* Vol. 1. Culiacán: Gobierno del Estado de Sinaloa.

Voss, S. F. 1982. *On the Periphery of Nineteenth-Century Mexico: Sonora and Sinaloa, 1810–1877.* Tucson: University of Arizona Press.

Wald, E. 2001. *Narcocorrido: A Journey into the Music of Drugs, Guns, and Guerrillas.* New York: Harper Collins Publishers.

Wangari, E., B. Thomas-Slayter, and D. Rocheleau. 1996. Gendered Visions for Survival: Semi-arid Regions in Kenya. In *Feminist Political Ecology: Global Issues and Local Experiences,* edited by D. Rocheleau, B. Thomas-Slayter, and E. Wangari, 127–54. New York: Routledge.

Wolf, E. 1982. *Europe and the People without History.* Berkeley: University of California Press.

References / 315

Wright, A. 1990. *The Death of Ramón González: The Modern Agricultural Dilemma*. Austin: University of Texas Press.

Yetman, D. 1998. *Scattered Round Stones: A Mayo Village in Sonora, Mexico.* Albuquerque: University of New Mexico Press.

Unpublished Primary Sources

Berlanga Robles, C. A. 1999. Evaluación de las Condiciones Actuales y del Cambio de los Paisajes de Humedales de la Costa Sur de Sinaloa, México: Una Aproximación con el Uso de Datos Provenientes de Sensores Remotos. Master's thesis, Universidad Nacional Autónoma de México.

Iribe Fonseca, L. 1994. Estudio de Servicio Social realizado en El Cerro. Unpublished manuscript.

Lobato, P. 1989. Las Cooperativas de Pescadores y sus Conflictos: Los Camaroneros de los Estuarios de Nayarit y del Sur de Sinaloa. Bachelor of Science thesis, Escuela Nacional de Antropología e Historia, México, D. F., México.

Ramírez-Zavala, J., A. Ruiz-Luna, and C. A. Berlanga-Robles. 1997. Estimación de las Tendencias de Cambio Ambiental en el Paisaje de Urías, Sinaloa, México, por Medio de un Análisis Multitemporal (1973–1997) con Imágenes LANDSAT. Unpublished manuscript.

Sault, N. 1985. Zapotec *Madrinas*: The Centrality of Women for *Compadrazgo* Groups in a Village of Oaxaca, Mexico. Ph.D. dissertation, University of California, Los Angeles.

Universidad Autónoma de Sinaloa and Consejo Ecológico de Mazatlán. 2000. La Problemática del Agua en Mazatlán: Cobertura y Tratamiento. Conference held on September 8, 2000, in Mazatlán, Mexico.

Municipal Archive of Escuinapa Sources: Chronological

Letter sent to the presidente municipal de Escuinapa by three members of the comisariado ejidal of Isla del Bosque, July 5, 1960.

Letter sent to Ingeniero Manuel Cazares, jefe de la Brigada de Ingenieros en los Estados de Sinaloa y Sonora, by the Juez Distrito del Estado, Licenciado Eduardo Lambarri Baquedano, August 27, 1960.

Letter sent to Francisco Alarcón, secretary general of the League of Agrarian Communities, Culiacán, Sinaloa, by two members of the Confederación Nacional Campesina, November 4, 1960.

Petition sent to the presidente municipal of Escuinapa by Filiberto Loera Martínez, Samuel Serna Loera, and Angel Alvarado Ramos, representatives of the campesinos from the faction José María Morelos y Pavón in Isla del Bosque, November 17, 1960.

Letter sent to Pedro Zamudio, presidente municipal of Escuinapa, by the board of directors of Ejido Isla del Bosque, November 25, 1960.

Report on the land transfer sent to the comisariado ejidal of Isla del Bosque by the Regional Agrarian Committee 15 of the municipality of Escuinapa, December 13, 1960.

Letter sent to Professor Roberto Barrios, director of the Department of Agrarian and

Colonization Issues, in Culiacán, by León García, head of the Office of Agrarian Reform in Escuinapa, March 13, 1961.

Letter sent to Luis Zenteno Mora, presidente del comisariado ejidal Isla del Bosque, by Gabriel Castañeda Landazuri, delegado de Asuntos Agrarios y Colonización, January 26, 1962.

Minutes of the meeting held in Isla del Bosque, concerning the division and transfer of parcels to ejidatarios of that settlement, September 8, 1962.

Official telegram sent to León García, jefe de la Oficina de Quejas, Palacio Nacional, México D. F., México by Ingeniero Jesús Aldana Sauceda, representative de la Delegación del Departamento de Asuntos Agrarios y Colonización en el Estado de Sinaloa, September 9, 1962.

Letter sent to Renato Vega Alvarado, gobernor of Sinaloa, by Ismael Burgueño, September 10, 1993.

Letter sent to Pedro Zamudio, presidente municipal of Escuinapa, by members of the comisariado ejidal of Isla del Bosque, n. d.

Index

Escutia, Héctor, 166, 168
estuaries, 56–57, 87, 88
ethnography, 20–22
ethnohistory, 50, 55; of El Cerro, 105–14; of Celaya, 164–70

factionalism, 161, 162, 180
families, 20, 73, 79, 217; Celaya, 169, 177–78; cooperation among, 266–68; health and, 148–49; and land, 289–90; powerful, 40, 41, 48–49; socio-economics of, 146–48, 209; survival of, 271–77
family planning, 151–52
feast days, 81, 195, 225–26, 283
Federal Law for Fisheries Department, 57
Federation of Sinaloan Growers Association (CAADES), 84
fertilizers, 86, 87, 227, 228
field work, 12–20
fiestas, 81, 195, 269, 283, 284
Fisheries Department, 59
Fisheries Law, 46
fishermen, 229–36
fishing, 7, 10, 34, 44, 87, 127, 135, 277; cooperatives, 61, 123, 124; in El Cerro, 118, 133–34; in Escuinapa, 75–76; for export, 83–85. *See also* shrimp
fishing areas: designated, 55–56
floods, 62–63, 65–66
Flores, Angel, 47
food, 224, 265, 275
forasteros, 146–47
foreigners, 41, 42, 44, 60, 298nn. 5, 6
frascas, 134–35, 299n. 1
fruit production, 79, 84–85, 224

gender, 12, 263; livestock and, 223–24; socioeconomics and, 208–9
General Coordination of the National Plan for Depressed Zones and Marginal Groups (COPLAMAR), 193
General Fisheries Law, 5
General Law on Cooperative Associations, 56

globalization, 71, 72, 84, 90, 95, 261, 265, 277
Group of 33, 48–49
Guzmán, Nuño de, 35
Gypsies, 74, 78–79, 97–98

Hacienda Las Cabras, 52, 177, 203, 207, 300n. 1; peones at, 164–68
haciendas, 41, 42–43, 46, 298n. 5
health care, 115, 126, 210–12, 300n. 1; in El Cerro, 148–52
Hernández, Tomás, 49
history: southern Sinaloa, 33–50
households, 8, 169, 202; agrarian reform and, 141–42; agriculture and, 226–28; cooperation among, 266–68; domestic violence in, 261–64; economy of, 132–36, 154, 182–83, 218, 222–25, 244–46, 254–55; environment and, 217, 218; migration and, 249–54; responsibilities of, 112–13; shrimp fishing by, 229–36; socioeconomics of, 137, 138—48, 204–9; struggle and survival of, 260–61, 265, 271–77, 278, 281; wealth of, 144–48; women's role in, 243–44
houses, 138, 142–43, 165, 168, 172–73, 197, 204–5
Huizache-Caimanero Lagoon Complex, 69–70, 117, 118
hydrological cycle, 69–70

Ibarra, Francisco de, 35, 36
identity, 17–19, 52, 64
illnesses, 115, 126 148, 150–51, 210, 212
income, 243, 265; cash, 219, 244–45; in Celaya, 175, 202; household, 120, 135, 137, 222; livestock as, 223, 224; from shrimp industry, 235–36
independence: struggle for, 40–41
indigenous peoples, 30, 32, 33–34, 37, 38, 40, 41, 45, 48, 60
Infantería de Marina, 231–32
inheritance: land, 111–12, 299n. 2
Instituto Mexicano del Seguro Social (IMSS), 210, 211–12

National Solidarity Program
(PRONASOL), 113, 152, 225
natural resources, 10, 11, 12, 32, 34, 68–
70, 90–91; aquatic, 201–2; Celaya's,
173–75; control of, 60, 114, 119, 128–
29, 137, 140; ejidos and, 128–29; El
Cerro's, 115–18; use of, 28–29, 45–46,
104–5, 165; water as, 66–67, 176–77
Nayarit, 42, 105–6, 122
neoliberalism, 20–21, 61, 104, 117–18
New Agrarian Reform Law, 16, 141, 186
North American Free Trade Agreement
(NAFTA), 21, 142, 206
Northern Hydraulic Plan, 66

Obregón, Alvaro, 45, 47
Office of the Attorney for Environmental
Defense (PROFEPA), 231–32
oral tradition, 63–64, 163, 188, 291, 292,
298–99n. 19, 301nn. 2, 3

pastureland, 117, 229
peones, 44, 52, 61, 123; and agrarian
reform, 47–48; on haciendas, 164–66,
167–68; land grants and, 166–67
pesticides, 86–87, 227, 228, 240–41
pigs, 206, 223, 300nn. 3, 4
piojillo, 136, 182, 219, 232
Plan Hidraúlico del Noroeste, 66
plantations: employment on, 236–44
poaching: 219–21, 229–32, 234–35
political ecology, 6, 11–12, 95, 119, 281; of
Celaya, 177–78; of El Cerro, 119
pollution, 86–87
population: in Celaya, 196–97
population growth, 56, 57, 176; in El
Cerro, 126–27, 153–54
Porfiriato, 42, 44, 48–49, 60
Portes Gil, Emilio, 45–46
poverty, 12, 21, 31, 103, 218, 256, 278; in
Celaya, 155, 157, 168–69, 170, 204,
207; and domestic violence, 264–65;
feminization of, 261, 277; urban, 81–82
presidentes de vigilancia, 262, 264
privatization, 42–43, 110–12, 249

Procuraduría Federal para la Defensa del
Medio Ambiente (PROFEPA), 231–32
Profe, El: murder of, 3–5, 279
Programa de Certificación de Derechos
Ejidales y Titulación de Solares
Urbanos (PROCEDE), 111
Programa de Educación, Salud, y
Alimentación (PROGRESA), 149–50,
211
Programa de Reforma del Sector Salud,
193
Programa Nacional de Desarrollo, 193
Programa Nacional de Solidaridad
(PRONASOL), 113, 152, 225
Program for Agrarian Reform, 47–48
promotora de salud, 151–52
property, 48, 164; private, 51, 67–68, 96,
113, 174
Proposition 187 (Calif.), 21, 256
prostitution, 245–46
pueblos, 33; characteristics of, 77–81;
municipal power in, 76–77

race, 37, 40
rainfall, 62–63, 65–66, 225–26
rainy season, 65, 80–81, 89, 109, 115–16,
177, 248, 283, 285; predicting, 225–26
ranching, 41, 42, 44, 64
ranchos, 77, 82–83, 95–96
reales de minas, 36–39, 41, 74
reciprocity, 266–68, 271
Reglamento de la Pesca Marítima y
Pluvial, 45
resistance, 217, 218, 231, 265; survival
strategies and, 271–77
Rincón, Francisco del, 84
Río Baluarte Growers Association, 84
Rio Las Cañas Growers Association, 84
rites of passage, 270–71
Rodríguez, Abelardo, 46
Rosalío, 219–20
Rosario (municipio), 55, 61, 64, 74–75,
99–100, 116, 150; agriculture in, 73, 84,
85, 237, 240; flood in, 62–63; land in,
122–23

Rosario (town), 28, 33, 42, 100, 150, 153, 246, 288; description of, 77–79; economy of, 83–85, 233, 235

Salinas de Gortari, Carlos, 20, 55, 104, 193
salt production, 38, 76, 173–74
Sánchez Celis, Leopoldo, 84, 107
savings, 223, 224, 273
schools, 153, 169, 187, 213, 248
seasons, 65, 114; work, 134–36
Senaide, Señora, 106, 107, 108
shell middens, 69, 75
Shrimp Acquaculture Program, 117
shrimp, 73, 116, 117–18, 121, 135, 165, 247–49, 280, 300n. 2; aquaculture, 4, 5, 13, 16, 19, 99, 100, 101, 246, 255; catching, 45–46, 69–70, 233–34; in Celaya, 158–59, 168, 173, 174–75, 201–2; cooperatives, 55–60, 299n. 1, 300n. 4; decline in, 87–88; environment and, 88–89; households and, 229–33, 236; marketing, 79, 80; poaching, 219–21, 234–35; regulations on, 45–46
Sinaloa (municipio), 68
síndico: in Celaya, 187–92, 259
slash-and-burn clearing, 167
slavery, 36, 38
smallholdings, 46, 48, 67, 85, 117, 168
social class, 36–37, 39–41, 48, 73, 82; in Celaya, 207–8; hierarchy of, 34, 40–41, 43, 57; post-independence, 41–42; resource access and, 60–61; in Rosario, 77, 79; and status, 138–39
socioeconomic stratification: in Celaya, 207–9; community, 137–44; household, 136–37, 144–48, 204–6
Spaniards, 37, 40, 43
Spanish conquest, 30, 32, 34–36, 60
"Story of the Storm of the Cow," 63–64
survival strategies, 217, 265–66, 277–78; household, 271–77, 281

Teacapán, 185, 197, 213, 300n. 1
terratenientes, 48, 49

Tijuana, 149, 158, 197, 251, 252–54
Toledo, José "Chepe," 166
Toledo, Natividad, 52, 164, 165, 166
Toledo Corro, Antonio, 52, 84, 164, 203
tortilla factory, 216(fig.), 289
Totorame, 33–34, 36
tourism, 67, 75, 76, 170, 283
trade: foreign, 41, 43
Traveling Cinema, 98
Trinidad, 102, 104, 105–6, 108–9, 111–12, 119, 267, 288–89, 290

Unidad Médica Rural, 210
Unión General de Obreros y Campesinos de México (UGOCM), 51, 52
United States, 42, 43, 44, 85, 158, 160, 197, 206, 240; migration to, 199, 250–52, 254, 256
urbanization, 31, 76

Victoria, 183, 184–85, 195, 204–5, 287; adultery and, 257–60
Villa Unión, 232, 297n. 3
violence, 5, 49, 55, 160–61; domestic, 130–31, 212, 261–65, 301nn. 1, 2

War of Independence, 40–41
water, 66–67, 114–15, 176–77
wealth: distribution of, 137, 138, 139(table), 140–44; households and, 144–46, 204, 205–6, 207
women, 12, 171, 195, 235, 260; and comadrazgo, 268–71; and domestic violence, 261–63, 301nn. 1, 2; house-hold role of, 243–44; migration of, 252–54; shrimp poaching by, 219–20; survival strategies of, 244–45 265–66, 271–78, 281; water and, 114, 115
work: in Celaya, 198–200, 207, 208, 286; in El Cerro, 133–34

Xiximes, 34, 38, 34, 297n. 3

About the Author

María L. Cruz-Torres is an anthropologist and associate professor of Women and Gender Studies and Transborder Chicana(o)/Latina(o) Studies at Arizona State University. She has conducted research on the social, economic, and environmental aspects of coastal communities and rural households in Puerto Rico, Key West, and Mexico.

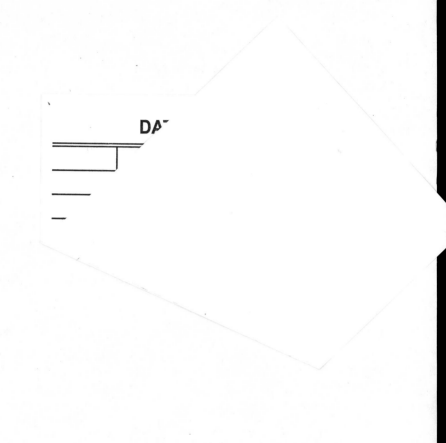

DA